Memory
Reconsolidation

Memory Reconsolidation

Edited by

Cristina M. Alberini

Center for Neural Science,
New York University

AMSTERDAM • BOSTON • HEIDELBERG • LONDON
NEW YORK • OXFORD • PARIS • SAN DIEGO
SAN FRANCISCO • SINGAPORE • SYDNEY • TOKYO

Academic Press is an Imprint of Elsevier

Academic Press is an imprint of Elsevier
32 Jamestown Road, London NW1 7BY, UK
225 Wyman Street, Waltham, MA 02451, USA
525 B Street, Suite 1800, San Diego, CA 92101-4495, USA

Notice
No responsibility is assumed by the publisher for any injury and/or damage to persons or property
as a matter of products liability, negligence or otherwise, or from any use or operation of any
methods, products, instructions or ideas contained in the material herein. Because of rapid advances
in the medical sciences, in particular, independent verification of diagnoses and drug dosages
should be made

British Library Cataloguing-in-Publication Data
A catalogue record for this book is available from the British Library

Library of Congress Cataloging-in-Publication Data
A catalog record for this book is available from the Library of Congress

ISBN : 978-0-12-386892-3

For information on all Academic Press publications
visit our website at www.store.elsevier.com

Typeset by TNQ Books and Journals

Printed and bound in United States of America
12 13 14 15   10 9 8 7 6 5 4 3 2 1

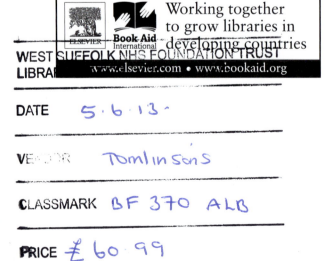

Contents

Preface

This book collects 14 chapters that discuss data and ideas about the dynamic nature of memory; in particular, they deal with the process evoked by memory retrieval and important for memory persistence, which is known as memory *reconsolidation*. The recognition of this process as important for memory storage is relatively recent, having occurred mainly through work done in the past 12 years.

Understanding how we form, store, and use memories over time has interested mankind for thousands of years. Aristotle, in his "On Memory and Reminiscence" written in 350 B.C.E., presented two important ideas about the dynamic nature of memory that are still currently the subject of many studies. First, he highlighted the link between memory and time, suggesting that memories occur in animals that perceive time. Second, he discussed how recollecting differs from relearning (Sorabji, 2006). Many years later—only slightly more than 100 years ago—a number of studies concluded that memory changes over time and continues to change for quite a while after learning. Experimental psychologists proposed the theory of memory *consolidation* to explain the detrimental effects of new learning experienced in close proximity to a previous learning event: The shorter the interval between the second learning and the original one, the greater the deficit. Hence, it was suggested that a newly formed memory undergoes changes after learning that are critical for its stabilization and storage. This was then supported by experimental evidence. Sherrington (1906) appreciated that neural activity often outlasts the stimulus, and later it was suggested that reverberating, self-re-exciting neural circuits are at the basis of memory storage (Hilgard & Marquis, 1940). Hebb proposed the idea that long-term memories are supported by stable structural changes and that a reverberating trace may cooperate with the structural change and carry the memory until the structural growth has occurred, at which point memory storage is fixed and stable. A large body of literature in animal models of retrograde amnesia supported this idea that over time memory becomes "fixed", as treatments administered soon after training profoundly disrupt memories, whereas treatments given at increasingly long intervals of time have a progressively less disruptive effect. Based on neuro-psychological studies of amnesia, experimental psychology, and behavioral neuroscience data, Squire, Cohen, and Nadel (1984) proposed that consolidation proceeds for a long time, up to several years in humans, and that it requires an intact medial temporal lobe. From all these observations, it appeared that memory consolidation takes a long time and progresses over time as a unitary process.

A few years ago, this theory of memory consolidation was challenged by studies reporting that memories that had become resistant to the amnesic effects of protein synthesis or neural activity/transmission blockers, and thus considered consolidated, became sensitive to that treatment again if, and only if, they were retrieved or reactivated. These studies, of which one of the most important was that of Nader, Schafe, and LeDoux (2000), proposed that memories can "reconsolidate" and that consolidation is not a unitary process. Similar observations had been reported in the 1960s but were then somewhat left out from the field or were considered not sufficiently convincing. The studies published in the 1990s by Susan Sara's laboratory and in 2000 by Nader *et al.* persuaded the community that it was important to investigate how and why memories that are considered consolidated again become sensitive to disruption and undergo another consolidation-like process in order to persist.

A great number of discussions, debates, divergent views, and controversies in the field emerged and have continued for the past 12 years, and several are still ongoing. In fact, in the past decade, several hundred studies have inquired about mechanisms, timing, functions, and meanings of memory reconsolidation in a multitude of species ranging from *Caenorhabditis elegans* to human. Addressing these questions is important not only for understanding how memory formation and storage works but also because it provides important information about changing memory stability in health and diseases.

Many diseases that affect memory, such as memory loss in aging, Alzheimer's disease, stroke, and dementia, would greatly benefit from the possibility of increasing memory strength or prolonging memory stability. Similarly, many diseases in which excessively strong memories cause symptoms and pathologies, such as post-traumatic stress disorder (PTSD) and addiction, can benefit from treatments that weaken memory stability. Reconsolidation and its mechanisms offer an opportunity for strengthening or weakening memory retention.

I had the privilege to edit this book on the exciting and debated topic of memory reconsolidation. I accepted enthusiastically because, in my view, this is a very important emerging field with high potential for clinical applications; hence, collecting its current state-of-the-art may stimulate new ideas, help critical thinking, and aid the progress of the field.

This book is intended for scientists, students, and experts who are interested in understanding where the field currently stands and what types of hypotheses, conclusions, and disagreements are discussed about memory reconsolidation. The reader will find chapters from some of the main contributors to the field of reconsolidation describing their work, views, and stance on debated issues. First, there is a brief historical chapter by Karim Nader. Karim's paper published in 2000 changed the field, and to Karim I express my appreciation for pioneering a new way of thinking about memory formation and storage. There is then a collection of interesting chapters on the reconsolidation of different types of memories in different species, including invertebrate conditioning, rodent Pavlovian conditioning, rodent temporal lobe-dependent memories, and human explicit and implicit memories. Furthermore, other chapters discuss boundary conditions and mechanisms in reconsolidation, the relationship between reconsolidation and extinction, and clinical applications based on memory reconsolidation in PTSD and addiction. Finally, a chapter discusses the role of consolidation and reconsolidation in psychotherapy and proposes a working hypothesis that may explain the role of memory traces in the Freudian unconscious. I deliberately left the authors completely free to express their points of view so that the controversies were not censured by the views of others.

I express my gratitude and thanks to all the authors who agreed to contribute a chapter to this book. It takes a great deal of knowledge, time, and passion. I deeply thank several colleagues who very generously gave me invaluable feedback for shaping this book: Yadin Dudai (Weizmann Institute of Science, Rehovot, Israel), Joe LeDoux (Center for Neural Science, New York University, New York), Maria Eugenia Pedreira and Arturo Romano (IFIBYNE-CONICET, Universidad de Buenos Aires, Buenos Aires, Argentina), and Xiaojing Ye, Sarah Johnson, and all the members of my laboratory (Center for Neural Science, New York University, New York).

REFERENCES

Hilgard, E. R., & Marquis, D. G. (1940). *Conditioning and Learning*. New York: Appleton-Century-Crofts.

Nader, K., Schafe, G. E., & LeDoux, J. E. (2000). Fear memories require protein synthesis in the amygdala for reconsolidation after retrieval. *Nature, 406*(6797), 722–726.

Sherrington, C. S. (1906). *The Integrative Action of the Nervous System*. New Haven, CT: Yale University Press.

Sorabji, R. (2006). *Aristotle on Memory* (2nd ed.). Chicago: University of Chicago Press.

Squire, L. R., Cohen, N. H., & Nadel, L. (1984). The medial temporal region and memory consolidation: A new hypothesis. In H. Weingartner, & E. Parker (Eds.), *Memory Consolidation* (pp. 185–210). Hillsdale, NJ: Erlbaum.

Contributors

Francois Ansermet University of Geneva, Geneva, Switzerland

Alain Brunet McGill University and Douglas Mental Health University Institute, Montreal, Quebec, Canada

Philip R. Corlett Department of Psychiatry, Yale University School of Medicine, Connecticut Mental Health Center, New Haven, Connecticut

Jacek Dębiec Molecular & Behavioral Neuroscience Institute and Department of Psychiatry, University of Michigan, Ann Arbor, Michigan

Einar Örn Einarrson Department of Psychology, McGill University, Montreal, Canada

Peter S.B. Finnie Department of Psychology, McGill University, Montreal, Canada

Rebecca Gomez Department of Psychology, The University of Arizona, Tucson, Arizona

Oliver Hardt Department of Psychology, McGill University, Montreal, Canada

Almut Hupbach Department of Psychology, Lehigh University, Bethlehem, Pennsylvania

Sarah A. Johnson Center for Neural Science, New York University, New York, New York

Carolyn E. Jones Department of Psychology, The University of Texas at Austin, Austin, Texas

Satoshi Kida Department of Bioscience, Faculty of Applied Bioscience, Tokyo University of Agriculture, Tokyo, Japan

Joseph E. LeDoux Center for Neural Science, New York University, New York, New York; and The Emotional Brain Institute, Nathan Kline Institute for Psychiatric Research, Orangeburg, New York

Jonathan L.C. Lee School of Psychology, University of Birmingham, Birmingham, United Kingdom

Michelle H. Lonergan McGill University and Douglas Mental Health University Institute, Montreal, Quebec, Canada

Pierre Magistretti University of Lausanne, Lausanne, Switzerland; EPFL, Lausanne, Switzerland; and KAUST, Thuwal, Kingdom of Saudi Arabia

Marie-H. Monfils Department of Psychology, The University of Texas at Austin, Austin, Texas

Lynn Nadel Department of Psychology, The University of Arizona, Tucson, Arizona

Karim Nader Department of Psychology, McGill University, Montreal, Canada

Lening A. Olivera-Figueroa Yale University School of Medicine, U.S. Department of Veteran Affairs Connecticut Healthcare System (VACHS), New Haven, Connecticut

María Eugenia Pedreira Laboratorio de Neurobiología de la Memoria, FCEN UBA, IFIBYNE-CONICET, Buenos Aires, Argentina

Elizabeth A. Phelps Department of Psychology and Center for Neural Science, New York University, New York, New York; and Nathan Kline Institute, Orangeburg, New York

Roger K. Pitman Harvard University, Cambridge, Massachusetts

Arturo Romano Laboratorio de Neurobiología de la Memoria, FCEN UBA, IFIBYNE-CONICET, Buenos Aires, Argentina

Daniela Schiller Departments of Psychiatry and Neuroscience, Icahn School of Medicine at Mt. Sinai, New York, New York

Jane R. Taylor Department of Psychiatry, Yale University School of Medicine, Connecticut Mental Health Center, New Haven, Connecticut

Xiaojing Ye Center for Neural Science, New York University, New York, New York

Chapter | one

The Discovery of Memory Reconsolidation

Karim Nader

McGill University, Montreal, Canada

This is an exciting time to be studying learning and memory. Prior to the year 2000, only initial acquisition and memory stabilization, or synaptic consolidation (Dudai, 2004; Kandel, 2001; Martin, Grimwood, & Morris, 2000), were so-called "active" processes, in that they required neurons to implement metabolic and morphological changes that are thought to depend on the synthesis of new RNA and proteins. Once these changes were in place, so it was commonly believed, all other memory processing phases were essentially akin to passive readouts of long-term memory (LTM). Although this was the mainstream opinion, there were some who did not agree with this model, pointing to the possibility that phases of plasticity may be present not just at the birth of a new memory (Lewis, 1979; Miller & Marlin, 1984; Spear & Mueller, 1984).

It is somewhat ironic that this once minority opinion has become the new de facto standard within the past 12 years, as described in more detail later. First, largely through the pioneering work of Todd Sacktor, we now know that memory maintenance appears to be maintenance as an active biological mechanism. There may be a continuous battle being played out between the forces of memory erasure versus maintenance (Migues *et al.*, 2010; Pastalkova *et al.*, 2006; Sacktor, 2010, Shema *et al.*, 2011). This body of work has identified the constitutively active protein kinase M zeta (PKMζ), an atypical isoform of protein kinase C, as critical for sustaining many types of LTM (Sacktor, 2008). It has been shown in many tasks and brain regions that transient inactivation of PKMζ results in the loss of established LTM. Work has shown that the persistent action of PKMζ keeps GluA2-containing AMPA receptors (GluA2 AMPARs) at the postsynaptic density (Migues *et al.*, 2010) and that this continuous regulation of GluA2 AMPAR trafficking maintains LTM (AMPARs are a core part of the biological substrate of memory, mediating the vast majority of excitatory neurotransmission in the brain).

Memory Reconsolidation. http://dx.doi.org/10.1016/B978-0-12-386892-3.00001-9

Second, retrieval is now firmly established as the opposite of the once envisioned passive readout of memory, and its mechanisms and consequences are the topic of much exciting research, to which the body of work assembled in this book gives testimony. All this work is based on the peculiar phenomenon that a fully consolidated memory, when recalled, can return to an unstable state from which, in order to persist, it has to be restabilized. This process of restabilization, which was first demonstrated by Lewis and Sherman's group (Misanin, Miller, & Lewis, 1968; Schneider & Sherman, 1968), is now referred to as reconsolidation. Now, for the second time in the history of our field, there is accumulating evidence that this memory process does indeed exist (Alberini, 2011; Dudai, 2012; Hardt, Wang, & Nader, 2009; Lewis, 1979; Miller & Springer, 1973; Nader & Hardt, 2009; Sara, 2000; Spear, 1973): Retrieval can cause the retrieved memory to reconsolidate, and disrupting this process will impair it.

Consolidation theory is a tale of two gradients describing conceptually related phenomena. On the one hand, there is the concept now referred to as synaptic consolidation. For more than 100 years, it has been known that new memories pass through qualitatively distinct phases over time (Ebbinghaus, 1885; Müller & Pilzecker, 1900; Ribot, 1881): Memories are unstable after acquisition and progressively stabilize over time. Müller and Pilzecker suggested that a perseveration—consolidation process mediates this stabilization. This process is now called "synaptic consolidation," which is thought to be a ubiquitous property of neurons throughout the brain (Dudai & Morris 2000; Kandel, 2001; Martin *et al.*, 2000). When this process is interrupted before completion, memory will be impaired.

The other time-dependent memory stabilization process was initially described by Theodule-Armand Ribot (1881). Studying patients suffering from amnesia, Ribot reported that patients could not recall recent events but had intact memories from the more remote past (Burnham, 1903; Ribot, 1881). Describing similar cases of retrograde amnesia, Russell and Nathan (1946) commented on the dynamic nature of memory as follows: "It seems likely that memory of events is not a static process" and "the normal activity of the brain must steadily strengthen distant memories so that with the passage of time these become less vulnerable to the effects of brain injury" (p. 299).

Another temporal gradient forms the basis for what is called "systems consolidation." This notion, proposing that prolonged consolidation reflected memory reorganization over brain systems, began to emerge in studies showing that damage to the medial temporal lobe (MTL) resulted in severe global amnesia, but mostly for recently acquired memories. In a landmark paper, the memory impairments were described for patient HM (the late Henry Molaison), who had most of his MTL removed to relieve intractable epilepsy (Scoville & Milner, 1957). Although Henry Molaison's intellectual abilities remained intact, the operation left him with a profound impairment in forming new episodic memories (memories of events) and an extensive loss of such memories extending back years before his surgery. He also suffered from anterograde amnesia, the inability to form new memories, which, interestingly, was not global. For instance, he was able to acquire new motor skills, the learning of which he had no conscious recollection. Results from this amnesic patient and others with similar MTL damage suggested that MTL structures, specifically the hippocampus, play a role in episodic, explicit, or declarative memory but not in implicit or nondeclarative memories, such as procedural memories, priming, and conditioned responses. Based on such dissociations provided by many case studies, the presence of a systems consolidation process was proposed in which the hippocampal region served to "prime activity" in cortical areas, where permanent storage took place (Milner, 1966; Squire, Stark, & Clark, 2004). Thus, the hippocampus was thought to be critical during the early, but not later, life of explicit, or episodic, memories.

It is important to note that the neurobiological mechanisms involved in systems consolidation likely engage synaptic consolidation mechanisms (Frankland & Bontempi, 2005). Therefore, reports of reconsolidation at the synaptic level have implications not just for theories of synaptic consolidation but also for theories of systems consolidation.

All consolidation theories posit that once consolidation is complete, a memory will remain in the consolidated state—that is, fixed and stable. In contrast to this expectation, overwhelming evidence suggests that consolidated memories can be transferred again into a labile state, from which they are restabilized by a reconsolidation process. Retrieval appears to be the key process that transfers memory from the stable to the unstable state. This idea is not new to cognitive psychology, in which memory malleability phenomena such as the misinformation effect and hindsight bias have been prominently studied for quite some time. The concept of memory reconsolidation now offers neurobiologically plausible mechanisms that might explain the molecular, cellular, circuit, and brain system processes that underpin these effects (Hardt, Einarsson, & Nader, 2010; Loftus & Yuille, 1984).

1.1 A BRIEF HISTORY

Three lines of evidence support the existence of a stabilization period on the order of hours after the acquisition of new memories. First, performance can be impaired if amnesic treatments such as electroconvulsive shock (Duncan, 1949) or protein synthesis inhibitors (Flexner, Flexner, & Stellar, 1965) are given after learning. Second, performance can be impaired if new competing learning occurs after the initial learning (Gordon & Spear, 1973). Third, retention can be enhanced by administration of various compounds after the initial learning, such as strychnine (McGaugh & Krivanek, 1970). Critically, all three manipulations are effective only when given soon after new learning and not when given after a delay. These findings gave rise to theories of synaptic consolidation (Glickman, 1961; Hebb, 1949; McGaugh, 1966).

The initial unstable trace is called "short-term memory," lasting on the order of hours. With time, the trace enters LTM, at which point it is considered to be consolidated and can no longer be affected by treatments such as those mentioned previously. Thus, if a memory is susceptible to enhancement or impairment, it is considered to be in a labile, nonconsolidated state, and if it is insensitive to administration of these amnesic treatments, then the memory is, by definition, consolidated (Dudai, 2004; McGaugh, 1966). Once a memory has become consolidated, it remains in the fixed state.

Consolidation theory became the central tenet around which the field of systems neuroscience of memory has evolved. Since that time, the field has enjoyed numerous successes in creating models at different levels of analysis to describe the changes that occur when a memory is converted from labile trace to a "fixed" one. These include long-term potentiation (Bliss & Lomo, 1973; Martin *et al.*, 2000) and the identification of transcription factors that act as gateways to LTM (Bourtchuladze *et al.*, 1994; Dash, Hochner, & Kandel, 1990; Kandel, 2001; Yin *et al.*, 1994).

Since its inception, there have been some challenges to consolidation theory. One emerged from a small number of studies demonstrating that a consolidated memory could destabilize and restabilize on the order of minutes to hours when reactivated. Again, there were three lines of evidence to support the existence of a restabilization period. First, performance can be impaired if amnesic treatments such as electroconvulsive shock (Misanin *et al.*, 1968; Schneider & Sherman, 1968) are given after reactivation. Second, performance can be impaired if new competing learning occurs after the reactivation (Gordon, 1977a). Third, retention can be enhanced by administration of various compounds, such as strychnine, after reactivation (Gordon 1977b). Critically, all three manipulations are effective only when given soon after reactivation but not when given after a delay. As had been the case for the consolidation concept, these findings gave rise to a theory to explain them, and new theories of memory were proposed (Lewis, 1979; Miller & Marlin, 1984; Miller & Springer, 1973; Spear & Mueller, 1984).

The implications of these findings, called, among other terms, cue-dependent amnesia, were that LTM was not the end of the road in terms of plasticity. Plasticity was merely momentarily paused when a memory was not used, but it could return when memory was reactivated. According to a model proposed by Lewis (1979), memory was in essence a dynamic process that took two states—the active state and the inactive state. The inactive state comprised dormant memories that were not being used, and in it they were insensitive to disruption. New and reactivated memories were in the active state and, as such, unstable and contained both new and reactivated traces. The model endowed memory with a principal dynamic nature. It could explain both the data on which consolidation theory was founded and the cue-dependent amnesia studies that consolidation theory could not explain. For reasons that remain unclear (Dudai, 2004), in the years following the first reconsolidation documentation in the 1970s, research on the phenomenon was very modestly present as a widely unrecognized small steady undercurrent in the mainstream of research on memory dynamics (Land, Bunsey, & Riccio, 2000; Litvin & Anokhin, 2000; Mactutus, Riccio, & Ferek, 1979; Przyby-slawski & Sara, 1997; Quartermain, McEwen, & Azmitia, 1972; Rodriguez, Rodriguez, Phillips, & Martinez, 1993; for a careful review of this literature, see Sara, 2000). In fact, no contemporary textbook on memory consolidation even made note of these earlier studies.

Research on the reconsolidation effect was greatly revitalized by the systematic demonstration of memory reconsolidation in a well-defined behavioral protocol: auditory fear conditioning in the rat (Nader, Schafe, & LeDoux, 2000). Directly targeting the brain circuitry critically mediating the behavior and its consolidation (basolateral nucleus of the amygdala) and using a drug with well-documented amnesic effects on memory consolidation (inhibition of protein synthesis with the antibiotic anisomycin), we showed that reminders could bring well-consolidated fear memories back to an unstable state, in which these reactivated memories could be disrupted by inhibiting protein synthesis in the amygdala. Also, as in the original finding, such impairments were not observed in the absence of reactivation. The conclusion using the definitions of the field of consolidation was that consolidated reactivated memories return to an unstable state from which they must restabilize in order to persist (Nader & Hardt, 2009).

Since publication of this study, reconsolidation has been demonstrated using a range of species, tasks, and amnesic agents (Table 1.1). The modern evidence for the existence of a reconsolidation period is once again based on the same three lines of evidence on which consolidation theory is rooted. First, performance can be impaired if amnesic treatments such as targeted infusions of protein synthesis inhibitors (Litvin & Anokhin, 2000; Milekic & Alberini, 2002; Nader et al., 2000) are given soon after reactivation. Second, performance can be impaired if new competing learning occurs in short temporal proximity to reactivation (Walker, Brakefield, Hobson, & Stickgold, 2003). Third, retention can be enhanced by administration of various compounds, such as activators of signaling pathways important for consolidation, after reactivation of the memory (Tronson, Wiseman, Olausson, & Taylor, 2006).

Evidence for reconsolidation does not derive solely from behavioral studies. Specifically, cellular and molecular correlates of reconsolidation have been found. For example, a cellular phenomenon akin to reconsolidation was shown for late long-term potentiation (Fonseca, Nagerl, & Bonhoeffer, 2006). The authors report that reactivation of the "consolidated" potentiated pathway returned it to an unstable state. If anisomycin was added at this point, then the potentiation was lost (Fonseca et al., 2006; Doyere, Debiec, Monfils, Schafe, & LeDoux, 2007). At the molecular level of analysis, a number of studies have demonstrated that blockade of reconsolidation leads to a reversal of molecular correlates of LTM (Miller & Marshall, 2005; Rose & Rankin, 2006; Valjent, Corbille, Bertran-Gonzalez, Hervé, & Girault,

TABLE 1.1 Examples of Paradigms in which Reconsolidation Has Been Reported[a]

Example	References
Experimental Paradigm	
Habituation	Rose and Rankin (2006)
Auditory fear conditioning	Nader et al. (2000)
Contextual fear conditioning	Debiec, LeDoux, and Nader (2002)
Instrumental learning	Sangha, Scheibenstock, and Lukowiak (2003); but see Hernandez and Kelley (2004)
Inhibitory avoidance	Anokhin, Tiunova, and Rose (2002); Litvin and Anokhin (2000); Milekic and Alberini (2002)
Motor sequence learning	Walker et al. (2003)
Incentive learning	Wang, Ostlund, Nader, and Balleine (2005)
Object recognition	Kelly, Laroche, and Davis (2003)
Spatial memory	Morris et al. (2006); Suzuki et al. (2004)
Memory for drug reward	Lee, Di Ciano, Thomas, and Everitt (2005); Miller and Marshall (2005); Valjent, Aubier, et al. (2006)
Episodic memory	Hupbach, Gomez, Hardt, and Nader (2007)
Treatment	
Protein synthesis inhibition	Nader et al. (2000)
RNA synthesis inhibition	Sangha et al. (2003)
Inhibition of kinase activity	Duvarci, Nader, and LeDoux (2005); Kelly et al. (2003)
Protein knockout mice	Bozon, Davis, and Laroche (2003)
Antisense	Lee, Everitt, and Thomas (2004); Taubenfeld, Milekic, Monti, and Alberini (2001)
Inducible knockout mice	Kida et al. (2002)
Receptor antagonists	Debiec and LeDoux (2004); Przybyslawski, Roullet, and Sara (1999); Suzuki et al. (2004)
Interference by new learning	Hupbach et al. (2007); Walker et al. (2003)
Potentiated reconsolidation by increase in kinase activity	Tronson et al. (2006)
Species	
Nematodes	Rose and Rankin (2006)
Honeybees	Stollhoff, Menzel, and Eisenhardt (2005)
Snails	Sangha et al. (2003)
Sea slugs	Cai, Pearce, Chen, and Glanzman (2012); Child, Epstein, Kuzirian, and Alkon (2003); Lee et al. (2012)

(Continued)

TABLE 1.1 Examples of Paradigms in which Reconsolidation Has Been Reported[a]—Continued

Example	References
Fish	Eisenberg, Kobilo, Berman, and Dudai (2003)
Crabs	Pedreira, Perez-Cuesta, and Maldonado (2002)
Chicks	Anokhin *et al.* (2002)
Mice	Kida *et al.* (2002)
Rats	Nader *et al.* (2000); rat pups: Gruest, Richer, and Hars (2004)
Humans	Hupbach *et al.* (2007); Walker *et al.* (2003)

[a]*This table lists examples from various experimental paradigms, treatments, and species for studies reporting evidence for a reconsolidation process since the year 2000.*
Source: *Modified from Nader and Hardt (2009).*

2006). One elegant study used *Caenorhabditis elegans* and a nonassociative task (habituation of the tap withdrawal effect) (Rose & Rankin, 2006). One molecular correlate of habituation in this system is a decrease in the number of postsynaptic AMPARs in the mechanosensory neuron mediating tap withdrawal (Rose, Kaun, Chen, & Rankin, 2003). When reconsolidation in this model was blocked by amnesic treatments, the amnesic animals had AMPAR levels comparable to those of naive animals in the mechanosensory neuron. This is striking evidence for the specificity of the impairments. Lastly, based on unpublished results from Lucas Johnson's lab, it appears that the same cells express a memory after reconsolidation has taken place as the ones that had consolidated it (Bergstrom *et al.*, 2011).

Given the richness of the data on reconsolidation mentioned previously, including the original findings, alternative interpretations are incapable of readily explaining the data set. Among these are nonspecific drug effects such as lesions (Rudy, Biedenkapp, Moineau, & Bolding, 2006), state-dependent learning (Millin, Moody, & Riccio, 2001), new learning (Eisenhardt & Menzel, 2007), facilitated extinction (Myers & Davis, 2002), and retrieval impairment (Cahill, McGaugh, & Weinberger, 2001; Squire, 2006; Vianna, Szapiro, McGaugh, Medina, & Izquierdo, 2001). All of these issues have been explicitly addressed in a review and have been refuted (Nader & Hardt, 2009). Indeed, Nader and Hardt described, and then applied, the traditional standards used to conclude that a consolidation period exists to the reactivation-induced phenomenon. They concluded that the reactivation data set met the standard to be considered a time-dependent stabilization period.

Of course, there remain different perspectives on reconsolidation that have been generating more experiments and more findings (Alberini, 2005; Dudai & Eisenberg, 2004; Lee, 2008; Tronson & Taylor, 2007; Walker & Stickgold, 2006). None of these new insights have challenged the basic fact that via reactivation, consolidated memory may return to an unstable state from which it must restabilize. Reconsolidation has been established as a fundamental memory process. Indeed, it seems that new information employs consolidation mechanisms to be stored. All subsequent modifications to these memories seem to engage reconsolidation mechanisms (Lee, 2008, 2009). Thus, consolidation is the exception, and reconsolidation is the memory process most prominently engaged throughout the lifetime of a memory.

It is a testament to the quality of the science performed by the original discoverers of reconsolidation that so many of the effects described approximately 30–40 years ago have now been rediscovered (Nader & Hardt, 2009). It is heartening that, as shown in Figure 1.1, as a consequence of this revival the classic papers that originally described these effects (Lewis, 1979; Misanin et al., 1968; Schneider & Sherman, 1968) have experienced renewed reception, as their rate of citation has been steadily increasing.

The term *reconsolidation* was introduced to the field as early as 1973 by Spear. Asking how consolidation theory would deal with the dynamic effects reported by Lewis and others, Skip Spear stated, "How will the dynamic aspects of memory be handled, that is, with successive learning trials or related successive experiences does the entire memory reconsolidate anew or merely the new information?" Since the publication of Nader et al. (2000), approximately 540 papers on the topic of reconsolidation have been published. Consistent with the impressions reported by Serge Laroche and colleagues, those domains are healthy and growing exponentially (Besnard, Caboche, & Laroche, 2012).

The authors of the chapters of this book are main contributors to this great wealth of knowledge and represent many of the leading thinkers in their fields. Many were at the forefront of the exciting debates and scientific discourses

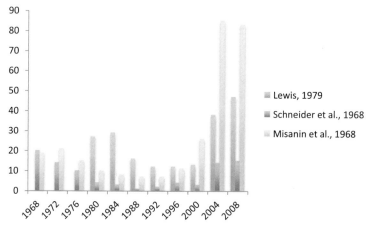

FIGURE 1.1 The number of citations per 4-year period for the two original papers reporting reconsolidation by Misanin et al. (1968) and Schneider et al. (1968). In addition, the rate of citations for Lewis (1970), reported in a conceptual paper in which he formulates a new model of memory processing, is also shown.

that arose after publication of our study in the year 2000. Thanks to Cristina Alberini's efforts, they are all united in this book, which, I have no doubt, will become one of the historic markers of our field that future generations will revisit to guide their own efforts in understanding more about this peculiar phenomenon of memory.

REFERENCES

Alberini, C. M. (2005). Mechanisms of memory stabilization: are consolidation and reconsolidation similar or distinct processes? *Trends in Neurosciences, 28*(1), 51−56.

Alberini, C. M. (2011). The role of reconsolidation and the dynamic process of long-term memory formation and storage. *Frontiers in Behavioral Neuroscience, 5*, 12.

Anokhin, K. V., Tiunova, A. A., & Rose, S. P. (2002). Reminder effects: Reconsolidation or retrieval deficit? Pharmacological dissection with protein synthesis inhibitors following reminder for a passive-avoidance task in young chicks. *European Journal of Neuroscience, 15*(11), 1759−1765.

Bergstrom, H., McDonald, C., et al. (2011). *Both consolidation and reconsolidation of Pavlovian fear conditioning engage a dedicated micro organization of neurons in the dorsolateral amygdala*. Washington, DC: Poster presented at the Society for Neuroscience Conference 2011, November, 12−16.

Besnard, A., Caboche, J., & Laroche, S. (2012). Reconsolidation of memory: a decade of debate. *Progress in Neurobiology, 99*(1), 61−80.

Bliss, T. V., & Lomo, T. (1973). Long-lasting potentiation of synaptic transmission in the dentate area of the anaesthetized rabbit following stimulation of the perforant path. *Journal of Physiology, 232*, 331−356.

Bourtchuladze, R., Frenguelli, B., Blendy, J., Cioffi, D., Schutz, G., & Silva, A. J. (1994). Deficient long-term memory in mice with a targeted mutation of the cAMP-responsive element-binding protein. *Cell, 79*(1), 59−68.

Bozon, B., Davis, S., & Laroche, S. (2003). A requirement for the immediate early gene zif268 in reconsolidation of recognition memory after retrieval. *Neuron, 40*(4), 695−701.

Burnham, W. H. (1903). Retroactive amnesia: illustrative cases and a tentative explanation. *American Journal of Psychology, 14*, 382−396.

Cahill, L., McGaugh, J. L., & Weinberger, N. M. (2001). The neurobiology of learning and memory: some reminders to remember. *Trends in Neurosciences, 24*(10), 578−581.

Cai, D., Pearce, K., Chen, S., & Glanzman, D. L. (2012). Reconsolidation of long-term memory in *Aplysia*. *Current Biology, 22*, 1783−1788. http://dx.doi.org/10.1016/j.cub.2012.07.038.

Child, F. M., Epstein, H. T., Kuzirian, A. M., & Alkon, D. L. (2003). Memory reconsolidation in *Hermissenda*. *Biology Bulletin, 205*(2), 218−219.

Dash, P. K., Hochner, B., & Kandel, E. R. (1990). Injection of the cAMP-responsive element into the nucleus of *Aplysia* sensory neurons blocks long-term facilitation. *Nature, 345*(6277), 718−721.

Debiec, J., & LeDoux, J. E. (2004). Disruption of reconsolidation but not consolidation of auditory fear conditioning by noradrenergic blockade in the amygdala. *Neuroscience, 129*(2), 267−272.

Debiec, J., LeDoux, J. E., & Nader, K. (2002). Cellular and systems reconsolidation in the hippocampus. *Neuron, 36*(3), 527−538.

Doyere, V., Debiec, J., Monfils, M. H., Schafe, G. E., & LeDoux, J. E. (2007). Synapse-specific reconsolidation of distinct fear memories in the lateral amygdala. *Nature Neuroscience, 10*(4), 414−416.

Dudai, Y. (2004). The neurobiology of consolidations, or, how stable is the engram? *Annual Review of Psychology, 55*, 51−86.

Dudai, Y. (2012). The restless engram: consolidations never end. *Annual Review of Neuroscience, 35*, 227−247.

Dudai, Y., & Eisenberg, M. (2004). Rites of passage of the engram: reconsolidation and the lingering consolidation hypothesis. *Neuron, 44*(1), 93−100.

Dudai, Y., & Morris, R. (2000). To consolidate or not to consolidate: what are the questions? In J. Bolhius (Ed.), *Brain, Perception, Memory: Advances in Cognitive Sciences* (pp. 149−162) Oxford: Oxford University Press.

Duncan, C. P. (1949). The retroactive effect of electroconvulsive shock. *Journal of Comparative & Physiological Psychology, 42*, 32−44.

Duvarci, S., Nader, K., & LeDoux, J. E. (2005). Activation of extracellular signal-regulated kinase-/mitogen-activated protein kinase cascade in the amygdala is required for memory reconsolidation of auditory fear conditioning. *European Journal of Neuroscience, 21*(1), 283−289.

Ebbinghaus, M. (1885). *Über das Gedächtnis*. Leipzig: Buehler.

Eisenberg, M., Kobilo, T., Berman, D. E., & Dudai, Y. (2003). Stability of retrieved memory: inverse correlation with trace dominance. *Science, 301*(5636), 1102−1104.

Eisenhardt, D., & Menzel, R. (2007). Extinction learning, reconsolidation and the internal reinforcement hypothesis. *Neurobiology of Learning and Memory, 87*(2), 167−173.

Flexner, L. B., Flexner, J. B., & Stellar, E. (1965). Memory and cerebral protein synthesis in mice as affected by graded amounts of puromycin. *Experimental Neurology, 13*(3), 264−272.

Fonseca, R., Nagerl, U. V., & Bonhoeffer, T. (2006). Neuronal activity determines the protein synthesis dependence of long-term potentiation. *Nature Neuroscience, 9*(4), 478−480.

Frankland, P. W., & Bontempi, B. (2005). The organization of recent and remote memories. *Nature Reviews Neuroscience, 6*(2), 119−130.

Glickman, S. (1961). Perseverative neural processes and consolidation of the memory trace. *Psychological Bulletin, 58*, 218−233.

Gordon, W. C. (1977a). Similarities of recently acquired and reactivated memories in interference. *American Journal of Psychology, 90*(2), 231−242.

Gordon, W. C. (1977b). Susceptibility of a reactivated memory to the effects of strychnine: a time-dependent phenomenon. *Physiology & Behavior, 18*(1), 95−99.

Gordon, W. C., & Spear, N. E. (1973). Effect of reactivation of a previously acquired memory on the interaction between memories in the rat. *Journal of Experimental Psychology, 99*(3), 349−355.

Gruest, N., Richer, P., & Hars, B. (2004). Memory consolidation and reconsolidation in the rat pup require protein synthesis. *Journal of Neuroscience, 24*(46), 10488−10492.

Hardt, O., Einarsson, E. O., & Nader, K. (2010). A bridge over troubled water: reconsolidation as a link between cognitive and neuroscientific memory research traditions. *Annual Review of Psychology, 61*, 141−167.

Hardt, O., Wang, S.-H., & Nader, K. (2009). Storage or retrieval deficit: the yin and yang of amnesia. *Learning & Memory, 16*, 224−230.

Hebb, D. O. (1949). *The Organization of Behavior*. New York: Wiley.

Hernandez, P. J., & Kelley, A. E. (2004). Long-term memory for instrumental responses does not undergo protein synthesis-dependent reconsolidation upon retrieval. *Learning & Memory, 11*, 748−754.

Hupbach, A., Gomez, R., Hardt, O., & Nader, K. (2007). Reconsolidation of episodic memories: a subtle reminder triggers integration of new information. *Learning & Memory, 14*, 47−53.

Kandel, E. R. (2001). The molecular biology of memory storage: a dialogue between genes and synapses. *Science, 294*(5544), 1030−1038.

Kelly, A., Laroche, S., & Davis, S. (2003). Activation of mitogen-activated protein kinase/extracellular signal-regulated kinase in hippocampal circuitry is required for consolidation and reconsolidation of recognition memory. *Journal of Neuroscience, 23*(12), 5354−5360.

Kida, S., Josselyn, S. A., Peña de Ortiz, S., Kogan, J. H., Chevere, I., Masushige, S., & Silva, A. J. (2002). CREB required for the stability of new and reactivated fear memories. *Nature Neuroscience, 5*(4), 348−355.

Land, C., Bunsey, M., & Riccio, D. C. (2000). Anomalous properties of hippocampal lesion-induced retrograde amnesia. *Psychobiology, 28*, 476−485.

Lee, J. L. (2008). Memory reconsolidation mediates the strengthening of memories by additional learning. *Nature Neuroscience, 11*(11), 1264−1266.

Lee, J. L. (2009). Reconsolidation: maintaining memory relevance. *Trends in Neurosciences, 32*(8), 413−420.

Lee, J. L., Di Ciano, P., Thomas, K. L., & Everitt, B. J. (2005). Disrupting reconsolidation of drug memories reduces cocaine-seeking behavior. *Neuron, 47*(6), 795−801.

Lee, J. L., Everitt, B. J., & Thomas, K. L. (2004). Independent cellular processes for hippocampal memory consolidation and reconsolidation. *Science, 304*(5672), 839−843.

Lee, S. H., Kwak, C., Shim, J., Kim, J. E., Choi, S. L., Kim, H. F., & Kaang, B. K. (2012). A cellular model of memory reconsolidation involves reactivation-induced destabilization and restabilization at the sensorimotor synapse in *Aplysia*. *Proceedings of the National Academy of Sciences USA, 109*, 14200−14205. http://dx.doi.org/10.1073/pnas.1211997109, (2012).

Lewis, D. J. (1979). Psychobiology of active and inactive memory. *Psychological Bulletin, 86*, 1054−1083.

Litvin, O. O., & Anokhin, K. V. (2000). Mechanisms of memory reorganization during retrieval of acquired behavioral experience in chicks: the effects of protein synthesis inhibition in the brain. *Neuroscience and Behavioral Physiology, 30*(6), 671−678.

Loftus, E. F., & Yuille, J. C. (1984). Departures from reality in human perception and memory. In H. Weingartner, & E. S. Parker (Eds.), *Memory Consolidation: Psychobiology of Cognition* (pp. 163−184). Hillsdale, NJ: Erlbaum.

Mactutus, C. F., Riccio, D. C., & Ferek, J. M. (1979). Retrograde amnesia for old (reactivated) memory: some anomalous characteristics. *Science, 204*, 1319−1320.

Martin, S. J., Grimwood, P. D., & Morris, R. G. (2000). Synaptic plasticity and memory: an evaluation of the hypothesis. *Annual Review of Neuroscience, 23*, 649−711.

McGaugh, J. L. (1966). Time-dependent processes in memory storage. *Science, 153*(742), 1351−1358.

McGaugh, J. L., & Krivanek, J. A. (1970). Strychnine effects on discrimination learning in mice: effects of dose and time of administration. *Physiology & Behavior, 5*(12), 1437−1442.

Migues, P. V., Hardt, O., Wu, D. C., Gamache, K., Sacktor, T. C., Wang, Y. T., & Nader, K. (2010). PKMzeta maintains memories by regulating GluR2-dependent AMPA receptor trafficking. *Nature Neuroscience, 13*(5), 630−634.

Milekic, M. H., & Alberini, C. M. (2002). Temporally graded requirement for protein synthesis following memory reactivation. *Neuron, 36*, 521−525.

Miller, C. A., & Marshall, J. F. (2005). Molecular substrates for retrieval and reconsolidation of cocaine-associated contextual memory. *Neuron, 47*(6), 873−884.

Miller, R. R., & Marlin, N. A. (1984). The physiology and semantics of consolidation: of mice and men. In H. Weingartner, & E. S. Parker (Eds.), *Memory Consolidation: Psychobiology of Cognition* (pp. 85−109). Hillsdale, NJ: Erlbaum.

Miller, R. R., & Springer, A. D. (1973). Amnesia, consolidation, and retrieval. *Psychological Review, 80*(1), 69−79.

Millin, P. M., Moody, E. W., & Riccio, D. C. (2001). Interpretations of retrograde amnesia: old problems redux. *Nature Reviews Neuroscience, 2*(1), 68−70.

Milner, B. (1966). Amnesia following operation on the temporal lobes. In C. W. M. Whitty, & O. L. Zangwill (Eds.), *Amnesia* (pp. 109−133). London: Butterworths.

Misanin, J. R., Miller, R. R., & Lewis, D. J. (1968). Retrograde amnesia produced by electroconvulsive shock after reactivation of a consolidated memory trace. *Science, 160*, 5540555.

Morris, R. G., Inglis, J., Ainge, J. A., Olverman, H. J., Tulloch, J., Dudai, Y., & Kelly, P. A. (2006). Memory reconsolidation: sensitivity of spatial memory to inhibition of protein synthesis in dorsal hippocampus during encoding and retrieval. *Neuron, 50*(3), 479−489.

Müller, G. E., & Pilzecker, A. (1900). Experimentelle Beitraege zur Lehre vom Gedaechtnis. *Zeitschrift für Psychologie.* Suppl. no.1: 1.

Myers, K. M., & Davis, M. (2002). Systems-level reconsolidation: reengagement of the hippocampus with memory reactivation. *Neuron, 36*(3), 340−343.

Nader, K., & Hardt, O. (2009). A single standard for memory: the case for reconsolidation. *Nature Reviews Neuroscience, 10*(3), 224−234.

Nader, K., Schafe, G., & LeDoux, J. E. (2000). Fear memories require protein synthesis in the amygdala for reconsolidation after retrieval. *Nature, 406,* 722−726.

Pastalkova, E., Serrano, P., Pinkhasova, D., Wallace, E., Fenton, A. A., & Sacktor, T. C. (2006). Storage of spatial information by the maintenance mechanism of LTP. *Science, 313*(5790), 1141−1144.

Pedreira, M. E., Perez-Cuesta, L. M., & Maldonado, H. (2002). Reactivation and reconsolidation of long-term memory in the crab *Chasmagnathus*: protein synthesis requirement and mediation by NMDA-type glutamatergic receptors. *Journal of Neuroscience, 22*(18), 8305−8311.

Przybyslawski, J., Roullet, P., & Sara, S. J. (1999). Attenuation of emotional and nonemotional memories after their reactivation: role of beta adrenergic receptors. *Journal of Neuroscience, 19*(15), 6623−6628.

Przybyslawski, J., & Sara, S. J. (1997). Reconsolidation of memory after its reactivation. *Behavioural Brain Research, 84*(1-2), 241−246.

Quartermain, D., McEwen, B. S., & Azmitia, E. C., Jr. (1972). Recovery of memory following amnesia in the rat and mouse. *Journal of Comparative & Physiological Psychology, 79*(3), 360−370.

Ribot, T. (1881). *Les Maladies de la Memoire.* New York: Appleton-Century-Crofts.

Rodriguez, W. A., Rodriguez, S. B., Phillips, M. Y., & Martinez, J. L., Jr. (1993). Post-reactivation cocaine administration facilitates later acquisition of an avoidance response in rats. *Behavioural Brain Research, 59*(1-2), 125−129.

Rose, J. K., Kaun, K. R., Chen, S. H., & Rankin, C. H. (2003). GLR-1, a non-NMDA glutamate receptor homolog, is critical for long-term memory in *Caenorhabditis elegans*. *Journal of Neuroscience, 23*(29), 9595−9599.

Rose, J. K., & Rankin, C. H. (2006). Blocking memory reconsolidation reverses memory-associated changes in glutamate receptor expression. *Journal of Neuroscience, 26,* 11582−11587.

Rudy, J. W., Biedenkapp, J. C., Moineau, J., & Bolding, K. (2006). Anisomycin and the reconsolidation hypothesis. *Learning & Memory, 13*(1), 1−3.

Russell, W. R., & Nathan, P. W. (1946). Traumatic amnesia. *Brain, 69,* 280−300.

Sacktor, T. C. (2008). PKMzeta, LTP maintenance, and the dynamic molecular biology of memory storage. *Progress in Brain Research, 169,* 27−40.

Sacktor, T. C. (2010). How does PKMzeta maintain long-term memory? *Nature Reviews Neuroscience, 12*(1), 9−15.

Sangha, S., Scheibenstock, A., & Lukowiak, K. (2003). Reconsolidation of a long-term memory in *Lymnaea* requires new protein and RNA synthesis and the soma of right pedal dorsal 1. *Journal of Neuroscience, 23*(22), 8034−8040.

Sara, S. J. (2000). Retrieval and reconsolidation: toward a neurobiology of remembering. *Learning & Memory, 7*(2), 73−84.

Schneider, A. M., & Sherman, W. (1968). Amnesia: a function of the temporal relation of footshock to electroconvulsive shock. *Science, 159*(3811), 219−221.

Scoville, W. B., & Milner, B. (1957). Loss of recent memory after bilateral hippocampal lesions. *Journal of Neurology and Psychiatry, 20,* 11−21.

Shema, R., Haramati, S., Ron, S., Hazvi, S., Chen, A., Sacktor, T. C., & Dudai, Y. (2011). Enhancement of consolidated long-term memory by overexpression of protein kinase Mzeta in the neocortex. *Science, 331,* 1207−1210.

Spear, N. (1973). Retrieval of memory in animals. *Psychological Review, 80,* 163−194.

Spear, N., & Mueller, C. (1984). Consolidation as a function of retrieval. In H. Weingarten, & E. Parker (Eds.), *Memory Consolidation: Psychobiology of Cognition* (pp. 111−147). London: Erlbaum.

Squire, L. R. (2006). Lost forever or temporarily misplaced? The long debate about the nature of memory impairment. *Learning & Memory, 13*(5), 522−529.

Squire, L. R., Stark, C. E., & Clark, R. E. (2004). The medial temporal lobe. *Annual Review of Neuroscience, 27,* 279−306.

Stollhoff, N., Menzel, R., & Eisenhardt, D. (2005). Spontaneous recovery from extinction depends on the reconsolidation of the acquisition memory in an appetitive learning paradigm in the honeybee (*Apis mellifera*). *Journal of Neuroscience, 25*(18), 4485−4492.

Suzuki, A., Josselyn, S. A., Frankland, P. W., Masushige, S., Silva, A. J., & Kida, S. (2004). Memory reconsolidation and extinction have distinct temporal and biochemical signatures. *Journal of Neuroscience, 24*(20), 4787−4795.

Taubenfeld, S. M., Milekic, M. H., Monti, B., & Alberini, C. H. (2001). The consolidation of new but not reactivated memory requires hippocampal C/EBPbeta. *Nature Neuroscience, 4*(8), 813−818.

Tronson, N. C., & Taylor, J. R. (2007). Molecular mechanisms of memory reconsolidation. *Nature Reviews Neuroscience, 8*(4), 262−275.

Tronson, N. C., Wiseman, S. L., Olausson, P., & Taylor, J. R. (2006). Bidirectional behavioral plasticity of memory reconsolidation depends on amygdalar protein kinase A. *Nature Neuroscience, 9*(2), 167−169.

Valjent, E., Aubier, B., Corbillé, A. G., Brami-Cherrier, K., Caboche, J., Topilko, P., & Hervé, D. (2006). Plasticity-associated gene Krox24/Zif268 is required for long-lasting behavioral effects of cocaine. *Journal of Neuroscience, 26*(18), 4956−4960.

Valjent, E., Corbille, A. G., Bertran-Gonzalez, J., Hervé, D., & Girault, J.-A. (2006). Inhibition of ERK pathway or protein synthesis during reexposure to drugs of abuse erases previously learned place preference. *Proceedings of the National Academy of Sciences of the USA, 103*(8), 2932−2937.

Vianna, M. R., Szapiro, G., McGaugh, J. L., Medina, J. H., & Izquierdo, I. (2001). Retrieval of memory for fear-motivated training initiates extinction requiring protein synthesis in the rat hippocampus. *Proceedings of the National Academy of Sciences of the USA, 98*(21), 12251−12254.

Walker, M. P., Brakefield, T., Hobson, J. A., & Stickgold, R. (2003). Dissociable stages of human memory consolidation and reconsolidation. *Nature, 425*(6958), 616−620.

Walker, M. P., & Stickgold, R. (2006). Sleep, memory, and plasticity. *Annual Review of Psychology, 57,* 139−166.

Wang, S. H., Ostlund, S. B., Nader, K., & Balleine, B. W. (2005). Consolidation and reconsolidation of incentive learning in the amygdala. *Journal of Neuroscience, 25*(4), 830−835.

Yin, J. C., Wallach, J. S., Del Vecchio, M., Wilder, E. L., Zhou, H., Quinn, W. G., & Tully, T. (1994). Induction of a dominant negative CREB transgene specifically blocks long-term memory in Drosophila. *Cell, 79*(1), 49−58.

Chapter | two

The Dynamic Nature of Memory

Karim Nader, Oliver Hardt, Einar Örn Einarsson, Peter S.B. Finnie
McGill University, Montreal, Canada

2.1 WHEN DOES RECONSOLIDATION OCCUR AND WHAT IS IT DOING?

2.1.1 Boundary conditions

One similarity between consolidation and reconsolidation is that there are experimental parameters that determine when they occur (Alberini, 2011; Dudai & Eisenberg, 2004; Nader & Hardt, 2009). Characteristics of a consolidated memory that seem to impede reconsolidation include its age (Baratti, Boccia Blake, & Acosta, 2008; Eisenberg & Dudai, 2004; Frankland *et al.*, 2006; Milekic & Alberini 2002; Suzuki *et al.*, 2004), training strength (Eisenberg, Kobilo, Berman, & Dudai, 2003; Suzuki *et al.*, 2004; Taylor, Olausson, Quinn, & Torregrossa, 2009; Wang, de Oliveira Alvares, & Nader, 2009; Winters, Tucci, & DaCosta-Furtado, 2009), and when learning reaches an asymptote (Garcia-DeLaTorre, Rodriguez-Ortiz, Arreguin-Martinez, Cruz-Castañeda, & Bermúdez-Rattoni, 2009; Lee, 2010; Morris *et al.*, 2006; Rodriguez-Ortiz, 2005; Rodríguez-Ortiz, Garcia-Delatorre, Benavidez, Ballesteros, & Bermudez-Rattoni, 2008).

Characteristics of the reactivation session may also act as boundaries to the induction of reconsolidation. Reconsolidation may not occur when the duration of the reactivation stimulus is significantly shorter (Bustos, Maldonado, & Molina, 2009; Lagasse, Devaud, & Mery, 2009) or longer (Eisenberg *et al.*, 2003; Lee, Milton, & Everitt, 2006; Mamiya *et al.*, 2009; Pedreira & Maldonado, 2003; Pérez-Cuesta & Maldonado, 2009; Suzuki *et al.*, 2004) than the stimulus that can induce extinction (Inda, Delgado-Garcia, & Carrion, 2005; Power, Berlau, McGaugh, & Steward, 2006; Rossato, Bevilaqua, Medina, Izquierdo, & Cammarota, 2006; Tronson, Wiseman, Olausson, & Taylor, 2006). Reconsolidation may also not be induced when reactivation occurs in a new environment (DeVietti & Holiday, 1972; Hupbach, Hardt, Gomez, & Nadel, 2008), when the reactivation stimulus is predictable (Forcato, Argibay, Pedreira, & Maldonado, 2009; Morris *et al.*, **15**

Memory Reconsolidation. http://dx.doi.org/10.1016/B978-0-12-386892-3.00002-0

2006; Osan, Tort, & Amaral, 2011; Pedreira, Pérez-Cuesta, & Maldonado, 2004; Robinson, Ross, & Franklin, 2011), when the reactivation stimulus is indirectly related to the memory being assessed (Debiec, Doyere, Nader, & LeDoux, 2006) or, as stated previously, when it is presented at long intervals after training. It has also recently been reported in one elegant study that reactivation during sleep is an additional condition under which sensitivity to interference is not observed (Diekelmann, Büchel, Born, & Rasch, 2011).

For most of these boundary conditions, however, there have been opposing findings. These include evidence for reconsolidation of old (Brunet *et al.*, 2008; Debiec, LeDoux, & Nader, 2002; Diergaarde, Schoffelmeer, & DeVries, 2006; Lee *et al.*, 2006; Robinson & Franklin, 2010; Romero-Granados, Fontán-Lozano, Delgado-Garcia, & Carrion, 2010; Wang *et al.*, 2009) and strongly trained memories (Suzuki *et al.*, 2004; Wang *et al.*, 2009). Specifically, remote or strongly trained memories may be rendered labile by longer reactivation sessions (Frankland *et al.*, 2006; Suzuki *et al.*, 2004) or by exposure to novel stimuli at reactivation (Lee, 2010; Winters *et al.*, 2009). Furthermore, it has been observed that strong memories can undergo reconsolidation if they are reactivated at remote time points (Robinson & Franklin, 2010; Wang *et al.*, 2009). Finally, it has been shown that even extinction may not prevent the induction of reconsolidation (Duvarci, Mamou, & Nadar, 2006; Pérez-Cuesta & Maldonado, 2009; Stollhoff, Menzel, & Eisenhardt, 2005). This final point is worth elaborating on because extinction per se may not represent a boundary condition on reconsolidation.

Reactivation can be an extinction trial. Extinction has long been interpreted not as the weakening or erasure of a previously acquired memory but, rather, as the formation of a new, inhibitory trace that in some manner competes with or suppresses the original memory (Bouton, 2004; Pavlov, 1927). Indeed, it appears that as unreinforced exposure to a previously conditioned stimulus gradually begins to reduce responding, infusions of amnestic drugs cease to disrupt extinction memory retention, leading to a higher level of performance in the amnesic group (Berman & Dudai, 2001; Lopez-Salon *et al.*, 2001).

The first modern prediction that significant extinction during memory reactivation could inhibit reconsolidation is stated in Debiec *et al.* (2002):

> *It is possible that extinction and reconsolidation compete on a molecular level. If extinction is expressed, it may be the dominant protein synthesis-dependent process, which in turn will be blocked by anisomycin infusions. On the other hand, in cases where a single reactivation session is not sufficient to induce significant extinction, reconsolidation may be the dominant protein synthesis-dependent process. Thus, anisomycin infusions would block reconsolidation and not extinction. (p. 533)*

Evidence in support of this prediction was published in the following year, including a paper by the Dudai group using two different species (Eisenberg *et al.*, 2003; Pedreira & Maldonado, 2003; Sangha, Scheibenstock, &

Lukowiak, 2003; Suzuki *et al.*, 2004). It was suggested that this effect could be explained by the trace dominance account. According to this notion, the memory driving the behavior may be primarily susceptible to disruption at retrieval (Eisenberg *et al.*, 2003). Thus, extinction may preclude reconsolidation because it encodes a new, independent memory trace. Results from a recent modeling study suggest that the transition that can occur during re-exposure to a conditioned stimulus (CS) may work along a novelty continuum (Osan *et al.*, 2011). As an animal progresses through a long unreinforced CS exposure, it may transition from mere memory retrieval to reconsolidation and to extinction, which may simply be related to the degree of similarity or novelty that exists between the re-exposure session and the initial training.

It is not surprising, then, that extinction memories have been observed to undergo reconsolidation following reactivation (Rossato, Bevilaqua, Izquierdo, Medina, & Cammarota, 2010), which suggests that these inhibitory traces share characteristics with many other memories. In this sense, extinction may not be a boundary per se but, rather, the boundary is the formation of a new memory. Supporting this position, exposure to a familiar context containing only new or only previously experienced objects does not induce lability of this memory, whereas a familiar context containing one new and one old object does (Rossato *et al.*, 2007). Also, Rodriguez-Ortiz, De la Cruz, Gutierrez, and Bermudez-Rattoni (2005) have reported that once learning that a certain flavored liquid is safe to drink reaches asymptote, it is resistant to disruption during additional exposures to the flavor. At near asymptotic responding, pairing malaise-inducing lithium−chloride with consumption of this liquid reduced its subsequent consumption, but additional reduction of consumption due to a second lithium−chloride pairing was impaired by the infusion of anisomycin. In fact, the consumption of liquid increased in this group, indicating that trace dominance caused anisomycin to impair only the active aversive memory trace. This supports the position that with sufficient novelty, a familiar experience can be encoded as a new, dissociable trace. Note that these authors interpret their findings as evidence for a phenomenon they refer to as "consolidation-update," which differs from reconsolidation in that it does not imply a complete recapitulation of the consolidation process but, rather, the encoding and integration of new information with existing knowledge via destabilization of only relevant parts of the neural ensemble that encodes a memory (Rodríguez-Ortiz *et al.*, 2008). This implies a gradient of destabilization during memory reactivation rather than an all-or-none phenomenon.

Regardless of the process engaged, it appears that encoding of a new trace has the ability to prevent destabilization of the initially retrieved trace in a manner that is not at all understood. In the case of extinction, mechanisms of reconsolidation could be engaged early in a reactivation session, and after a certain amount of time, extinction mechanisms may be engaged, inhibiting reconsolidation from proceeding. This might involve suppression of the nuclear transcription factor κB (NF-κB) (de la Fuente, Freudenthal,

& Romano, 2011; Merlo, Freudenthal, Maldonado, & Romano, 2005; Merlo & Romano, 2008), activation of CB1 receptors (de Oliveira Alvares, Pasqualini Genro, Diehl, Molina, & Quillfeldt, 2008), or alterations in calcineurin activity (de la Fuente *et al.*, 2011). It is also possible that either reconsolidation or extinction is engaged only at the termination of a reactivation session (i.e., offset of a CS), which would each induce plasticity mechanisms in functionally distinct neural ensembles (for related findings, see Pedreira *et al.*, 2004).

Further complicating this boundary, if reconsolidation of a trace has already progressed beyond a certain point (perhaps the removal or degradation of synaptic proteins), it might not be possible to prevent this destabilization, and thus the new learning (extinction or otherwise) may be mediated by an alteration of the original memory trace. Specifically, when extinction follows soon after a reactivation session, some researchers have found that this memory does not exhibit evidence for the return of a conditioned response (Clem & Huganir, 2010; Flavell, Barber, & Lee, 2011; Monfils, Cowansage, Klann, & LeDoux, 2009; Rao-Ruiz *et al.*, 2011; Schiller *et al.*, 2010), such as spontaneous recovery, reinstatement, or renewal, which are normally observed for extinguished memories (Bouton, 2004). This has led some to conclude that post-reactivation extinction works via "reconsolidation update" to be functionally identical to a reconsolidation blockade (Clem & Huganir, 2010; Flavell *et al.*, 2011; Marin, 2011; Monfils *et al.*, 2009; Rao-Ruiz *et al.*, 2011). However, this effect has not been consistently observed (Chan, Leung, Westbrook, & McNally, 2010; Costanzi, Cannas, Saraulli, Rossi-Arnaud, & Cestari, 2011; Soeter & Kindt, 2012).

2.1.2 Functions of reconsolidation

The boundaries discussed previously have collectively led to two semidistinct theories regarding the function of reconsolidation (for discussion, see Alberini, 2011; Davis *et al.*, 2010). Both support the idea that a malleable phase following retrieval could serve an important function in maintaining memory relevance in a changing environment: Infrequently reactivated memories may be lost, whereas those that continue to be necessary (as evidenced by their continued retrieval and usefulness to predict outcomes) will be preserved.

RECONSOLIDATION REFLECTS "LINGERING CONSOLIDATION"

Evidence that older or stronger memories (i.e., those at a putative learning asymptote) are not destabilized by reactivation has led to the suggestion that reconsolidation may simply be a part of an extended, lingering consolidation process (Alberini 2005, 2011; Dudai, 2004). This is partially based on observations that responses learned over time gradually strengthen, a phenomenon known as incubation (Eysenck, 1968; Gabriel, 1968; Pickens, Golden, Adams-Deutsch, Nair, & Shaham, 2009), and is further bolstered by reports that repeated reactivations can accelerate incubation (Forcato, Rodríguez, & Pedreira, 2011) and the progression of a memory toward a reconsolidation-resistant state (Inda, Muravieva, & Alberini, 2011). This could be due to a process such as synaptic re-entry reinforcement (Wittenberg, Sullivan, & Tsien, 2002), wherein reactivation during awake experience or during rest may induce processes that facilitate the establishment and modification of associations between previously experienced stimuli in order to extract biologically significant predictors (Rasch & Born, 2007; Sara, 2010). Lingering consolidation is also partially supported by the occurrence of retrograde amnesia, wherein recent memory is generally more susceptible to loss than remote memory that has had more time to fully stabilize (Squire & Bayley, 2007).

Under this rationale, it has been suggested that cases of memory "updating" should often be mediated via the formation and consolidation of a new trace (Alberini, 2011). Citing dissociable mechanisms of consolidation and reconsolidation (inhibitory avoidance consolidation requires transcription factor CCAAT enhancer binding protein β (C/EBPβ) in the hippocampus, but reconsolidation requires C/EBPβ in the amygdala) (Taubenfeld, Milekic, Monti, & Alberini, 2001; Tronel, Milekic, & Alberini, 2005), Tronel and colleagues showed that acquisition of a second-order inhibitory avoidance task is not prevented by blocking amygdalar C/EBPβ (Tronel et al., 2005). Specifically, animals trained to avoid a section of a chamber containing a salient visual cue (light), a process that required hippocampal C/EBPβ activity, could transfer this response to another chamber when the light was presented during the rats' exposure to this environment (known as second-order conditioning). Blocking C/EBPβ in amygdala had no effect on acquisition of this second-order response. However, it impaired retention of the previously acquired first-order memory. The interpretation presented by these authors was that linking new information to a fear memory could induce its reconsolidation, but the second-order trace was encoded independently as a new memory trace. This was taken as evidence that updating a memory relies on consolidation. However, whether second-order conditioning would even be expected to induce memory updating is debatable because it is conceptualized to involve the formation of a direct association between the second-order CS and the unconditioned stimulus (US) that is resistant to extinction of the first-order CS (Rizley & Rescorla, 1972; Rodríguez-Ortiz et al., 2008; Tronson & Taylor, 2007). Furthermore, as discussed next, other work has demonstrated that updating an existing memory (the representation of a conditioning chamber) during immediate shock in this environment engages reconsolidation-specific mechanisms in the hippocampus (Lee, 2010).

RECONSOLIDATION AS A MECHANISM FOR MEMORY UPDATING

The second major theory of reconsolidation function stems from the aforementioned evidence that old and/or strongly encoded memories at learning asymptote can still be made labile by exposure to novel, unexpected, or long reactivation stimuli. It is also based on findings such as those of Hupbach and colleagues, which show that newly learned items can intrude into old knowledge if existing memories are first retrieved (Hupbach, Gomez, Hardt, & Nader, 2007). Together, this work has led to the conclusion that memory may be maintained in a permanently modifiable form that permits the updating of each trace when relevant new information is encountered (Abraham & Robins, 2005; Dudai, 2004; Forcato, Rodríguez, Pedreira, & Maldonado, 2010; Hupbach *et al.*, 2007, 2008; Jones, Bukoski, Nadel, & Fellous, 2012; Lee, 2009; Lukowiak, Fras, Smyth, Wong, & Hittel, 2007; Morris *et al.*, 2006; Sara, 2000; Tronson & Taylor, 2007).

We propose that these two theories of reconsolidation function (strengthening of consolidation and memory updating) are not entirely incompatible. It is quite clear that the age and strength of a memory can indeed make it more resistant to destabilization following some types of reactivation, but it appears that this resistance might not apply to all possible reactivation parameters (Lee, 2010; Suzuki *et al.*, 2004; Winters *et al.*, 2009). To reconcile these positions, several authors have proposed that reconsolidation should only occur when the actual features or outcomes of an event do not match what was predicted, based on past experience (Lee, 2009; Wang & Morris, 2010), such as when a water maze platform is no longer in the previous location or when a well-explored environment contains new features. This is founded on the work of Rescorla and Wagner (1972), which suggests that surprise will dictate when learning occurs. If an animal continues to learn incrementally over successive encounters with a task, then this should be added to the memory of the previous trial (Wang & Morris, 2010). In this way, even repeated trials of the same training procedure could induce reconsolidation as long as there is still something new to learn (Morris, Inglis *et al.*, 2006; Rodriguez-Ortiz, 2005). For instance, Lee (2008) demonstrated that a weakly trained contextual fear memory was strengthened via reconsolidation when another conditioning trial was administered in the same context. However, an efficient biological system would not be expected to expend energy in re-encoding information that is already adequately stored. In this way, reconsolidation should cease to occur when additional exposures to a task closely match what is encoded, which may be reflected in the tendency of brain activity to be reduced over multiple exposures to the same event (Grill-Spector, Henson, & Martin, 2006). Importantly, additional training may not be necessary to bring a sub-asymptotic learned response to asymptote. As discussed previously, there may be enough time to allow sufficient offline reactivation for the brain to identify and strengthen task-relevant information to an asymptote (Inda *et al.*, 2011).

Several studies support these predictions. Morris *et al.* (2006) and Rodriguez-Ortiz *et al.* (2008) each demonstrated that when animals were given more training trials in a water maze task, their memories were not rendered labile by the same reactivations that destabilized more weakly trained memories. In a similar manner, Winters *et al.* (2009) reported that changing the texture of flooring during a reactivation trial was sufficient to induce lability of a well-trained object recognition memory that would not undergo reconsolidation during additional exposure to the objects in the unaltered context. Furthermore, although it might be expected that over time a weak recognition memory should fade, Winters *et al.* reported that when reactivation was delivered 2 days instead of 1 day after training, inclusion of the novel flooring was necessary to induce lability. Although other valid interpretations of these results have been presented (Alberini, 2011), we believe that the simplest explanation is that the new flooring requires remodeling of the well-encoded Y-maze context representation via reconsolidation-mediated memory update, the disruption of which also impairs retrieval of the object memories.

Perhaps the most convincing evidence that reconsolidation serves to update memory with new information comes from a study mentioned previously (Lee, 2010). In this study, short exposure to a conditioning chamber allowed additional re-exposure to induce reconsolidation. This was indicated by a reduced capacity for this context representation to subsequently facilitate fear conditioning during an immediate footshock procedure (Fanselow, 1986) if this re-exposure was preceded by infusion of a drug known to selectively disrupt reconsolidation in hippocampus (Zif268 antisense; see Lee, Everitt, & Thomas, 2004). If animals had already been given a long exploration session, presumably sufficient to encode this environment, additional exposure did not induce reconsolidation, as evidenced by insensitivity to Zif268 antisense infusion. However, the well-encoded context memory could be made labile when animals were given immediate shock in this environment, indicating that task-relevant novelty at the time of reactivation could cause reconsolidation. This "update" of the context memory to include the footshock relied on hippocampal immediate early gene (IEG) Zif268 but not BDNF activity, which have been shown to be necessary for reconsolidation and consolidation, respectively (Lee *et al.*, 2004). When Zif268 activity was inhibited during immediate shock, it not only prevented the memory update but also impaired the previously encoded context memory. Those animals infused with Zif268 antisense at immediate shock exposure could not be retrained by a later immediate shock session, whereas animals that had merely undergone blockade of reconsolidation update by proteasome inhibition were later able to acquire a contextual fear response. Finally, animals already strongly fear-conditioned to the training context did not undergo reconsolidation when given immediate shock in this environment. Together, these findings indicate that learning which has reached asymptotic levels can still be made labile by exposure to an unpredicted outcome. Most critically, encoding of the unexpected event in a familiar context relies on purportedly reconsolidation-specific mechanisms. Blocking these mechanisms disrupted both updating and retention of the previously consolidated context memory.

The findings of Lee *et al.* (2004) clearly differ from those of Tronel and colleagues (2005) (albeit using a different task). First, Lee *et al.* found that consolidation and reconsolidation processes require distinct mechanisms within a single brain region instead of the same mechanism in different regions. Second, they observed that both strengthening a contextual memory trace and the addition of a new conditioned response induced and required reconsolidation. Tronel and colleagues might have predicted that this process should be mediated by consolidation of a distinct memory and that blocking reconsolidation would have disrupted retention of the context memory representation. It is not simple to reconcile these inconsistent findings, although we expect that the Tronel study may have utilized a procedure that causes a direct association between a second-order stimulus and a fear response that does not directly rely on the "updating" of the existing associative memory.

Evidence that old memories may become labile and get updated by new information presented during reactivation is not as direct (Wichert, Wolf, & Schwabe, 2011). Debiec and colleagues (2002) showed that even 45-day-old contextual fear memories could be impaired by anisomycin infusion after unreinforced context exposure, but the role for memory updating in this task is not conclusive. Some studies using the "event arena" provide evidence for the rapid incorporation of new information into gradually acquired "schemas" via a process that is reminiscent of reconsolidation (Tse *et al.*, 2007, 2011). In this task, it was found that training rats to find specific foods at specific spatial locations for each of several different flavor cues resulted in gradually improved performance in a manner that required a functional hippocampus throughout the weeks of training. Once the task was well acquired, new odor—location pairs could be rapidly encoded in a manner that was only briefly hippocampus-dependent. Importantly, it was observed that this rapid incorporation only occurred when new paired associates were presented in the same environment, which might serve to reactivate the proper memory trace (Tse *et al.*, 2007). Furthermore, exposure to only new or only old pairs did not induce the same increase of IEG expression in various cortical regions (prelimbic and retrosplenial cortices) that was observed when two new pairs were presented after several old pairs (Tse *et al.*, 2011). This suggests that retrieval of the old pairs prior to new encoding might have facilitated incorporation of new information into schemas via plasticity of an existing cortical memory network. Critically, it could also indicate that the gradual transition of memory into cortical regions over weeks or months of training might not prevent its updating when relevant new information is encountered. Indeed, retrieval of these rapidly encoded pairs 24 hr after training was impaired by infusion of an AMPA receptor antagonist into the prelimbic cortex, which might not be predicted for newly acquired hippocampus-dependent memories if updating is mediated by consolidation. Moreover, lesioning the hippocampus 48 hr after rapid encoding of new pairs had no effect on retention, which suggests that these memories had rapidly transitioned to a cortically-mediated state.

This work does not directly implicate reconsolidation, but if future studies were to demonstrate that exposure to new paired associates induced lability of the well-trained old pairs in cortical regions, then it would provide convincing evidence. To further dissociate whether updating of the schema relied on reconsolidation, it could be assessed whether blocking the proteasome pathway in cortical regions or hippocampus during the training of new pairs would impair their acquisition. If so, would inhibiting Zif268 in hippocampus during the presentation of new pairs block this form of memory updating? Related work in our lab indicates that hippocampus and cortical regions (anterior cingulate) work together to process the storage and reconsolidation of remote contextual fear memories (Einarsson, Pors, & Nader, unpublished observations).

PARTIAL OR COMPLETE DESTABILIZATION OF A MEMORY FOLLOWING REACTIVATION?

This discussion also highlights our considerable uncertainty about how "independently" encoded memories about similar stimuli or events can be integrated and retrieved (see the discussion of updating-consolidation by Rodriguez-Ortiz and Bermudez-Rattoni (2007)). One possibility is that reactivation of a memory may only destabilize part of the trace. Although an amnesic treatment may block this labile portion, the other parts could remain intact. Under some conditions (e.g., when anisomycin is applied after extinction), it might be expected that this remaining nonlabilized portion of the memory could mediate expression of the behavior being measured, and thus it might be concluded that reconsolidation has not been induced when it actually has.

For example, Debiec and colleagues (2006) demonstrated that in a second-order auditory fear conditioning task (in which an auditory tone (CS1) was first associated with shock and then was paired with another distinct tone (CS2)), fear responding to CS1 was not impaired when reconsolidation was disrupted by basolateral amygdala (BLA) application of anisomycin after CS2 re-exposure. However, responding to both CS1 and CS2 was impaired when anisomycin was infused after CS1 reactivation. This suggests that these memory traces might exist within a network that can be either partially or entirely labilized depending on the reactivation cue used. Similarly, Winters, Tucci, Jacklin, Reid, and Newsome (2011) demonstrated that anisomycin infused into perirhinal cortex could impair an object recognition memory following reactivation that included one novel object, a novel contextual feature, or re-exposure to the original objects in context. However, only reactivation that included a new contextual feature (a textured floor insert) was impaired by anisomycin infused into hippocampus. Although the authors hypothesized that the altered context apparently causes a reorganization of the memory into a hippocampus-dependent state, another interpretation is that not all of the memory is destabilized when aspects of it are modified. Instead, the hippocampal-mediated portion of the trace is only destabilized by context-related novelty. If only hippocampal infusions had been used, it would have appeared that only new contextual information engaged reconsolidation of this type of memory. Critically, this result also demonstrates that blocking the labilized hippocampus-mediated portion still impairs the putatively perirhinal-mediated memory for the objects. Relatedly, Rodriguez-Ortiz and Bermudez-Rattoni (2007) proposed that as a learning asymptote is approached, progressively less of a trace may return to a vulnerable state during re-exposure to the task, as evidenced by a decreasing impairment induced by post-reactivation application of amnesic treatments. Thus, the neuronal ensemble mediating the memory may only be partially destabilized to update aspects of an experience that are not already well encoded (or that are new). This position would also predict that if a reactivation cue is dissimilar to a memory, the smaller portion of that memory will be destabilized to encode the new information, although this position is not yet strongly supported empirically.

RECONSOLIDATION AND THE SIMILARITY OF EXPERIENCES

One parsimonious way of conceptualizing the results discussed so far is that mismatch between the memory of a previously experienced event and a current episode might determine whether or not reconsolidation will be observed (Pedreira & Perez-Cuesta, 2004), as elegantly modeled by Osan and colleagues (2011). A large degree of similarity (i.e., when additional training is presented to an animal at behavioral asymptote for that task) may fail to induce consolidation and reconsolidation entirely because no new information need be encoded. A small degree of similarity between a memory and reactivation (i.e., when extinction is induced) may engage memory encoding but may not cause the destabilization of an existing memory and will instead establish a new memory trace. This position would predict that only moderate task-related novelty would engage reconsolidation (or would destabilize enough of the trace that its disruption causes a behavioral impairment, as reviewed previously).

However, at a behavioral level, this hypothesis presents a problem for empirical falsifiability. For instance, when a weakly fear-conditioned animal is given unreinforced re-exposure to the CS, a short presentation may only engage retrieval (the CS presentation; Biedenkapp & Rudy, 2004), but a long re-exposure may induce extinction (Eisenberg et al., 2003). When a moderate duration is used, perhaps yet unencoded information about the CS is stored or the feared CS acts as its own secondary reinforcer to strengthen the memory, engaging reconsolidation. But what is a moderate CS duration? Providing an independent measure for mismatch, other than the occurrence of reconsolidation, is a necessary requirement. Without one, whether or not a reactivation cue "matches" a given memory is dependent on the observation of reconsolidation. This might be complicated more so following strong training, when the re-exposure duration capable of evoking reconsolidation may shrink or close altogether (Suzuki et al., 2004), potentially because the animal can acquire no new information about the predictive relationship. In this instance, no CS re-exposure duration should be sufficient to initiate reconsolidation. Rather, other types of mismatch might be necessary during reactivation—perhaps revaluation of the US (Wang, Ostlund, Nader, & Balleine, 2005) or inclusion of new physical features during the task (Rossato et al., 2007). Thus, defining what constitutes similarity or dissimilarity could be immensely complicated; we present this interpretation only as a simple explanation of conditions that may induce reconsolidation.

In summary, we conclude that the available evidence supports the position that reconsolidation mediates memory updating when task-related novelty is experienced. Although factors such as strength or age can apparently decrease the susceptibility of a memory to undergo reconsolidation when reactivation is similar to training, one possibility is that novel information might always be able to destabilize at least part of a related trace.

2.1.3 Challenges in the interpretation of boundary conditions

It follows from the aforementioned behavioral studies that there is a clear inter-pretive limitation when attempting to identify true reconsolidation boundary conditions. Typically, boundary conditions are concluded to exist if application of post-reactivation amnesic agents does not lead to memory impairment. However, in most studies, only a single reactivation procedure has been used. Thus, the evidence for the transformation of a trace from a normal labile state to a static form is based on negative findings with a single reactivation procedure. The problem is confounded by the fact that there is no single univer-sally effective reactivation procedure that is always observed to induce recon-solidation. We know that different reactivation procedures can have different efficacies at inducing reconsolidation (DeVietti & Holiday, 1972; Lee, 2010; Suzuki *et al.*, 2004). For example, in the elegant study by Kida's group (Suzuki *et al.*, 2004), which examined the effects of training strength on the ability of a memory to undergo reconsolidation, it was reported that contextual fear memories acquired with one "pairing" of context and shock were sensitive to post-reactivation infusions of anisomycin into dorsal hippocampus. Memo-ries acquired with three shocks, however, were insensitive to the identical amnesic treatment. If these authors had stopped there and interpreted the data, they may have suggested that memory strength is an important regulator of reconsolidation. The subsequent experiment performed by these authors shows the difficulty in interpreting the negative results in the manner just discussed. The authors tested whether a longer reactivation trial would be able to induce reconsolidation in the memories acquired with three shocks. When the reactivation session was extended, the stronger memory was observed to undergo reconsolidation.

This is a clear demonstration that a negative finding on some experimental parameter does not mean the memory cannot undergo reconsolidation. This is why we need a more rigorous approach to this issue. Currently, in many studies, if a negative finding is obtained using one reactivation procedure, then a boundary conditioning is stated to exist. However, it will always be possible that another reactivation procedure could destabilize the memory (e.g., one that is more or less similar to the original event). Given that the parameter space for potential reactivation procedures is in principle infinite, a purely behavioral approach to describing boundary conditions can only lead to a long list of nega-tive findings. It does not differentiate between a memory that will never undergo reconsolidation from one that may simply require a different reactivation protocol. Therefore, it remains very difficult to prove, using purely behavioral approaches, that boundary conditions exist (Wang *et al.*, 2009).

We have highlighted a complementary approach to help resolve this situation (Wang *et al.*, 2009). Specifically, we aimed to identify some of the molecular mechanisms that correlate with boundary conditions and that inhibit reconsolidation from occurring. The discovery of such molecular signatures would permit strong predictions that could unambiguously be addressed experimentally; if memory strength, age, or extinction are robust boundary conditions, then the putative molecular mechanisms mediating boundary conditions should be fully expressed under the respective experimental conditions. Conversely, when a memory does reconsolidate (e.g., after weak training or short retention intervals), then the mechanisms mediating boundary conditions should be minimally expressed. This strategy would significantly complement the behavioral studies described previously in their search for true boundary conditions, and it could help resolve some of the conflicting findings in the field. In addition, it could create a framework to guide future research on boundary conditions.

2.1.4 A general principle that could mediate boundary conditions

One general principle that could mediate boundary conditions is the downregulation of mechanisms that allow memories to destabilize, thereby keeping them in a stable state in which they are insensitive to amnesic agents after reactivation while still allowing them to be expressed behaviorally.

As discussed previously, we have shown that the mechanisms mediating destabilization within the BLA can be dissociated from those mediating expression of the learned behavior (Ben Mamou, Gamache, & Nader, 2006). Infusing the GluN2b antagonist ifenprodil into the BLA prior to memory reactivation prevented fear memory from destabilizing, making it insensitive to post-reactivation amnesic treatment, although the conditioned response was still expressed during reactivation (a phenotype similar to memories at putative boundary conditions). Thus, we reasoned that the presence or absence of the GluN2b subunit could act as a molecular indicator for whether or not a memory would undergo reconsolidation.

In order to test the application of this approach to find convergence between behavioral and molecular markers of reconsolidation, Wang *et al.* (2009) performed a number of parametric behavioral experiments to identify how strength of training can affect the ability of an auditory fear memory to undergo reconsolidation within the BLA. They found that memories trained with 10 tone–shock pairings were resistant to post-reactivation amnesic treatments. Three different reactivation procedures each led to negative findings when the memory was reactivated 2 days after learning. Wang *et al.* went on to report that the memory returned to a state that was sensitive to post-reactivation amnesic treatments if a 30-day interval was inserted between learning and reactivation. Typically when boundary conditions are discussed, they are implicitly discussed as permanent inhibition on reconsolidation. Their finding, however, indicates for the first time that boundary conditions may be transient in nature, which has obvious clinical and theoretical implications.

We found the time course of the 30-day transition of memory back to a reconsolidation-sensitive state intriguing. When it is observed, systems consolidation (the transition of contextual fear memory from dependent on to independent of the dorsal hippocampus) also typically takes approximately 30 days in rodents (Kim & Fanselow, 1992). Given that all conditioning happens within a specific environment, contextual conditioning will naturally occur in our auditory fear paradigm. Therefore, we reasoned that it was possible that this hippocampus-dependent contextual representation could theoretically inhibit reconsolidation of auditory fear conditioning in the BLA up to approximately 30 days. To test this hypothesis, Wang *et al.* (2009) gave electrolytic lesions of the dorsal hippocampus prior to strong training, with the intent of impairing the hippocampal representation. The prediction was that strong memories should then be able to undergo reconsolidation within the BLA 2 days after learning. This is exactly what was observed, which indicates that one brain area can inhibit reconsolidation from occurring elsewhere. It remains an empirical question whether the hippocampus is the only memory system that can inhibit reconsolidation in other systems. Indeed, we might predict that extinction could form an inhibitory memory trace in hippocampus or prefrontal cortex, which could suppress the induction of reconsolidation in amygdala (Mamiya *et al.*, 2009).

Given these results by Wang *et al.* (2009), we predicted that stronger auditory fear conditioning might induce a boundary condition on reconsolidation by reducing the expression of GluN2B subunits in the BLA. This decrease is a plausible effect because the ability of training differences to affect NMDAR subtype composition has previously been described in a study showing decreased GluN2B in amygdala following strong fear conditioning (Zinebi *et al.*, 2003). We thus predicted that increasing the strength of fear training could lead to a corresponding decrease in GluN2B expression in the BLA and weak training to a small (or no) decrease in GluN2B levels (with all comparisons relative to baseline established by naive animals). Behaviorally, these differences in GluN2B expression would manifest as different probabilities that a memory would undergo reconsolidation after reactivation. This is exactly what was found. Two days after strong training, a time point when the memory does not undergo reconsolidation, the level of the GluN2B subunit was reduced by 50%. However, this was at control levels 60 days after training, a time point when the memory does undergo reconsolidation. These findings also provide positive molecular evidence to support the negative behavioral findings that define boundary conditions.

These findings show a relationship between reconsolidation and the level of GluN2B subunits, but they provide no direct evidence for a functional relationship. One manner in which Wang and colleagues (2009) tested for a functional relationship between the level of GluN2B subunits and reconsolidation was to examine expression of these receptors 2 days after conditioning in animals with hippocampus lesions. At that time point, the strong memories do not undergo reconsolidation. However, pretraining lesions of the dorsal hippocampus were observed to permit these memories to undergo reconsolidation in the BLA. They found that GluN2B receptor subunits were at control levels, thus demonstrating a potential functional relationship between the presence and the absence of the GluN2B subunits and the ability of the memory to undergo reconsolidation in their task.

This metaplastic restriction on the induction of plasticity and reconsolidation might exist to prevent excitotoxicity (Abraham, 2008; Zinebi *et al.*, 2003), and the apparent return of GluN2B to basal levels could be an amygdala-specific process that permits re-evaluation of intensely fearful stimuli (for discussion, see Wang & Morris, 2010). In nature, few places or stimuli will forever predict danger or reward, so it may be adaptive to have a system that allows an organism to re-evaluate previously established contingencies.

We believe that these findings provide a principle to help conceptualize the conditions that enable or inhibit a memory from undergoing reconsolidation. The boundary conditions are manifested by downregulation of some mechanism critical for destabilizing the memory (in the previous case, GluN2B). This will in turn allow the memory to be expressed normally and to remain insensitive to post-reactivation amnesic treatment. To date, the approach of correlating molecular markers for reconsolidation and its boundary conditions has only been demonstrated for extinction (Mamiya *et al.*, 2009) and strength of training (Wang *et al.*, 2009). None of the other reported constraints on reconsolidation have met this criterion; therefore, suspected boundaries to reconsolidation could simply reflect reactivation parameters that are ineffective. Using a molecular marker such as GluN2B downregulation could help highlight when a specific memory lies beyond a reconsolidation boundary.

2.2 POSSIBLE LINKS BETWEEN RECONSOLIDATION AND MEMORY MAINTENANCE MECHANISMS

The previously described change of plasticity characteristics due to past experience is a phenomenon referred to as metaplasticity (Abraham, 2008; Abraham & Bear, 1996). This has been extensively studied *in vitro* and *ex vivo*, with several impressive demonstrations of how synaptic plasticity or learning can be affected by prior behavioral experience (Quinlan, Lebel, Brosh, & Barkai, 2004; Zelcer *et al.*, 2006). Most often this involves a priming stimulus or experience, which changes the threshold and/or direction of subsequent plasticity induction (Abraham, 2008). For instance, an early study (Huang, Colino, Selig, & Malenka, 1992) demonstrated that activation of NMDARs could raise the stimulation threshold for induction of long-term potentiation (LTP). However, when behavioral manipulations have been used, they typically consist of nonspecific or long-lasting manipulations (i.e., environmental enrichment and sensory deprivation) and are often studied in developing neurons or organisms (Abraham, 2008). Thus, it is not yet apparent whether similar mechanisms mediate the storage of information under typical learning conditions. Elsewhere, we have described in detail the possible links between the mechanisms of metaplasticity that could contribute to the phenomena described previously (Finnie & Nader, 2012). Here, we only briefly revisit these issues.

2.2.1 PKMζ and the regulation of GluA2-containing AMPAR endocytosis

The constitutively active, atypical isoform of protein kinase C, protein kinase M-zeta (PKMζ), appears to be necessary for the maintenance of long-term memory and synaptic potentiation (Sacktor & Fento, 2011; Sacktor et al., 1993). Inhibiting its activity via a number of experimental manipulations, such as the infusion of the ζ-pseudosubstrate inhibitory peptide (ZIP), is observed to dramatically impair memory retention (Pastalkova et al., 2006; Serrano et al., 2008), whereas its genetic overexpression has been observed to enhance long-term memory (Shema et al., 2011). It is thought that PKMζ is involved in maintaining GluA2-containing AMPAR insertion by opposing its regulated endocytosis (Migues et al., 2010). Migues and colleagues found that infusing a peptide, GluA2$_{3Y}$, that prevents this endocytic process (Ahmadian et al., 2004) also prevents the memory- and LTP-impairing effects of ZIP. PKMζ appears to exist in a positive feedback loop through which it might induce its own local synthesis (Cai, Pearce, Chen, & Glanzman, 2011; Ogasawara & Kawato, 2010) in order to preserve the structure of the postsynaptic density via the maintenance of GluA2.

2.2.2 PKMζ could prevent memory destabilization

It might be expected that this kinase might not just mediate the maintenance of memory storage but could also selectively control the entry of memory into a plastic state following retrieval (Dudai, 2009). Because disrupting GluA2 AMPAR insertion at the cell membrane is observed to cause plastic changes at the membrane and disruption of memory maintenance, preserving this association between GluA2 AMPARs and postsynaptic scaffolding proteins could potentially cause a synapse and the memory it encodes to remain stable during reactivation under some conditions. For instance, we have collected preliminary evidence that strongly trained auditory fear memories (five CS−US pairings) may be more insensitive to the amnesic effects of ZIP (Migues, Finnie, and Nader, unpublished observations). Thus, one possibility is that learning could increase PKMζ expression or change its structural localization such that it cannot be readily removed (even by the maximum dissolvable concentration of ZIP). The sustained PKMζ activity may be sufficient to retain memory, or it may re-engage its own production to recover any lost synaptic strength (for discussion of PKMζ as a bistable switch, see Ogasawara & Kawato, 2010). However, training strength has not always been observed to limit ZIP effectiveness (Kwapis et al., 2009). Clearly, more work is needed to identify how PKMζ activity is regulated at the synapse and whether under some conditions it could persist despite plasticity-initiation processes such as calcium influx.

2.2.3 Does blocking GluA2 endocytosis prevent memory modification?

Recently, a highly relevant study demonstrated behavioral and cellular effects of applying membrane-permeable GluA2$_{3Y}$ peptide during reactivation of contextual fear memory on the reconsolidation-update extinction procedure (Rao-Ruiz et al., 2011). First, it was reported that GluA2$_{3Y}$ blocked the GluA2 endocytosis otherwise observed to occur between 1 and 4 hr after reactivation and also the insertion of GluA2 that occurred 7 hr post-reactivation. Although it was claimed that preventing GluA2 endocytosis via this mechanism might not entirely prevent the induction of reconsolidation, because GluA2$_{3Y}$ actually caused an increase in post-retrieval fear expression, it was reported to prevent memory updating during the reconsolidation time window. Using a reconsolidation-update protocol, in which reactivation just prior to extinction has been observed to cause a permanent reduction in conditioned responding (Monfils et al., 2009), animals infused with the GluA2$_{3Y}$ peptide into the dorsal hippocampus CA1 region before reactivation exhibited significant post-extinction spontaneous recovery relative to rats given control peptide. This potentially suggests that the extinction was not mediated by reconsolidation update but, rather, by consolidation of an inhibitory trace. Thus, GluA2$_{3Y}$ might have prevented the putatively reconsolidation-dependent weakening of the conditioned fear memory that has been proposed previously (Clem & Huganir, 2010; Flavell et al., 2011; Monfils et al., 2009; Schiller et al., 2010). Rao-Ruiz and colleagues concluded that reconsolidation update may not reflect memory "erasure" (Clem & Huganir, 2010; Maren, 2011) but, rather, a long-term reduction in fear expression via a re-evaluation and modification of the original fear trace (as discussed by Soeter & Kindt, 2012).

Rao-Ruiz et al. (2011) argue that maintenance of GluA2 by PKMζ may not necessarily prevent the induction of reconsolidation, but it may reduce interference or loss of memory perhaps by preventing memory updating during retrieval (while still permitting reactivation-induced strengthening). Taken one step further, if the removal of GluA2-containing AMPARs following reactivation reflects the destabilization of memory, then this finding indicates that experience-induced memory strengthening may not necessarily require labilization at all—just the insertion of new AMPARs. If endogenous conditions exist under which AMPARs can be maintained at the synapse (e.g., when GluA2$_{3Y}$ is administered), then perhaps under some conditions a synapse and the memory it encodes can be strengthened during reactivation without placing it into a state in which it can be weakened or disrupted pharmacologically.

However, we believe that this ingenious study by Rao-Ruiz and colleagues (2011) has not conclusively demonstrated that reconsolidation continues to be induced with GluA2$_{3Y}$ onboard during reactivation. First, the memory strengthening reported for animals given GluA2$_{3Y}$ prior to two reactivation sessions could merely be due to the artificial maintenance of GluA2 at the synapse because perhaps freezing would have been similarly elevated if animals had been given no reactivation between training and test 48 hr later (this was not directly evaluated). Second, it is not yet convincingly established that extinction following memory reactivation is mediated by reconsolidation. Work by Flavell and colleagues (2011) has demonstrated that blocking L-VGCCs (which is known to block the induction of reconsolidation for some tasks) also causes post-reactivation extinction to produce transient rather than persistent behavioral inhibition. Although this finding suggests that Rao-Ruiz *et al.* may be studying a reconsolidation-mediated process, it is possible that they have simply provided an elegant characterization of mechanisms mediating a phenomenon of persistent extinction.

Thus, an important question is whether anisomycin or another amnestic treatment would still impair memory following reactivation if GluA2$_{3Y}$ were first applied, or if the sustained AMPARs at the membrane would cause the memory not to destabilize. This experiment is ongoing in our lab. In either case, this intriguing study provides evidence that at least some forms of memory modification may be prevented by the inhibition of regulated GluA2 endocytosis. This position is further supported by a report that GluA2$_{3Y}$ can block an ocular dominance shift following monocular deprivation in young mice (Yang *et al.*, 2011). Ocular dominance development was unimpaired by GluA2$_{3Y}$ in mice without monocular deprivation. Because visual development could be considered a form of memory encoding, these results suggest that updating this memory with novel information (visual input from the nondominant eye) requires GluA2 endocytosis. It has also been reported that GluA2$_{3Y}$ can prevent both the depotentiation of amygdala synapses and the reduction in conditioned auditory fear following extinction (Kim *et al.*, 2007). Thus, GluA2 endocytosis may be necessary to properly encode and/or integrate new inhibitory memories.

Finally, an unexpected twist in this literature is the observation that acquisition of a conditioned drug approach behavior increased PKMζ expression in nucleus accumbens core, but infusion of ZIP into this structure led to a subsequent memory retention impairment only in animals given reactivation after infusion (Crespo *et al.*, 2012). Because ZIP is normally observed to affect memory in the absence of reactivation (for review, see Sacktor, 2011), one tentative interpretation is that in some cases reactivation may permit PZMζ activity to be more readily disrupted, perhaps via structural synaptic changes and/or removal of a portion of PKMζ molecules from the synapse.

2.2.4 PKMζ and GluA2 maintenance summary

It is not clear if or how PKMζ or other GluA2 maintenance mechanisms might be retained to prevent plasticity induction, but it is a possibility that deserves further attention. As discussed by Dudai (2009), this could provide a mechanism for the controlled destabilization of select synapses during both reconsolidation and regulated forgetting or memory decay. Therefore, it is worth investigating what endogenous systems mediate the weakening of PKMζ's stabilizing grasp on synapses and whether some types of behavioral experience (e.g., strong training) might cause it to persist at the synapse despite stimulation that might otherwise initiate plasticity.

2.2.5 Epigenetic regulation

Epigenetic changes could stably alter the expression of specific genes necessary for plasticity. They are known to influence the storage and maintenance of long-term memory (Levenson & Sweatt, 2005; Swank & Sweatt, 2001) but also the capacity of previously activated synapses to undergo additional changes (Lubin & Sweatt, 2007; Maddox & Schafe, 2011). Lubin and Sweatt reported that contextual fear memory reactivation caused an upregulation of NF-κB signaling via IkKα, which elevated histone H3 phosphorylation. Blocking this cascade was found to impair reconsolidation, but pharmacologically elevating histone acetylation was found to rescue this impairment. Epigenetic regulation might also control the conditions under which a memory might undergo extinction (for review, see Stafford & Lattal, 2011). Via epigenetic mechanisms, it could be imagined that expression of plasticity-related genes may be suppressed following some types of memory encoding to prevent changes to the stored information.

2.3 MEMORY MALLEABILITY PHENOMENA AND MEMORY RECONSOLIDATION

Here, we briefly discuss how the reconsolidation account may explain some well-documented (human) memory distortion phenomena, based on the idea that the paradigms used to study them always incorporate some form of memory reactivation.

2.3.1 Misleading post-event information

In the classic study (Loftus, Miller, & Burns, 1978), participants viewed slides of a car accident and were later asked questions about it. The critical misleading question asked whether there was a "stop" or a "yield" sign at the intersection where the car made the fatal turn. In a subsequent recognition test, participants had to decide which of two slides they had originally seen (the critical pair showed a slide with the car and a stop sign, and the other one showed a car with a yield sign). Participants presented with the misleading information chose more often the wrong slide—that is, the one consistent with the misinformation.

The experimental design invoked to demonstrate the misinformation effect essentially is an instance of a reconsolidation protocol, and the effect could be explained as a process that allows new information to be included into the existing memory representation because it became plastic after reactivation (Hupbach *et al.*, 2007).

2.3.2 Hindsight bias

In a typical hindsight bias experiment, participants are asked to respond to difficult questions to which they usually do not know the answers and thus have to estimate (e.g., "How high is the Eiffel Tower?"). Sometime afterward, they are given the actual solutions, and finally they are asked to recall their original answers. Typically, the remembered answer is biased such that, in hindsight, it is closer to the additional information presented in the second phase than it initially had been.

In the SARA model (Pohl, Eisenhauer, & Hardt, 2003), to explain the bias, presentation of supplemental information automatically initiates an encoding process that transfers this information to long-term memory, during which related memories are also retrieved. As a consequence of retrieval, the associations of the related memories are increased in strength, so that they are more likely to be recalled later. Subsequent information retrieval hence is biased toward the supplemental information and similar, related memories. This process corresponds directly to the reconsolidation hypothesis.

2.3.3 Forgetting and reconsolidation

Thorndike's (1914) laws of use and disuse suggest that retrieval can cause memory strengthening, slowing forgetting. Indeed, repeated retrieval can improve memory retention, as demonstrated by hypermnesia (the overall increase in the number of remembered items as a function of repeated retrieval; Erdelyi & Becker, 1974) and reminiscence (the recall of items on later tests that were not recalled on earlier ones; Ballard, 1913). Another widely studied forgetting mechanism is interference. A substantial body of data on memory interference phenomena has been produced using the paired-associates technique. Typically, participants first study a list of word pairs (A−B) and later are presented with another list, in which words from the first list are paired with new ones (A−C). Finally, they are provided with A as a cue to retrieve C. Interference manifests as a performance impairment relative to a control group that did not study A−B initially.

We propose that memory reconsolidation processes following retrieval mediate some of these forgetting effects. The beneficial effects of repeated testing could be a function of reconsolidation processes strengthening reactivated memory (Gordon, 1981). Interference effects, on the other hand, could be a function of memory modifications initiated by retrieval of existing memory in the presence of new information. The fact that interference effects are small when memory for A−B is tested soon after learning of the

A—C list, but larger when tested at time points more remote, directly supports the suggestion that reconsolidation processes underpin these distortions (for a similar account of interference in rats, see Gordon, 1977): A defining characteristic of memory reconsolidation is intact post-reactivation short-term memory but impaired post-reactivation long-term memory (Nader & Hardt, 2009). This pattern has also been observed in a set of studies on reconsolidation of human episodic memory (Hupbach *et al.*, 2007, 2008).

2.4 CONCLUSION

Memory storage is often viewed as if it were fixed and permanent. We have noted that flexibility is a core characteristic of memory systems, and that this has long been a subject of study in cognitive psychology. Indeed, it is difficult to imagine how a system designed to maintain memories in static form could allow widespread remodeling of even the most fundamentally important learned information, such as that observed in cortical ocular dominance columns of adult animals in response to visual deprivation (Sawtell *et al.*, 2003). Although this could be driven by processes that resemble homeostasis more than reconsolidation (Goel & Lee, 2007; Mrsic-Flogel *et al.*, 2007; but see Ranson, Cheetham, Fox, & Sengpiel, 2012), it highlights that even very old synaptic connections in the brain may be susceptible to experience-dependent plasticity given the proper conditions. Determining how the brain is capable of maintaining some semblance of stability, and also how this stability can be lifted given appropriate learning situations, should be a focus of continued research. This is of particular relevance to the field of reconsolidation, in which the effects of acute learning events on the retention of existing memories are explored.

The mechanisms recruited to destabilize a retrieved memory might be expected to vary dramatically depending on training and reactivation characteristics. Even for a specific type of memory task, such as contextual fear conditioning, we doubt that there is a single pattern of mechanisms for plasticity initiation triggered by all reactivation procedures. A short re-exposure to the conditioned context may trigger different destabilization mechanisms than a longer re-exposure, and reinforced reactivation may also recruit its own complement of mechanisms. Furthermore, the duration of time between when a memory was acquired and its reactivation might alter the mechanisms of plasticity because memory age is observed to reduce, but not prevent, the propensity of plasticity induction (Suzuki *et al.*, 2004; Winters *et al.*, 2009). These rather intuitive predictions tend to get lost in the search for consolidation, reconsolidation, or extinction-specific mechanisms. However, we do not expect distinct mechanisms for different training conditions. Rather, we expect that the relative involvement of each of many plasticity-induction mechanisms could vary depending on training and reactivation characteristics.

Here, we attempted to extend the idea that memories may only rarely, if ever, be stored in a truly stable, unmodifiable form. For this to be true, it could necessitate the existence of neurophysiological mechanisms to change the sensitivity of memory-encoding neuronal networks to different types of behavioral input. We reviewed several metaplasticity systems that could augment the sensitivity of neurons and synapses to different forms of activity in a manner that might alter when and how plasticity is induced. We anticipate that future work will rule out the involvement of most of these mechanisms, so we present these speculative ideas largely in the hope that others with far more ingenuity and technical ability will test these possibilities on the road to a clearer understanding of how memory is "stored."

REFERENCES

Abraham, W. C. (2008). Metaplasticity: tuning synapses and networks for plasticity. *Nature Review Neuroscience, 9*, 387.

Abraham, W. C., & Bear, M. F. (1996). Metaplasticity: the plasticity of synaptic plasticity. *Trends in Neuroscience, 19*, 126–130.

Abraham, W. C., & Robins, A. (2005). Memory retention—The synaptic stability versus plasticity dilemma. *Trends in Neuroscience, 28*, 73–78.

Alberini, C. M. (2005). Mechanisms of memory stabilization: are consolidation and reconsolidation similar or distinct processes? *Trends in Neuroscience, 28*, 51–56.

Alberini, C. M. (2011). The role of reconsolidation and the dynamic process of long-term memory formation and storage. *Frontiers in Behavioral Neuroscience, 5*, 12.

Ballard, P. B. (1913). Obliviescence and reminiscence. *British Journal of Psychology Monograph Supplements, 1*, 1–82.

Baratti, C. M., Boccia, M. M., Blake, M. G., & Acosta, G. B. (2008). Reactivated memory of an inhibitory avoidance response in mice is sensitive to a nitric oxide synthase inhibitor. *Neurobiology of Learning and Memory, 89*, 426–440.

Ben Mamou, C., Gamache, K., & Nader, K. (2006). NMDA receptors are critical for unleashing consolidated auditory fear memories. *Nature Neuroscience, 9*, 1237–1239.

Berman, D. E., & Dudai, Y. (2001). Memory extinction, learning anew, and learning the new: dissociations in the molecular machinery of learning in cortex. *Science, 291*(5512), 2417–2419.

Biedenkapp, J. C., & Rudy, J. W. (2004). Context memories and reactivation: constraints on the reconsolidation hypothesis. *Behavioral Neuroscience, 118*(5), 956–964.

Bouton, M. E. (2004). Context and behavioral processes in extinction. *Learning & Memory, 11*, 485–494.

Brunet, A., Orr, S. P., Tremblay, J., Robertson, K., Nader, K., & Pitman, R. K. (2008). Effect of post-retrieval propranolol on psychophysiologic responding during subsequent script-driven traumatic imagery in post-traumatic stress disorder. *Journal of Psychiatric Research, 42*, 503–506.

Bustos, S. G., Maldonado, H., & Molina, V. A. (2009). Disruptive effect of midazolam on fear memory reconsolidation: decisive influence of reactivation time span and memory age. *Neuropsychopharmacology, 34*, 446–457.

Cai, D., Pearce, K., Chen, S., & Glanzman, D. L. (2011). Protein kinase M maintains long-term sensitization and long-term facilitation in *Aplysia*. *Journal of Neuroscience, 31*, 6421–6431.

Chan, W. Y., Leung, H. T., Westbrook, R. F., & McNally, G. P. (2010). Effects of recent exposure to a conditioned stimulus on extinction of Pavlovian fear conditioning. *Learning & Memory, 17*, 512–521.

Clem, R. L., & Huganir, R. L. (2010). Calcium-permeable AMPA receptor dynamics mediate fear memory erasure. *Science, 330*, 1108–1112.

Costanzi, M., Cannas, S., Saraulli, D., Rossi-Arnaud, C., & Cestari, V. (2011). Extinction after retrieval: effects on the associative and nonassociative components of remote contextual fear memory. *Learning & Memory, 18*, 508–518.

Crespo, J. A., Stöckl, P., Ueberall, F., Jenny, M., Saria, A., & Zernig1, G. (2012). Activation of PKCzeta and PKMzeta in the nucleus accumbens core is necessary for the retrieval, consolidation and reconsolidation of drug memory. *PLoS ONE, 7*(2), e30502.

Davis, S., Renaudineau, S., Poirier, R., Poucet, B., Save, E., & Laroche, S. (2010). The formation and stability of recognition memory: what happens upon recall? *Frontiers in Behavioral Neuroscience, 4*, 177.

de la Fuente, V., Freudenthal, R., & Romano, A. (2011). Reconsolidation or extinction: transcription factor switch in the determination of memory course after retrieval. *Journal of Neuroscience, 31*, 5562–5573.

de Oliveira Alvares, L., Pasqualini Genro, B., Diehl, F., Molina, V. A., & Quillfeldt, J. A. (2008). Opposite action of hippocampal CB1 receptors in memory reconsolidation and extinction. *Neuroscience, 154*, 1648–1655.

Debiec, J., Doyere, V., Nader, K., & LeDoux, J. E. (2006). Directly reactivated, but not indirectly reactivated, memories undergo reconsolidation in the amygdala. *Proceedings of National Academy of Sciences of the United States of America, 103*, 3428–3433.

Debiec, J., LeDoux, J. E., & Nader, K. (2002). Cellular and systems reconsolidation in the hippocampus. *Neuron, 36*, 527–538.

DeVietti, T. L., & Holiday, J. H. (1972). Retrograde amnesia produced by electroconvulsive shock after reactivation of a consolidated memory trace: a replication. *Bulletin of the Psychonomic Society, 29*, 137–138.

Diekelmann, S., Büchel, C., Born, J., & Rasch, B. (2011). Labile or stable: opposing consequences for memory when reactivated during waking and sleep. *Nature Neuroscience, 14*, 381–386.

Diergaarde, L., Schoffelmeer, A., & DeVries, T. J. (2006). β-Adrenoceptor mediated inhibition of long-term reward-related memory reconsolidation. *Behavioural Brain Research, 170*, 333–336.

Dudai, Y. (2004). The neurobiology of consolidations, or, how stable is the engram? *Annual Review of Psychology, 55*, 51–86.

Dudai, Y. (2009). Predicting not to predict too much: how the cellular machinery of memory anticipates the uncertain future. *Philosophical Transactions of the Royal Society of London - Series B: Biological Sciences, 364*, 1255–1262.

Dudai, Y., & Eisenberg, M. (2004). Rites of passage of the engram: reconsolidation and the lingering consolidation hypothesis. *Neuron, 44*, 93–100.

Duvarci, S., Mamou, C. B., & Nader, K. (2006). Extinction is not a sufficient condition to prevent fear memories from undergoing reconsolidation in the basolateral amygdala. *European Journal of Neuroscience, 24*, 249–260.

Eisenberg, M., & Dudai, Y. (2004). Reconsolidation of fresh, remote, and extinguished fear memory in Medaka: old fears don't die. *European Journal of Neuroscience, 20*, 3397–3403.

Eisenberg, M., Kobilo, T., Berman, D. E., & Dudai, Y. (2003). Stability of retrieved memory: inverse correlation with trace dominance. *Science, 301*, 1102–1104.

Erdelyi, M. H., & Becker, J. (1974). Hypermnesia for pictures: incremental memory for pictures but not for words in multiple recall trials. *Cognitive Psychology, 6*, 159–171.

Eysenck, H. J. (1968). A theory of the incubation of anxiety-fear responses. *Behaviour Research and Therapy, 6*, 309–321.

Fanselow, M. S. (1986). Associative vs. topographical accounts of the immediate shock-freezing deficit in rats: implications for the response selection rules governing species-specific defensive reactions. *Learning & Motivation, 17*, 16–39.

Finnie, P. S., & Nader, K. (2012). The role of metaplasticity mechanisms in regulating memory destabilization and reconsolidation. *Neuroscience and Biobehavioral Reviews, 36*(7), 1667–1707.

Flavell, C. R., Barber, D. J., & Lee, J. L. (2011). Behavioural memory reconsolidation of food and fear memories. *National Communications, 2*, 504.

Forcato, C., Argibay, P. F., Pedreira, M. E., & Maldonado, H. (2009). Human reconsolidation does not always occur when a memory is retrieved: the relevance of the reminder structure. *Neurobiology of Learning and Memory, 91*, 50–57.

Forcato, C., Rodríguez, M. L., & Pedreira, M. E. (2011). Repeated labilization-reconsolidation processes strengthen declarative memory in humans. *PLoS ONE, 6*, e23305.

Forcato, C., Rodríguez, M. L., Pedreira, M. E., & Maldonado, H. (2010). Reconsolidation in humans opens up declarative memory to the entrance of new information. *Neurobiology of Learning and Memory, 93*, 77–84.

Frankland, P. W., Ding, H.-K., Takahashi, E., Suzuki, A., Kida, S., & Silva, A. J. (2006). Stability of recent and remote contextual fear memory. *Learning & Memory, 13*, 451–457.

Gabriel, M. (1968). Effects of intersession delay and training level on avoidance extinction and intertrial behavior. *Journal of Comparative & Physiological Psychology, 66*, 412–416.

Garcia-DeLaTorre, P., Rodriguez-Ortiz, C. J., Arreguin-Martinez, J. L., Cruz-Castañeda, P., & Bermúdez-Rattoni, F. (2009). Simultaneous but not independent anisomycin infusions in insular cortex and amygdala hinder stabilization of taste memory when updated. *Learning & Memory, 16*, 514–519.

Goel, A., & Lee, H.-K. (2007). Persistence of experience-induced homeostatic synaptic plasticity through adulthood in superficial layers of mouse visual cortex. *Journal of Neuroscience, 27*, 6692–6700.

Gordon, W. C. (1977). Similarities of recently acquired and reactivated memories in interference. *American Journal of Community Psychology, 90*(2), 231–242.

Gordon, W. C. (1981). Mechanisms of cue-induced retention enhancements. In N. E. Spear, & J. A. Kleim (Eds.), *Information Processing in Animals: Memory Mechanisms* (pp. 319–339). Hillsdale, NJ: Erlbaum.

Grill-Spector, K., Henson, R., & Martin, A. (2006). Repetition and the brain: neural models of stimulus-specific effects. *Trends in Cognitive Sciences (Regular Education), 10*, 14–23.

Huang, Y. Y., Colino, A., Selig, D. K., & Malenka, R. C. (1992). The influence of prior synaptic activity on the induction of long-term potentiation. *Science, 255*, 730–733.

Hupbach, A., Gomez, R., Hardt, O., & Nadel, L. (2007). Reconsolidation of episodic memories: a subtle reminder triggers integration of new information. *Learning & Memory, 14*, 47–53.

Hupbach, A., Hardt, O., Gomez, R., & Nadel, L. (2008). The dynamics of memory: context-dependent updating. *Learning and Memory, 15*(8), 574–579.

Inda, M., Delgado-Garcia, J., & Carrion, M. (2005). Acquisition, consolidation, reconsolidation, and extinction of eyelid conditioning responses require *de novo* protein synthesis. *Journal of Neuroscience, 25*, 2070–2080.

Inda, M. C., Muravieva, E. V., & Alberini, C. M. (2011). Memory retrieval and the passage of time: from reconsolidation and strengthening to extinction. *Journal of Neuroscience, 31*, 1635–1643.

Jones, B., Bukoski, E., Nadel, L., & Fellous, J. M. (2012). Remaking memories: reconsolidation updates positively motivated spatial memory in rats. *Learning & Memory, 19*, 91–98.

Kim, J., Lee, S., Park, K., Hong, I., Song, B., Son, S., & Choi, S. (2007). Amygdala depotentiation and fear extinction. *Proceedings of National Academy of Sciences of the United States of America, 104*, 20955–20960.

Kim, J. J., & Fanselow, M. S. (1992). Modality-specific retrograde amnesia of fear. *Science, 256*, 675–677.

Kumar, S. S., Bacci, A., Kharazia, V., & Huguenard, J. R. (2002). A developmental switch of AMPA receptor subunits in neocortical pyramidal neurons. *Journal of Neuroscience, 22*, 3005–3015.

Kwapis, J. L., Jarome, T. J., Lonergan, M. E., & Helmstetter, F. J. (2009). Protein kinase Mzeta maintains fear memory in the amygdala but not in the hippocampus. *Behavioral Neuroscience, 123*, 844–850.

Lagasse, F., Devaud, J.-M., & Mery, F. (2009). A switch from cycloheximide-resistant consolidated memory to cycloheximide-sensitive reconsolidation and extinction in Drosophila. *Journal of Neuroscience, 29*, 2225–2230.

Lee, J., Milton, A., & Everitt, B. J. (2006). Cue-induced cocaine seeking and relapse are reduced by disruption of drug memory reconsolidation. *Journal of Neuroscience, 26*, 5881−5887.

Lee, J. L. (2008). Memory reconsolidation mediates the strengthening of memories by additional learning. *Nature Neuroscience, 11*, 1264−1266.

Lee, J. L. (2009). Reconsolidation: maintaining memory relevance. *Trends in Neuroscience, 32*, 413−420.

Lee, J. L. (2010). Memory reconsolidation mediates the updating of hippocampal memory content. *Frontiers in Behavioral Neuroscience, 4*, 168.

Lee, J. L., Everitt, B. J., & Thomas, K. L. (2004). Independent cellular processes for hippocampal memory consolidation and reconsolidation. *Science, 304*, 839−843.

Lee, J. L., Milton, A. L., & Everitt, B. J. (2006). Reconsolidation and extinction of conditioned fear: inhibition and potentiation. *Journal of Neuroscience, 26*, 10051−10056.

Levenson, J. M., & Sweatt, J. D. (2005). Epigenetic mechanisms in memory formation. *Nature Review Neuroscience, 6*, 108−118.

Loftus, E. F., Miller, D. G., & Burns, H. J. (1978). Semantic integration of verbal information into a visual memory. *Journal of Experimental Psychology: Human Learning and Memory, 4*(1), 19−31.

Lopez-Salon, M., Alonso, M., Vianna, M. R., Viola, H., Mello e Souza, T., Izquierdo, I., & Medina, J. H. (2001). The ubiquitin−proteasome cascade is required for mammalian long-term memory formation. *European Journal of Neuroscience, 14*(11), 1820−1826.

Lubin, F. D., & Sweatt, J. D. (2007). The IkappaB kinase regulates chromatin structure during reconsolidation of conditioned fear memories. *Neuron, 55*(6), 942−957.

Lukowiak, K., Fras, M., Smyth, K., Wong, C., & Hittel, K. (2007). Reconsolidation and memory infidelity in *Lymnaea*. *Neurobiology of Learning and Memory, 87*, 547−560.

Maddox, S. A., & Schafe, G. E. (2011). Epigenetic alterations in the lateral amygdala are required for reconsolidation of a Pavlovian fear memory. *Learning & Memory, 18*, 579−593.

Mamiya, N., Fukushima, H., Suzuki, A., Matsuyama, Z., Homma, S., Frankland, P. W., & Kida, S. (2009). Brain region-specific gene expression activation required for reconsolidation and extinction of contextual fear memory. *Journal of Neuroscience, 29*, 402−413.

Maren, S. (2011). Seeking a spotless mind: Extinction, deconsolidation, and erasure of fear memory. *Neuron, 70*, 830−845.

Merlo, E., Freudenthal, R., Maldonado, H., & Romano, A. (2005). Activation of the transcription factor NF-kappaB by retrieval is required for long-term memory reconsolidation. *Learning & Memory, 12*, 23−29.

Merlo, E., & Romano, A. (2008). Memory extinction entails the inhibition of the transcription factor NF-kappaB. *PLoS ONE, 3*, e3687.

Migues, P. V., Hardt, O., Wu, D. C., Gamache, K., Sacktor, T. C., Wang, Y. T., & Nader, K. (2010). PKMzeta maintains memories by regulating GluR2-dependent AMPA receptor trafficking. *Nature Neuroscience, 13*(5), 630−634.

Milekic, M. H., & Alberini, C. M. (2002). Temporally graded requirement for protein synthesis following memory reactivation. *Neuron, 36*, 521−525.

Monfils, M. H., Cowansage, K. K., Klann, E., & LeDoux, J. E. (2009). Extinction−reconsolidation boundaries: key to persistent attenuation of fear memories. *Science, 324*, 951−955.

Morris, R. G. M., Inglis, J., Ainge, J. A., Olverman, H. J., Tulloch, J., Dudai, Y., & Kelly, P. A. (2006). Memory reconsolidation: Sensitivity of spatial memory to inhibition of protein synthesis in dorsal hippocampus during encoding and retrieval. *Neuron, 50*, 479−489.

Mrsic-Flogel, T. D., Hofer, S. B., Ohki, K., Reid, R. C., Bonhoeffer, T., & Hübener, M. (2007). Homeostatic regulation of eye-specific responses in visual cortex during ocular dominance plasticity. *Neuron, 54*, 961−972.

Nader, K., & Hardt, O. (2009). A single standard for memory: the case for reconsolidation. *Nature Review Neuroscience, 10*, 224−234.

Ogasawara, H., & Kawato, M. (2010). The protein kinase Mζ network as a bistable switch to store neuronal memory. *BMC Systems Biology, 4*, 181.

Osan, R., Tort, A. B., & Amaral, O. B. (2011). A mismatch-based model for memory reconsolidation and extinction in attractor networks. *PLoS ONE, 6*, e23113.

Pastalkova, E., Serrano, P., Pinkhasova, D., Wallace, E., Fenton, A. A., & Sacktor, T. C. (2006). Storage of spatial information by the maintenance mechanism of LTP. *Science, 313*(5790), 1141−1144.

Pavlov, I. P. (1927). *Conditioned Reflexes*. New York: Dover.

Pedreira, M. E., & Maldonado, H. (2003). Protein synthesis subserves reconsolidation or extinction depending on reminder duration. *Neuron, 38*, 863−869.

Pedreira, M. E., Pérez-Cuesta, L. M., & Maldonado, H. (2004). Mismatch between what is expected and what actually occurs triggers memory reconsolidation or extinction. *Learning & Memory, 11*, 579−585.

Pérez-Cuesta, L. M., & Maldonado, H. (2009). Memory reconsolidation and extinction in the crab: mutual exclusion or coexistence? *Learning & Memory, 16*, 714−721.

Pickens, C. L., Golden, S. A., Adams-Deutsch, T., Nair, S. G., & Shaham, Y. (2009). Long-lasting incubation of conditioned fear in rats. *Biological Psychiatry, 65*, 881−886.

Pohl, R. F., Eisenhauer, M., & Hardt, O. (2003). SARA: a cognitive process model to simulate the anchoring effect and hindsight bias. *Memory, 11*(4-5), 337−356.

Power, A. E., Berlau, D. J., McGaugh, J. L., & Steward, O. (2006). Anisomycin infused into the hippocampus fails to block "reconsolidation" but impairs extinction: the role of re-exposure duration. *Learning & Memory, 13*, 27−34.

Quinlan, E. M., Lebel, D., Brosh, I., & Barkai, E. (2004). A molecular mechanism for stabilization of learning-induced synaptic modifications. *Neuron, 41*(2), 185−192.

Ranson, A., Cheetham, C. E. J., Fox, K., & Sengpiel, F. (2012). Homeostatic plasticity mechanisms are required for juvenile, but not adult, ocular dominance plasticity. *Proceedings of National Academy of Sciences of the United States of America, 109*, 1311−1316.

Rao-Ruiz, P., Rotaru, D. C., van der Loo, R. J., Mansvelder, H. D., Stiedl, O., Smit, A. B., & Spijker, S. (2011). Retrieval-specific endocytosis of GluA2-AMPARs underlies adaptive reconsolidation of contextual fear. *Nature Neuroscience, 14*, 1302−1308.

Rasch, B., & Born, J. (2007). Maintaining memories by reactivation. *Current Opinion in Neurobiology, 17*, 698−703.

Rescorla, R. A., & Wagner, A. R. (1972). A theory of Pavlovian conditioning: Variations in the effectiveness of reinforcement and non-reinforcement. In A. H. Black, & W. F. Prokasy (Eds.), *Classical Conditioning II: Current Research and Theory* (pp. 64−69). New York: Appleton-Century-Crofts.

Rizley, R. C., & Rescorla, R. A. (1972). Associations in second-order conditioning and sensory preconditioning. *Journal of Comparative & Physiological Psychology, 81*, 1−11.

Robinson, M. J. F., & Franklin, K. B. J. (2010). Reconsolidation of a morphine place preference: impact of the strength and age of memory on disruption by propranolol and midazolam. *Behavioural Brain Research, 213*, 201−207.

Robinson, M. J. F., Ross, E. C., & Franklin, K. B. (2011). The effect of propranolol dose and novelty of the reactivation procedure on the reconsolidation of a morphine place preference. *Behavioural Brain Research, 216*, 281−284.

Rodriguez-Ortiz, C. J. (2005). Protein synthesis underlies post-retrieval memory consolidation to a restricted degree only when updated information is obtained. *Learning & Memory, 12*, 533−537.

Rodriguez-Ortiz, C. J., & Bermudez-Rattoni, F. (2007). Memory reconsolidation or updating consolidation? In F. Bermudez-Rattoni (Ed.), *Neural Plasticity and Memory: From Genes to Brain Imaging* Boca Raton, FL: CRC Press.

Rodríguez-Ortiz, C. J., De la Cruz, V., Gutierrez, R., & Bermudez-Rattoni, F. (2005). Protein synthesis underlies post-retrieval memory consolidation to a restricted degree only when updated information is obtained. *Learning & Memory, 12*, 533−537.

Rodríguez-Ortiz, C. J., Garcia-DeLaTorre, P., Benavidez, E., Ballesteros, M. A., & Bermudez-Rattoni, F. (2008). Intrahippocampal anisomycin infusions disrupt previously consolidated spatial memory only when memory is updated. *Neurobiology of Learning and Memory, 89*, 352–359.

Romero-Granados, R., Fontán-Lozano, A., Delgado-García, J. M., & Carrion, A. M. (2010). From learning to forgetting: behavioral, circuitry, and molecular properties define the different functional states of the recognition memory trace. *Hippocampus, 20*, 584–595.

Rossato, J. I., Bevilaqua, L. R., Izquierdo, I., Medina, J. H., & Cammarota, M. (2010). Retrieval induces reconsolidation of fear extinction memory. *Proceedings of National Academy of Sciences of the United States of America, 107*, 21801–21805.

Rossato, J. I., Bevilaqua, L. R., Medina, J. H., Izquierdo, I., & Cammarota, M. (2006). Retrieval induces hippocampal-dependent reconsolidation of spatial memory. *Learning & Memory, 13*, 431–440.

Rossato, J. I., Bevilaqua, L. R., Myskiw, J. C., Medina, J. H., Izquierdo, I., & Cammarota, M. (2007). On the role of hippocampal protein synthesis in the consolidation and reconsolidation of object recognition memory. *Learning & Memory, 14*, 36–46.

Sacktor, T. C., & Fenton, A. A. (2011). Appropriate application of ZIP for PKMζ inhibition, LTP reversal, and memory erasure. *Hippocampus, 22*, 645–647.

Sacktor, T. C., Osten, P., Valsamis, H., Jiang, X., Naik, M. U., & Sublette, E. (1993). Persistent activation of the zeta isoform of protein kinase C in the maintenance of long-term potentiation. *Proceedings of National Academy of Sciences of the United States of America, 90*(18), 8342–8346.

Sangha, S., Scheibenstock, A., & Lukowiak, K. (2003). Reconsolidation of a long-term memory in *Lymnaea* requires new protein and RNA synthesis and the soma of right pedal dorsal 1. *Journal of Neuroscience, 23*(22), 8034–8040.

Sara, S. J. (2000). Retrieval and reconsolidation: toward a neurobiology of remembering. *Learning & Memory, 7*, 73–84.

Sara, S. J. (2010). Reactivation, retrieval, replay and reconsolidation in and out of sleep: connecting the dots. *Frontiers in Behavioral Neuroscience, 4*, 185.

Sawtell, N. B., Frenkel, M. Y., Philpot, B. D., Nakazawa, K., Tonegawa, S., & Bear, M. F. (2003). NMDA receptor-dependent ocular dominance plasticity in adult visual cortex. *Neuron, 38*, 977–985.

Schiller, D., Monfils, M. H., Raio, C. M., Johnson, D. C., LeDoux, J. E., & Phelps, E. A. (2010). Preventing the return of fear in humans using reconsolidation update mechanisms. *Nature, 463*, 49–53.

Serrano, P., Friedman, E. L., Kenney, J., Taubenfeld, S. M., Zimmerman, J. M., Hanna, J., & Fenton, A. A. (2008). PKMzeta maintains spatial, instrumental, and classically conditioned long-term memories. *PLoS Biol, 6*(12), 2698–2706.

Shema, R., Haramati, S., Ron, S., Hazvi, S., Chen, A., Sacktor, T. C., & Dudai, Y. (2011). Enhancement of consolidated long-term memory by overexpression of protein kinase Mzeta in the neocortex. *Science, 33*, 1207–1210.

Soeter, M., & Kindt, M. (2012). Stimulation of the noradrenergic system during memory formation impairs extinction learning but not the disruption of reconsolidation. *Neuropsychopharmacology, 37*, 1204–1215.

Squire, L. R., & Bayley, P. J. (2007). The neuroscience of remote memory. *Current Opinion in Neurobiology, 17*, 185–196.

Stafford, J. M., & Lattal, K. M. (2011). Is an epigenetic switch the key to persistent extinction? *Neurobiology of Learning and Memory, 96*, 35–40.

Stollhoff, N., Menzel, R., & Eisenhardt, D. (2005). Spontaneous recovery from extinction depends on the reconsolidation of the acquisition memory in an appetitive learning paradigm in the honeybee (*Apis mellifera*). *Journal of Neuroscience, 25*, 4485–4492.

Suzuki, A., Josselyn, S. A., Frankland, P. W., Masushige, S., Silva, A. J., & Kida, S. (2004). Memory reconsolidation and extinction have distinct temporal and biochemical signatures. *Journal of Neuroscience, 24*, 4787–4795.

Swank, M. W., & Sweatt, J. D. (2001). Increased histone acetyltransferase and lysine acetyltransferase activity and biphasic activation of the ERK/RSK cascade in insular cortex during novel taste learning. *Journal of Neuroscience, 21*, 3383–3391.

Taubenfeld, S. M., Milekic, M. H., Monti, B., & Alberini, C. H. (2001). The consolidation of new but not reactivated memory requires hippocampal C/EBPbeta. *Nature Neuroscience, 4,* 813−818.

Taylor, J. R., Olausson, P., Quinn, J. J., & Torregrossa, M. M. (2009). Targeting extinction and reconsolidation mechanisms to combat the impact of drug cues on addiction. *Neuropharmacology, 56*(Suppl. 1), 186−195.

Thorndike, E. L. (1914). *Educational Psychology.* New York: Teachers College, Columbia University.

Tronel, S., Milekic, M. H., & Alberini, C. M. (2005). Linking new information to a reactivated memory requires consolidation and not reconsolidation mechanisms. *PLoS Biology, 3,* e293.

Tronson, N. C., & Taylor, J. R. (2007). Molecular mechanisms of memory reconsolidation. *Nature Review Neuroscience, 8,* 262−275.

Tronson, N. C., Wiseman, S. L., Olausson, P., & Taylor, J. R. (2006). Bidirectional behavioral plasticity of memory reconsolidation depends on amygdalar protein kinase A. *Nature Neuroscience, 9,* 167−169.

Tse, D., Langston, R. F., Kakeyama, M., Bethus, I., Spooner, P. A., Wood, E. R., & Morris, R. G. M. (2007). Schemas and memory consolidation. *Science, 316,* 76−82.

Wang, S.-H., de Oliveira Alvares, L., & Nader, K. (2009). Cellular and systems mechanisms of memory strength as a constraint on auditory fear reconsolidation. *Nature Neuroscience, 12,* 905−912.

Wang, S.-H., & Morris, R. G. M. (2010). Hippocampal-neocortical interactions in memory formation, consolidation, and reconsolidation. *Annual Review of Psychology, 61,* 49−79, C41-44.

Wang, S.-H., Ostlund, S. B., Nader, K., & Balleine, B. W. (2005). Consolidation and reconsolidation of incentive learning in the amygdala. *Journal of Neuroscience, 25*(4), 830−835.

Wichert, S., Wolf, O. T., & Schwabe, L. (2011). Reactivation, interference, and reconsolidation: are recent and remote memories likewise susceptible? *Behavioral Neuroscience, 125,* 699−704.

Winters, B. D., Tucci, M. C., & DaCosta-Furtado, M. (2009). Older and stronger object memories are selectively destabilized by reactivation in the presence of new information. *Learning & Memory, 16,* 545−553.

Winters, B., Tucci, M., Jacklin, C., D. L., Reid, J. M., & Newsome, J. (2011). On the dynamic nature of the engram: evidence for circuit-level reorganization of object memory traces following reactivation. *Journal of Neuroscience, 31,* 17719−17728.

Wittenberg, G. M., Sullivan, M. R., & Tsien, J. Z. (2002). Synaptic reentry reinforcement based network model for long-term memory consolidation. *Hippocampus, 12,* 637−647.

Yang, K., Xiong, W., Yang, G., Kojic, L., Tian Wang, Y., & Cynader, M. (2011). The regulatory role of long-term depression in juvenile and adult mouse ocular dominance plasticity. *Scientific Reports, 1.* http://dx.doi.org/10.1038/srep00203.

Zelcer, I., Cohen, H., Richter-Levin, G., Lebiosn, T., Grossberger, T., & Barkai, E. (2006). A cellular correlate of learning-induced metaplasticity in the hippocampus. *Cerebral Cortex, 16,* 460−468.

Zinebi, F., Xie, J., Liu, J., Russell, R. T., Gallagher, J. P., McKernan, M. G., & Shinnick-Gallagher, P. (2003). NMDA currents and receptor protein are downregulated in the amygdala during maintenance of fear memory. *Journal of Neuroscience, 23*(32), 10283−10291.

Chapter three

Mechanisms and Functions of Hippocampal Memory Reconsolidation

Jonathan L.C. Lee

University of Birmingham, Birmingham, United Kingdom

One of the many intriguing features of mammalian memories is their longevity. That an individual event can lead to a long-lasting memory, which can persist for years, is a central feature of ongoing behavior. Therefore, a great deal of research has been dedicated to the understanding of the laying down and maintenance of long-term memories. Moreover, a significant proportion of that research has been conducted on hippocampal-dependent memories. Foremost among the reasons for the focus on hippocampal memories is the fact that the hippocampus has long been thought to be an important locus of memory, particularly human declarative memory (Wang & Morris, 2010). Thus, any mechanistic understanding gained from the study of animal models of hippocampal memory might translate to conscious human memories. Furthermore, at the physiological level, the mechanism of synaptic plasticity that is thought to support behavioral memories has been studied most thoroughly in the hippocampus (Martin & Morris, 2002).

In humans, the hippocampus supports episodic recollection of events in our past. In the absence of a functional hippocampus, an individual is impaired both in the recollection of past events and in the laying down of new episodic memories (Cipolotti & Bird, 2006). However, at the mechanistic level, human studies are not informative concerning the cellular processes that support long-term memory. Instead, experiments on rodents are particularly useful. In rats and mice, the hippocampus has been implicated in a number of memory paradigms, including contextual fear conditioning, inhibitory avoidance conditioning, conditioned place preference, and spatial learning in the water maze. An important common feature of these paradigms is that they all depend on the long-term encoding of a spatial representation of the experimental environment in order to

43

Memory Reconsolidation. http://dx.doi.org/10.1016/B978-0-12-386892-3.00003-2

support adaptive behavior at the memory test. Both contextual fear and inhibitory avoidance conditioning depend on expressing the fearful response to appropriate contextual cues. Conditioned place preference relies on similar mechanisms in order to express an appetitive Pavlovian response to the reward-paired context, and successful navigation to the platform location in the water maze is acutely dependent on a detailed spatial representation of the testing room.

Using such paradigms in rodents (as well as nonhippocampal memory settings), there is now a wealth of evidence supporting the hypothesis that initial learning leads to a process of cellular memory consolidation that is necessary to encode the memory into a long-term form. This consolidation process is critically dependent on the synthesis of new proteins under the control of cell surface and intracellular signaling mechanisms (Wang, Hu, & Tsien, 2006). Many of these basic mechanisms of cellular memory consolidation mirror those identified as being important for hippocampal long-term potentiation (LTP; Martin & Morris, 2002). Therefore, LTP has come to be viewed as a useful cellular analog of behavioral memory formation.

Although the analysis of cellular memory consolidation has proved useful and informative in terms of the initial formation of a long-term memory trace, it only partially addresses the issue of how memories are maintained and modified with new information. The cellular and structural synaptic plasticity associated with memory consolidation can explain memory stability, especially when allied with emerging mechanisms of memory maintenance such as PKMζ (Sacktor, 2011). However, an emphasis on the mechanisms of memory stability is not immediately consistent with the reality that memories are adaptive and modifiable. It is within such a conceptual setting that the phenomenon of memory reconsolidation becomes particularly interesting.

3.1 HIPPOCAMPAL MEMORY RECONSOLIDATION

For the purposes of this review, the term *reconsolidation* is used simply to reflect the process (regardless of its mechanism and function) that is impaired when a reactivated memory is disrupted, leading to long-lasting amnesia. The phenomenon of reactivation-dependent amnesia has been widely observed across species and memory types (Nader & Hardt, 2009). A classical demonstration of reconsolidation impairment will observe that when a memory is reactivated through re-exposure to either training cues, outcome or context, the concurrent administration of an amnestic agent results in a long-lasting amnesia. Critically, the amnesia is not observed following amnestic agent administration alone, strongly suggesting that stimulus re-exposure engages a phase of synaptic plasticity that is disrupted by the amnestic agent.

Whereas one of the original demonstrations of what has come to be known as memory reconsolidation (Misanin, Miller, & Lewis, 1968) used an auditory fear conditioning procedure that has subsequently been shown to depend critically on the amygdala (Nader, Schafe, & LeDoux, 2000), the other initial demonstration (Schneider & Sherman, 1968) as well as many subsequent studies instead used variants of inhibitory avoidance procedures. However, although the hippocampus is critically important for inhibitory avoidance, it remains unclear whether this extends to inhibitory avoidance memory reconsolidation (Taubenfeld, Milekic, Monti, & Alberini, 2001). The memories that support inhibitory avoidance undoubtedly undergo reconsolidation as systemic administration of protein synthesis inhibitors results in reactivation-dependent amnesia (Milekic & Alberini, 2002). However, infusion of protein synthesis inhibitors directly into the hippocampus did not replicate this effect (Cammarota, Bevilaqua, Medina, & Izquierdo, 2004; Taubenfeld *et al.*, 2001). In contrast, there are demonstrations that other hippocampal manipulations, such as nicotinic or glucocorticoid receptor antagonism or inhibition of NF-κB activity or the mammalian target of rapamycin, did disrupt inhibitory avoidance memory reconsolidation (M. Boccia *et al.*, 2007; M. M. Boccia, Blake, Krawczyk, & Baratti, 2010; Jobim *et al.*, 2012; Nikzad, Vafaei, Rashidy-Pour, & Haghighi, 2011), suggesting that the contribution of the hippocampus remains to be defined fully. Given this level of uncertainty, we focus mainly on three other models: contextual fear conditioning, pure contextual learning, and spatial learning. These settings have provided some of the key findings in understanding the underlying principles and adaptive function of hippocampal memory reconsolidation.

3.1.1 Contextual fear memory reconsolidation

Contextual fear conditioning is perhaps the simplest form of learning from an operational perspective. A rodent subject is introduced to a new experimental context and a few minutes later subjected to one or more electric footshocks, such that upon subsequent return to the context it will show the characteristic fear behavior of freezing. Debiec *et al.* (2002) were the first to demonstrate that this form of hippocampal-dependent memory undergoes reconsolidation. Moreover, they showed that intradorsal hippocampal infusions of the protein synthesis inhibitor anisomycin impaired contextual fear memory reconsolidation in rats. Given that these findings have been replicated using a number of different plasticity-associated interventions (Barnes, Kirtley, & Thomas, 2012; de Oliveira Alvares, Pasqualini Genro, Diehl, Molina, & Quillfeldt, 2008; Gafford, Parsons, & Helmstetter, 2011; J. L. C. Lee, Everitt, & Thomas, 2004; Lubin & Sweatt, 2007; Suzuki *et al.*, 2004), there is strong evidence that the reactivation of contextual fear memories initiates a phase of synaptic plasticity that is necessary to restabilize the memory. Moreover, the mechanisms of hippocampal memory reconsolidation largely recapitulate those observed to be important for consolidation both in the hippocampus and in other neural loci (for review, see Alberini, 2005).

It is important at this stage to note that there are two distinct phases to the reconsolidation process: the initial memory destabilization through reactivation, followed by restabilization through reconsolidation. Importantly, these are mechanistically separate. Most research has been directed at understanding the restabilization phase, but there is also emerging understanding concerning the reactivation and destabilization process. Importantly, in the context of this review, *reactivation* refers to a process that destabilizes memories. Therefore, memories might be retrieved without being reactivated and destabilized. In contrast, memory reactivation always leads to memory destabilization. In studies of contextual fear memory reconsolidation, the initial destabilization appears to be dependent on cell surface mechanisms (CB1 receptors and L-type voltage-gated calcium channels; Suzuki, Mukawa, Tsukagoshi, Frankland, & Kida, 2008), as well as intracellular protein degradation at the proteasome (S. H. Lee *et al.*, 2008), in the hippocampus.

The original study by Debiec *et al.* (2002) also showed, rather surprisingly, that the reactivation of a remote contextual fear memory that had undergone systems consolidation rendered that memory once again vulnerable to the amnestic effect of hippocampal protein synthesis inhibition. However, this finding was not replicated in a subsequent study on mice (Frankland *et al.*, 2006). Although systemically applied protein synthesis inhibition did disrupt the reconsolidation of a contextual fear memory, the dorsal hippocampus did not appear to be a primary neural locus because intrahippocampal infusions of anisomycin were without effect. Given that the age of a memory sometimes acts as a boundary condition upon memory reconsolidation in other settings (Eisenberg & Dudai, 2004; Milekic & Alberini, 2002), reconsolidation in old memories is an area that requires further investigation. Indeed, there does appear to be an impact of memory age upon the propensity of a contextual fear memory to undergo reconsolidation. In mice, Suzuki *et al.* (2004) demonstrated that older memories required a greater duration of context re-exposure (10 min) in order to successfully reactivate the context fear memory than did younger memories (3 min). However, the method used to disrupt reconsolidation was a systemic injection of anisomycin, and a similar pattern of results also used systemic administration of midazolam (Bustos, Maldonado, & Molina, 2009). Because contextual fear memories depend on plasticity in both the hippocampus and the amygdala (Rudy, Huff, & Matus-Amat, 2004), it remains unclear whether the increased context exposure triggered reactivation of plasticity in the hippocampus, allowing anisomycin and midazolam to disrupt reconsolidation, or whether the primary locus of effect was in the amygdala.

One further constraining factor on contextual fear memory reconsolidation is the apparent balance between reconsolidation and extinction. Operationally, the most common form of memory reactivation consists of a brief extinction session. The conditioned stimulus is presented in the absence of the footshock outcome. Whereas a reinforced reactivation procedure is equally effective in inducing reconsolidation for both context fear and other memories (Duvarci & Nader, 2004; Lee, 2008), unreinforced reactivation remains the prototypical method in reconsolidation studies. However, extinction itself critically involves synaptic plasticity that serves to inhibit, rather than maintain, memory expression. It appears, therefore, that when the reactivation session is long enough to engage extinction processes, this results in amnestic treatment impairing extinction, rather than reconsolidation, leading to preserved, rather than impaired, memory expression. This has been observed across a number of paradigms, including contextual fear conditioning (Eisenberg, Kobilo, Berman, & Dudai, 2003; Lee, Milton, & Everitt, 2006; Pedreira & Maldonado, 2003; Suzuki *et al.*, 2004). Therefore, it has been suggested that extinction acts as a boundary condition on reconsolidation. In other words, when extinction is engaged, reconsolidation does not take place.

An important question concerns the neural localization of the extinction/reconsolidation balance. The amnestic agent used in the contextual fear conditioning setting was again applied systemically (Suzuki *et al.*, 2004), and so this does not demonstrate that the amnestic target was in the hippocampus. In fact, when amnestic interventions have been targeted to a particular neural locus, the evidence has been mixed on whether extinction inhibits reconsolidation from taking place. The initial observation emerged from a study of insular cortex plasticity for conditioned taste aversion (Eisenberg *et al.*, 2003), whereas extinction does not appear to inhibit reconsolidation plasticity in the amygdala for auditory fear memories (Duvarci, Mamou, & Nader, 2006). Therefore, it has not been clear until recently whether extinction places a restriction on hippocampal reconsolidation plasticity.

The observation that there is a balance between reconsolidation and extinction in the hippocampus has resulted from the identification of selective cellular mechanisms of hippocampal memory reconsolidation and extinction. The transcription factor NF-κB appears to be specifically involved in reconsolidation because inhibition of NF-κB activity impaired memory reconsolidation with a short reactivation session but did not disrupt extinction with a long reactivation session (de la Fuente, Freudenthal, & Romano, 2011). Moreover, there was no evidence that NF-κB inhibition disrupted reconsolidation when the long reactivation session was used. Accordingly, NF-κB activity was induced only by the short, and not the long, reactivation session. Therefore, it seems that when a long reactivation session is used, which likely engages extinction, NF-κB-dependent reconsolidation processes in the hippocampus are not functionally engaged. This is in line with the suggestion that extinction places a boundary condition on hippocampal memory reconsolidation, but de la Fuente *et al.* go further to show that it is a cellular mechanism in the hippocampus that inhibits reconsolidation from taking place. The phosphatase calcineurin shows a function that is doubly dissociable from that of NF-κB. Calcineurin inhibition impaired contextual fear memory extinction but not reconsolidation. Moreover, the activation of calcineurin by extinction is the mechanism by which NF-κB is inhibited. Thus, when calcineurin was inhibited, the long reactivation session did activate NF-κB. Therefore, hippocampal contextual fear memory reconsolidation is inhibited by extinction in a process that involves the activation of calcineurin.

3.1.2 Reconsolidation of unemotional context memories

The traditional understanding of the contribution of the hippocampus to contextual fear conditioning is that the hippocampus supports the contextual representation that is associated with the footshock information in the amygdala. This is in accordance with the role of the hippocampus in spatial learning, and there is ample evidence implicating the amygdala, as well as the hippocampus, in contextual fear conditioning (Fendt & Fanselow, 1999; LeDoux, 2000; Maren, 2001). Given such a scheme, it would be hypothesized that what is undergoing reconsolidation in the hippocampus in the contextual fear setting is the contextual representation. Thus, if the contextual representation is disrupted, conditioned fear will not be expressed to the context as observed.

One initial exploration of this hypothesis found no support for the prediction that hippocampal contextual representations undergo reconsolidation. Biedenkapp and Rudy (2004) conducted an elegant study making use of an experimental paradigm (the context pre-exposure facilitation effect) that isolates pure contextual memories. Rats will associate a footshock event with the retrieved memory for a context, thereby displaying normal contextual fear at a subsequent test. However, if the contextual memory is impaired, there is nothing with which the footshock can be associated, and so there is an impairment in contextual fear. By targeting the context memory for reactivation and reconsolidation, the integrity of that memory can then be assessed by its ability subsequently to support a contextual fear response. However, Biedenkapp and Rudy observed that even under a number of different conditions, the infusion of anisomycin into the hippocampus did not disrupt the reconsolidation of the contextual representation.

We have shown contrasting evidence using the same procedure (Lee, 2010). Rather than using a general protein synthesis inhibitor, we focused on the inhibition of the synthesis of a particular protein, Zif268, which has been strongly implicated in memory reconsolidation (Bozon, Davis, & Laroche, 2003; Lee et al., 2004; Maddox, Monsey, & Schafe, 2011). When antisense oligodeoxynucleotides were infused into the hippocampus to inhibit the translation of Zif268 mRNA, they successfully disrupted the reconsolidation of the pure contextual memory representation. The reason why the two studies (Biedenkapp & Rudy, 2004; Lee, 2010) contrast markedly in their results is not clear, but one potentially important difference is the strength of the contextual memory at the time of memory reactivation. Biedenkapp and Rudy gave their rats more context exposure than Lee, and this might be expected to have led to the formation of a stronger and more stable contextual representation.

3.1.3 Reconsolidation of spatial memories

The hypothesis that the discrepancy between the studies of Biedenkapp and Rudy (2004) and Lee (2010) results from differential strength of initial context learning is supported by evidence from spatial learning studies. The initial studies of spatial memory were conducted in a radial arm maze, showing that systemic administration of MK-801 or propranolol impaired memory reconsolidation (Przybyslawski, Roullet, & Sara, 1999; Przybyslawski & Sara, 1997). Although spatial learning, unlike contextual fear conditioning, is not dependent on the amygdala, there is evidence that it is supported by plasticity in the lateral entorhinal cortex (Stranahan, Salas-Vega, Jiam, & Gallagher, 2011), as well as in the hippocampus. Moreover, recall of spatial memories induces the expression of immediate-early gene Arc/Arg3.1 in the lateral entorhinal cortex (Gusev, Cui, Alkon, & Gubin, 2005). Given that Arc/Arg3.1 protein is important for memory reconsolidation in the amygdala (Maddox & Schafe, 2011), the entorhinal upregulation of Arc/Arg3.1 might reflect functional plasticity that is involved in the reconsolidation of spatial memories. As such, it cannot be asserted that the effect of systemically applied MK-801 and propranolol on the reconsolidation of spatial memories is mediated by the hippocampus.

Kim *et al.* (2011) demonstrated that infusion of the NMDA receptor antagonist AP5 directly into the hippocampus impaired the reconsolidation of spatial memories in the water maze. This adds to a growing body of evidence implicating a number of plasticity-associated mechanisms in the hippocampal reconsolidation of spatial memories, including protein synthesis (Rossato, Bevilaqua, Medina, Izquierdo, & Cammarota, 2006), mRNA synthesis (Da Silva *et al.*, 2008), protein degradation (Artinian *et al.*, 2008), and protein kinase C (Bonini *et al.*, 2007). Moreover, the mechanisms of spatial memory destabilization in the hippocampus mirror those of contextual fear memory destabilization (Kim *et al.*, 2011). However, what is more interesting is the methodology used to reactivate the spatial memory in order that amnestic treatment is successful in disrupting the subsequent reconsolidation process. Several studies have used the equivalent of a brief extinction trial (i.e., a brief probe trial without the platform present) in order to reactivate the spatial memory (Bonini *et al.*, 2007; Da Silva *et al.*, 2008; Kim *et al.*, 2011; Rossato *et al.*, 2006). However, others have successfully used different methods of memory reactivation, such as a further training trial (Artinian *et al.*, 2008), or simply exposure to the test environment without any further learning (Artinian, De Jaeger, Fellini, de Saint Blanquat, & Roullet, 2007). This variety may suggest that spatial memories are easily reactivated, but two further studies indicated otherwise.

Of the previously discussed studies, only in the study by Artinian *et al.* (2007) was an analysis of different methods of memory reactivation performed, which found that exposure to the training environment alone was sufficient. However, both Morris *et al.* (2006) and Rodriguez-Ortiz *et al.* (2008) describe clear conditions under which spatial memories appear to be difficult, or even impossible, to reactivate. When reactivation consisted of additional learning, a spatial memory that had been learned with 20 previous trials was effectively reactivated and disrupted by intrahippocampal infusions of anisomycin. In contrast, when training consisted of 40 trials, the same reactivation and infusion was without effect (Rodriguez-Ortiz *et al.*, 2008). This suggests that stronger memories become more resistant to reconsolidation impairments, and this is further supported by Morris *et al.* (2006), who demonstrated that a spatial memory trained with 24 trials was not effectively reactivated by a probe test trial. Instead, use of a delayed matching-to-sample procedure that changed the location of the platform on each day such that an "encoding mode" was engaged at reactivation resulted in intrahippocampal anisomycin-produced amnestic effects. These two studies together indicate that only when further learning or an encoding mode is engaged at memory reactivation is reconsolidation triggered. Thus, when the spatial memory has been well trained, reconsolidation is less likely to be observed and disrupted. Note, however, that the failure of well-learned spatial memories to undergo reconsolidation might, in fact, be related not to a boundary condition on reconsolidation within the hippocampus but, rather, to the apparent shift of neuroanatomical dependence of spatial memories, at least in part, to extrahippocampal areas with extended training (Packard & McGaugh, 1996; Pouzet, Zhang, Feldon, & Rawlins, 2002).

Cross-study comparisons provide conflicting support for the hypothesis that spatial memory reconsolidation is only engaged with further learning. Some successful spatial memory reconsolidation studies used training limited to 12 trials (Artinian *et al.*, 2007; Artinian *et al.*, 2008; Kim *et al.*, 2011). In contrast, others used stronger training with 40 trials (Bonini *et al.*, 2007; Da Silva *et al.*, 2008; Rossato *et al.*, 2006). A focus on the number of training trials, however, may not be particularly informative because across laboratories and studies there is unlikely to be a strong link between training intensity and the strength of the learned spatial memory. What appears to be of most importance according to Rodrigues-Ortiz *et al.* (2008) is whether learning has progressed to asymptotic levels of performance. As such, if there is nothing further to be learned, the memory is not reactivated, whereas if the memory is incompletely learned, further training engages the reconsolidation process. Morris *et al.* (2006) were able to demonstrate spatial memory reconsolidation in a procedure in which learning was necessary on each day in order to perform correctly. Therefore, there was no such thing as incomplete or asymptotic learning in that setting, and the hypothesized necessity for an encoding mode is not inconsistent with the notion that additional learning is a requirement for reconsolidation to occur.

3.2 RECONSOLIDATION AT THE NEUROPHYSIOLOGICAL LEVEL

Given that the contribution of the hippocampus to contextual fear conditioning, context memories, and spatial navigation is ultimately supported by neurophysiological processes, it would be expected that reconsolidation impairments should be observed at the neurophysiological level. Strong support for this comes from a study showing a reconsolidation-like phenomenon in an *in vitro* LTP setting. Fonseca *et al.* (2006) induced tetanic LTP in hippocampal slices and showed that under the normal testing conditions of continual test stimulation at 1-min intervals, the delayed application of anisomycin to the slice had no impact on the persistence of the late phase of LTP (L-LTP). Similarly, if anisomycin was applied during a rest period in which no test stimulation was given, L-LTP was also unaffected. In contrast, if the slice experienced a rest period and then was restimulated at the time of anisomycin application, L-LTP subsequently decayed. Therefore, the period of rest between tetanic stimulation and restimulation may be an analog of the delay between learning and memory reactivation. As such, the test stimulation may have reactivated the potentiated synapses, necessitating a reconsolidation-like process that was disrupted by anisomycin, leading to the decay of LTP. However, there are obvious differences between the time course of reconsolidation in behavioral memories and the LTP phenomenon. Perhaps most important is the contrast between the age of the memory at this time of its reactivation. In behavioral studies, memory reactivation takes place at least 24 hr after learning. The interval is much shorter in the study by Fonseca *et al.* However, LTP as a phenomenon takes place over a shorter time course than learning and memory. Nevertheless, it remains to be determined to what extent the phenomenon described by Fonseca *et al.* is an effective neurophysiological analog of memory reconsolidation at the behavioral level.

The *in vitro* demonstration of a reconsolidation-like phenomenon in LTP has not yet been extended to *in vivo* settings, although interventions that impair behavioral memory reconsolidation have concurrent effects on neurophysiological correlates *in vivo*, at least in the amygdala (Doyere, Debiec, Monfils, Schafe, & Ledoux, 2007). One hippocampal study that is of relevance assessed the stability of hippocampal place fields in mice after manipulations that equate to impairments of consolidation and reconsolidation (Agnihotri, Hawkins, Kandel, & Kentros, 2004). The systemic administration of anisomycin impaired the long-term, but not the short-term, stability of newly formed place fields, just as it impairs the consolidation of spatial memories (Artinian *et al.*, 2008). However, when anisomycin was injected after re-exposure to a familiar environment, there was no effect on the subsequent stability of the previously-formed place fields. This appears to suggest that the plasticity that supports the stability of hippocampal place fields does not undergo reconsolidation. Given that the contribution of the hippocampus to memory tasks such as contextual fear conditioning and spatial learning is thought to depend on the representation of space encoded in hippocampal place cells, the dichotomy between the clear observations of memory reconsolidation in these settings and the failure to demonstrate a reconsolidation-like phenomenon at the neurophysiological level might seem puzzling. However, the interpretation of negative findings in reconsolidation studies is not straightforward. Just as the failure to demonstrate that pure context memories reconsolidate (Biedenkapp & Rudy, 2004) has subsequently been shown likely to be due to parametric conditions (Lee, 2010), that there has been a single negative finding in relation to the stability of familiar hippo-campal place fields does not allow any conclusions regarding whether or not the underlying plasticity undergoes reconsolidation. The strongest conclusion that we can draw is that under the conditions tested, reconsolidation does not take place. Indeed, Agnihotri *et al.* (2004) noted that a salient difference between their study and those of memory reconsolidation was the extent of prior training. They familiarized their mice to the environment at least 10 times for an undisclosed period. This is likely to have resulted in a stable spatial representation equivalent to that used in the study by Biedenkapp and Rudy, in which reconsolidation was not observed. Perhaps then, the reconsolidation of hippocampal place fields might be disrupted if those place fields were acquired in only a mildly familiar environment, exposed only to the extent used by Lee (2010).

3.3 BOUNDARY CONDITIONS ON HIPPOCAMPAL MEMORY RECONSOLIDATION

In the previous review of hippocampal memory reconsolidation, a number of potential boundary conditions have been observed. These boundary conditions are descriptions of parametric or conceptual constraints upon the reconsolidation process, thereby determining whether or not reconsolidation takes place under a given set of conditions. Ultimately, these conditions determine whether or not the method of reactivation used is successful in destabilizing the memory and hence triggering its reconsolidation. To summarize, the boundary conditions observed are as follows:

- Older memories are more difficult or even perhaps impossible to reactivate.
- Extinction may prevent reconsolidation from occurring.
- Stronger or more fully learned memories are more difficult or perhaps impossible to reactivate.
- The engagement of an "encoding mode" may be necessary to reactivate a memory.

These apparently different boundary conditions have been argued to reflect potentially a single overriding conceptual constraint upon memory reconsolidation—that of the need for memory updating (Lee, 2009). Strong or fully learned memories are less likely to necessitate any updating upon new experience, and so if reconsolidation serves to update memories, there would be no need to engage the reconsolidation process under those conditions. Effectively, the notion of an encoding mode is very much complementary to the need for further plasticity in order to update a memory. Moreover, given that extinction involves the formation of a new inhibitory memory (Bouton, 2004), the recruitment of such an additional modulatory memory obviates the need for updating the original memory, and hence reconsolidation would not be triggered when extinction takes place. Finally, and perhaps most speculatively, the simple passage of time may render new experiences more likely to be encoded as a new memory rather than being integrated into an existing memory. We have speculated that central concepts in learning theories that determine whether or not learning takes place (e.g., a prediction error signal) may also be viewed as the ultimate determinant of whether or not a memory reconsolidates. However, there remains no evidence with which to evaluate such a tentative hypothesis.

3.4 MEMORY RECONSOLIDATION UPDATES MEMORIES

Many have speculated that the plasticity that characterizes memory reconsolidation may serve a purpose of updating memories with new information (Dudai, 2004, 2006; Dudai & Eisenberg, 2004; Hupbach, Gomez, Hardt, & Nadel, 2007; Sara, 2000; Tronson & Taylor, 2007; Winters, Tucci, & DaCosta-Furtado, 2009). Therefore, the hypothesized requirement for new information to be present at the time of memory retrieval in order for the memory to be reactivated and undergo reconsolidation is consistent with such a function for the reconsolidation process. However, until recently, there was little or no evidence actually implicating reconsolidation in the adaptive function of memory updating. Part of the problem is that there is the theoretical and practical challenge of separating the contribution of reconsolidation from that of new learning. Consider, for example, the simplest form of memory updating: strengthening a memory with another learning episode. How is it possible to dissociate the relative contributions of reconsolidation and new learning? Undoubtedly, the memory becomes stronger with further learning. However, this could be due to new learning in the absence of any reconsolidation of the original memory, to reconsolidation-mediated updating in the absence of any separate new learning, or to a combination of the two.

There are numerous studies showing that reconsolidation is engaged when a memory is strengthened. In studies of spatial memories, we have already seen that some demonstrations of reconsolidation impairments were observed when the reactivation session took the form of a training trial (Artinian *et al.*, 2008; Rodriguez-Ortiz *et al.*, 2008). By definition, a training trial reactivation is likely to result in memory strengthening, and Rodrigues-Ortiz *et al.* showed explicitly that reconsolidation was only impaired when the reactivation training trial did result in memory strengthening. Similarly, we have shown that in the study of pure contextual memories, those memories can undergo reconsolidation upon simple re-exposure to the context (Lee, 2010). Given that the learning of a contextual representation is acquired through simple exposure to the context, such a reactivation session is a further training trial that might result in a stronger contextual representation. However, in the same manner as for spatial memories, reconsolidation was only observed and disrupted when the initial context exposure was limited and hence when reactivation is likely to have strengthened the context memory. In contrast, when initial exposure was extended, subsequent re-exposure may not have strengthened the memory, and this may explain why reconsolidation was not engaged under these conditions. Finally, explicit further training on a contextual fear memory task engages reconsolidation, such that intrahippocampal infusions of anisomycin disrupt reconsolidation, resulting in amnesia (Lee, 2008). This replicates a prior finding using intra-amygdala infusions in a tone fear setting (Duvarci & Nader, 2004). Therefore, given that reconsolidation is engaged when memories are strengthened, we can exclude the possibility that memory strengthening occurs purely through new learning mechanisms in the absence of the reconsolidation process.

Given that reconsolidation is taking place when memories are strengthened, and possibly also in other forms of memory updating (Winters *et al.*, 2009), the question that remains is to what extent do reconsolidation and new learning each contribute to memory updating? It is here that the practical challenge emerges. In their original demonstration that memory strengthening engages the reconsolidation of auditory fear memories, Duvarci and Nader (2004) speculated that the impact of anisomycin to produce amnesia was mediated by its disruption of both reconsolidation and consolidation of new learning, both of which depend on *de novo* protein synthesis. We have already seen that, in general, the cellular mechanisms of reconsolidation recapitulate those engaged by consolidation. However, in the hippocampus for contextual fear memories, we have the methodology selectively to interfere with consolidation and reconsolidation. Studies of contextual fear conditioning- and memory retrieval-induced gene expression revealed the tantalizing possibility that there may be dissociable mechanisms of consolidation and reconsolidation. Learning induced the expression of BDNF, but not Zif268, in the hippocampus (Hall, Thomas, & Everitt, 2000), whereas retrieval resulted in the upregulation of Zif268 (Hall, Thomas, & Everitt, 2001). Although it was unclear whether or not BDNF was regulated by contextual fear memory retrieval, we subsequently demonstrated that this apparent dissociation was functionally meaningful (Lee *et al.*, 2004). Knockdown of BDNF in the dorsal hippocampus through the infusion of antisense oligodeoxynucleotides impaired contextual fear memory consolidation, whereas knockdown of Zif268 disrupted contextual fear memory reconsolidation. Importantly, these mechanisms of contextual fear memory consolidation and reconsolidation were truly doubly dissociable in that BDNF knockdown had no effect on reconsolidation and Zif268 knockdown did not impair consolidation. Therefore, it is possible selectively to disrupt the consolidation and reconsolidation of contextual fear memories, thereby dissociating their relative contributions to memory updating.

The dissociable nature of hippocampal consolidation and reconsolidation mechanisms is thus far limited to the contextual fear conditioning setting, although there is also evidence that the consolidation and reconsolidation of the memories that underlie inhibitory avoidance behavior are doubly dissociable at the neuroanatomical level (Milekic, Pollonini, & Alberini, 2007; Taubenfeld *et al.*, 2001). Therefore, in the following discussion, we focus on the analysis of whether reconsolidation mediates the updating of memories in the contextual fear paradigm.

3.4.1 Reconsolidation updates memory strength

Using BDNF and Zif268 antisense oligodeoxynucleotides, we selectively disrupted consolidation and reconsolidation in a memory-strengthening procedure (Lee, 2008). Whereas BDNF knockdown had no impact on the strengthening of the memory with an additional training trial, Zif268 knockdown resulted in a long-lasting amnesia. This means that reconsolidation alone was responsible for strengthening the memory because disruption of the consolidation process had no effect. Therefore, when additional learning takes place, the existing memory is destabilized and then strengthened through its reconsolidation. This explains why impairment of reconsolidation by knocking down Zif268 resulted in amnesia rather than simply a failure to increase the strength of the memory. The reconsolidation process is required to restabilize the strengthened memory trace, and if it is interrupted, the memory does not restabilize normally. Because the memory has already destabilized, its subsequent failure to reconsolidate results in amnesia. This scheme is further supported by the effects of preventing memory destabilization in the first place. As noted previously, a handful of destabilization mechanisms have been discovered for contextual fear memories, including protein degradation at the proteasome (Lee *et al.*, 2008). Preventing hippocampal proteasomal protein degradation stops contextual fear memories from destabilizing, and so the reconsolidation phase is not required. As such, proteasome inhibition protects against the amnestic effects of protein synthesis inhibition in a reconsolidation setting. This is also true in a memory strengthening setting, with an interesting additional observation that proteasome inhibition also prevents the additional learning from strengthening the contextual fear memory (Lee, 2008). Because memory strengthening first requires that the existing memory be destabilized in order to be strengthened through reconsolidation, preventing initial destabilization both impairs the ability of the additional learning to strengthen the memory and renders protein synthesis inhibition ineffective.

The hypothesis that memory reconsolidation strengthens memories is not limited to contextual fear memories. There is further evidence that reconsolidation strengthens inhibitory avoidance memories. Brief reactivation of inhibitory avoidance memories on three occasions results in an enhancement of subsequent avoidance performance, suggesting that the process of destabilizing and restabilizing a memory through reconsolidation can strengthen a memory independently of any additional training (Inda, Muravieva, & Alberini, 2011). This might also account for the phenomenon of fear memory incubation (Pickens, Golden, Adams-Deutsch, Nair, & Shaham, 2009), especially if it can be assumed that memories can be implicitly reactivated in the absence of any direct behavioral memory retrieval (Alberini, 2005). One important question, however, is whether the brief reactivations caused memory strengthening through reconsolidation or simply through the consolidation of new information. The retrieval of fear memories is itself highly motivating and capable of reinforcing new learning, as is evident in the setting of second-order conditioning. Therefore, an alternative interpretation of the findings of Inda *et al.*, or indeed any demonstration that retrieval strengthens a memory, is that the new fear learning motivated by the retrieved avoidance memory subsequently combined with the original memory in an additive manner to enhance behavioral performance. However, it is not the case that reconsolidation was not engaged in the strengthening setting because Inda *et al.* clearly show that systemic inhibition of protein synthesis impaired the reactivated memory. On the other hand, without selectively disrupting consolidation and reconsolidation mechanisms, it is difficult to conclude that the observed memory strengthening was truly a result of memory reconsolidation. Indeed, following the interpretative rationale of Lee (2008), it is a clear hypothesis that knockdown of C/EBPβ in the amygdala (the reconsolidation mechanism; Milekic *et al.*, 2007) would result in amnesia under the conditions employed by Inda *et al.*, whereas knockdown in the hippocampus (the consolidation mechanism; Taubenfeld *et al.*, 2001) would have no behavioral effect under the same conditions.

3.4.2 Reconsolidation updates memory content

Whereas memory strengthening is relatively easily studied, determining the contribution of memory reconsolidation to the updating of memory content is more challenging. Given the role of the hippocampus in spatial/contextual representation, an ideal approach would be to use a paradigm in which the contextual representation is updated. However, there are different levels of qualitatively updating of contextual representations. At perhaps the most extreme end is the addition of completely new information, such as salient footshock, to a previously neutral contextual representation. This is exactly what is achieved in the context pre-exposure facilitation of the immediate shock deficit (Fanselow, 1990). This is a paradigm that we have previously seen is useful in isolating the role of the hippocampus in pure contextual representations. The retrieved memory for the pure contextual representation is associated with the delivery of a footshock, resulting in conditioned freezing to subsequent exposure to the context. The standard neural interpretation of this effect is that the hippocampus mediates the pure context representation and its retrieval, whereas the amygdala associates the contextual representation with footshock (Fanselow, 2000; LeDoux, 2000; Maren, 2001; Rudy *et al.*, 2004). However, given that the hippocampus is acutely responsive to contextual fear conditioning, in addition to the formation of a neutral contextual representation (Hall *et al.*, 2000; Impey *et al.*, 1998; Tischmeyer & Grimm, 1999; von Hertzen & Giese, 2005), we hypothesized that the association of the contextual representation with footshock information might represent a substantial qualitative updating of the hippocampal memory from a neutral to an emotionally-salient state. As such, hippocampal memory reconsolidation might be critically required.

Using the same experimental strategy as for our memory strengthening study, we demonstrated that Zif268-dependent reconsolidation mechanisms in the dorsal hippocampus were necessary for the updating of hippocampal memories (Lee, 2010). When Zif268 was knocked down in the hippocampus during the footshock updating phase, no contextual fear was subsequently observed. In contrast, knockdown of BDNF had no effect. Again, the contrast between the effects of Zif268 knockdown and those of proteasome inhibition was particularly informative. After Zif268 knockdown, even a further attempt to associate footshock with the retrieved contextual representation in the absence of any neural manipulation was unsuccessful, indicating that the contextual representation had also been disrupted by impairing memory reconsolidation. In contrast, proteasome inhibition impaired the first attempt to associate footshock with the contextual representation, but it had no effect on the second attempt in the absence of neural manipulation. This is consistent with the hypothesis that updating the content of the contextual representation requires that it first be destabilized by protein degradation at the proteasome and then reconsolidated with the new information via Zif268-dependent mechanisms.

De Oliveira Alvares *et al.* (2012) have taken a conceptually different approach to demonstrating the role of hippocampal memory reconsolidation in the modification of memory content. They made use of the observation that contextual fear memories are initially specific, such that fear is expressed selectively in the fear conditioned context, but over time and through the process of systems consolidation they generalize, such that fear is expressed in similar but distinct contexts (Wiltgen & Silva, 2007). Thus, a 2-day-old memory is specific, but a 28-day-old memory is generalized. However, when the contextual fear memory was reactivated three times at weekly intervals, the 28-day-old memory remained specific to the conditioning context (de Oliveira Alvares *et al.*, 2012). The authors acknowledge that the effect of weekly memory reactivation might be mediated equally as much by new learning as it is by memory reconsolidation. However, the resultant memory became dependent on the hippocampus at the 28-day test, when usually 28-day-old contextual fear memories are unaffected by hippocampal inactivation. This may be problematic for an account that new learning alone mediates the maintained specificity of reactivated memories (de Oliveira Alvares *et al.*, 2012). If each reactivation simply adds a new independent memory trace, the original memory should still generalize over time, leading to a generalized response at the 28-day test. Nevertheless, that the reactivation seemingly delays the time course of systems consolidation, and hence renders the 28-day-old memory dependent on the hippocampus, does not exclude the possibility that new independent learning contributes to this process. Ultimately, without demonstrating the selective functional involvement of reconsolidation mechanisms in this phenomenon, it is impossible to link it definitively to reconsolidation, rather than consolidation, processes. Therefore, it would be a clear prediction that hippocampal Zif268 knockdown at each (or indeed only the final) reactivation would result in amnesia. BDNF knockdown would have no effect, and proteasome inhibition would disrupt the effect of reactivation, leaving the contextual fear memory to generalize as normal over the 28 days.

3.4.3 Exploiting the function of reconsolidation in updating memories

If memory reconsolidation serves to update memories, we might be able to manipulate this behaviorally to diminish problematic memories using nonpharmacological means. The reactivation of a memory results in a period of plasticity that serves to integrate new information. If the new information were designed to update and diminish the memory, subsequent memory expression would be reduced. This approach has been pioneered by Monfils, Cowansage, Klann, and LeDoux (2009) in an auditory fear conditioning setting. By reactivating the fear memory and then after a short interval training rats that the auditory stimulus no longer predicted the footshock, Monfils *et al.* showed that the fear memory was persistently diminished, and the auditory stimulus even appeared to have been revalued as being a predictor of safety rather than fear (for further details, see Chapter 8).

Two studies have demonstrated that the combination of memory reactivation and extinction training is also effective in diminishing contextual fear. First, in mice, extinguishing the memory 2 hr after memory reactivation resulted in a persistent reduction in subsequent contextual freezing (Rao-Ruiz *et al.*, 2011). Whereas simply extinguished mice showed the normal spontaneous recovery of contextual fear just through the passage of time (17 days), mice subjected to the reactivation and extinction procedure displayed no recovery. This indicates that the memory was updated and revalued rather than being modulated by a new inhibitory memory as is the case for extinction alone (Bouton, 2004). In the second study, we showed similar results in rats, with a shorter reactivation–extinction interval of 1 hr (Flavell, Barber, & Lee, 2011). Rather than using spontaneous recovery as the measure of persistent memory impairment, we reconditioned the rats and showed that reactivation and extinction resulted in a retardation of reconditioning, consistent with the previous observation in the auditory fear setting (Monfils *et al.*, 2009). Moreover, the persistent memory impairment was critically dependent on memory destabilization. Preventing contextual fear memory destabilization with the L-type voltage-gated calcium channel blocker nimodipine (Suzuki *et al.*, 2008) abolished the effect of memory reactivation to transform extinction training into memory updating. Therefore, the effect of reactivation and extinction does appear to be genuinely mediated by a behavioral hijacking of the reconsolidation-mediated memory updating process.

3.5 SUMMARY AND IMPLICATIONS

As previously reviewed, there is emerging evidence that one function of the reconsolidation process is to allow memories to be updated in terms of both their strength and their content. This can be exploited experimentally to produce persistent memory impairments both pharmacologically and behaviorally. These conclusions are based on an analysis of hippocampal contextual fear memory reconsolidation, facilitated by the finding that the cellular mechanisms of hippocampal memory consolidation and reconsolidation are doubly dissociable, allowing for the selective disruption of the reconsolidation process. Therefore, one important question is whether such conceptual advances also apply to other hippocampal memories and nonhippocampal memories.

It is not known whether a dissociation between the functions of BDNF and Zif268 also exists for the consolidation and reconsolidation of spatial memories. What is known is that the dichotomy does appear to apply to pure contextual memories (Lee, 2010) as well as to contextual fear memories. Furthermore, the distinction between BDNF and Zif268 is not a singular, fortunate, dissociation. In a microarray study, overlapping but distinct patterns of hippocampal gene expression were observed for the consolidation and reconsolidation of contextual fear memories (Barnes *et al.*, 2012). This led to the identification of a further mechanism, interleukin-1, which is selectively involved in reconsolidation. Moreover, an analysis of the literature reveals a potential difference between consolidation and reconsolidation at the level of intracellular signaling cascades. The MEK inhibitor U0126 impairs the consolidation (Trifilieff *et al.*, 2006), but not the reconsolidation (Chen *et al.*, 2005; Fischer *et al.*, 2007), of contextual fear memories. It will therefore be important to determine to what extent the consolidation and reconsolidation of spatial memories and other hippocampal-dependent tasks are separable at the mechanistic level.

In contrast to the selectivity of contextual fear memory consolidation and reconsolidation mechanisms, there does not appear to be any evidence for such a distinction in other neural loci. The scope of any comparison is limited, and only the amygdala substrates of auditory fear conditioning have been studied with comparable depth. Focusing on the amygdala, however, reveals an interesting difference from the hippocampus. For example, MEK inhibition impairs both the consolidation (Schafe *et al.*, 2000) and the reconsolidation (Duvarci, Nader, & LeDoux, 2005) of auditory fear memories. Moreover, Zif268 is required for both processes (Maddox *et al.*, 2011). The one study that has shown a selective disruption of either consolidation or reconsolidation used the β-adrenergic receptor antagonist propranolol (Debiec & LeDoux, 2004). Systemic or intra-amygdala application of propranolol impaired auditory fear memory reconsolidation. In contrast, systemic propranolol had no effect on the consolidation of auditory fear memories. Therefore, although it is likely that intra-amygdala propranolol would also have been ineffective, this was not tested. Moreover, the use of a single, albeit standard, dose of propranolol does not rule out a functional role for β-adrenergic receptors in amygdala memory consolidation processes, especially given the fact that reconsolidation is seemingly more vulnerable to disruption than consolidation (Mactutus, Riccio, & Ferek, 1979; Przybyslawski *et al.*, 1999). Therefore, there is currently no evidence that in the amygdala, or indeed any nonhippocampal locus, there are dissociable mechanisms of consolidation and reconsolidation.

At this point, it is useful to note that the reconsolidation literature has been characterized by an emphasis on the question of whether reconsolidation recapitulates the initial consolidation process (Alberini, 2005). Therefore, the demonstration that hippocampal memory consolidation depended on BDNF, whereas reconsolidation required Zif268, was most commonly interpreted as reconsolidation differing from consolidation (Lee *et al.*, 2004). However, in the lifetime of a memory, that memory has several opportunities to undergo reconsolidation, compared to only one initial consolidation event. Therefore, if the two processes are mechanistically separable, perhaps the most salient question is why initial consolidation should differ from reconsolidation rather than the other way round. Indeed, it has been noted that the concept of initial consolidation may be meaningless in that all new memories involve the "reorganization of pre-existing memories" (McKenzie & Eichenbaum, 2011). McKenzie and Eichenbaum were concerned mainly with the question of how reconsolidation relates to systems-level consolidation, whereas the question posed here is specifically related to cellular-level consolidation. Nevertheless, an analogy can be made in that all memory-supporting synaptic plasticity occurs upon the background of prior synaptic plasticity and so the concept of new learning (and hence consolidation as being distinct from reconsolidation) may be flawed. Clearly, at the operational and behavioral levels, the distinction between new learning and memory updating is obvious. However, this is an externally applied categorization that need not map onto the reality of its neurophysiological underpinnings. Indeed, the limited evidence suggests that outside the hippocampus, the common mechanisms of consolidation and reconsolidation are completely consistent with the hypothesis that, mechanistically, consolidation does equal reconsolidation because all new learning involves the reconsolidation of prior synaptic plasticity.

Regardless of whether the mechanistic dissociation between consolidation and reconsolidation exists in nonhippocampal regions, the question remains whether reconsolidation serves to update nonhippocampal memories. Certainly, the evidence from hippocampal spatial memories is consistent with the hypothesis that reconsolidation is intimately linked with memory updating (Morris *et al.*, 2006; Rodriguez-Ortiz *et al.*, 2008). There is also consistent evidence in both insular cortex-dependent taste memories (Rodriguez-Ortiz, De la Cruz, Gutierrez, & Bermudez-Rattoni, 2005) and the object recognition setting (Winters *et al.*, 2009), the latter likely being dependent on plasticity in the perirhinal cortex (Winters, Tucci, Jacklin, Reid, & Newsome, 2011). From an evolutionary perspective, the fact that updating appears to be a critical trigger for memory reconsolidation in a species as phylogenetically different as the *Chasmagnathus* crab (Pedreira, Perez-Cuesta, & Maldonado, 2004) is further evidence that reconsolidation generally serves to modify memories. Therefore, although the tools may not exist to determine conclusively the contribution of memory reconsolidation to the updating of nonhippocampal memories, it remains possible, or even likely, that this is a universal function of memory reconsolidation.

One pertinent issue, if reconsolidation updates memories, is that all types of memories should undergo reconsolidation under appropriate conditions, given that all memories are capable of being updated. Although it is clearly impossible to state the veracity of such a statement without testing all memories in all species, we can make some headway by focusing on salient cases. In rodent models, there were three particular settings in which reconsolidation had yet to be observed: the memories underlying instrumental responding (Hernandez & Kelley, 2004), appetitive Pavlovian memories supporting goal-tracking behavior (Pavlovian conditioned approach; Blaiss & Janak, 2007), and pure contextual memories (Biedenkapp & Rudy, 2004). We have already seen that the last of these may be explained by boundary conditions, given that we have successfully demonstrated the disruption of contextual memory reconsolidation (Lee, 2010). Moreover, we have data showing that the reconsolidation of goal-tracking memories can be disrupted by systemic injections of MK-801, although there are strict boundary conditions in relation to the balance between reconsolidation and extinction (Reichelt & Lee, 2012). In relation to instrumental memories, Hernandez and Kelley noted that the extensive level of training used in their study may have rendered the underlying memories more difficult, or even impossible, to reactivate. Therefore, their negative finding does not preclude the possibility that instrumental memories do undergo reconsolidation. Moreover, instrumental responding, especially after extensive training, can be supported by both action−outcome associations and stimulus−response habits (Dickinson, 1985). Therefore, both memories would have to be disrupted in order to reduce instrumental responding. It has already been demonstrated that the incentive memories that modulate instrumental performance do undergo reconsolidation (Wang, Ostlund, Nader, & Balleine, 2005). Therefore, we hypothesize that the memories underlying instrumental performance do reconsolidate in order to update them, and the present lack of supportive data is due to the issues of isolating the contributory associations. Hence, it is not unreasonable to maintain that all memories, at least in rodents, do undergo reconsolidation.

Finally, memory reconsolidation has also been demonstrated and disrupted in humans. In the absence of the variety of amnestic treatments that can be applied in rodents, human memory reconsolidation has been impaired by the interference generated by new learning (Forcato *et al.*, 2007; Hupbach *et al.*, 2007; Walker, Brakefield, Hobson, & Stickgold, 2003) and by the systemic administration of propranolol (Brunet *et al.*, 2011; Kindt, Soeter, & Vervliet,

2009). However, propranolol has been effective only in disrupting behavioral fear memory and psychophysiological traumatic memory expression (Brunet *et al.*, 2008; Kindt *et al.*, 2009), leaving the putatively hippocampal-dependent declarative memory of the learning episode intact (Kindt *et al.*, 2009). Although systemic propranolol does disrupt the reconsolidation of contextual fear memories in rats (Muravieva & Alberini, 2010), the central locus of effect remains unclear, and it remains possible that reconsolidation processes in the amygdala, but not the hippocampus, are functionally dependent on β-adrenergic receptor activation. Therefore, the lack of propranolol-induced declarative memory impairment in humans is not inconsistent with current understanding of hippocampal memory reconsolidation. Instead, the efficacy with which interference impairs the reconsolidation of episodic memories in humans (Forcato *et al.*, 2007; Hupbach *et al.*, 2007) suggests that the study of rodent hippocampal memory reconsolidation may be of some relevance to the understanding of human declarative memory persistence.

REFERENCES

Agnihotri, N. T., Hawkins, R. D., Kandel, E. R., & Kentros, C. (2004). The long-term stability of new hippocampal place fields requires new protein synthesis. *Proceedings of National Academy of Sciences of the United States of America, 101*(10), 3656−3661. http://dx.doi.org/10.1073/pnas.0400385101.

Alberini, C. M. (2005). Mechanisms of memory stabilization: are consolidation and reconsolidation similar or distinct processes? *Trends in Neuroscience, 28*(1), 51−56.

Artinian, J., De Jaeger, X., Fellini, L., de Saint Blanquat, P., & Roullet, P. (2007). Reactivation with a simple exposure to the experimental environment is sufficient to induce reconsolidation requiring protein synthesis in the hippocampal CA3 region in mice. *Hippocampus, 17*(3), 181−191. http://dx.doi.org/10.1002/hipo.20256.

Artinian, J., McGauran, A. M., De Jaeger, X., Mouledous, L., Frances, B., & Roullet, P. (2008). Protein degradation, as with protein synthesis, is required during not only long-term spatial memory consolidation but also reconsolidation. *European Journal of Neuroscience, 27*(11), 3009−3019. http://dx.doi.org/10.1111/EJN6262, [pii] 10.1111/j.1460-9568.2008.06262.x.

Barnes, P., Kirtley, A., & Thomas, K. L. (2012). Quantitatively and qualitatively different cellular processes are engaged in CA1 during the consolidation and reconsolidation of contextual fear memory. *Hippocampus, 22*, 149−171. http://dx.doi.org/10.1002/hipo.20879.

Biedenkapp, J. C., & Rudy, J. W. (2004). Context memories and reactivation: constraints on the reconsolidation hypothesis. *Behavioral Neuroscience, 118*(5), 956−964.

Blaiss, C. A., & Janak, P. H. (2007). Post-training, but not post-reactivation, administration of amphetamine and anisomycin modulates Pavlovian conditioned approach. *Neurobiology of Learning and Memory, 87*(4), 644−658.

Boccia, M., Freudenthal, R., Blake, M., de la Fuente, V., Acosta, G., Baratti, C., & Romano, A. (2007). Activation of hippocampal nuclear factor-kappa B by retrieval is required for memory reconsolidation. *Journal of Neuroscience, 27*(49), 13436−13445. http://dx.doi.org/10.1523/27/49/13436, [pii] 10.1523/JNEUROSCI.4430-07.2007.

Boccia, M. M., Blake, M. G., Krawczyk, M. C., & Baratti, C. M. (2010). Hippocampal alpha7 nicotinic receptors modulate memory reconsolidation of an inhibitory avoidance task in mice. *Neuroscience, 171*(2), 531−543. http://dx.doi.org/10.1016/S0306-4522(10)01135-8, [pii] 10.1016/j.neuroscience.2010.08.027.

Bonini, J. S., Da Silva, W. C., Bevilaqua, L. R., Medina, J. H., Izquierdo, I., & Cammarota, M. (2007). On the participation of hippocampal PKC in acquisition, consolidation and reconsolidation of spatial memory. *Neuroscience, 147*(1), 37−45. http://dx.doi.org/10.1016/S0306-4522(07)00476-9, [pii] 10.1016/j.neuroscience.2007. 04.013.

Bouton, M. E. (2004). Context and behavioral processes in extinction. *Learning & Memory, 11*(5), 485−494. http://dx.doi.org/10.1101/11/5/485, [pii] 10.1101/lm.78804.

Bozon, B., Davis, S., & Laroche, S. (2003). A requirement for the immediate early gene Zif268 in reconsolidation of recognition memory after retrieval. *Neuron, 40*(4), 695−701.

Brunet, A., Orr, S. P., Tremblay, J., Robertson, K., Nader, K., & Pitman, R. K. (2008). Effect of post-retrieval propranolol on psychophysiologic responding during subsequent script-driven traumatic imagery in post-traumatic stress disorder. *Journal of Psychiatric Research, 42*(6), 503−506.

Brunet, A., Poundja, J., Tremblay, J., Bui, E., Thomas, E., Orr, S. P., & Pitman, R. K. (2011). Trauma reactivation under the influence of propranolol decreases posttraumatic stress symptoms and disorder: 3 open-label trials. *Journal of Clinical Psychopharmacology, 31*(4), 547−550. http://dx.doi.org/10.1097/JCP.0b013e318222f36000004714-201108000-00032, [pii].

Bustos, S. G., Maldonado, H., & Molina, V. A. (2009). Disruptive effect of midazolam on fear memory reconsolidation: decisive influence of reactivation time span and memory age. *Neuropsychopharmacology, 34*(2), 446−457. http://dx.doi.org/10.1038/ npp200875, [pii] 10.1038/npp.2008.75.

Cammarota, M., Bevilaqua, L. R., Medina, J. H., & Izquierdo, I. (2004). Retrieval does not induce reconsolidation of inhibitory avoidance memory. *Learning & Memory, 11*(5), 572−578.

Chen, X., Garelick, M. G., Wang, H., Lil, V., Athos, J., & Storm, D. R. (2005). PI3 kinase signaling is required for retrieval and extinction of contextual memory. *Nature Neuroscience, 8*(7), 925−931. http://dx.doi.org/10.1038/nn1482, [pii] 10.1038/nn1482.

Cipolotti, L., & Bird, C. M. (2006). Amnesia and the hippocampus. *Current Opinion in Neurology & Neurosurgery, 19*(6), 593−598. http://dx.doi.org/10.1097/01.wco. 0000247608.42320.f900019052-200612000-00015, [pii].

Da Silva, W. C., Bonini, J. S., Bevilaqua, L. R., Medina, J. H., Izquierdo, I., & Cammarota, M. (2008). Inhibition of mRNA synthesis in the hippocampus impairs consolidation and reconsolidation of spatial memory. *Hippocampus, 18*(1), 29−39. http://dx.doi.org/10.1002/hipo.20362.

de la Fuente, V., Freudenthal, R., & Romano, A. (2011). Reconsolidation or extinction: transcription factor switch in the determination of memory course after retrieval. *Journal of Neuroscience, 31*(15), 5562−5573. http://dx.doi.org/10.1523/31/15/5562, [pii] 10.1523/ JNEUROSCI.6066-10.2011.

de Oliveira Alvares, L., Einarsson, E. O., Santana, F., Crestani, A. P., Haubrich, J., Cassini, L. F., & Quillfeldt, J. A. (2012). Periodically reactivated context memory retains its precision and dependence on the hippocampus. *Hippocampus, 22*(5), 1092−1095. http://dx.doi.org/10.1002/hipo.20983.

de Oliveira Alvares, L., Pasqualini Genro, B., Diehl, F., Molina, V. A., & Quillfeldt, J. A. (2008). Opposite action of hippocampal CB1 receptors in memory reconsolidation and extinction. *Neuroscience, 154*(4), 1648−1655. http://dx.doi.org/10.1016/S0306-4522(08)00750-1, [pii] 10.1016/j.neuroscience.2008.05.005.

Debiec, J., & LeDoux, J. E. (2004). Disruption of reconsolidation but not consolidation of auditory fear conditioning by noradrenergic blockade in the amygdala. *Neuroscience, 129*(2), 267−272.

Debiec, J., LeDoux, J. E., & Nader, K. (2002). Cellular and systems reconsolidation in the hippocampus. *Neuron, 36*(3), 527−538.

Dickinson, A. (1985). Actions and habits: the development of behavioural autonomy. *Philosophical Transactions of the Royal Society of London. Series B, Biological Sciences, 308*(1135), 67−78.

Doyere, V., Debiec, J., Monfils, M. H., Schafe, G. E., & Ledoux, J. E. (2007). Synapse-specific reconsolidation of distinct fear memories in the lateral amygdala. *Nature Neuroscience, 10*(4), 414−416.

Dudai, Y. (2004). The neurobiology of consolidations, or, how stable is the engram? *Annual Review of Psychology, 55*, 51–86.

Dudai, Y. (2006). Reconsolidation: the advantage of being refocused. *Current Opinion in Neurobiology, 16*(2), 174–178.

Dudai, Y., & Eisenberg, M. (2004). Rites of passage of the engram: reconsolidation and the lingering consolidation hypothesis. *Neuron, 44*(1), 93–100.

Duvarci, S., Mamou, C. B., & Nader, K. (2006). Extinction is not a sufficient condition to prevent fear memories from undergoing reconsolidation in the basolateral amygdala. *European Journal of Neuroscience, 24*(1), 249–260.

Duvarci, S., & Nader, K. (2004). Characterization of fear memory reconsolidation. *Journal of Neuroscience, 24*(42), 9269–9275.

Duvarci, S., Nader, K., & LeDoux, J. E. (2005). Activation of extracellular signal-regulated kinase-mitogen-activated protein kinase cascade in the amygdala is required for memory reconsolidation of auditory fear conditioning. *European Journal of Neuroscience, 21*(1), 283–289.

Eisenberg, M., & Dudai, Y. (2004). Reconsolidation of fresh, remote, and extinguished fear memory in medaka: old fears don't die. *European Journal of Neuroscience, 20*(12), 3397–3403.

Eisenberg, M., Kobilo, T., Berman, D. E., & Dudai, Y. (2003). Stability of retrieved memory: inverse correlation with trace dominance. *Science, 301*(5636), 1102–1104.

Fanselow, M. S. (1990). Factors governing one-trial contextual conditioning. *Animal Learning and Behavior, 18*(3), 264–270.

Fanselow, M. S. (2000). Contextual fear, gestalt memories, and the hippocampus. *Behavioural Brain Research, 110*(1-2), 73–81.

Fendt, M., & Fanselow, M. S. (1999). The neuroanatomical and neurochemical basis of conditioned fear. *Neuroscience and Biobehavioral Reviews, 23*(5), 743–760.

Fischer, A., Radulovic, M., Schrick, C., Sananbenesi, F., Godovac-Zimmermann, J., & Radulovic, J. (2007). Hippocampal Mek/Erk signaling mediates extinction of contextual freezing behavior. *Neurobiology of Learning and Memory, 87*(1), 149–158. http://dx. doi.org/10.1016/S1074-7427(06)00091-8, [pii] 10.1016/j.nlm.2006.08.003.

Flavell, C. R., Barber, D. J., & Lee, J. L. (2011). Behavioural memory reconsolidation of food and fear memories. *National Communications, 2*, 504. http://dx.doi.org/10.1038/ncomms1515, [pii] 10.1038/ncomms1515.

Fonseca, R., Nagerl, U. V., & Bonhoeffer, T. (2006). Neuronal activity determines the protein synthesis dependence of long-term potentiation. *Nature Neuroscience, 9*(4), 478–480.

Forcato, C., Burgos, V. L., Argibay, P. F., Molina, V. A., Pedreira, M. E., & Maldonado, H. (2007). Reconsolidation of declarative memory in humans. *Learning & Memory, 14*(4), 295–303.

Frankland, P. W., Ding, H. K., Takahashi, E., Suzuki, A., Kida, S., & Silva, A. J. (2006). Stability of recent and remote contextual fear memory. *Learning & Memory, 13*(4), 451–457.

Gafford, G. M., Parsons, R. G., & Helmstetter, F. J. (2011). Consolidation and reconsolidation of contextual fear memory requires mammalian target of rapamycin-dependent translation in the dorsal hippocampus. *Neuroscience, 182*, 98–104. http://dx.doi.org/10.1016/S0306-4522(11)00281-8, [pii] 10.1016/j.neuroscience.2011.03.023.

Gusev, P. A., Cui, C., Alkon, D. L., & Gubin, A. N. (2005). Topography of Arc/Arg3.1 mRNA expression in the dorsal and ventral hippocampus induced by recent and remote spatial memory recall: Dissociation of CA3 and CA1 activation. *Journal of Neuroscience, 25*(41), 9384–9397. http://dx.doi.org/10.1523/25/41/9384, [pii] 10. 1523/JNEUROSCI.0832-05.2005.

Hall, J., Thomas, K. L., & Everitt, B. J. (2000). Rapid and selective induction of BDNF expression in the hippocampus during contextual learning. *Nature Neuroscience, 3*(6), 533–535.

Hall, J., Thomas, K. L., & Everitt, B. J. (2001). Cellular imaging of Zif268 expression in the hippocampus and amygdala during contextual and cued fear memory retrieval: selective activation of hippocampal CA1 neurons during the recall of contextual memories. *Journal of Neuroscience, 21*(6), 2186−2193.

Hernandez, P. J., & Kelley, A. E. (2004). Long-term memory for instrumental responses does not undergo protein synthesis-dependent reconsolidation upon retrieval. *Learning & Memory, 11*(6), 748−754.

Hupbach, A., Gomez, R., Hardt, O., & Nadel, L. (2007). Reconsolidation of episodic memories: a subtle reminder triggers integration of new information. *Learning & Memory, 14*(1-2), 47−53.

Impey, S., Smith, D. M., Obrietan, K., Donahue, R., Wade, C., & Storm, D. R. (1998). Stimulation of cAMP response element (CRE)-mediated transcription during contextual learning. *Nature Neuroscience, 1*(7), 595−601.

Inda, M. C., Muravieva, E. V., & Alberini, C. M. (2011). Memory retrieval and the passage of time: from reconsolidation and strengthening to extinction. *Journal of Neuroscience, 31*(5), 1635−1643. http://dx.doi.org/10.1523/31/5/1635, [pii] 10.1523/JNEUROSCI. 4736-10.2011.

Jobim, P. F., Pedroso, T. R., Christoff, R. R., Werenicz, A., Maurmann, N., Reolon, G. K., & Roesler, R. (2012). Inhibition of mTOR by rapamycin in the amygdala or hippocampus impairs formation and reconsolidation of inhibitory avoidance memory. *Neurobiology of Learning and Memory, 97*, 105−112. http://dx.doi.org/10.1016/S1074-7427(11)00176-6, [pii] 10.1016/j.nlm.2011.10.002.

Kim, R., Moki, R., & Kida, S. (2011). Molecular mechanisms for the destabilization and restabilization of reactivated spatial memory in the Morris water maze. *Molecular Brain, 4*, 9. http://dx.doi.org/10.1186/1756-6606-4-9, [pii] 10.1186/1756-6606-4-9.

Kindt, M., Soeter, M., & Vervliet, B. (2009). Beyond extinction: erasing human fear responses and preventing the return of fear. *Nature Neuroscience, 12*(3), 256−258. http://dx.doi.org/10.1038/nn.2271, [pii] 10.1038/nn.2271.

LeDoux, J. E. (2000). Emotion circuits in the brain. *Annual Review of Neuroscience, 23*, 155−184.

Lee, J. L. C. (2008). Memory reconsolidation mediates the strengthening of memories by additional learning. *Nature Neuroscience, 11*(11), 1264−1266. http://dx.doi.org/10. 1038/nn.2205, [pii] 10.1038/nn.2205.

Lee, J. L. C. (2009). Reconsolidation: maintaining memory relevance. *Trends in Neuroscience, 32*(8), 413−420. http://dx.doi.org/10.1016/S0166-2236(09)00102-7, [pii] 10. 1016/j.tins.2009.05.002.

Lee, J. L. C. (2010). Memory reconsolidation mediates the updating of hippocampal memory content. *Frontiers in Behavioral Neuroscience, 4*, 168. http://dx.doi.org/10.3389/fnbeh. 2010.00168.

Lee, J. L. C., Everitt, B. J., & Thomas, K. L. (2004). Independent cellular processes for hippocampal memory consolidation and reconsolidation. *Science, 304*(5672), 839−843.

Lee, J. L. C., Milton, A. L., & Everitt, B. J. (2006). Reconsolidation and extinction of conditioned fear: inhibition and potentiation. *Journal of Neuroscience, 26*(39), 10051−10056.

Lee, S. H., Choi, J. H., Lee, N., Lee, H. R., Kim, J. I., Yu, N. K., & Kaang, B. K. (2008). Synaptic protein degradation underlies destabilization of retrieved fear memory. *Science, 319*(5867), 1253−1256.

Lubin, F. D., & Sweatt, J. D. (2007). The IkappaB kinase regulates chromatin structure during reconsolidation of conditioned fear memories. *Neuron, 55*(6), 942−957. http:// dx.doi.org/10.1016/S0896-6273(07)00585-5, [pii] 10.1016/j.neuron.2007.07.039.

Mactutus, C. F., Riccio, D. C., & Ferek, J. M. (1979). Retrograde amnesia for old (reactivated) memory: some anomalous characteristics. *Science, 204*, 1319−1320.

Maddox, S. A., Monsey, M. S., & Schafe, G. E. (2011). Early growth response gene 1 (Egr-1) is required for new and reactivated fear memories in the lateral amygdala. *Learning & Memory, 18*(1), 24−38. http://dx.doi.org/10.1101/18/1/24, [pii] 10.1101/lm.1980211.

Maddox, S. A., & Schafe, G. E. (2011). The activity-regulated cytoskeletal-associated protein (Arc/Arg3.1) is required for reconsolidation of a Pavlovian fear memory. *Journal of Neuroscience, 31*(19), 7073−7082. http://dx.doi.org/10.1523/31/19/7073, [pii] 10.1523/JNEUROSCI.1120-11.2011.

Maren, S. (2001). Neurobiology of Pavlovian fear conditioning. *Annual Review of Neuroscience, 24,* 897−931.

Martin, S. J., & Morris, R. G. (2002). New life in an old idea: the synaptic plasticity and memory hypothesis revisited. *Hippocampus, 12*(5), 609−636. http://dx.doi.org/10. 1002/hipo.10107.

McKenzie, S., & Eichenbaum, H. (2011). Consolidation and reconsolidation: two lives of memories? *Neuron, 71*(2), 224−233. http://dx.doi.org/10.1016/S0896-6273(11)00594-0, [pii] 10.1016/j.neuron.2011.06.037.

Milekic, M. H., & Alberini, C. M. (2002). Temporally graded requirement for protein synthesis following memory reactivation. *Neuron, 36*(3), 521−525.

Milekic, M. H., Pollonini, G., & Alberini, C. M. (2007). Temporal requirement of C/EBPbeta in the amygdala following reactivation but not acquisition of inhibitory avoidance. *Learning & Memory, 14*(7), 504−511.

Misanin, J. R., Miller, R. R., & Lewis, D. J. (1968). Retrograde amnesia produced by electroconvulsive shock after reactivation of a consolidated memory trace. *Science, 160,* 554−555.

Monfils, M. H., Cowansage, K. K., Klann, E., & LeDoux, J. E. (2009). Extinction-reconsolidation boundaries: key to persistent attenuation of fear memories. *Science, 324*(5929), 951−955. http://dx.doi.org/10.1126/1167975, [pii] 10.1126/science.1167975.

Morris, R. G., Inglis, J., Ainge, J. A., Olverman, H. J., Tulloch, J., Dudai, Y., & Kelly, P. A. (2006). Memory reconsolidation: sensitivity of spatial memory to inhibition of protein synthesis in dorsal hippocampus during encoding and retrieval. *Neuron, 50*(3), 479−489.

Muravieva, E. V., & Alberini, C. M. (2010). Limited efficacy of propranolol on the reconsolidation of fear memories. *Learning & Memory, 17*(6), 306−313. http://dx.doi.org/10. 1101/17/6/306, [pii] 10.1101/lm.1794710.

Nader, K., & Hardt, O. (2009). A single standard for memory: the case for reconsolidation. *Nature Reviews Neuroscience, 10,* 224−234.

Nader, K., Schafe, G. E., & LeDoux, J. E. (2000). Fear memories require protein synthesis in the amygdala for reconsolidation after retrieval. *Nature, 406*(6797), 722−726.

Nikzad, S., Vafaei, A. A., Rashidy-Pour, A., & Haghighi, S. (2011). Systemic and intrahippocampal administrations of the glucocorticoid receptor antagonist RU38486 impairs fear memory reconsolidation in rats. *Stress, 14*(4), 459−464. http://dx.doi.org/10. 3109/10253890.2010.548171.

Packard, M. G., & McGaugh, J. L. (1996). Inactivation of hippocampus or caudate nucleus with lidocaine differentially affects expression of place and response learning. *Neurobiology of Learning and Memory, 65*(1), 65−72.

Pedreira, M. E., & Maldonado, H. (2003). Protein synthesis subserves reconsolidation or extinction depending on reminder duration. *Neuron, 38*(6), 863−869.

Pedreira, M. E., Perez-Cuesta, L. M., & Maldonado, H. (2004). Mismatch between what is expected and what actually occurs triggers memory reconsolidation or extinction. *Learning & Memory, 11*(5), 579−585.

Pickens, C. L., Golden, S. A., Adams-Deutsch, T., Nair, S. G., & Shaham, Y. (2009). Long-lasting incubation of conditioned fear in rats. *Biological Psychiatry, 65*(10), 881−886. http://dx.doi. org/10.1016/S0006-3223(08)01592-8, [pii] 10.1016/j.biopsych.2008.12.010.

Pouzet, B., Zhang, W. N., Feldon, J., & Rawlins, J. N. (2002). Hippocampal lesioned rats are able to learn a spatial position using non-spatial strategies. [Research Support, Non-U.S. Gov't]. *Behavioural Brain Research, 133*(2), 279−291.

Przybyslawski, J., Roullet, P., & Sara, S. J. (1999). Attenuation of emotional and nonemotional memories after their reactivation: role of beta adrenergic receptors. *Journal of Neuroscience, 19*(15), 6623−6628.

Przybyslawski, J., & Sara, S. J. (1997). Reconsolidation of memory after its reactivation. *Behavioural Brain Research, 84*(1-2), 241−246.

Rao-Ruiz, P., Rotaru, D. C., van der Loo, R. J., Mansvelder, H. D., Stiedl, O., Smit, A. B., & Spijker, S. (2011). Retrieval-specific endocytosis of GluA2-AMPARs underlies adaptive reconsolidation of contextual fear. *Nature Neuroscience, 14*(10), 1302−1308. http://dx. doi.org/10.1038/nn.2907, [pii] 10.1038/nn.2907.

Reichelt, A. C., & Lee, J. L. (2012). Appetitive Pavlovian goal-tracking memories reconsolidate only under specific conditions. *Learning & Memory, 20*(1), 51−60.

Rodriguez-Ortiz, C. J., De la Cruz, V., Gutierrez, R., & Bermudez-Rattoni, F. (2005). Protein synthesis underlies post-retrieval memory consolidation to a restricted degree only when updated information is obtained. *Learning & Memory, 12*(5), 533−537.

Rodriguez-Ortiz, C. J., Garcia-DeLaTorre, P., Benavidez, E., Ballesteros, M. A., & Bermudez-Rattoni, F. (2008). Intrahippocampal anisomycin infusions disrupt previously consolidated spatial memory only when memory is updated. *Neurobiology of Learning and Memory, 89*(3), 352−359.

Rossato, J. I., Bevilaqua, L. R., Medina, J. H., Izquierdo, I., & Cammarota, M. (2006). Retrieval induces hippocampal-dependent reconsolidation of spatial memory. *Learning & Memory, 13*(4), 431−440.

Rudy, J. W., Huff, N. C., & Matus-Amat, P. (2004). Understanding contextual fear conditioning: insights from a two-process model. *Neuroscience & Biobehavioral Reviews, 28*(7), 675−685. http://dx.doi.org/10.1016/S0149-7634(04)00093-4, [pii] 10.1016/j.neubiorev.2004.09.004.

Sacktor, T. C. (2011). How does PKMzeta maintain long-term memory? *Nature Reviews Neuroscience, 12*(1), 9−15. http://dx.doi.org/10.1038/nrn2949, [pii] 10.1038/nrn2949.

Sara, S. J. (2000). Retrieval and reconsolidation: toward a neurobiology of remembering. *Learning & Memory, 7*(2), 73−84.

Schafe, G. E., Atkins, C. M., Swank, M. W., Bauer, E. P., Sweatt, J. D., & LeDoux, J. E. (2000). Activation of ERK/MAP kinase in the amygdala is required for memory consolidation of Pavlovian fear conditioning. *Journal of Neuroscience, 20*(21), 8177−8187.

Schneider, A. M., & Sherman, W. (1968). Amnesia: a function of the temporal relation of footshock to electroconvulsive shock. *Science, 159*, 219−222.

Stranahan, A. M., Salas-Vega, S., Jiam, N. T., & Gallagher, M. (2011). Interference with reelin signaling in the lateral entorhinal cortex impairs spatial memory. *Neurobiology of Learning and Memory, 96*(2), 150−155. http://dx.doi.org/10.1016/S1074-7427(11)00061-X, [pii] 10.1016/j.nlm.2011.03.009.

Suzuki, A., Josselyn, S. A., Frankland, P. W., Masushige, S., Silva, A. J., & Kida, S. (2004). Memory reconsolidation and extinction have distinct temporal and biochemical signatures. *Journal of Neuroscience, 24*(20), 4787−4795.

Suzuki, A., Mukawa, T., Tsukagoshi, A., Frankland, P. W., & Kida, S. (2008). Activation of LVGCCs and CB1 receptors required for destabilization of reactivated contextual fear memories. *Learning & Memory, 15*(6), 426−433.

Taubenfeld, S. M., Milekic, M. H., Monti, B., & Alberini, C. M. (2001). The consolidation of new but not reactivated memory requires hippocampal C/EBP beta. *Nature Neuroscience, 4*(8), 813−818.

Tischmeyer, W., & Grimm, R. (1999). Activation of immediate early genes and memory formation. *Cellular and Molecular Life Sciences, 55*(4), 564−574.

Trifilieff, P., Herry, C., Vanhoutte, P., Caboche, J., Desmedt, A., Riedel, G., & Micheau, J. (2006). Foreground contextual fear memory consolidation requires two independent phases of hippocampal ERK/CREB activation. *Learning & Memory, 13*(3), 349−358.

Tronson, N. C., & Taylor, J. R. (2007). Molecular mechanisms of memory reconsolidation. *Nature Reviews Neuroscience, 8*(4), 262−275.

von Hertzen, L. S., & Giese, K. P. (2005). Memory reconsolidation engages only a subset of immediate-early genes induced during consolidation. *Journal of Neuroscience, 25*(8), 1935−1942.

Walker, M. P., Brakefield, T., Hobson, J. A., & Stickgold, R. (2003). Dissociable stages of human memory consolidation and reconsolidation. *Nature, 425*(6958), 616−620.

Wang, H., Hu, Y., & Tsien, J. Z. (2006). Molecular and systems mechanisms of memory consolidation and storage. *Progress in Neurobiology, 79*(3), 123−135. http://dx.doi.org/10.1016/S0301-0082(06)00059-1, [pii] 10.1016/j.pneurobio.2006.06.004.

Wang, S. H., & Morris, R. G. (2010). Hippocampal-neocortical interactions in memory formation, consolidation, and reconsolidation. *Annual Review of Psychology, 61* (49-79), C41−C44. http://dx.doi.org/10.1146/annurev.psych.093008.100523.

Wang, S. H., Ostlund, S. B., Nader, K., & Balleine, B. W. (2005). Consolidation and reconsolidation of incentive learning in the amygdala. *Journal of Neuroscience, 25*(4), 830−835.

Wiltgen, B. J., & Silva, A. J. (2007). Memory for context becomes less specific with time. *Learning & Memory, 14*(4), 313−317. http://dx.doi.org/10.1101/14/4/313, [pii] 10.1101/lm.430907.

Winters, B. D., Tucci, M. C., & DaCosta-Furtado, M. (2009). Older and stronger object memories are selectively destabilized by reactivation in the presence of new information. *Learning & Memory, 16*(9), 545−553. http://dx.doi.org/10.1101/16/9/545, [pii] 10.1101/lm.1509909.

Winters, B. D., Tucci, M. C., Jacklin, D. L., Reid, J. M., & Newsome, J. (2011). On the dynamic nature of the engram: Evidence for circuit-level reorganization of object memory traces following reactivation. *Journal of Neuroscience, 31*(48), 17719−17728. http://dx.doi.org/10.1523/31/48/17719, [pii] 10.1523/JNEUROSCI. 2968-11.2011.

Chapter four

Reconsolidation of Pavlovian Conditioned Defense Responses in the Amygdala

Jacek Dębiec*, Joseph E. LeDoux[†]

* *University of Michigan, Ann Arbor, Michigan*
[†] *New York University, New York, New York; and The Emotional Brain Institute, Nathan Kline Institute for Psychiatric Research, Orangeburg, New York*

4.1 AMYGDALA AND DEFENSE FEAR CONDITIONING

Pavlovian defense conditioning, also called fear conditioning, is the most commonly used experimental model of fear learning (Fanselow & Poulos, 2005; Johansen *et al.*, 2011; LeDoux, 2000, 2012; Maren, 2005). In fear conditioning, an intrinsically neutral conditioned stimulus (CS), such as an odor, sound, or light, is paired with an innately aversive unconditioned stimulus (US), such as an electric shock. The most widespread variant of fear conditioning used in rodent studies is auditory fear conditioning, which involves the pairing of a tone with footshock. The CS naturally triggers mild and transient responses, such as altering and orientation. After pairing with the US, however, the CS acquires the ability to elicit hardwired and stereotyped defense responses, such as freezing. The performance and maintenance of defense behaviors is supported by associated autonomic nervous responses, such as changes in respiration, heart rate, and blood pressure, as well as the release of stress hormones.

Although several brain structures are involved in detection and responses to threat, it is well-established that a key site involved in processing fear is the amygdala (Davis, 1992; Fanselow & Poulos, 2005; Johansen *et al.*, 2011; LeDoux, 2000; Maren, 2005; Phelps & LeDoux, 2005). The regions within the amygdala that are most relevant to fear conditioning are the lateral (LA), basal (B), and central (CE) nuclei of the amygdala, as well as a discrete group of neurons known as intercalated masses (ITM) (Fanselow & Poulos,

69

Memory Reconsolidation. http://dx.doi.org/10.1016/B978-0-12-386892-3.00004-4

2005; Lang & Davis, 2006; LeDoux, 2000, 2007; Maren, 2005; Pare, Quirk & LeDoux, 2004).

The LA serves as the major sensory gateway of the amygdala. It receives inputs from all sensory modalities, including pathways conveying information about the CS and the US. The B receives projections from the hippocampus, entorhinal, and polymodal associative cortices, areas that convey information about the environmental context in which threat is occurring (LeDoux, 2007). The LA sends direct and indirect (via B and ITM) projections to the CE. The CE is the major output area of the amygdala. It projects to the brain stem and hypothalamic structures directly controlling particular behavioral, autonomic, and endocrine defense responses. Damage or pharmacological inactivation of the CE disrupts innate, as well as learned, fear reactions. The ITM have an inhibitory control over the CE (Pare & Duvarci, 2012).

The convergence of the CS and the US pathways defines the LA as a site where synaptic plasticity underlying defense conditioning occurs. During fear conditioning, the weak signal produced in the LA neurons by the CS is enhanced by the concurrent stimulation of the US pathways. This enhancement of signaling is believed to initiate Hebbian plasticity mechanisms, leading to synaptic modifications that strengthen the CS pathway and endow the CS with the ability to elicit fear responses (Blair et al., 2001; Johansen et al., 2011).

Fear learning processes controlled by synaptic plasticity in the LA occur in stages. The initial stage of acquisition of defense conditioning, which occurs during the CS–US pairing, is followed by memory consolidation processes. Numerous studies identified molecular mechanisms underlying acquisition and consolidation of fear memories (Johansen et al., 2011; Rodrigues et al., 2004; Schafe et al., 2001; Sigurdsson et al., 2007). In general, memory acquisition and consolidation are initiated by stimulations of the receptors at the synapses, which in turn activate second messengers and downstream intracellular signaling cascades, including protein kinases and transcription factors, leading to gene expression and protein synthesis (Kandel, 2001). Existing studies indicate that the LA stores critical elements of conditioned fear responses following their consolidation; for example, damage or pharmacological inactivation of the LA impairs retrieval of conditioned defense responses elicited by the CS without affecting fear triggered directly by the US (Johansen et al., 2011; LeDoux, 2007; LeDoux & Fanselow, 1999).

Defense conditioning, due to its survival importance, produces lasting memories. A single CS–US pairing may establish conditioned responses that last throughout the whole life of an organism. However, multiple exposures to the CS unaccompanied by the US trigger extinction processes. Fear extinction is commonly understood as a form of safety learning in which an organism learns that the CS no longer predicts the aversive event (Bouton et al., 2006; Milad & Quirk, 2012; Myers & Davis, 2007; Sotres-Bayon et al., 2006). Fear extinction is controlled by several sites in the rodent brain, including the ventral prefrontal cortex, the hippocampus, and the amygdala (Milad & Quirk, 2012; Myers & Davis, 2007; Pare & Duvarci, 2012; Sotres-Bayon *et al.*, 2007, 2009). The LA is especially involved in the acquisition of extinction (Sotres-Bayon *et al.*, 2007, 2009).

In summary, existing research on Pavlovian defense conditioning provides evidence that the amygdala, and specifically the LA, is critical for the acquisition, consolidation, and storage of conditioned fear, as well as the acquisition of fear extinction.

4.2 MOLECULAR MECHANISMS OF MEMORY RECONSOLIDATION

In the original report of the reconsolidation of Pavlovian conditioned fear in the amygdala, Nader *et al.* (2000) used a standard consolidation protocol and a commonly used consolidation blocker (the protein synthesis inhibitor anisomycin). The drug was infused directly into the LA, the brain site where fear conditioning consolidation processes occur (Rodrigues *et al.*, 2004; Schafe & LeDoux, 2000). According to the protocol used in consolidation studies, in order to conclusively demonstrate consolidation, pharmacologic manipulations have to be administered following training leaving short-term memory (STM) intact and long-term memory (LTM) affected. Nader and colleagues applied this standard in their study and showed that post-retrieval intra-amygdala drug administration spares post-retrieval STM and disrupts post-retrieval LTM.

The successful use of this combination of a standard consolidation protocol and consolidation blocker in a brain region known to be involved in consolidation as a way of studying reconsolidation raised the question whether reconsolidation recapitulates consolidation processes at the cellular and molecular level (Alberini, 2005, 2011; Dudai, 2004, 2012; Nader & Hardt, 2009). Further research using a variety of species and learning tasks demonstrated that although consolidation and reconsolidation are distinct phenomena (Bahar *et al.*, 2004; Debiec & LeDoux, 2004; Lee *et al.*, 2004; Tronel *et al.*, 2005; von Hertzen & Giese, 2005), they frequently share temporal, anatomical, and biochemical properties but also have unique requirements (for review, see Tronson & Taylor, 2007; Cain *et al.*, 2008; Johansen *et al.*, 2011).

Initiation of reconsolidation of Pavlovian fear in the LA requires glutamatergic signaling (Ben Mamou *et al.*, 2006; Kim *et al.*, 2010). Pharmacological blockade of N-methyl-D-aspartate receptors in the LA prior to an exposure to the CS immunizes the reactivated memory against subsequent administration of reconsolidation blockers (Ben Mamou *et al.*, 2006). Consistently, pre-retrieval enhancement of glutamatergic transmission in the LA augments fear memories (Ben Mamou *et al.*, 2006). Pre-retrieval interference with another class of glutamatergic receptors, α-amino-3-hydroxyl-5-methyl-4isoxazole-proprionate receptors (AMPARs), had no effect on fear memory reconsolidation (Ben Mamou *et al.*, 2006).

Studies have demonstrated that molecular processes downstream of gluta-matergic activation, including activation of protein kinases, transcription factors, gene expression, and protein synthesis, are also implicated in reconsolidation of Pavlovian fear (for review, see Tronson & Taylor, 2007). Post-retrieval blockade of protein kinase A (PKA) disrupts and augmentation enhances reconsolidation of fear memories (Tronson *et al.*, 2006). Similarly, post-reactivation blockade of mitogen-activated protein kinase (MAPK) impairs reconsolidation of Pavlovian fear (Doyere *et al.*, 2007; Duvarci *et al.*, 2005). Downstream of PKA and MAPK, acute disruption of the transcription factor cyclic adenosine monophosphate-responsive element binding protein (CREB) function in the mice forebrain following reactivation of auditory fear conditioning impairs reconsolidation of fear memories (Kida *et al.*, 2002; Tronson *et al.*, 2012). Recent studies demonstrated that blocking the immediate early genes: early growth response gene-I (EGR-I), activity-regulated cytoskeletal-associated protein (Arc/Arg3.1) gene, and the neuronal PAS domain protein 4 (Npas4) gene in LA disrupts reconsolidation of Pavlovian auditory fear (Lee *et al.*, 2005; Maddox & Schafe, 2011a; Maddox *et al.*, 2011; Ploski *et al.*, 2011). Intra-LA blockade of *de novo* matrix RNA synthesis following CS exposure impaired fear memories (Duvarci *et al.*, 2008). Several reports showed the requirement of protein synthesis for the reconsolidation of conditioned fear (Debiec *et al.*, 2006, 2010; Duvarci & Nader, 2004; Jarome *et al.*, 2012; Nader *et al.*, 2000; Wang *et al.*, 2009), whereas one study demonstrated the requirement of protein degradation for the reconsolidation of auditory fear conditioning (Jarome *et al.*, 2011). Both consolidation and reconsolidation of auditory fear conditioning are sensitive to actin filament arrest in the LA (Rehberg *et al.*, 2010). One publication reported the involvement of translational regulator mammalian target of rapamycin (mTOR) in the reconsolidation of auditory fear (Jarome *et al.*, 2006). Another report demonstrated that similarly to consolidation processes (Monsey *et al.*, 2011), reconsolidation of auditory fear conditioning is subject to epigenetic control (Maddox & Schafe, 2011b).

It has been well-established that emotional memories are sensitive to noradrenergic modulation (Roozendaal & McGaugh, 2011). A number of studies reported involvement of norepinephrine in the consolidation of emotional memories (Roozendaal & McGaugh, 2011). We have found that post-retrieval noradrenergic stimulation enhances and blockade impairs Pavlovian fear (Debiec & LeDoux, 2004; Debiec *et al.*, 2011). Norepinephrine release is normally associated with arousal. The susceptibility of fear memory reconsolidation processes to modulation by norepinephrine suggests that one of the functions of reconsolidation is updating the memory with the new information accompanying memory retrieval (Debiec *et al.*, 2011). If retrieval of fear memories is accompanied by threatening events, memory trace becomes strengthened. The dysfunction of this noradrenergic-regulated memory updating mechanism may account for the development of pathologic memories, such as in post-traumatic stress disorder or phobias (Debiec, 2012; Debiec & LeDoux,

2006; Debiec *et al.*, 2011). One study demonstrated that another stress response-mediating system, the glucocorticoid system, is also involved in reconsolidation of auditory fear in the LA, supporting the idea that arousal and stress accompanying memory retrieval contribute to strengthening of fear memories (Jin *et al.*, 2007).

Despite sharing molecular pathways, consolidation and reconsolidation of Pavlovian fear are distinct processes. The differences between consolidation and reconsolidation have been best described in other learning paradigms. In contextual fear conditioning preparation, memory consolidation requires brain-derived neurotrophic factor (BDNF) but not the transcription factor Zif268, whereas reconsolidation involves Zif268 but not BDNF (Lee *et al.*, 2004). In inhibitory avoidance paradigm, consolidation but not reconsolidation recruits the expression of the transcription factor CCAAT enhancer binding protein β (C/EBPβ) in the hippocampus (Taubenfeld *et al.*, 2001). Using the Pavlovian fear conditioning paradigm, we observed that reconsolidation, but not consolidation, is modulated by the noradrenergic system (Debiec & LeDoux, 2004; Debiec *et al.*, 2011). Indeed, noradrenergic transmission in the LA has been shown to be involved in the acquisition but not consolidation of Pavlovian fear (Bush *et al.*, 2010).

Together, studies using pharmacological post-retrieval manipulations demonstrate that fear memories through reconsolidation processes in the LA are actively maintained and modified (augmented or blunted).

4.3 RELATIONSHIPS BETWEEN MEMORY EXTINCTION AND RECONSOLIDATION PROCESSES

Studies described so far demonstrate that critical elements of Pavlovian fear memory are stored, maintained, and updated in the lateral amygdala. It is commonly accepted that extinction of acquired fear through multiple exposures to a learned cue results in an establishment of a new memory trace (Bouton *et al.*, 2006; Milad & Quirk, 2012; Myers & Davis, 2007; Sotres-Bayon *et al.*, 2006). Return of the CS-triggered defense responses, either spontaneously (spontaneous recovery) or using post-extinction behavioral manipulations such as testing in a different context (renewal) or exposure to the US (reinstatement), supports the hypothesis that fear memory and safety (extinction) memory are encoded in discrete traces. Contrary to extinction procedures that do not permanently eliminate conditioned fear, pharmacological disruption of reconsolidation has been shown to have lasting effects (Duvarci & Nader, 2004). As a new learning experience, extinction undergoes acquisition and consolidation, which involve all the previously described molecular stages (Orsini & Maren, 2012; Quirk & Mueller, 2008). Several studies using various species and learning tasks established that memory reconsolidation and extinction are distinct phenomena (Eisenberg *et al.*, 2003; Lee *et al.*, 2006; Pedreira & Maldonado, 2003; Pedreira *et al.*, 2004; Perez-Cuesta & Maldonado, 2009).

However, we have found that under certain conditions, reconsolidation and extinction may be paralleled (Debiec *et al.*, 2006; Diaz-Mataix *et al.*, 2011).

To study this, we used a second-order fear conditioning procedure. Second-order fear conditioning is a variant of fear conditioning. It begins with a standard fear conditioning procedure, in which a CS is paired with a noxious US (Gewirtz & Davis, 2000). This CS, now called a first-order CS (CS1), is subsequently paired with a new distinct neutral stimulus, a second-order CS (CS2), in the absence of the US. Consequently, the CS2 also acquires the ability to elicit defense responses. Using second-order fear conditioning, we found that extinction of CS2 and disruption of reconsolidation of CS2 memory spare the CS1 memory while at the same time impairing the memory for CS2 (Debiec *et al.*, 2006). In contrast, in the same training paradigm, both extinction of CS1 and disruption of reconsolidation of CS1 memory affect responding to both CS1 and CS2 (Debiec *et al.*, 2006).

We further explored the relation of multiple memories using a procedure in which two distinct CSs were each paired with a distinct US (electric shock to foot pads or eyelids). Reconsolidation was then triggered by exposure to one of the CSs or USs. We found that disruption of reconsolidation in the LA after exposure to a US affects defense responding to the CS that was previously paired with this US, leaving freezing to the other CS intact (Debiec *et al.*, 2010; Diaz-Mataix *et al.*, 2011). Similarly, using the same training protocol, extinction of responding to one CS leaves freezing to the other CS intact (Diaz-Mataix *et al.*, 2011). These findings suggest that fear memory traces and extinction memory traces share certain elements and/or similar architecture. Indeed, combining extinction and reconsolidation protocols by a brief CS exposure prior to extinction training has been shown to lastingly eliminate Pavlovian fear memories (Monfils *et al.*, 2009; Schiller *et al.*, 2010). In other words, a single pre-extinction CS exposure renders extinguished memory immune to reinstatement and renewal procedures. Another study suggests that reconsolidation−extinction interference protocol resulting in memory erasure may be associated with alterations in AMPARs in the LA (Clem & Huganir, 2010).

Although behaviorally and pharmacologically dissociable, reconsolidation and extinction of Pavlovian fear appear to interact in the LA. It is thus conceivable that fear memory trace and extinction memory trace share neural and/or molecular elements allowing modification of memories by combining reconsolidation and extinction approaches.

4.4 ORGANIZATION OF FEAR MEMORY ASSOCIATIONS

Pavlovian fear conditioning involves establishment of associations between neural representations of learning events (Konorski, 1967). The organization of associations developed during a learning experience puzzled early learning theorists (Hull, 1943; Konorski, 1967; Rizley & Rescorla, 1972). Typically, the strength of proposed associations is assessed using various post-training manipulations (Gewirtz & Davis, 2000). In this approach, especially second-order conditioning procedures, compared to first-order learning protocols, were found to be useful, offering a tool for analyzing the structure of associations and the number of possible associations (Gewirtz & Davis, 2000). In second-order conditioning, the CS2 may become associated with the CS1, forming a CS2—CS1 association. Alternatively, the CS2 may become associated with the US, establishing a CS2—US association, or with the fear response, producing a CS2—response memory. Manipulating the value of the CS memory reveals the structure of existing associations. For example, extinction of responding to CS1 resulting in attenuation of responding to CS2 suggests that during second-order learning, a CS2—CS1 association is developed (Gewirtz & Davis, 2000). In contrast, if extinction of responding to CS1 has no effect on memory for CS2, the existence of CS2—US or CS2—response associations would be more plausible (Rizley & Rescorla, 1972). Some authors have proposed to use this approach in analyzing the structure of Pavlovian fear conditioning in the amygdala (Gewirtz & Davis, 2000). We used this methodology, combining extinction procedures with reconsolidation protocols (Debiec et al., 2006, 2010; Diaz-Mataix et al., 2011; Doyere et al., 2007). We found that when two distinct auditory CSs are paired with the same US, exposure to one of these CSs followed by the intra-LA microinfusions of a reconsolidation blocker results in a selective disruption of responding to this CS (Debiec et al., 2010; Doyere et al., 2007). However, an exposure to the shared US followed by the disruption of reconsolidation affects responding to both CSs (Debiec et al., 2010). These findings suggest that in our protocol, each distinct CS has a distinct representation in the LA, although each of these representations is associated with a shared element (representation of the US). However, if these same distinct CSs are used in a second-order conditioning protocol, the post-CS1 disruption of reconsolidation in the LA or extinction of CS1 both affect freezing responding to the CS2 (Debiec et al., 2006). This demonstrates that the same representation of the auditory CS, depending on the learning conditions, forms distinct associations. In another series of experiments, we used two distinct auditory CSs, each paired with a distinct US (either electric foot- or eyelid shock) (Debiec et al., 2010; Diaz-Mataix et al., 2011). Using reconsolidation protocols, we found that exposure to one of the USs followed by the pharmacological disruption of reconsolidation in the LA selectively affects responding to the CS that was paired with this US, leaving responding to the other US intact (Debiec et al., 2010; Diaz-Mataix et al., 2011). These findings were paralleled by the extinction experiments as described in the previous section (Diaz-Mataix et al., 2011). US-selective character of reconsolidation processes suggests that the amygdala distinguishes between these USs and encodes their specific sensory values.

Our findings demonstrate that reconsolidation protocols in combination with extinction procedures provide a powerful tool to gain insights into the architecture of fear memories in the LA.

4.5 CONCLUSIONS

Studies of Pavlovian fear conditioning have elucidated the role of the amygdala in the acquisition, consolidation, and storage of fear memories. Reconsolidation research expanded this knowledge, revealing the contributions of the amygdala to the maintenance and updating of fear memories. Combinations of reconsolidation and extinction protocols proved to be useful in shedding light on the character and nature of fear associations in the amygdala.

ACKNOWLEDGMENTS

We would like to express our gratitude to our colleagues and co-investigators in reconsolidation studies: Drs. Valérie Doyère, Karim Nader, Glenn E. Schafe, Lorenzo Diaz-Mataix, David Bush and Marie-H. Monfils. JD has been supported by the 2010 NARSAD Young Investigator Award from the Brain & Behavior Research Foundation. JEL has been supported by P50 MH058911, R01 MH038774 and R01 MH046516 grants.

REFERENCES

Alberini, C. M. (2005). Mechanisms of memory stabilization: are consolidation and reconsolidation similar or distinct processes? [Review]. *Trends in Neuroscience, 28*(1), 51–56.

Alberini, C. M. (2011). The role of reconsolidation and the dynamic process of long-term memory formation and storage. *Frontiers in Behavioral Neuroscience, 5*, 12.

Ben Mamou, C., Gamache, K., & Nader, K. (2006). NMDA receptors are critical for unleashing consolidated auditory fear memories. *Nature Neuroscience, 9*(10), 1237–1239.

Blair, H. T., Schafe, G. E., Bauer, E. P., Rodrigues, S. M., & LeDoux, J. E. (2001). Synaptic plasticity in the lateral amygdala: a cellular hypothesis of fear conditioning. *Learning & Memory, 8*(5), 229–242. http://dx.doi.org/10.1101/lm.30901.

Bouton, M. E., Westbrook, R. F., Corcoran, K. A., & Maren, S. (2006). Contextual and temporal modulation of extinction: behavioral and biological mechanisms. *Biological Psychiatry, 60*(4), 352–360. http://dx.doi.org/10.1016/j.biopsych.2005.12.015.

Debiec, J. (2012). Memory reconsolidation processes and posttraumatic stress disorder: promises and challenges of translational research. *Biological Psychiatry, 71*(4), 284–285. http://dx.doi.org/10.1016/j.biopsych.2011.12.009.

Debiec, J., Bush, D. E., & LeDoux, J. E. (2011). Noradrenergic enhancement of reconsolidation in the amygdala impairs extinction of conditioned fear in rats—A possible mechanism for the persistence of traumatic memories in PTSD. *Depression and Anxiety, 28*(3), 186–193. http://dx.doi.org/10.1002/da.20803.

Debiec, J., Diaz-Mataix, L., Bush, D. E., Doyere, V., & Ledoux, J. E. (2010). The amygdala encodes specific sensory features of an aversive reinforcer. *Nature Neuroscience, 13*(5), 536–537. http://dx.doi.org/10.1038/nn.2520.

Debiec, J., Doyere, V., Nader, K., & Ledoux, J. E. (2006). Directly reactivated, but not indirectly reactivated, memories undergo reconsolidation in the amygdala. *Proceedings of National Academy of Science of the United States of America, 103*(9), 3428–3433. http://dx.doi.org/10.1073/pnas.0507168103.

Debiec, J., & Ledoux, J. E. (2004). Disruption of reconsolidation but not consolidation of auditory fear conditioning by noradrenergic blockade in the amygdala. *Neuroscience, 129*(2), 267–272. http://dx.doi.org/10.1016/j.neuroscience.2004.08.018.

Debiec, J., & LeDoux, J. E. (2006). Noradrenergic signaling in the amygdala contributes to the reconsolidation of fear memory: treatment implications for PTSD. *Annals of the New York Academy of Sciences, 1071*, 521–524. http://dx.doi.org/10.1196/annals. 1364.056.

Diaz-Mataix, L., Debiec, J., LeDoux, J. E., & Doyere, V. (2011). Sensory-specific associations stored in the lateral amygdala allow for selective alteration of fear memories. *Journal of Neuroscience, 31*(26), 9538−9543. http://dx.doi.org/10.1523/JNEUROSCI. 5808-10.2011.

Doyere, V., Debiec, J., Monfils, M. H., Schafe, G. E., & LeDoux, J. E. (2007). Synapse-specific reconsolidation of distinct fear memories in the lateral amygdala. *Nature Neuroscience, 10*(4), 414−416. http://dx.doi.org/10.1038/nn1871.

Dudai, Y. (2004). The neurobiology of consolidations, or, how stable is the engram? *Annual Review of Psychology, 55*, 51−86. http://dx.doi.org/10.1146/annurev.psych.55.090902. 142050.

Dudai, Y. (2012). The Restless Engram: Consolidations Never End. *Annual Review of Neuroscience, 35*, 227−247. http://dx.doi.org/10.1146/annurev-neuro-062111-150500.

Duvarci, S., & Nader, K. (2004). Characterization of fear memory reconsolidation. *Journal of Neuroscience, 24*(42), 9269−9275. http://dx.doi.org/10.1523/JNEUROSCI.2971-04. 2004.

Duvarci, S., Nader, K., & LeDoux, J. E. (2005). Activation of extracellular signal-regulated kinase-/mitogen-activated protein kinase cascade in the amygdala is required for memory reconsolidation of auditory fear conditioning. *European Journal of Neuroscience, 21*(1), 283−289. http://dx.doi.org/10.1111/j.1460-9568.2004.03824.x.

Duvarci, S., Nader, K., & LeDoux, J. E. (2008). *De novo* mRNA synthesis is required for both consolidation and reconsolidation of fear memories in the amygdala. *Learning & Memory, 15*(10), 747−755. http://dx.doi.org/10.1101/lm.1027208.

Fanselow, M. S., & LeDoux, J. E. (1999). Why we think plasticity underlying Pavlovian fear conditioning occurs in the basolateral amygdala [Review]. *Neuron, 23*(2), 229−232.

Jin, X. C., Lu, Y. F., Yang, X. F., Ma, L., & Li, B. M. (2007). Glucocorticoid receptors in the basolateral nucleus of amygdala are required for postreactivation reconsolidation of auditory fear memory. *European Journal of Neuroscience, 25*(12), 3702−3712. http://dx.doi.org/10.1111/j.1460-9568.2007.05621.x.

Johansen, J. P., Cain, C. K., Ostroff, L. E., & LeDoux, J. E. (2011). Molecular mechanisms of fear learning and memory [Review]. *Cell, 147*(3), 509−524. http://dx.doi.org/10.1016/j. cell.2011.10.009.

Kandel, E. R. (2001). The molecular biology of memory storage: a dialogue between genes and synapses. *Science, 294*(5544), 1030−1038. http://dx.doi.org/10.1126/science.1067020.

Kim, J., Song, B., Hong, I., Lee, J., Park, S., Eom, J. Y., Lee, C. J., Lee, S., & Choi, S. (2010). Reactivation of fear memory renders consolidated amygdala synapses labile. *Journal of Neuroscience, 30*(28), 9631−9640. http://dx.doi.org/10.1523/JNEUROSCI. 0940-10.2010.

Lang, P. J., & Davis, M. (2006). Emotion, motivation, and the brain: reflex foundations in animal and human research. *Progress in Brain Research, 156*, 3−29. http://dx.doi.org/ 10.1016/S0079-6123(06)56001-7.

LeDoux, J. E. (2000). Emotion circuits in the brain [Review]. *Annual Review of Neuroscience, 23*, 155−184. http://dx.doi.org/10.1146/annurev.neuro.23.1.155.

LeDoux, J. (2007). The amygdala [Review]. *Current Biology, 17*(20), R868−874. http://dx. doi.org/10.1016/j.cub.2007.08.005.

Lee, J. L., Everitt, B. J., & Thomas, K. L. (2004). Independent cellular processes for hippocampal memory consolidation and reconsolidation. *Science, 304*(5672), 839−843. http://dx.doi.org/10.1126/science.1095760.

Lee, J. L., Di Ciano, P., Thomas, K. L., & Everitt, B. J. (2005). Disrupting reconsolidation of drug memories reduces cocaine-seeking behavior. *Neuron, 47*(6), 795−801. http://dx. doi.org/10.1016/j.neuron.2005.08.007.

Lee, J. L., Milton, A. L., & Everitt, B. J. (2006). Reconsolidation and extinction of conditioned fear: inhibition and potentiation. *Journal of Neuroscience, 26*(39), 10051−10056. http://dx.doi.org/10.1523/JNEUROSCI.2466-06.2006.

Maddox, S. A., Monsey, M. S., & Schafe, G. E. (2011). Early growth response gene 1 (Egr-1) is required for new and reactivated fear memories in the lateral amygdala. *Learning & Memory, 18*(1), 24−38. http://dx.doi.org/10.1101/lm.1980211.

Maddox, S. A., & Schafe, G. E. (2011a). The activity-regulated cytoskeletal-associated protein (Arc/Arg3.1) is required for reconsolidation of a Pavlovian fear memory. *Journal of Neuroscience, 31*(19), 7073−7082. http://dx.doi.org/10.1523/JNEUROSCI. 1120-11.2011.

Maddox, S. A., & Schafe, G. E. (2011b). Epigenetic alterations in the lateral amygdala are required for reconsolidation of a Pavlovian fear memory. *Learning & Memory, 18*(9), 579−593. http://dx.doi.org/10.1101/lm.2243411.

Maren, S. (2005). Synaptic mechanisms of associative memory in the amygdala. *Neuron, 47*(6), 783−786. http://dx.doi.org/10.1016/j.neuron.2005.08.009.

Milad, M. R., & Quirk, G. J. (2012). Fear extinction as a model for translational neuroscience: ten years of progress. *Annual Review of Psychology, 63*, 129−151. http://dx.doi. org/10.1146/annurev.psych.121208.131631.

Monfils, M. H., Cowansage, K. K., Klann, E., & LeDoux, J. E. (2009). Extinction-reconsolidation boundaries: key to persistent attenuation of fear memories. *Science, 324*(5929), 951−955. http://dx.doi.org/10.1126/science.1167975.

Myers, K. M., & Davis, M. (2007). Mechanisms of fear extinction. *Molecular Psychiatry, 12*(2), 120−150. http://dx.doi.org/10.1038/sj.mp.4001939.

Nader, K., & Hardt, O. (2009). A single standard for memory: the case for reconsolidation. *Nature Reviews Neuroscience, 10*(3), 224−234. http://dx.doi.org/10.1038/nrn2590.

Nader, K., Schafe, G. E., & Le Doux, J. E. (2000). Fear memories require protein synthesis in the amygdala for reconsolidation after retrieval. *Nature, 406*(6797), 722−726. http://dx. doi.org/10.1038/35021052.

Orsini, C. A., & Maren, S. (2012). Neural and cellular mechanisms of fear and extinction memory formation. *Neuroscience & Biobehavioral Reviews, 36*(7), 1773−1802. http:// dx.doi.org/10.1016/j.neubiorev.2011.12.014.

Pare, D., & Duvarci, S. (2012). Amygdala microcircuits mediating fear expression and extinction. *Current Opinion in Neurobiology, 22*, 717−723. http://dx.doi.org/10.1016/ j.conb.2012.02.014.

Pare, D., Quirk, G. J., & Ledoux, J. E. (2004). New vistas on amygdala networks in conditioned fear. *Journal of Neurophysiology, 92*(1), 1−9. http://dx.doi.org/10.1152/jn.00153. 2004.

Phelps, E. A., & LeDoux, J. E. (2005). Contributions of the amygdala to emotion processing: from animal models to human behavior. *Neuron, 48*(2), 175−187. http://dx.doi.org/10. 1016/j.neuron.2005.09.025.

Rehberg, K., Bergado-Acosta, J. R., Koch, J. C., & Stork, O. (2010). Disruption of fear memory consolidation and reconsolidation by actin filament arrest in the basolateral amygdala. *Neurobiol Learning and Memory, 94*(2), 117−126. http://dx.doi.org/10. 1016/j.nlm.2010.04.007.

Rodrigues, S. M., Schafe, G. E., & LeDoux, J. E. (2004). Molecular mechanisms underlying emotional learning and memory in the lateral amygdala. *Neuron, 44*(1), 75−91. http:// dx.doi.org/10.1016/j.neuron.2004.09.014.

Schafe, G. E., Nader, K., Blair, H. T., & LeDoux, J. E. (2001). Memory consolidation of Pavlovian fear conditioning: a cellular and molecular perspective. *Trends in Neuroscience, 24*(9), 540−546.

Schiller, D., Monfils, M. H., Raio, C. M., Johnson, D. C., Ledoux, J. E., & Phelps, E. A. (2010). Preventing the return of fear in humans using reconsolidation update mechanisms. *Nature, 463*(7277), 49−53. http://dx.doi.org/10.1038/nature08637.

Sigurdsson, T., Doyere, V., Cain, C. K., & LeDoux, J. E. (2007). Long-term potentiation in the amygdala: a cellular mechanism of fear learning and memory. *Neuropharmacology, 52*(1), 215−227. http://dx.doi.org/10.1016/j.neuropharm.2006.06.022.

Sotres-Bayon, F., Cain, C. K., & LeDoux, J. E. (2006). Brain mechanisms of fear extinction: historical perspectives on the contribution of prefrontal cortex. *Biological Psychiatry, 60*(4), 329−336. http://dx.doi.org/10.1016/j.biopsych.2005.10.012.

Sotres-Bayon, F., Bush, D. E., & LeDoux, J. E. (2007). Acquisition of fear extinction requires activation of NR2B-containing NMDA receptors in the lateral amygdala. *Neuropsychopharmacology, 32*(9), 1929−1940. http://dx.doi.org/10.1038/sj.npp.1301316.

Sotres-Bayon, F., Diaz-Mataix, L., Bush, D. E., & LeDoux, J. E. (2009). Dissociable roles for the ventromedial prefrontal cortex and amygdala in fear extinction: NR2B contribution. *Cerebral Cortex, 19*(2), 474−482. http://dx.doi.org/10.1093/cercor/bhn099.

Tronson, N. C., & Taylor, J. R. (2007). Molecular mechanisms of memory reconsolidation. *Nature Reviews Neuroscience, 8*(4), 262−275. http://dx.doi.org/10.1038/nrn2090.

Tronson, N. C., Wiseman, S. L., Olausson, P., & Taylor, J. R. (2006). Bidirectional behavioral plasticity of memory reconsolidation depends on amygdalar protein kinase A. *Nature Neuroscience, 9*(2), 167−169. http://dx.doi.org/10.1038/nn1628.

Wang, S. H., de Oliveira Alvares, L., & Nader, K. (2009). Cellular and systems mechanisms of memory strength as a constraint on auditory fear reconsolidation. *Nature Neuroscience, 12*(7), 905−912. http://dx.doi.org/10.1038/nn.2350.

Chapter five

Memory Reconsolidation: Lingering Consolidation and the Dynamic Memory Trace

Cristina M. Alberini, Sarah A. Johnson, Xiaojing Ye

New York University, New York, New York

5.1 DEFINITIONS OF MEMORY CONSOLIDATION AND RECONSOLIDATION

5.1.1 Memory consolidation

Memory consolidation is a fundamental process of long-term memory formation, as, in fact, has been described to occur in a multitude of different types of memories, species, and memory systems. It refers to the stabilization process of a newly formed long-term memory. Initially, the memory is in a fragile state and can be disrupted by several types of interference, including behavioral, pharmacological, and electrical. Over time, the memory becomes resilient to these forms of interference through the process known as consolidation (Alberini, Bambah-Mukku, & Chen, 2012; Davis & Squire, 1984; McGaugh, 2000). Memory consolidation involves synaptic and broad cellular events that include transcriptional, translational, and post-translational mechanisms, as well as their feedback and feedforward regulation. These molecular changes start with the initial encoding and evolve with time because memory consolidation seems to occur in stages (Alberini, 2008, 2009; Dudai, 1996, 2012; McGaugh, 2000; Squire & Alvarez, 1995). For example, the consolidation of medial temporal lobe-dependent memories, in addition to the cellular consolidation events just described, also involves a redistribution of the memory trace, such that it transitions from hippocampal-dependent to hippocampal-independent (Squire & Alvarez, 1995; Squire, Clark, & Knowlton,

81

Memory Reconsolidation. http://dx.doi.org/10.1016/B978-0-12-386892-3.00005-6

2001; Squire, Stark, & Clark, 2004). Hence, memory consolidation appears to consist of multiple stages, which can be delineated based on the type of interference to which a memory trace is susceptible over time—for example, those that target molecular versus system mechanisms.

5.1.2 Memory reconsolidation

For several decades, it was believed that memory consolidation, at least the initial synaptic and cellular consolidation phase, was a unique process. A newly formed memory requires gene expression for several hours, after which it becomes stable and resilient to transcription and translation disruption (McGaugh, 2000). However, studies performed during the past decade, extending findings from the 1960s, demonstrate that the initial gene expression-dependent phase required for memory consolidation is not unique to a newly encoded memory. In fact, memories that have become resistant to disruption by inhibitors of gene expression, if reactivated, for example, by a retrieval event, again become temporarily labile. During this period, similar to what is seen during the initial consolidation, memories can be disrupted by molecular interference. Over time, the reactivated memories again become stable and resilient to disruption. This restabilization process has been termed *memory reconsolidation* (Alberini, 2005; Dudai & Eisenberg, 2004; Lewis, 1979; Nader, Schafe, & LeDoux, 2000; Sara, 2000). Although the term reconsolidation, as well as interpretations of findings about the reconsolidation process, is still highly debated, the existence of a temporal window of reacquired fragility following memory reactivation is supported by numerous studies. This post-reactivation fragility opens an opportunity for memory disruption or enhancement, and it has been reported in a wide range of species, from *Caenorhabditis elegans* to human, with respect to different types of learning, including aversive and appetitive, suggesting that it is a fundamental process underlying memory formation (Dudai & Eisenberg, 2004; Nader & Hardt, 2009).

5.2 CONSOLIDATION AND RECONSOLIDATION OF SINGLE TRIAL INHIBITORY AVOIDANCE CONDITIONING

5.2.1 What are the advantages of studying inhibitory avoidance and what information will we gain?

Inhibitory avoidance (IA) is a fear-based conditioning paradigm in which a single learning trial leads to the formation of a long-lasting memory. In this paradigm, animals learn to suppress a natural response, such as moving out of a brightly lit area into a darkened area (i.e., step-through inhibitory avoidance) or stepping down off a small starting platform (i.e., step-down passive avoidance) following conditioning to an aversive stimulus. A typical step-through IA task in rodents occurs as follows: During the training session, the animal is placed in a conditioning chamber that is divided into two compartments separated by an automated sliding door. One compartment is brightly lit, and the other is dark. The animal is placed in the lit chamber with the door closed. After a brief initial period to acclimate to the chamber (normally 10 sec), the door is opened, allowing the animal to cross to the dark compartment, upon which the door closes and a footshock is delivered via a grid floor. Memory retention can then be assessed at any time by returning the animal to the conditioning chamber and measuring its latency to enter the dark (shock) compartment. The retention level is a function of the intensity of the footshock used during training. In general, a maximum testing time is set (cut-off time; e.g., in our studies, 9 or 15 min), after which the animal is returned to its home cage. As a fear- and context-based conditioning paradigm, IA memory formation critically involves many brain regions similar to those mediating contextual fear conditioning, including the hippocampus, amygdala, anterior cingulate cortex, and prelimbic/infralimbic cortex (Ambrogi Lorenzini, Baldi, Bucherelli, Sacchetti, & Tassoni, 1997, 1999; Izquierdo *et al.*, 1997; Malin, Ibrahim, Tu, & McGaugh, 2007; McGaugh, 2004; McIntyre, Power, Roozendaal, & McGaugh, 2003; Zhang, Fukushima, & Kida, 2011). However, unlike contextual fear conditioning, IA is a form of instrumental learning (also called operant conditioning) because it requires that the subject takes a natural action during training and subsequently learns and decides to suppress the action (Staddon & Cerutti, 2003). IA provides several advantages for multilevel investigation of memory mechanisms, including molecular, behavioral, and translational. First, as described, it is easily learned with a single training trial, thus allowing the investigation of the temporal evolution of molecular and cellular events underlying the formation of a single memory trace. Second, this single trial induces a robust and long-lasting memory, thus allowing for tracing the reorganization of memory over time. Third, a single memory trace is also advantageous for isolating the responses associated with memory reactivation. Conversely, in tasks based on multiple training sessions, it is difficult, if not impossible, to determine the exact temporal evolution of the mechanisms underlying each learning trial and their contribution to the whole memory trace. IA has been widely accepted as a rodent model of human aversive/traumatic episodic memories. Hence, studying this task may provide important knowledge for designing and developing novel therapeutic approaches for disorders caused or precipitated by trauma and stress. At the same time, elucidating the mechanisms by which a temporal lobe-dependent memory is strengthened through consolidation may also offer the identification of strategies and tools that mediate memory enhancement and prevent memory loss. As such, it may lead to the discovery of new treatments that could combat numerous disease-based and aging-related cognitive impairments.

5.2.2 Mechanisms underlying the consolidation of IA memory

In order to understand the mechanisms and functions of IA memory reconsolidation, it is first important to highlight what is known with regard to the initial consolidation of IA memory. As with many other contextual and spatial (or, in humans, episodic and declarative) learning paradigms, both aversive and nonaversive, the consolidation of IA memory requires an intact hippocampus; in fact, lesion or inactivation of the hippocampus leads to both retrograde and anterograde amnesia (Lorenzini, Baldi, Bucherelli, Sacchetti, & Tassoni, 1996; Rossato *et al.*, 2004). Similar to that of many other memory paradigms investigated, the consolidation of IA requires post-translational, translational, and transcriptional mechanisms in both hippocampus and amygdala. In the hippocampus, IA consolidation requires the activation of cAMP-dependent protein kinase A (PKA) (Bernabeu, Cammarota, Izquierdo, & Medina, 1997), cAMP response element binding protein (CREB) (Bernabeu *et al.*, 1997; Impey *et al.*, 1998), the expression of CCAAT enhancer binding proteins (C/EBPβ and C/EBPδ isoforms) (Taubenfeld, Milekic, Monti, & Alberini, 2001; Taubenfeld, Wiig, Bear, & Alberini, 1999), mammalian target of rapamycin (mTOR) (Jobim *et al.*, 2012; Slipczuk *et al.*, 2009), and brain-derived neurotrophic factor (BDNF) (Slipczuk *et al.*, 2009), just to name a few. In addition, our laboratory found that in the hippocampus, IA consolidation also requires the activation of glucocorticoid receptors (GRs), whose engagement recruits the BDNF−CREB−C/EBPβ-dependent gene cascade (Chen, Bambah-Mukku, Pollonini, & Alberini, 2012). Moreover, hippocampal C/EBPβ-dependent target genes, whose regulation is critical for IA memory consolidation, include muscle-specific tyrosine kinase receptor (MuSK) (Garcia-Osta *et al.*, 2006) and insulin-like growth factor II (IGF-II) (Chen *et al.*, 2011). Similarly, in amygdala, IA consolidation requires *de novo* protein synthesis (Milekic, Pollonini, & Alberini, 2007), NMDA receptor- and AMPA receptor-dependent signaling (Bonini *et al.*, 2003; Jerusalinsky *et al.*, 1992), protein kinase C (Bonini, Cammarota, Kerr, Bevilaqua, & Izquierdo, 2005), CREB (Canal, Chang, & Gold, 2008), mTOR (Jobim *et al.*, 2012), corticotropin-releasing hormone (Roozendaal, Brunson, Holloway, McGaugh, & Baram, 2002), and C/EBPδ (Arguello, Ye, *et al.*, in press). However, unlike in the hippocampus, Induction of C/EBPβ is not required in the amygdala for IA consolidation (Tronel, Milekic, & Alberini, 2005; Milekic *et al.*, 2007) (Figure 5.1).

Our laboratory has been particularly interested in identifying the temporal evolution of these molecular cascades activated following IA learning in rats and their functional requirements in the hippocampus. We have found that the requirement of the CREB−C/EBP-target gene cascade, as well as *de novo* protein synthesis in general, lasts for more than 1 day after training, ends by 48 hr after training, and appears to involve feedforward autoregulation of BDNF and MuSK expression and function. Interfering with the initial phase of these changes completely prevents IA memory formation; interfering with the same molecular pathways later, but within the first 24 hr, leads to the establishment of a weaker memory that, however, rapidly decays. Finally, interfering with the same mechanisms at later times (e.g., 48 hr post-training) no longer has an effect on memory retention (Chen *et al.*, 2011; Garcia-Osta *et al.*, 2006; Taubenfeld *et al.*, 2001a, 2001b; Bambah-Mukku *et al.*, unpublished data).

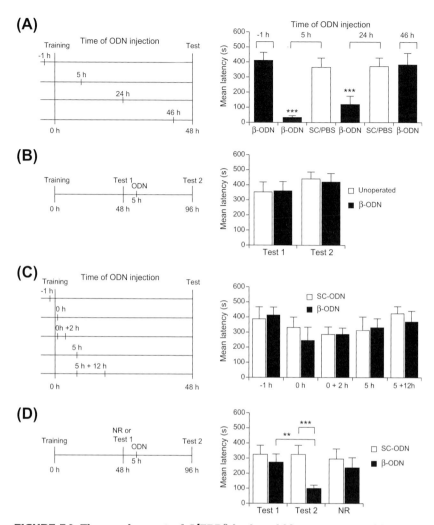

FIGURE 5.1 The requirement of C/EBPβ in dorsal hippocampus and basolateral amygdala (BLA) during consolidation and reconsolidation. Experimental schedules are shown beside each graph. (A) Dorsal hippocampal injection of C/EBPβ antisense oligodeoxynucleotide (β-ODN) at 5 or 24 hr after IA training significantly blocks memory retention at 48 hr, compared to scramble oligodeoxynucleotide (SC-ODN) or vehicle (PBS)-injected controls. Injection of β-ODN 1 hr before or 46 hr after training does not produce any significant memory impairment. (B) Dorsal hippocampal β-ODN injection at 5 hr after testing does not interfere with reconsolidation of IA memory. (C) C/EBPβ in the BLA is not required for IA memory consolidation. β-ODN or SC-ODN was injected bilaterally into the BLA at the following time points: 1 hr before training (−1 hr), immediately after (0 hr), 0 + 2 hr, 5 hr, or 5 + 12 hr after training. No significant difference in latency was observed among β-ODN- and SC-ODN-injected rats at any of the injection time points. (D) β-ODN injection into BLA 5 hr after reactivation impairs memory. Rats injected with β-ODN 5 hr after memory reactivation (Test 1) had significantly lower retention latencies when retested 48 hr later (Test 2, 96 hr post-training) compared to rats injected with SC-ODN or latencies at Test 1. **$P < 0.01$, ***$P < 0.001$. *Source*: Reprinted by permission from Taubenfeld *et al.* (2001) (A and B) and from Milekic *et al.* (2007) (C and D).

Together, the molecular interference studies have been mainly restricted to investigating changes occurring rapidly after training and thus far, as mentioned previously, seem to suggest that these changes are completed by 24–48 hr after training. They have also been mostly carried out in hippocampus and amygdala but not yet in cortical regions, where, with the passage of time, memory consolidation seems to redistribute the memory trace.

Indeed, a number of studies noted that medial temporal lobe (MTL)-dependent memories undergo a consolidation process that can take weeks in animals and up to years in humans. Clinical studies of retrograde amnesia find that damage to the MTL structures, including hippocampus and adjacent cortices, impairs recent memories in a temporally graded manner but spares remote memories, whereas damage that involves the neocortex of lateral and anterior temporal lobes produces a constant loss of memory across the passage of time. Thus, the MTL seems to be necessary for the formation and maintenance of a memory for a limited time (McGaugh, 2000; Squire & Alvarez, 1995). This conclusion is further supported by findings from experimental studies in animal models (Squire et al., 2001). For example, using contextual fear conditioning, Kim and Fanselow (1992) showed that lesion of the hippocampus on 1, 7, 14, or 28 days after training results in a temporally graded retrograde amnesia because 1-day memory is mostly impaired, whereas 28-day memory is spared. Similarly, in rats trained on a step-down IA task, blocking AMPA receptor signaling in the dorsal hippocampus and amygdala impaired a 1-day-old but not a 31-day-old memory (Izquierdo et al., 1997; Quillfeldt et al., 1996). Collectively, these findings suggest that there is a reorganization of the memory trace: Over time, the MTL regions are no longer essential for maintaining the information but, rather, memory storage and retrieval is mainly supported by the neocortex. This process is also termed system consolidation (Dudai, 2004).

In agreement with this temporally graded requirement of MTL in memory maintenance, neuroimaging studies in humans have shown that when subjects recall memories ranging from 1 to 30 years old, there is an anatomical redistribution of activity: The MTL structures exhibit greater activity during the recall of younger memories compared to older memories, whereas activity in the frontal, temporal, and parietal lobes shows the opposite pattern (Smith & Squire, 2009). Similarly, a series of studies has examined the activation of different brain regions by the retrieval of young versus old memories in rodents using functional mapping of neural activity (e.g., the induction of activity-related genes, uptake of 2-deoxyglucose, and neuronal firing patterns) with a variety of behavioral tasks (Frankland & Bontempi, 2005; Gusev & Gubin, 2010a, 2010b; Ross & Eichenbaum, 2006; Sacco & Sacchetti, 2010; Takehara-Nishiuchi, & McNaughton, 2008; Teixeira, Pomedli, Maei, Kee, & Frankland, 2006; Wiltgen, Brown, Talton, & Silva, 2004). In general, these studies find greater activation of dorsal hippocampus by the retrieval of recent compared to remote memories, whereas an opposite pattern is observed in a number of cortical regions.

Very few studies have explored the underlying mechanisms of this reorganization of memory traces over time. A recent report suggests that neurogenesis in adult hippocampus may regulate the temporal window within which contextual fear memory becomes independent from the hippocampus (Kitamura *et al.*, 2009). Other investigations found that dendritic spine growth in caudal anterior cingulate cortex correlates with and is required for remote contextual fear memory storage, whereas the hippocampus is required for driving spine growth in this region (Restivo, Vetere, Bontempi, & Ammassari-Teule, 2009; Vetere *et al.*, 2011).

Interestingly, there seems to be a critical link between sleep and system consolidation. *In vivo* recordings show that the patterns of neuronal firing in the hippocampus and other brain regions that occur during exploration of a novel environment or spatial tasks reoccur in the same order during subsequent sleep. This "implicit" memory reactivation mostly occurs during slow wave sleep. It has been suggested that during this stage of sleep, the neocortical slow oscillation may facilitate the interaction between the hippocampus and the neocortex, leading to redistribution of the memory trace (Born & Wilhelm, 2012; Diekelmann & Born, 2010; Marshall, Helgadottir, Molle, & Born, 2006; Molle, Yeshenko, Marshall, Sara, & Born, 2006; Sirota, Csicsvari, Buhl, & Buzsaki, 2003).

Animal studies also indicate that the rearrangement of the memory representation from hippocampal to cortical areas occurs together with a qualitative transformation. Using both social transmission of food preference and contextual fear conditioning tasks in rats, Winocur *et al.* (2007) report that when memories are assessed 1 day after training, performance is significantly better in the training context compared to a different context. However, as time elapses, this context specificity is lost and rats show increased memory expression in the different context. Similar results have also been reported for contextual fear conditioning in mice (Wiltgen & Silva, 2007). Thus, the initial memory, which would be highly detailed and context specific, seems to become one that is more general (Moscovitch *et al.*, 2005; Winocur, Moscovitch, & Bontempi, 2010).

An important question that remains to be addressed is whether the initial molecular consolidation that occurs in the MTL, such as that identified in the hippocampus of IA trained rats, redistributes with the trace as memory undergoes system consolidation, or whether different molecular/cellular mechanisms are engaged in the different brain regions and/or over time.

5.2.3 Mechanisms of IA memory reconsolidation

While the molecular mechanisms underlying memory consolidation were in the process of being uncovered, Nader *et al.* (2000) published their landmark study showing that memory for auditory fear conditioning could once again become sensitive to inhibition of *de novo* protein synthesis in the amygdala following retrieval, thus suggesting that memory can undergo a process of reconsolidation as well as identifying an underlying cellular process (see Chapter 2). This result changed the way the field viewed memory consolidation, which was, until then, mainly seen as a unitary stabilization process. This in turn prompted us to ask a number of questions about reconsolidation using the IA task in rats. First, are the initial IA consolidation and reconsolidation similar or different processes? Second, how does the passage of time influence the process of reconsolidation? Third, why does memory become labile after reactivation and need to reconsolidate? What function does reconsolidation serve? Finally, can we use reconsolidation mechanisms to disrupt pathogenic memories or to enhance healthy, adaptive memories?

Our studies, in agreement with studies examining different kinds of memories and different species, revealed that reconsolidation is a partial recapitulation of the initial consolidation (Alberini, 2005; Dudai & Eisenberg, 2004; von Hertzen & Giese, 2005). Specifically, in IA, *de novo* protein synthesis is required in both hippocampus and basolateral amygdala for IA memory consolidation, but it is only required in the basolateral amygdala for reconsolidation (Milekic *et al.*, 2007; Taubenfeld *et al.*, 2001a). In addition, C/EBPβ and C/EBPδ are required for both consolidation and reconsolidation of IA (although in different brain regions), and there are important distinctions in the critical functional implication of brain areas in the two processes. Specifically, C/EBPβ-dependent gene expression in the hippocampus is necessary for IA consolidation but not reconsolidation (Taubenfeld *et al.*, 2001a) (Figure 5.1). In contrast, C/EBPβ-dependent gene expression in the amygdala is required for IA memory reconsolidation but not for its initial consolidation (Milekic *et al.*, 2007; Tronel *et al.*, 2005) (Figure 5.1), whereas C/EBPδ is required in the hippocampus for IA consolidation and in the BLA for both consolidation and reconsolidation (Arguello, Ye, *et al.*, in press).

In agreement with the conclusions reached with these IA studies, other model systems, including other species, have found that consolidation and reconsolidation have distinct signatures. For example, Lee *et al.* (2004) reported that contextual fear conditioning consolidation requires hippocampal BDNF but not Zif268 expression, whereas the reconsolidation process requires hippocampal Zif268 but not BDNF expression (for more details, see Chapter 3). In addition, whereas protein synthesis is generally critical in the lateral amygdala for both consolidation and reconsolidation of auditory fear conditioning memory, inhibiting cap-dependent translation impairs consolidation but not reconsolidation of this memory (Hoeffer *et al.*, 2011). Finally, a comprehensive analysis of gene expression in the hippocampus of mice trained in contextual fear conditioning revealed that reconsolidation only induces a subset of molecules that are activated during consolidation (von Hertzen & Giese, 2005). Collectively, our studies in IA together with studies utilizing different memory tasks suggest that (1) consolidation and reconsolidation processes may engage distinct brain circuits and (2) even within the same brain region, they may recruit different or a subset of molecular mechanisms involved in the initial consolidation.

5.3 MEMORY RECONSOLIDATION AND THE PASSAGE OF TIME

Time is an extremely important parameter in memory formation and storage, allowing the selection of what is stored as long-term memory, regulating how long information will be stored, and allowing for continuous changes and updating of information. Memory consolidation takes time to be completed, evolves through different stages, and, thus, memory storage changes with time. How do these changes influence memory reconsolidation?

5.3.1 Temporal dynamics of memory reconsolidation

Understanding the temporal boundaries limiting reconsolidation is critical for understanding how memories are maintained and for the development of effective clinical approaches that target the reconsolidation process. Studies from our laboratory and others have revealed that the passage of time critically influences the ability of a memory to undergo reconsolidation; the older a memory becomes, the less susceptible it is to disruption following its reactivation. For example, in rat IA, 2- and 7-day-old memories are disrupted by protein synthesis inhibitors administered systemically after retrieval, whereas 14- and 28-day-old memories are resistant to the same treatment (Milekic & Alberini, 2002) (Figure 5.2). Similar findings have been reported for a variety of species, including rat (Bustos, Maldonado, & Molina, 2009), mouse (Boccia, Blake, Acosta, & Baratti, 2006; Frankland *et al.*, 2006; Suzuki *et al.*, 2004), chick (Litvin & Anokhin, 2000), and medaka fish (Eisenberg & Dudai, 2004); different types of behavioral paradigms, including both aversive and appetitive memories; and a range of pharmacological disruptions

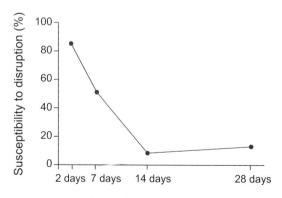

FIGURE 5.2 Temporally graded decreases of susceptibility to disruption of a reactivated memory. The percent (%) susceptibility to disruption by anisomycin injected immediately after retrieval of an IA memory was calculated using the following formula: [(mean latency [sec] of test one − mean latency [sec] of test two) / (mean latency [sec] of test one) × 100. *Source*: Reprinted by permission from Milekic *et al.* (2002).

(Alberini, 2011). Typically, in animal studies, the resilience to post-reactivation disruption occurs over a time window of weeks.

Importantly, as detailed later, memory reactivation and the post-reactivation fragility allow for not only memory disruption but also enhancement (Carbo Tano, Molina, Maldonado, & Pedreira, 2009; Chen *et al.*, 2011; de Souza *et al.*, 2004; Frenkel, Maldonado, & Delorenzi, 2005; Tronson, Wiseman, Olausson, & Taylor, 2006). In our lab, Chen *et al.* (2011) found that administration of IGF-II into dorsal hippocampus after retrieval of a 1-day-old memory, but not a 2-week-old memory, leads to a significant enhancement in memory retention, indicating that the enhancing effect of IGF-II in the hippocampus is restricted to a temporal window that exactly coincides with the reconsolidation-sensitive temporal period (Figure 5.3).

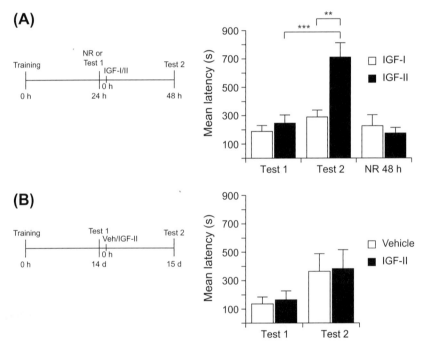

FIGURE 5.3 Post-retrieval IGF-II administration enhances memory, and the effect is temporally limited. Experimental schedules are shown beside each graph. (A) Rats were tested 24 hr post-IA training, and immediately after test (memory reactivation) they were injected with IGF-II or IGF-I bilaterally into dorsal hippocampus. Non-reactivated rats (NR) were trained and injected at the same time points without testing. Rats were tested again 48 hr post-training. Rats that received post-retrieval IGF-II injection had significantly enhanced retention latency compared to those injected with IGF-I or non-reactivated. **$P < 0.01$, ***$P < 0.001$. (B) Rats trained in IA task were tested on 14 days post-training, and immediately after test they were injected with IGF-II or vehicle bilaterally into dorsal hippocampus. They were tested again 1 day later. IGF-II injection did not enhance the 14-day-old IA memory. *Source*: Reprinted by permission from Chen *et al.* (2011).

Other studies report that in some cases, even older memories can be vulnerable to disruption in certain circumstances and that post-retrieval memory fragility is a function of the strength of training, strength of reactivation, and passage of time (Suzuki *et al.*, 2004; for more details, see Chapter 6). Other investigations have also used long reactivation sessions to show that old memories or stronger memories can be disrupted by post-reactivation interference, at least to a certain extent (Bustos *et al.*, 2009; Diergaarde, Schoffelmeer, & De Vries, 2006; Eisenberg, Kobilo, Berman, & Dudai, 2003). However, all these results are in agreement with the general conclusion that the passage of time makes the memory stronger and less susceptible to post-reactivation interference. Furthermore, it is important to keep in mind that reactivation by retrieval of a conditioned response can (as in many studies of reconsolidation) evoke two processes—reconsolidation of the original memory trace and extinction learning, which teaches the animals that a conditioned stimulus (CS) is no longer paired with an unconditioned stimulus (US) and results in decreased expression of the conditioned response. Competition of the two traces seems to control the behavioral outcome (Eisenberg *et al.*, 2003). Long-lasting reactivation sessions preferentially evoke extinction over reconsolidation (Pedreira & Maldonado, 2003; Power, Berlau, McGaugh, & Steward, 2006; Suzuki *et al.*, 2004). Thus, when investigating whether and how the length of the reactivation session may influence the susceptibility of reactivated memories to disruption, it is important to exclude the possibility that memory disruption results from a facilitated extinction.

In line with the notion that memory evolves over time, using rat IA, Inda, Muravieva, and Alberini (2011) in our laboratory explored how the passage of time interacts with memory reactivation to regulate memory strength. It was found that multiple reactivations by brief exposure to the CS, which evoked memory reconsolidation, given within the first week after IA training led to significant memory strengthening. However, the same behavioral reactivations given 2 weeks after training, when memory already appeared to be stronger as a result of the passage of time, could not induce memory reconsolidation or strengthening. Interestingly, when the same reactivations were given 4 weeks after training, when memory had partially decayed, they actually produced extinction instead of reconsolidation and strengthening (Figure 5.4). These findings not only support the hypothesis that the function of memory reconsolidation is, at least in part, to strengthen memory retention during the temporal window of system consolidation (discussed later) but also show that memory storage is temporally dynamic. First, over time, without explicit reactivations, memory strengthens and becomes refractory to both reactivation-dependent interference and strengthening. Second, reactivation of a young memory preferentially triggers reconsolidation over extinction, whereas reactivation of an old memory preferentially triggers extinction over reconsolidation. These results have important clinical implications because the same post-reactivation intervention may affect different processes, depending on the age and state of the memory.

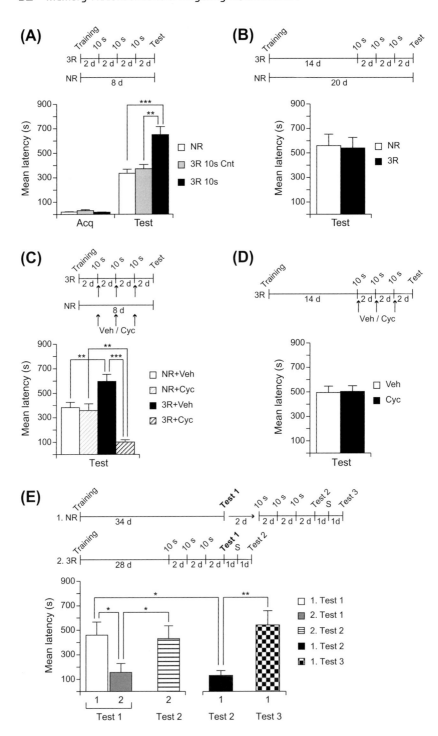

Some authors disagree with this conclusion. They view reconsolidation as a general process that occurs following memory retrieval without temporal constraints, and they explain temporal boundaries as experimental limitations (Nader & Einarsson, 2010). For example, Nader *et al.* (2000) showed that both 2-day- and 2-week-old auditory fear conditioning memories in rats were disrupted by post-retrieval bilateral injection of the protein synthesis inhibitor anisomycin into the lateral and basal nuclei of the amygdala. Similarly, injection of Zif268 antisense before re-exposure to a cocaine-associated cue at 3 and 27 days after cocaine self-administration impaired subsequent cocaine-seeking behaviors (Lee, Milton, & Everitt, 2006). Furthermore, in contrast to some studies showing that contextual fear memories in mice become less sensitive to post-retrieval interference as memories age (Frankland *et al.*, 2006; Suzuki *et al.*, 2004), Debiec *et al.* (2002) reported that 3- to 45-day-old contextual fear memories in rats were disrupted by post-retrieval bilateral injection of aniso-mycin into hippocampus. Interestingly, lesion of the hippocampus 45 days after training did not result in memory impairment, suggesting that by this time the contextual fear memory is independent of the hippocampus; however, reactiva-tion of the memory caused the trace to again become dependent on the hippo-campus. It is not clear what contributes to these conflicting results. One

◄————————————————————————

FIGURE 5.4 Memory reactivation leads to reconsolidation and strengthening in a recent memory and extinction in a remote memory. Experimental schedules are shown beside each graph. (A) Rats were trained (Acq), and 2 days later memory was reactivated with three 10—sec context exposures with a 2-day inter-reactivation interval (3R). A control group was trained and received three 10-sec exposures to a different context (Context B; Cnt), whereas another control group remained in the home cage (NR). At testing (Test), the 3R group showed a significant increase in latency compared with the NR group. (B) Rats that underwent three reactivations (3R) 14 days after training or NR had similar, strong latencies when tested 20 days after training. (C) Rats were trained and received 3R beginning 2 days later, or NR, as in panel A. Both groups were injected immediately after each reactivation, or at a paired time point, with either cycloheximide (Cyc) or vehicle (Veh), and they were tested 8 days after training. At testing, 3R significantly increased latency, whereas Cyc prevented this increase. (D) Rats underwent the same training and reactivation protocol as in panel B, and they were injected with either Cyc or Veh after each reactivation as in panel C. At testing, no difference was found between groups. (E) Reactivation of a 4-week-old memory led to a facilitation of extinction. Rats were trained and divided into two groups. The first group (1) was tested 34 days after training. The second group (2) underwent 3R starting 28 days after training. Both groups were tested 34 days after training (test 1). At test 1, group 2 had a significantly lower latency than group 1. To verify whether this loss of memory was due to extinction, group 2 received a footshock reminder (S) 1 day after test 1 and was tested again the following day (test 2). Group 2 showed reinstatement of memory retention as, in fact, at test 2 showed significantly higher retention than at test 1. After test 1, group 1 received 3R and was tested 2 days later (test 2). Again, these animals showed extinction because their latency was significantly lower than that at test 1. A reminder footshock given 1 day later resulted in significant reinstatement of the memory at test 3 the following day. *$P <$ 0.05, **$P <$ 0.01, ***$P <$ 0.001. *Source*: Reprinted with permission from Inda *et al.* (2011).

possibility, as discussed previously, is that memory reactivation triggers both reconsolidation and extinction processes. At least under certain conditions, inhibiting hippocampal protein synthesis or other forms of molecular interference can result in enhanced extinction of contextual fear (Cai, Blundell, Han, Greene, & Powell, 2006; Fischer, Sananbenesi, Schrick, Spiess, & Radulovic, 2004). Thus, it is important to determine whether the retrieval-dependent impairment in memory expression is due to blocking reconsolidation or facilitating extinction. In addition, the temporal window for the stabilization process and circuitry storage distribution is likely to be different for different memories and modalities of training (e.g., training intensity). However, the answer may be that both conclusions are correct and that different types of memories follow different consolidation processes or stages. For example, one possibility that remains to be investigated is that the temporal window of reconsolidation in medial temporal lobe-dependent memories is limited because these memories undergo system consolidation and trace redistribution, whereas cue-dependent memories (e.g., implicit memories) do not undergo such redistribution, and their storage might therefore be more restricted and mechanistically distinct. A different distribution of the memory storage, together with a change in quality of the mechanisms underlying memory storage, may be the answer to these controversies.

5.4 FUNCTIONS OF MEMORY RECONSOLIDATION: UPDATING AND STRENGTHENING

Why do memories undergo reconsolidation? Given that during reconsolidation memory may be lost if interference occurs, what purpose does the post-reactivation destabilization of a memory trace serve? Two non-mutually exclusive hypotheses have been proposed to address this question: (1) Reconsolidation serves as an opportunity for memory updating, allowing new information to be incorporated into existing memory traces, and (2) reconsolidation provides an opportunity or a mechanism for strengthening and enhancing memory retention.

5.4.1 Reconsolidation and memory updating

At least two forms of memory updating have been investigated to date: the linking of novel, distinct information to an old memory trace and the addition of information regarding the same experience (i.e., incremental learning). Although both can be defined as memory updating, these processes are likely controlled by very different underlying mechanisms.

With respect to the first form of memory updating, that of incorporation of new information into an existing trace, in our laboratory, Tronel et al. (2005) found that second-order conditioning—that is, the association of a novel and distinct conditioned stimulus (CS2) to a previously formed association (CS1−US)—is mediated by consolidation mechanisms. This conclusion was reached using a molecular requirement that doubly dissociates consolidation from reconsolidation of IA memory in rats, namely that C/EBPβ is required in the dorsal hippocampus for consolidation but not reconsolidation, whereas C/EBPβ is required in the basolateral amygdala for reconsolidation but not consolidation.

Specifically, inhibition of C/EBPβ in the amygdala after reactivation of IA memory (CS1−US) in a new context (i.e., CS2) did not prevent the formation of the CS2−(CS1−US) association through second-order conditioning because rats subsequently tested in this new context showed clear memory. However, as would be predicted, inhibition of C/EBPβ in the amygdala interfered with reconsolidation of the first trace (i.e., CS1−US) because rats no longer showed memory for the original context (Figure 5.5). In contrast, second-order

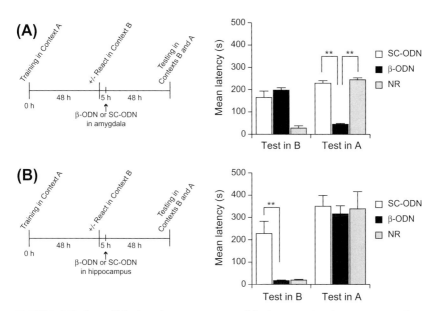

FIGURE 5.5 Consolidation, but not reconsolidation, mechanisms are required to associate new information with a reactivated memory. Experimental schedules are shown beside each graph. Rats were trained in IA in a shuttlebox (context A), which included a contextual cue (light turned on). Memory was reactivated with the same contextual cue (light turned on) 48 hr later in an otherwise distinct shuttlebox context (context B). Memory for either the original trace or the second-order trace was assessed 48 hr after reactivation by testing the latency in context A or context B, respectively. (A) Amygdala injection of C/EBPβ antisense oligodeoxynucleotide (β-ODN) after memory reactivation disrupted the memory for context A without affecting the memory for context B. In contrast, the same treatment strongly impaired memory of context A, compared to SC-ODN injection. Memory of context A was not affected in rats that did not receive reactivation. (B) Hippocampal injection of β-ODN blocked the formation of an association between new and reactivated information without affecting the stability of the reactivated memory. β-ODN injection into the hippocampi of rats 5 hr after memory reactivation significantly impaired memory retention for context B 48 hr later, compared with SC-ODN injection. However, the same β-ODN injection did not affect the memory of context A, which remained similar to that of both control groups that received either SC-ODN injection after reactivation or β-ODN injection in the absence of reactivation. **P < 0.01. *Source*: Reprinted with permission from Tronel *et al.* (2005).

conditioning was prevented by inhibition of C/EBPβ in the dorsal hippocampus, suggesting that this memory underwent a new process of consolidation. Disruption of C/EBPβ in the hippocampus did not affect the reconsolidation of the original memory (Figure 5.5). Together, these data indicate that reconsolidation does not mediate memory updating through second-order conditioning but, rather, that updating engages a new consolidation process. In fact, disrupting the reconsolidation of the original CS1−US memory does not affect the new CS2−(CS1−US) association, supporting the conclusion that the two memories exist completely independent of each other.

Our findings that memory updating requires consolidation, for the purpose of adding new information to an existing trace, suggest that this form of updating is not a primary function of reconsolidation. In fact, given that memories are continuously updated throughout the life span, how could a reconsolidation-based mechanism that is temporally restricted and mainly occurs when a memory is recent be the process that mediates all updating of old memories? New information is constantly integrated into a network of memory traces, and this seems to occur via new consolidation processes. We speculate that for very long-lasting memories, it would be less adaptive that the updating of an existing memory would transform the original memory into a new one, whereas it seems more advantageous that to provide behavioral adaptability and choices, the old memories continue to coexist with new memories that comprise both old and new linked information. An example of this situation is extinction, whereby a new extinction memory trace coexists with the original conditioning trace. Memory updating, consolidation, and reconsolidation are all important pieces of the dynamic memory trace and storage, and understanding these processes and how they evolve over time is key for developing effective treatments of psychopathologies, whether they are pharmacological, behavioral, or the combination of approaches. This knowledge will also be critical for developing more effective psychotherapeutic treatments (see Chapter 14).

Data from other memory paradigms and other model organisms support the conclusion that integrating new information occurs through consolidation and that two related traces can continue to exist in parallel after updating. For example, Debiec *et al.* (2006), using rat auditory fear conditioning, found that disrupting the reconsolidation of a CS1−US memory by inhibiting amygdala protein synthesis after reactivation does not affect the formation of a new, related second-order association (i.e., CS2−CS1−US). Similar results were also found with associative memories in the crab *Chasmagnathus* (Suárez, Smal, & Delorenzi, 2010), as well as in humans (Forcato, Rodríguez, Pedreira, & Maldonado, 2010). Hence, we conclude that the primary function of reconsolidation must be different from that of linking an existing, reactivated memory to a novel, distinct experience. In general terms, we can infer that memory updating via formation of complex networks requires memory reactivation but not reconsolidation, and that reconsolidation of a reactivated memory does not alter the entire network of updated associative memories.

Other studies have tested whether reconsolidation mediates memory updating by examining the contribution of the repetition of similar training trials compared to that of encoding new information. These studies concluded that with multiple learning trials or reactivations, memory does indeed become labile. However, the fragility is seen only when learning is in a non-asymptotic mode. Specifically, inhibition of protein synthesis after repeated training trials during a non-asymptotic phase of learning returns memory performance to a pretraining chance level, suggesting that the original trace had remained labile. This effect has been shown using spatial learning (Meiri & Rosenblum, 1998; Touzani, Puthanveettil, & Kandel, 2007) and motor learning (Luft, Buitrago, Kaelin-Lang, Dichgans, & Schulz, 2004; Luft, Buitrago, Ringer, Dichgans, & Schulz, 2004). In contrast, when performance on a task has reached ceiling levels, and memory has therefore reached an asymptotic phase, memory is resistant to disruption by post-reactivation amnesic treatments (Morris *et al.*, 2006; Rodriguez-Ortiz, De la Cruz, Gutiérrez, & Bermudez-Rattoni, 2005; Winters, Tucci, & DaCosta-Furtado, 2009).

Interestingly, memory becomes labile once again if conditions are adjusted to induce a new phase of encoding. For example, using a delayed matching-to-place task in rats requiring that they locate a platform in a water maze, Morris *et al.* (2006) found that reconsolidation of a well-trained spatial memory is engaged only when there is a shift in location of the escape platform, representing a mismatch in contextual information that triggers updating of their cognitive representation of space. With a combination of taste recognition and taste aversion learning in rats, Rodriguez-Ortiz *et al.* (2005) found that inhibition of protein synthesis in the gustatory cortex disrupted a well-trained memory for saccharin taste only when malaise was introduced in conjunction with reactivation, another situation in which a mismatch between prior and current conditions triggers updating of the memory for familiar taste. Winters *et al.* (2009) noted a similar effect using spontaneous object recognition in rats: Inhibition of NMDA receptor function interfered with expression of the original object memory when reactivation introduced new contextual information but not when reactivation was identical to the initial training sessions.

As in studies discussed previously in relation to memory updating, it is unclear whether disruption of the memory occurs, because during reactivation the rat associates old information (e.g., the water maze, saccharin taste, or objects) with novel information (e.g., a new platform location, malaise, or new contextual cues), and the interference disrupts the consolidation of a new memory trace containing information about the contextual mismatch rather than the reconsolidation of the original trace. Much like the case for extinction learning in conditioning paradigms, two memory traces could potentially coexist and both contribute to the expression of behavior in the tasks described previously. Also, because both consolidation and reconsolidation are sensitive to similar forms of molecular disruption, using an interference approach that does not doubly dissociate the two processes cannot irrefutably demonstrate that reconsolidation mediates this type of updating.

Thus, an alternative interpretation from that offered by authors who suggest that reconsolidation mediates memory updating when novel information is linked to an existing trace is twofold. First, in agreement with the authors' conclusions, during a learning curve, post-trial application of amnesic treatments disrupts memory retention only when the memory is not at an asymptotic level. However, when retention has reached an asymptotic level and no further learning or increased retention is evident, a previously consolidated memory remains stable and resistant to disruption. Second, if new events are then presented and associated with this memory, a new trace is formed that is labile because it undergoes consolidation. If part of the old information is incorporated in a new trace, its retention might be disrupted if the new trace is challenged by amnesic treatments, following the rules of the predominant active trace (Eisenberg *et al.*, 2003).

Hence, we speculate that for memories that undergo system consolidation through the medial temporal lobe, reconsolidation is engaged only to change the strength of the original memory; in other words, reactivation of the memory strengthens or further consolidates the original memory without changing its content.

5.4.2 Reconsolidation and memory strengthening

Although inducing fragility of a memory trace through reactivation or retrieval can open it to interference, it appears to offer an equivalent opportunity for enhancement and strengthening. In fact, we propose that during the temporal window in which system consolidation occurs, memory strengthening through reactivation or retrieval is the chief function of reconsolidation.

Although it is intuitive to predict that repeated training sessions would reinforce memory formation and result in memory strengthening, as observed in situations of asymptotic memory performance described previously, it is less obvious to expect the same effect from non-reinforced exposures. As discussed in previous sections, presentation of stimuli under non-reinforced conditions (i.e., in the absence of the unconditioned aversive stimulus or reinforcer, such as a footshock or food reward; US) leads to extinction, a distinct learning process that is also protein synthesis dependent (Berman & Dudai, 2001; Power *et al.*, 2006; Santini, Ge, Ren, Peña de Ortiz, & Quirk, 2004). However, brief exposure to a non-reinforced reminder may not result in extinction but, rather, may preferentially induce reconsolidation and enhancement of the memory. In other words, reactivation of a memory can result in its strengthening through reconsolidation or suppression through extinction, and the bias toward either of these processes would be determined by the dominant state of the trace (Eisenberg *et al.*, 2003).

As mentioned previously, we have found that brief, repeated 10-sec exposures to the IA context (i.e., memory reactivations) given during the first week after training, while the IA memory trace is still undergoing system consolidation, lead to memory strengthening and prevent forgetting (Inda *et al.*, 2011). This strengthening of IA memory is contingent upon *de novo* protein synthesis because memory retention is disrupted by systemic injections of the protein synthesis inhibitor cycloheximide prior to each of the three reactivations. However, when the same brief reactivations were given 2 weeks after IA training, at a time when the memory is stronger and known to be resistant to the effects of protein synthesis inhibitors administered after retrieval (Milekic & Alberini, 2002), we found no effects of reactivation or post-retrieval molecular interference (Figure 5.4). Interestingly, with older IA memories beginning 28 days after training, a time at which memory has decayed, the three reactivations led to extinction (Inda *et al.*, 2011) (Figure 5.4). Thus, whereas reactivation of a recent memory leads to its strengthening through reconsolidation, the reactivation of a remote memory promotes its extinction, suggesting there is in fact a temporal boundary on the time period within which reconsolidation can be harnessed to improve memory. This period may overlap with the period of system consolidation.

The fact that memory strengthens over time without explicit reactivations leads us to speculate, as others have (Diekelmann, Büchel, Born, & Rasch, 2011), that reconsolidation is induced through implicit reactivations, and that this may be the mechanism through which memory becomes stronger and resilient to disruption. In support, studies of the incubation of conditioned fear, anxiety, and conditioned reward-seeking suggest that memory is strengthened over time, in the absence of explicit retraining, reactivation, or retrieval (Bindra & Cameron, 1953; Grimm, Fyall, & Osincup, 2005; Lu, Grimm, Hope, & Shaham, 2004; Pickens *et al.*, 2011; Pickens, Golden, Adams-Deutsch, Nair, & Shaham, 2009). Although the mechanisms underlying regulated implicit reactivation are far from clear, sleep appears to play an important role in the consolidation of long-term memories and may provide an opportunity for lingering consolidation to take place over time (Diekelmann & Born, 2010; Graves, Pack, & Abel, 2001; Stickgold, Hobson, Fosse, & Fosse, 2001).

Overall, it is clear from our work and the work of others that reconsolidation serves the important function of strengthening memory traces when partially or fully reactivated, but only within a defined window of time after the initial training. Given these temporal boundaries, interesting questions arise regarding the interplay of reconsolidation and system consolidation, and the temporal boundaries of system consolidation.

5.5 MEMORY STRENGTHENING VIA RECONSOLIDATION: MECHANISMS AND POTENTIAL APPLICATIONS

5.5.1 Molecular, cellular, and systems mechanisms of strengthening through reconsolidation

Very little is known about the molecular and cellular mechanisms responsible for memory enhancement through reconsolidation. However, targeting these mechanisms may represent an important strategy for delaying memory loss and combating cognitive impairments. Early studies suggested that one potential mechanism through which reconsolidation may strengthen memory is by increasing attention and arousal. DeVietti, Conger, and Kirkpatrick (1977) demonstrated that stimulation of the mesencephalic reticular formation, targeting noradrenergic fibers originating in the locus coeruleus, in conjunction with memory retrieval, enhanced subsequent memory performance. Others went on to demonstrate that direct stimulation of the locus coeruleus during retrieval enhanced memory for a maze task and that this enhancement was mediated by β-adrenergic receptor activation (Devauges & Sara, 1991; Sara, 2000). Indeed, it is possible that memory reactivation re-engages neuromodulatory processes affecting components of the trace, which in turn facilitates retrieval and memory strengthening.

More recent molecular investigations have identified factors that, if given in tandem with memory reactivation, enhance memory retention, suggesting that they boost reconsolidation mechanisms. For example, activation of PKA in the amygdala by infusing 6-BNZ–cAMP after retrieval of an auditory fear conditioning memory leads to subsequent enhancement of the memory (Tronson, Wiseman, Olausson, & Taylor, 2006). Similarly, increasing brain levels of angiotensin II following reactivation of a contextual fear memory in the crab *Chasmagnathus* leads to strengthening of the trace (Frenkel, Maldonado, & Delorenzi, 2005). It is interesting to note that in this particular study, the authors induced release of angiotensin II through water deprivation, an ethologically relevant circumstance during which identifying and remembering potential survival tactics would be beneficial. This finding suggests that factors released in response to internal states at times when memory activation is critical may support reconsolidation, and particularly memory strengthening (or, in other conditions, perhaps extinction).

Furthermore, as mentioned previously, we have recently shown that infusion of IGF-II in the dorsal hippocampus after retrieval of IA memory significantly strengthens the memory, and the effect occurs only at the times at which reconsolidation takes place (i.e., 1 but not 14 days after training; Chen *et al.*, 2011) (Figure 5.3).

The identification of mechanisms underlying memory strengthening via reconsolidation is important and has immediate translational potential. For example, normal aging is accompanied by cognitive decline, and its effects can significantly impede day-to-day functioning in older adults. Interestingly, age-related memory loss is not ubiquitous, in that it does not affect all individuals, and does not impact all types of memory. Rather, deficits most often manifest in declarative or episodic memory function—that is, explicit memory for information encountered during the course of daily living. These deficits seem to affect most profoundly the processes of long-term memory. In fact, when tracked over the human life span, short-term and early phases of long-term memory are spared, whereas the formation of long-term memory is significantly attenuated (Cansino, 2009). A similar pattern is observed in studies of middle-aged and older animals, such that working and short-term memory in hippocampal-dependent tasks remain intact, whereas probe tests given after longer retention intervals indicate memory loss (Bizon *et al.*, 2009; Countryman & Gold, 2007; Gallagher & Rapp, 1997; LaSarge *et al.*, 2007; Robitsek, Fortin, Koh, Gallagher, & Eichenbaum, 2008).

This pattern of memory decline suggests that consolidation and reconsolidation gradually become less effective as we age. Understanding the impact of normal aging on mechanisms of memory consolidation, and particularly reconsolidation, is therefore important because reconsolidation mechanisms could potentially be boosted through memory retrieval or pharmacological interventions to lessen the impact of age-related memory loss. Although studies investigating the effects of normal aging on molecular mechanisms of consolidation and reconsolidation are sparse, several lines of evidence suggest that decline of these functions could be linked to impairment of long-term memory on hippocampal-dependent tasks. For example, loss of input from the entorhinal cortex to the dentate gyrus via fibers of the perforant path has been observed in older rats, and this decreased connectivity is reflected by a failure to induce and maintain long-term potentiation, relative to younger rats (Burke & Barnes, 2006). Induction of factors required for memory consolidation in the hippocampus is also compromised in some circumstances; aged rats do not show increased hippocampal expression of pCREB and C/EBPβ in response to contextual fear conditioning (Monti, Berteotti, & Contestabile, 2005), and aged rats impaired in a spatial Morris water maze task show reduced CREB protein levels, relative to young and unimpaired rats (Brightwell, Gallagher, & Colombo, 2004).

5.6 PHARMACOLOGICAL DISRUPTION OF RECONSOLIDATION: WEAKENING PATHOGENIC MEMORIES

The re-emergence of research focusing on memory reconsolidation has stimulated interest in the medical community, particularly among mental health professionals treating disorders that are based on maladaptive memories. Two examples that have been investigated in animal models and in humans are post-traumatic stress disorder (PTSD) and drug addiction, both of which can be viewed as the result of dysfunctional memory processes.

PTSD can develop after an exposure to an emotionally or physically traumatic event, and the illness is characterized by repeated, intrusive memories of the experienced trauma. Patients suffering from PTSD have difficulty sleeping and feel detached or estranged, and these symptoms can be so severe and persistent so as to significantly impair the person's daily life. A behavioral model of PTSD onset has been proposed: The traumatic event (US) triggers a strong hormonal stress response, which mediates the formation of a robust and enduring memory for the trauma. Subsequent recall of the event in response to cues and reminders (CS) releases more stress hormones (conditioned response) and even further consolidates the memory leading to PTSD symptoms, such as flashbacks, nightmares, and anxiety (Pitman & Delahanty, 2005). The persistence of PTSD can be explained in terms of a trauma-induced strengthening of the memory trace. Specifically, it is hypothesized that noradrenergic hyperactivity and stress hormones facilitate the encoding and consolidation of the memory (O'Donnell, Hegadoren, & Coupland, 2004; Pitman, 1989; Yehuda *et al.*, 2006).

Although it is not possible to precisely reproduce PTSD in an animal model, fear conditioning in rodents can be used to mimic and elucidate some aspects of PTSD, including the processing of fearful stimuli and the encoding of emotional memory. Thus, it is possible to closely approximate some of the PTSD symptoms in an animal model that can be used for preclinical research. In principle, forms of pharmacological and behavioral interference thus far found to be effective in disrupting fear memory reconsolidation or enhancing extinction (not discussed in this chapter) could potentially be useful for identifying new treatments that can be tested in clinical trials. Some of the compounds found to disrupt reconsolidation, including antagonists of β-adrenergic receptor, glucocorticoid receptors (GRs), or rapamycin, are already used in clinical pharmacology for treating other diseases. Hence, they are the most readily available potential therapies for targeting reconsolidation in PTSD and addiction.

Antagonists of the β-adrenergic receptor, such as propranolol and rapamycin, have already been explored at clinical levels. Propranolol, which is most commonly used to treat hypertension, has been administered in concert with the retrieval of a fearful or traumatic event in both animals and humans. Przybyslawski, Roullet, and Sara (1999) provided one of the first reports on the effect of propranolol on memory reconsolidation. Using rat IA, these authors found that systemic administration of propranolol after the reactivation of an IA memory disrupted the memory on subsequent tests. However, we recently reached the opposite conclusion. Because the shock used by Przybyslawski *et al.* was very weak (0.2 mA), we set out to determine whether the reconsolidation of a memory induced by a greater shock, which may more closely approximate a traumatic event, was sensitive to propranolol treatment. Hence, we tested the effect of the same propranolol treatment in rats given either before or after the retrieval of an inhibitory avoidance memory evoked by a 0.6- or 0.9-mA footshock. We found that although these memories could be disrupted by several other treatments, such as anisomycin or the GR antagonist RU38486, propranolol had no effect (Muravieva & Alberini, 2010). These divergent results could be related to several differences in the protocols used. However, to provide solid preclinical information, it is important that the potency and generalization of the propranolol treatment on fear memories are established. Using auditory fear conditioning, Debiec and LeDoux (2004) found that propranolol injected either systemically or into the lateral nucleus of the amygdala after reactivation of a 1-day- or 2-month-old memory weakened the fear response when tested 48 hr later (see also Chapter 4). In agreement, in recent studies based on contextual–auditory Pavlovian fear conditioning, we found that systemic propranolol injection following a retrieval elicited by cue exposure interferes with the reconsolidation of both cued and contextual fear conditioning. On the other hand, propranolol administered after contextual reactivation only affects contextual fear conditioning and has no effect on the auditory fear conditioning. Thus, it seems that the efficacy of systemically administered propranolol in disrupting the reconsolidation of fear memories might be limited (Muravieva & Alberini, 2010).

Other studies have reported divergent effects of propranolol on memory reconsolidation (for discussion of human studies, see Chapter 9). Whereas the reconsolidation of eyeblink conditioning potentiation and conditioning to natural or drug-associated reward is disrupted by propranolol (Diergaarde *et al.*, 2006; Kindt, Soeter, & Vervliet, 2009; Milton, Lee, & Everitt, 2008), the reconsolidation of appetitive Pavlovian memories in rats (Lee & Everitt, 2008) and that of neutral and emotional verbal memories in humans (Tollenaar, Elzinga, Spinhoven, & Everaerd, 2009) are not. Interestingly, declarative measures for the acquired contingency between the CS and the US (Kindt *et al.*, 2009) are insensitive to propranolol treatment, but the fear response is sensitive. Hence, as Kindt *et al.* suggested, propranolol may target the fear response but not the cognitive or explicit components of that response. Further studies should address this question and will be important to determine whether blocking the noradrenergic mechanisms during the reconsolidation of fear/traumatic memories indeed mainly disrupts the emotional component without much interfering with the explicit/declarative representation.

Another pharmacologically targeted pathway for the potential treatment of PTSD, which we have investigated using IA, is the glucocorticoid pathway. The endogenous stress hormone corticosterone bidirectionally modulates memory retention (McGaugh & Roozendaal, 2002; Roozendaal *et al.*, 2002). Low doses increase memory retention, whereas high doses disrupt it. Recent studies have reported that glucocorticoids, when administered after the reactivation of a contextual fear memory, have an amnesic effect on the original memory and provide evidence that a possible mechanism for this effect is an enhancement of extinction of the expression of the original memory (Abrari, Rashidy-Pour, Semnanian, & Fathollahi, 2008; Cai, Blundell, Han, Greene, & Powell, 2006). A study from our laboratory, however, revealed that intra-amygdala blockade of glucocorticoid receptors with the antagonist mifepristone (RU38486) after reactivation of IA memory in rats significantly disrupts the original memory, probably interfering with its reconsolidation process (Tronel & Alberini, 2007). Further investigations have also shown that systemic administration of RU38486, either before or after retrieval, consistently weakens IA retention in a dose-dependent manner (Nikzad, Vafaei, Rashidy-Pour, & Haghighi, 2011; Taubenfeld, Riceberg, New, & Alberini, 2009). The efficacy of treatment appears to be a function of the intensity of the initial trauma. Highly traumatic IA memories are not disrupted with RU38486 administered systemically after retrieval given 1 day after training. However, these memories become sensitive to this intervention after 1 week. Hence, according to the results in the IA paradigm, for stronger or highly traumatic memories, there is a temporal window for effective intervention, which begins sometime (days in animals) after the trauma, perhaps because the stress is very high, and ends when the memory is consolidated and resilient to interference. In fact, changing the timing and number of interventions successfully disrupts the highly traumatic IA memories (Taubenfeld *et al.*, 2009) (Figure 5.6). Furthermore, we found that one or two treatments are sufficient to maximally disrupt the memory, and that the treatment selectively targets the reactivated memory without interfering with the retention of another non-reactivated

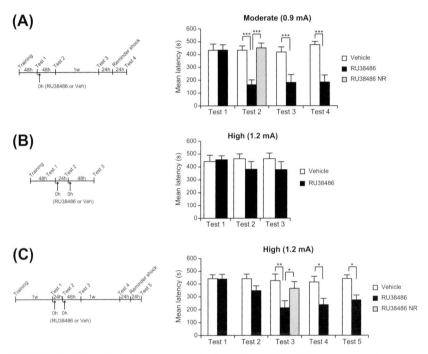

FIGURE 5.6 Preclinical assessment for disrupting IA memory via post-retrieval inhibition of glucocorticoid receptors with systemic injection of RU38486, a glucocorticoid receptor antagonist. Experimental schedules are shown beside each graph. (A) IA memory in rats trained with a moderate (0.9 mA) foot-shock is disrupted by systemic RU38486 injection given immediately after retrieval (test 1). The retention latencies in the rats that received post-retrieval RU38486 (30 mg/kg body weight) were significantly lower 48 hr later (test 2), 1 week later (test 3), and after a reminder shock (test 4), compared to the vehicle-injected group. NR, rats that received RU38486 in the absence of reactivation. (B) IA memory in rats trained with high-intensity footshock (1.2 mA) is not affected by two treatments consisting of post-retrieval RU38486 injection (30 mg/kg body weight) given 48 hr after training and 1 day later, and tested 48 hr after the last injection. (C) Extending the time between training and memory reactivation allows high-intensity traumatic memory to be disrupted by post-retrieval RU38486 injection. The experiment schedule was similar to that in panel B, except that the first reactivation started at 1 week after IA training. Rats that received two subsequent post-retrieval RU38486 injection had significantly lower retention latencies in subsequent tests compared to the vehicle-injected rats or rats that received RU38486 in the absence of memory retrieval. * $P < 0.05$, ** $P < 0.01$, *** $P < 0.001$. *Source:* Reprinted with permission from Taubenfeld *et al.* (2009).

memory (Taubenfeld *et al.*, 2009). In light of these results, the glucocorticoid pathway appears to be a promising site of pharmacologic intervention for trauma-related pathologies, including PTSD. Another compound that has been employed as a successful pharmacological interference of traumatic memory reconsolidation in both animal fear conditioning (Blundell, Kouser, & Powell, 2008; Helmstetter, Parsons, & Gafford, 2008) and human PTSD is rapamycin (Sirolimus). Interestingly, it appears that more recently developed PTSD may be more amenable to treatment with rapamycin (Suris *et al.*, 2012).

A novel and very interesting alternative to pharmacological disruption, which uses a behavioral design, has recently been provided by animal and human studies based on sequential retrieval (i.e., reconsolidation) and extinction. Extinction training after retrieval of a contextually conditioned fear memory leads to a long-lasting memory reduction if it is presented within the post-retrieval reconsolidation temporal window (Monfils, Cowansage, Klann, & LeDoux, 2009; Schiller *et al.*, 2010) (see Chapters 8 and 9). Further studies should be able to elucidate underlying mechanisms of this interesting approach.

Another pathology for which treatment may take advantage of reconsolidation studies is addiction. Substance abuse generally leads to a chronic condition believed to result from an addict's inability to permanently abstain from drug use. Drug addicts repeatedly relapse to drug seeking even after years of abstinence. This pathologic behavior is frequently induced by the recall of memories and environmental stimuli that are intimately connected to the rewarding effects of the drug (O'Brien, Childress, McLellan, & Ehrman, 1992). Therefore, disruption of memory reconsolidation provides an unprecedented potential strategy to weaken or eliminate memories that facilitate drug addiction. Promising results have been achieved in animals dependent on morphine or cocaine by injecting, after memory reactivation, inhibitors of protein synthesis, extracellular signal-regulated kinase (ERK), β-adrenergic receptors, or matrix metalloproteinases—or by disrupting the expression of the immediate early gene Zif268 either peripherally or within specific brain regions, such as the amygdala, hippocampus, or nucleus accumbens (Brown *et al.*, 2007; Fricks-Gleason, & Marshall, 2008; Lee, Di Ciano, Thomas, & Everitt, 2005; Milekic, Brown, Castellini, & Alberini, 2006; Miller & Marshall, 2005; Robinson & Franklin, 2010; Sorg, 2012; Valjent, Corbillé, Bertran-Gonzalez, Hervé, & Girault, 2006).

In some of these studies, inhibitors were injected in animals that had acquired a place preference in response to the drug of abuse, a learning known as conditioned place preference. Animals learned to associate euphoria of the drug with a specific location, choosing to spend more time in that location. Administration of several of these inhibitors after reactivation of the drug-related memory interfered with its reconsolidation and abolished the place preference. Other studies investigated a different type of task in which animals form a CS–drug association during drug self-administration training, a model of drug seeking (Lee *et al.*, 2005; Lee, Milton, & Everitt, 2006).

These studies particularly showed that infusion of Zif268 antisense oligodeoxy-nucleotides into the basolateral amygdala, prior to the reactivation of a CS–cocaine association, abolished its impact on the learning of a new cocaine-seeking response or on the maintenance of cocaine seeking, as well as relapse to a previously established drug-seeking behavior. Furthermore, the same group later demonstrated that conditioned withdrawal could be disrupted following reactivation of a CS-withdrawal association (Hellemans, Everitt, & Lee, 2006).

We have also found that disrupting the reconsolidation of a conditioned place preference induced in rats by morphine also leads to a loss of motivational withdrawal evoked in the same place. Interestingly, the hippocampus has a critical role in linking the place preference memory to the context-conditioned withdrawal because interfering with hippocampal molecular mechanisms after the reactivation of morphine conditioned place preference significantly weakens the motivational withdrawal. Thus, targeting the reconsolidation of memories induced by drugs of abuse may prove to be an important strategy for attenuating context-conditioned withdrawal and relapse in opiate addicts (Taubenfeld, Muravieva, Garcia-Osta, & Alberini, 2010). Notably, a protocol of design similar to those employed by Monfils *et al.* (2009) and Schiller *et al.* (2010) has been reported to be successful in disrupting conditioned craving in recovering heroin addicts (Xue *et al.*, 2012).

From all these investigations, it emerges that agents or strategies that disrupt memory reconsolidation represent potentially important approaches for developing novel treatments aimed at weakening pathogenic memories. It is important that future studies determine precisely what response is affected by the post-reactivation treatments, as well as how the age of a memory changes its sensitivity to treatments.

5.7 A MODEL FOR MEMORY RECONSOLIDATION IN HIPPOCAMPAL-DEPENDENT MEMORIES

Memories of a single event that become very long-lasting are evoked by the experience of a salient or emotional event. In contrast, emotionally weaker memories require multiple training trials (i.e., incremental learning) to become equally long-lasting. Let's consider the consolidation and reconsolidation of a long-term memory evoked by a strongly emotional event. The formation of this memory will be processed by the medial temporal lobe through molecular, cellular, and circuitry changes that evolve over an extended time (i.e., weeks in rats and months to years in humans), together with changes occurring in the amygdala. An initial phase of consolidation takes place during the first 1 or 2 days after learning. During this phase, memory is disrupted by treatments that interfere with the synthesis of a number of proteins; however, after this time, it becomes resistant to the same amnesic treatments. This may be interpreted as indicating that consolidation is completed. However, the memory still lies, for some time, in a sensitive, critical phase, during which it can again return to a labile state if reactivated, for example, by retrievals (retraining or reminders), and while in this fragile state, its retention can be bidirectionally modulated. This is the phase of memory recon-solidation. With the passage of time, a gradient of memory stabilization sets in, along with increased resistance to post-retrieval interference. This may be the result of the redistribution of the memory trace and/or the change in the type of trace that underlies the memory.

How does the passage of time contribute to memory strengthening and consolidation? It is possible that the memory trace strengthens because it undergoes implicit reactivations (thus reconsolidations), perhaps as a conse-quence of constitutive brain activity, such as circadian rhythms or sleep (Diekelmann & Born, 2010; Dudai, 2012; Stickgold et al., 2001). A salient, aversive or traumatic event is also frequently recalled over and over, especially during the first days or weeks (Rubin, Boals, & Berntsen, 2008). Cues often trigger the retrieval of aversive or traumatic experiences. Perhaps these reacti-vations, both implicit and explicit, serve the biologically important function of consolidating an aversive (important) memory without repeating the aversive experience. Thus, we suggest that through retrieval or reactivation, reconsolida-tion strengthens or consolidates important memories. Similarly, multiple trials of weaker learning events would produce the same outcome through rounds of consolidations that occur during incremental learning experiences. Hence, for hippocampal-dependent memories, we suggest that reconsolidation is a phase of strengthening that contributes to system memory consolidation.

Reactivation of the memory trace also has another important function, which is to update memories and add new information to the past experience. If the infor-mation is a repetition of a previous experience, its reactivations may overlap and perhaps even override the network of the original trace and ultimately lead to strengthening of the same behavior. If the new information encountered is novel and distinct from the recalled experience, the new trace may become linked to the reactivated trace and create a new, parallel memory that coexists with the orig-inal one. Importantly, as this new memory is established via a new consolidation process, new associations can be made even when the old reactivated memory is insensitive to post-reactivation interference (Morris et al., 2006; Rodriguez-Ortiz et al., 2005; Winters et al., 2009). Hence, trace activation and reactivation likely create a complex network of stored experiences that is highly dynamic, thus allowing us to adapt to the changing environment.

A better understanding of the dynamics of memory consolidation, reconso-lidation, and forgetting should help in the development of novel strategies that can either weaken pathogenic memories of memory components or, when advantageous, enhance memory strength.

ACKNOWLEDGMENTS

This work was supported by grants from the National Institute of Mental Health (R01 MH074736, R01 MH065635), National Institute of Drugs of Abuse (R21 CEBRA DA017672), and the Hirschl, NARSAD, and Philoctetes Foundations to Cristina M. Alberini. We also thank all the members of the Alberini laboratory for their invaluable contributions to the work discussed in this chapter and for their helpful feedback on the manuscript.

REFERENCES

Abrari, K., Rashidy-Pour, A., Semnanian, S., & Fathollahi, Y. (2008). Administration of corticosterone after memory reactivation disrupts subsequent retrieval of a contextual conditioned fear memory: dependence upon training intensity. *Neurobiology of Learning and Memory, 89*(2), 178−184. http://dx.doi.org/10.1016/j.nlm.2007.07.005.

Alberini, C. M. (2005). Mechanisms of memory stabilization: are consolidation and reconsolidation similar or distinct processes? *Trends in Neurosciences, 28*(1), 51−56. http://dx.doi.org/10.1016/j.tins.2004.11.001.

Alberini, C. M. (2008). The role of protein synthesis during the labile phases of memory: revisiting the skepticism. *Neurobiology of Learning and Memory, 89*(3), 234−246. http://dx.doi.org/10.1016/j.nlm.2007.08.007.

Alberini, C. M. (2009). Transcription factors in long-term memory and synaptic plasticity. *Physiological Reviews, 89*(1), 121−145. http://dx.doi.org/10.1152/physrev.00017.2008.

Alberini, C. M. (2011). The role of reconsolidation and the dynamic process of long-term memory formation and storage. *Frontiers in Behavioral Neuroscience, 5*, 12. http://dx.doi.org/10.3389/fnbeh.2011.00012.

Alberini, C. M., Bambah-Mukku, D., & Chen, D. Y. (2012). Memory consolidation and its underlying mechanisms. In K. P. Giese (Ed.), *Memory mechanisms in health and disease*. London: World Scientific Publishing.

Ambrogi Lorenzini, C. G., Baldi, E., Bucherelli, C., Sacchetti, B., & Tassoni, G. (1997). Role of ventral hippocampus in acquisition, consolidation and retrieval of rat's passive avoidance response memory trace. *Brain Research, 768*(1-2), 242−248, doi: S0006-8993(97)00651-3.

Ambrogi Lorenzini, C. G., Baldi, E., Bucherelli, C., Sacchetti, B., & Tassoni, G. (1999). Neural topography and chronology of memory consolidation: a review of functional inactivation findings. *Neurobiology of Learning and Memory, 71*(1), 1−18, S1074-7427(98)93865-5.

Arguello, A. A., Ye, X., Bozdagi, O., Pollonini, G., Tronel, S., Bambah-Mukku, D., Huntley, G. W., Platano, D., & Alberini, C. M. (2013). CCAAT enhancer binding protein delta plays an essential role in memory consolidation and reconsolidation. *Journal of Neuroscience* (in press).

Berman, D. E., & Dudai, Y. (2001). Memory extinction, learning anew, and learning the new: dissociations in the molecular machinery of learning in cortex. *Science, 291*(5512), 2417−2419. http://dx.doi.org/10.1126/science.1058165.

Bernabeu, R., Bevilaqua, L., Ardenghi, P., Bromberg, E., Schmitz, P., Bianchin, M., & Medina, J. H. (1997). Involvement of hippocampal cAMP/cAMP-dependent protein kinase signaling pathways in a late memory consolidation phase of aversively motivated learning in rats. *Proceedings of the National Academy of Sciences of the United States of America, 94*(13), 7041−7046.

Bernabeu, R., Cammarota, M., Izquierdo, I., & Medina, J. H. (1997). Involvement of hippocampal AMPA glutamate receptor changes and the cAMP/protein kinase A/CREB-P signalling pathway in memory consolidation of an avoidance task in rats. *Brazilian Journal of Medical and Biological Research, 30*(8), 961−965.

Bindra, D., & Cameron, L. (1953). Changes in experimentally produced anxiety with the passage of time: incubation effect. *Journal of Experimental Psychology, 45*(3), 197−203.

Bizon, J. L., Lasarge, C. L., Montgomery, K. S., McDermott, A. N., Setlow, B., & Griffith, W. H. (2009). Spatial reference and working memory across the lifespan of male Fischer 344 rats. *Neurobiology of Aging, 30*(4), 646−655. http://dx.doi.org/10.1016/j.neurobiolaging.2007.08.004.

Blundell, J., Kouser, M., & Powell, C. M. (2008). Systemic inhibition of mammalian target of rapamycin inhibits fear memory reconsolidation. *Neurobiology of Learning and Memory, 90*(1), 28−35. http://dx.doi.org/10.1016/j.nlm.2007.12.004.

Boccia, M. M., Blake, M. G., Acosta, G. B., & Baratti, C. M. (2006). Post-retrieval effects of icv infusions of hemicholinium in mice are dependent on the age of the original memory. *Learning & Memory, 13*(3), 376−381, 13/3/376 10.1101/lm.150306.

Bonini, J. S., Cammarota, M., Kerr, D. S., Bevilaqua, L. R., & Izquierdo, I. (2005). Inhibition of PKC in basolateral amygdala and posterior parietal cortex impairs consolidation of inhibitory avoidance memory. *Pharmacology, Biochemistry, & Behavior, 80*(1), 63−67, S0091-3057(04)00332-6.

Bonini, J. S., Rodrigues, L., Kerr, D. S., Bevilaqua, L. R., Cammarota, M., & Izquierdo, I. (2003). AMPA/kainate and group-I metabotropic receptor antagonists infused into different brain areas impair memory formation of inhibitory avoidance in rats. *Behavioural Pharmacology, 14*(2), 161−166. http://dx.doi.org/10.1097/01.fbp.0000063621.43827.8c.

Born, J., & Wilhelm, I. (2012). System consolidation of memory during sleep. *Psychological Research, 76*(2), 192−203. http://dx.doi.org/10.1007/s00426-011-0335-6.

Brightwell, J. J., Gallagher, M., & Colombo, P. J. (2004). Hippocampal CREB1 but not CREB2 is decreased in aged rats with spatial memory impairments. *Neurobiology of Learning and Memory, 81*(1), 19−26.

Brown, T. E., Forquer, M. R., Cocking, D. L., Jansen, H. T., Harding, J. W., & Sorg, B. A. (2007). Role of matrix metalloproteinases in the acquisition and reconsolidation of cocaine-induced conditioned place preference. *Learning & Memory, 14*(3), 214−223. http://dx.doi.org/10.1101/lm.476207.

Burke, S. N., & Barnes, C. A. (2006). Neural plasticity in the ageing brain. *Nature Reviews Neuroscience, 7*(1), 30−40. http://dx.doi.org/10.1038/nrn1809.

Bustos, S. G., Maldonado, H., & Molina, V. A. (2009). Disruptive effect of midazolam on fear memory reconsolidation: decisive influence of reactivation time span and memory age. *Neuropsychopharmacology, 34*(2), 446−457, npp200875.

Cai, W.-H., Blundell, J., Han, J., Greene, R. W., & Powell, C. M. (2006). Postreactivation glucocorticoids impair recall of established fear memory. *Journal of Neuroscience, 26*(37), 9560−9566. http://dx.doi.org/10.1523/JNEUROSCI.2397-06.2006.

Canal, C. E., Chang, Q., & Gold, P. E. (2008). Intra-amygdala injections of CREB antisense impair inhibitory avoidance memory: role of norepinephrine and acetylcholine. *Learning & Memory, 15*(9), 677−686. http://dx.doi.org/10.1101/15/9/677, [pii] 10.1101/lm.904308.

Cansino, S. (2009). Episodic memory decay along the adult lifespan: a review of behavioral and neurophysiological evidence. *International Journal of Psychophysiology, 71*(1), 64−69. http://dx.doi.org/10.1016/j.ijpsycho.2008.07.005.

Carbo Tano, M., Molina, V. A., Maldonado, H., & Pedreira, M. E. (2009). Memory consolidation and reconsolidation in an invertebrate model: the role of the GABAergic system. *Neuroscience, 158*(2), 387−401. http://dx.doi.org/10.1016/S0306-4522(08)01591-1, [pii] 10.1016/j.neuroscience.2008.10.039.

Chen, D. Y., Bambah-Mukku, D., Pollonini, G., & Alberini, C. M. (2012). Glucocorticoid receptors recruit the CaMKIIα, BDNF-CREB pathways to mediate memory consolidation. *Nature Neuroscience, 15*(12), 1707−1714. http://dx.doi.org/10.1038/nn.3266.

Chen, D. Y., Stern, S. A., Garcia-Osta, A., Saunier-Rebori, B., Pollonini, G., Bambah-Mukku, D., & Alberini, C. M. (2011). A critical role for IGF-II in memory consolidation and enhancement. *Nature, 469*(7331), 491−497. http://dx.doi.org/10.1038/nature09667, [pii] 10.1038/nature09667.

Countryman, R. A., & Gold, P. E. (2007). Rapid forgetting of social transmission of food preferences in aged rats: relationship to hippocampal CREB activation. *Learning & Memory, 14*(5), 350−358. http://dx.doi.org/10.1101/lm.524907.

Davis, H. P., & Squire, L. R. (1984). Protein synthesis and memory: a review. *Psychological Bulletin, 96*(3), 518−559.

de Souza, F. A., Sanchis-Segura, C., Fukada, S. Y., de Bortoli, V. C., Zangrossi, H., Jr., & de Oliveira, A. M. (2004). Intracerebroventricular effects of angiotensin II on a step-through passive avoidance task in rats. *Neurobiology of Learning and Memory, 81*(1), 100−103, S1074742703000959.

Dębiec, J., Doyère, V., Nader, K., & LeDoux, J. E. (2006). Directly reactivated, but not indirectly reactivated, memories undergo reconsolidation in the amygdala. *Proceedings of the National Academy of Sciences of the United States of America, 103*(9), 3428−3433. http://dx.doi.org/10.1073/pnas.0507168103.

Dębiec, J., & LeDoux, J. E. (2004). Disruption of reconsolidation but not consolidation of auditory fear conditioning by noradrenergic blockade in the amygdala. *Neuroscience, 129*(2), 267–272. http://dx.doi.org/10.1016/j.neuroscience.2004.08.018.

Dębiec, J., LeDoux, J. E., & Nader, K. (2002). Cellular and systems reconsolidation in the hippocampus. *Neuron, 36*(3), 527–538.

Devauges, V., & Sara, S. J. (1991). Memory retrieval enhancement by locus coeruleus stimulation: evidence for mediation by beta-receptors. *Behavioural Brain Research, 43*(1), 93–97.

DeVietti, T. L., Conger, G. L., & Kirkpatrick, B. R. (1977). Comparison of the enhancement gradients of retention obtained with stimulation of the mesencephalic reticular formation after training or memory reactivation. *Physiology & Behavior, 19*(4), 549–554.

Diekelmann, S., & Born, J. (2010). The memory function of sleep. *Nature Reviews Neuroscience, 11*(2), 114–126. http://dx.doi.org/10.1038/nrn2762.

Diekelmann, S., Büchel, C., Born, J., & Rasch, B. (2011). Labile or stable: opposing consequences for memory when reactivated during waking and sleep. *Nature Neuroscience, 14*(3), 381–386. http://dx.doi.org/10.1038/nn.2744.

Diergaarde, L., Schoffelmeer, A. N., & De Vries, T. J. (2006). Beta-adrenoceptor mediated inhibition of long-term reward-related memory reconsolidation. *Behavioural Brain Research, 170*(2), 333–336. http://dx.doi.org/10.1016/j.bbr.2006.02.014.

Dudai, Y. (1996). Consolidation: fragility on the road to the engram. *Neuron, 17*(3), 367–370.

Dudai, Y. (2004). The neurobiology of consolidations, or, how stable is the engram? *Annual Review of Psychology, 55,* 51–86. http://dx.doi.org/10.1146/annurev.psych.55.090902.142050.

Dudai, Y. (2012). The restless engram: consolidations never end. *Annual Review of Neuroscience, 35,* 227–247. http://dx.doi.org/10.1146/annurev-neuro-062111-150500.

Dudai, Y., & Eisenberg, M. (2004). Rites of passage of the engram: reconsolidation and the lingering consolidation hypothesis. *Neuron, 44*(1), 93–100. http://dx.doi.org/10.1016/j.neuron.2004.09.003.

Eisenberg, M., & Dudai, Y. (2004). Reconsolidation of fresh, remote, and extinguished fear memory in Medaka: old fears don't die. *European Journal of Neuroscience, 20*(12), 3397–3403. http://dx.doi.org/10.1111/j.1460-9568.2004.03818.x.

Eisenberg, M., Kobilo, T., Berman, D. E., & Dudai, Y. (2003). Stability of retrieved memory: inverse correlation with trace dominance. *Science, 301*(5636), 1102–1104. http://dx.doi.org/10.1126/science.1086881 301/5636/1102.

Fischer, A., Sananbenesi, F., Schrick, C., Spiess, J., & Radulovic, J. (2004). Distinct roles of hippocampal *de novo* protein synthesis and actin rearrangement in extinction of contextual fear. *Journal of Neuroscience, 24*(8), 1962–1966. http://dx.doi.org/10.1523/JNEUROSCI.5112-03.2004.

Forcato, C., Rodríguez, M. L. C., Pedreira, M. E., & Maldonado, H. (2010). Reconsolidation in humans opens up declarative memory to the entrance of new information. *Neurobiology of Learning and Memory, 93*(1), 77–84. http://dx.doi.org/10.1016/j.nlm.2009.08.006.

Frankland, P. W., & Bontempi, B. (2005). The organization of recent and remote memories. *Nature Reviews Neuroscience, 6*(2), 119–130. http://dx.doi.org/10.1038/nrn1607.

Frankland, P. W., Ding, H. K., Takahashi, E., Suzuki, A., Kida, S., & Silva, A. J. (2006). Stability of recent and remote contextual fear memory. *Learning & Memory, 13*(4), 451–457. http://dx.doi.org/10.1101/lm.183406.

Frenkel, L., Maldonado, H., & Delorenzi, A. (2005). Memory strengthening by a real-life episode during reconsolidation: an outcome of water deprivation via brain angiotensin II. *European Journal of Neuroscience, 22*(7), 1757–1766. http://dx.doi.org/10.1111/EJN4373, [pii] 10.1111/j.1460-9568.2005.04373.x.

Fricks-Gleason, A. N., & Marshall, J. F. (2008). Post-retrieval beta-adrenergic receptor blockade: effects on extinction and reconsolidation of cocaine-cue memories. *Learning & Memory, 15*(9), 643–648. http://dx.doi.org/10.1101/lm.1054608.

Gallagher, M., & Rapp, P. R. (1997). The use of animal models to study the effects of aging on cognition. *Annual Review of Psychology, 48,* 339–370. http://dx.doi.org/10.1146/annurev.psych.48.1.339.

Garcia-Osta, A., Tsokas, P., Pollonini, G., Landau, E. M., Blitzer, R., & Alberini, C. M. (2006). MuSK expressed in the brain mediates cholinergic responses, synaptic plasticity, and memory formation. *Journal of Neuroscience, 26*(30), 7919−7932, 26/30/7919 10.1523/JNEUROSCI.1674-06.2006.

Graves, L., Pack, A., & Abel, T. (2001). Sleep and memory: a molecular perspective. *Trends in Neurosciences, 24*(4), 237−243.

Grimm, J. W., Fyall, A. M., & Osincup, D. P. (2005). Incubation of sucrose craving: effects of reduced training and sucrose pre-loading. *Physiology & Behavior, 84*(1), 73−79. http://dx.doi.org/10.1016/j.physbeh.2004.10.011.

Gusev, P. A., & Gubin, A. N. (2010a). Arc/Arg3.1 mRNA global expression patterns elicited by memory recall in cerebral cortex differ for remote versus recent spatial memories. *Frontiers in Integrative Neuroscience, 4*, 15. http://dx.doi.org/10.3389/fnint.2010.00015.

Gusev, P. A., & Gubin, A. N. (2010b). Recent and remote memory recalls modulate different sets of stereotypical interlaminar correlations in Arc/Arg3.1 mRNA expression in cortical areas. *Brain Research, 1352*, 118−139. http://dx.doi.org/10.1016/S0006-8993(10)01490-3, [pii] 10.1016/j.brainres.2010.06.064.

Hellemans, K. G. C., Everitt, B. J., & Lee, J. L. C. (2006). Disrupting reconsolidation of conditioned withdrawal memories in the basolateral amygdala reduces suppression of heroin seeking in rats. *Journal of Neuroscience, 26*(49), 12694−12699. http://dx.doi.org/10.1523/JNEUROSCI.3101-06.2006.

Helmstetter, F. J., Parsons, R. G., & Gafford, G. M. (2008). Macromolecular synthesis, distributed synaptic plasticity, and fear conditioning. *Neurobiology of Learning and Memory, 89*(3), 324−337. http://dx.doi.org/10.1016/j.nlm.2007.09.002.

Hoeffer, C. A., Cowansage, K. K., Arnold, E. C., Banko, J. L., Moerke, N. J., Rodriguez, R., & Klann, E. (2011). Inhibition of the interactions between eukaryotic initiation factors 4E and 4G impairs long-term associative memory consolidation but not reconsolidation. *Proceedings of the National Academy of Sciences of the United States of America, 108*(8), 3383−3388, 1013063108 10.1073/pnas.1013063108.

Impey, S., Smith, D. M., Obrietan, K., Donahue, R., Wade, C., & Storm, D. R. (1998). Stimulation of cAMP response element (CRE)-mediated transcription during contextual learning. *Nature Neuroscience, 1*(7), 595−601. http://dx.doi.org/10.1038/2830.

Inda, M. C., Muravieva, E. V., & Alberini, C. M. (2011). Memory retrieval and the passage of time: from reconsolidation and strengthening to extinction. *Journal of Neuroscience, 31*(5), 1635−1643. http://dx.doi.org/10.1523/JNEUROSCI.4736-10.2011.

Izquierdo, I., Quillfeldt, J. A., Zanatta, M. S., Quevedo, J., Schaeffer, E., Schmitz, P. K., & Medina, J. H. (1997). Sequential role of hippocampus and amygdala, entorhinal cortex and parietal cortex in formation and retrieval of memory for inhibitory avoidance in rats. *European Journal of Neuroscience, 9*(4), 786−793.

Jerusalinsky, D., Ferreira, M. B., Walz, R., Da Silva, R. C., Bianchin, M., Ruschel, A. C., & Izquierdo, I. (1992). Amnesia by post-training infusion of glutamate receptor antagonists into the amygdala, hippocampus, and entorhinal cortex. *Behavioral and Neural Biology, 58*(1), 76−80.

Jobim, P. F., Pedroso, T. R., Christoff, R. R., Werenicz, A., Maurmann, N., Reolon, G. K., & Roesler, R. (2012). Inhibition of mTOR by rapamycin in the amygdala or hippocampus impairs formation and reconsolidation of inhibitory avoidance memory. *Neurobiology of Learning and Memory, 97*(1), 105−112. http://dx.doi.org/10.1016/S1074-7427(11)00176-6, [pii] 10.1016/j.nlm.2011.10.002.

Kim, J. J., & Fanselow, M. S. (1992). Modality-specific retrograde amnesia of fear. *Science, 256*(5057), 675−677.

Kindt, M., Soeter, M., & Vervliet, B. (2009). Beyond extinction: erasing human fear responses and preventing the return of fear. *Nature Neuroscience, 12*(3), 256−258. http://dx.doi.org/10.1038/nn.2271.

Kitamura, T., Saitoh, Y., Takashima, N., Murayama, A., Niibori, Y., Ageta, H., & Inokuchi, K. (2009). Adult neurogenesis modulates the hippocampus-dependent period of associative fear memory. *Cell, 139*(4), 814−827. http://dx.doi.org/10.1016/S0092-8674(09)01309-9, [pii] 10.1016/j.cell.2009.10.020.

LaSarge, C. L., Montgomery, K. S., Tucker, C., Slaton, G. S., Griffith, W. H., Setlow, B., & Bizon, J. L. (2007). Deficits across multiple cognitive domains in a subset of aged Fischer 344 rats. *Neurobiology of Aging, 28*(6), 928−936. http://dx.doi.org/10.1016/j. neurobiolaging.2006.04.010.

Lee, J. L. C., Everitt, B. J., & Thomas, K. L. (2004). Independent cellular processes for hippocampal memory consolidation and reconsolidation. *Science, 304*(5672), 839−843. http://dx.doi.org/10.1126/science.1095760 1095760.

Lee, J. L. C., Di Ciano, P., Thomas, K. L., & Everitt, B. J. (2005). Disrupting reconsolidation of drug memories reduces cocaine-seeking behavior. *Neuron, 47*(6), 795−801. http://dx. doi.org/10.1016/j.neuron.2005.08.007.

Lee, J. L. C., Milton, A. L., & Everitt, B. J. (2006). Cue-induced cocaine seeking and relapse are reduced by disruption of drug memory reconsolidation. *Journal of Neuroscience, 26*(22), 5881−5887. http://dx.doi.org/10.1523/JNEUROSCI.0323-06.2006.

Lewis, D. J. (1979). Psychobiology of active and inactive memory. *Psychological Bulletin, 86*(5), 1054−1083.

Litvin, O. O., & Anokhin, K. V. (2000). Mechanisms of memory reorganization during retrieval of acquired behavioral experience in chicks: the effects of protein synthesis inhibition in the brain. *Neuroscience and Behavioral Physiology, 30*(6), 671−678.

Lorenzini, C. A., Baldi, E., Bucherelli, C., Sacchetti, B., & Tassoni, G. (1996). Role of dorsal hippocampus in acquisition, consolidation and retrieval of rat's passive avoidance response: a tetrodotoxin functional inactivation study. *Brain Research, 730*(1-2), 32−39.

Lu, L., Grimm, J. W., Hope, B. T., & Shaham, Y. (2004). Incubation of cocaine craving after withdrawal: a review of preclinical data. *Neuropharmacology, 47*(Suppl. 1), 214−226. http://dx.doi.org/10.1016/j.neuropharm.2004.06.027.

Luft, A. R., Buitrago, M. M., Kaelin-Lang, A., Dichgans, J., & Schulz, J. B. (2004). Protein synthesis inhibition blocks consolidation of an acrobatic motor skill. *Learning & Memory, 11*(4), 379−382. http://dx.doi.org/10.1101/lm.72604.

Luft, A. R., Buitrago, M. M., Ringer, T., Dichgans, J., & Schulz, J. B. (2004). Motor skill learning depends on protein synthesis in motor cortex after training. *Journal of Neuroscience, 24*(29), 6515−6520. http://dx.doi.org/10.1523/JNEUROSCI.1034-04.2004.

Malin, E. L., Ibrahim, D. Y., Tu, J. W., & McGaugh, J. L. (2007). Involvement of the rostral anterior cingulate cortex in consolidation of inhibitory avoidance memory: interaction with the basolateral amygdala. *Neurobiology of Learning and Memory, 87*(2), 295−302. http://dx.doi.org/10.1016/S1074-7427(06)00134-1, [pii] 10.1016/j.nlm.2006.09.004.

Marshall, L., Helgadottir, H., Molle, M., & Born, J. (2006). Boosting slow oscillations during sleep potentiates memory. *Nature, 444*(7119), 610−613. http://dx.doi.org/10.1038/nature05278.

McGaugh, J. L. (2000). Memory—A century of consolidation. *Science, 287*(5451), 248−251.

McGaugh, J. L. (2004). The amygdala modulates the consolidation of memories of emotionally arousing experiences. *Annual Review of Neuroscience, 27*, 1−28. http://dx.doi.org/10.1146/annurev.neuro.27.070203.144157.

McGaugh, J. L., & Roozendaal, B. (2002). Role of adrenal stress hormones in forming lasting memories in the brain. *Current Opinion in Neurobiology, 12*(2), 205−210.

McIntyre, C. K., Power, A. E., Roozendaal, B., & McGaugh, J. L. (2003). Role of the basolateral amygdala in memory consolidation. *Annals of the New York Academy of Sciences, 985*, 273−293.

Meiri, N., & Rosenblum, K. (1998). Lateral ventricle injection of the protein synthesis inhibitor anisomycin impairs long-term memory in a spatial memory task. *Brain Research, 789*(1), 48−55.

Milekic, M. H., & Alberini, C. M. (2002). Temporally graded requirement for protein synthesis following memory reactivation. *Neuron, 36*(3), 521−525, S0896627302009765.

Milekic, M. H., Brown, S. D., Castellini, C., & Alberini, C. M. (2006). Persistent disruption of an established morphine conditioned place preference. *Journal of Neuroscience, 26*(11), 3010−3020. http://dx.doi.org/10.1523/JNEUROSCI.4818-05.2006.

Milekic, M. H., Pollonini, G., & Alberini, C. M. (2007). Temporal requirement of C/EBPbeta in the amygdala following reactivation but not acquisition of inhibitory avoidance. *Learning & Memory, 14*(7), 504−511. http://dx.doi.org/10.1101/14/7/504, [pii] 10. 1101/lm.598307.

Miller, C. A., & Marshall, J. F. (2005). Molecular substrates for retrieval and reconsolidation of cocaine-associated contextual memory. *Neuron, 47*(6), 873−884. http://dx.doi.org/10. 1016/j.neuron.2005.08.006.

Milton, A. L., Lee, J. L., & Everitt, B. J. (2008). Reconsolidation of appetitive memories for both natural and drug reinforcement is dependent on β-adrenergic receptors. *Learning & Memory, 15*(2), 88−92. http://dx.doi.org/10.1101/lm.825008.

Molle, M., Yeshenko, O., Marshall, L., Sara, S. J., & Born, J. (2006). Hippocampal sharp wave-ripples linked to slow oscillations in rat slow-wave sleep. *Journal of Neurophysiology, 96*(1), 62−70. http://dx.doi.org/10.1152/jn.00014.2006.

Monfils, M.-H., Cowansage, K. K., Klann, E., & LeDoux, J. E. (2009). Extinction-reconsolidation boundaries: key to persistent attenuation of fear memories. *Science, 324*(5929), 951−955. http://dx.doi.org/10.1126/science.1167975.

Monti, B., Berteotti, C., & Contestabile, A. (2005). Dysregulation of memory-related proteins in the hippocampus of aged rats and their relation with cognitive impairment. *Hippocampus, 15*(8), 1041−1049. http://dx.doi.org/10.1002/hipo.20099.

Morris, R. G. M., Inglis, J., Ainge, J. A., Olverman, H. J., Tulloch, J., Dudai, Y., & Kelly, P. A. T. (2006). Memory reconsolidation: sensitivity of spatial memory to inhibition of protein synthesis in dorsal hippocampus during encoding and retrieval. *Neuron, 50*(3), 479−489. http://dx.doi.org/10.1016/j.neuron.2006.04.012.

Moscovitch, M., Rosenbaum, R. S., Gilboa, A., Addis, D. R., Westmacott, R., Grady, C., & Nadel, L. (2005). Functional neuroanatomy of remote episodic, semantic and spatial memory: a unified account based on multiple trace theory. *Journal of Anatomy, 207*(1), 35−66. http://dx.doi.org/10.1111/JOA421, [pii] 10.1111/j.1469-7580.2005. 00421.x.

Muravieva, E. V., & Alberini, C. M. (2010). Limited efficacy of propranolol on the reconsolidation of fear memories. *Learning & Memory, 17*(6), 306−313. http://dx.doi.org/10. 1101/lm.1794710.

Nader, K., & Einarsson, E. O. (2010). Memory reconsolidation: an update. *Annals of the New York Academy of Sciences, 1191*, 27−41. http://dx.doi.org/10.1111/NYAS5443, [pii] 10. 1111/j.1749-6632.2010.05443.x.

Nader, K., & Hardt, O. (2009). A single standard for memory: the case for reconsolidation. *Nature Reviews Neuroscience, 10*(3), 224−234. http://dx.doi.org/10.1038/nrn2590.

Nader, K., Schafe, G. E., & Le Doux, J. E. (2000). Fear memories require protein synthesis in the amygdala for reconsolidation after retrieval. *Nature, 406*(6797), 722−726. http://dx. doi.org/10.1038/35021052.

Nader, K., Schafe, G. E., & LeDoux, J. E. (2000). The labile nature of consolidation theory. *Nature Reviews Neuroscience, 1*(3), 216−219. http://dx.doi.org/10.1038/35044580.

Nikzad, S., Vafaei, A. A., Rashidy-Pour, A., & Haghighi, S. (2011). Systemic and intrahippocampal administrations of the glucocorticoid receptor antagonist RU38486 impairs fear memory reconsolidation in rats. *Stress, 14*(4), 459−464. http://dx.doi.org/10. 3109/10253890.2010.548171.

O'Brien, C. P., Childress, A. R., McLellan, A. T., & Ehrman, R. (1992). Classical conditioning in drug-dependent humans. *Annals of the New York Academy of Sciences, 654*, 400−415.

O'Donnell, T., Hegadoren, K. M., & Coupland, N. C. (2004). Noradrenergic mechanisms in the pathophysiology of post-traumatic stress disorder. *Neuropsychobiology, 50*(4), 273−283. http://dx.doi.org/10.1159/000080952.

Pedreira, M. E., & Maldonado, H. (2003). Protein synthesis subserves reconsolidation or extinction depending on reminder duration. *Neuron, 38*(6), 863−869, S0896627303003520.

Pickens, C. L., Airavaara, M., Theberge, F., Fanous, S., Hope, B. T., & Shaham, Y. (2011). Neurobiology of the incubation of drug craving. *Trends in Neurosciences, 34*(8), 411−420. http://dx.doi.org/10.1016/j.tins.2011.06.001.

Pickens, C. L., Golden, S. A., Adams-Deutsch, T., Nair, S. G., & Shaham, Y. (2009). Long-lasting incubation of conditioned fear in rats. *Biological Psychiatry, 65*(10), 881−886. http://dx.doi.org/10.1016/j.biopsych.2008.12.010.

Pitman, R. K. (1989). Post-traumatic stress disorder, hormones, and memory. *Biological Psychiatry, 26*(3), 221−223.

Pitman, R. K., & Delahanty, D. L. (2005). Conceptually driven pharmacologic approaches to acute trauma. *CNS Spectrums, 10*(2), 99−106.

Power, A. E., Berlau, D. J., McGaugh, J. L., & Steward, O. (2006). Anisomycin infused into the hippocampus fails to block "reconsolidation" but impairs extinction: The role of re-exposure duration. *Learning & Memory, 13*(1), 27−34, 13/1/27 10.1101/lm.91206.

Przybyslawski, J., Roullet, P., & Sara, S. J. (1999). Attenuation of emotional and nonemotional memories after their reactivation: role of beta adrenergic receptors. *Journal of Neuroscience, 19*(15), 6623−6628.

Quillfeldt, J. A., Zanatta, M. S., Schmitz, P. K., Quevedo, J., Schaeffer, E., Lima, J. B., & Izquierdo, I. (1996). Different brain areas are involved in memory expression at different times from training. *Neurobiology of Learning and Memory, 66*(2), 97−101. http://dx.doi.org/10.1006/S1074-7427(96)90050-7, [pii] 10.1006/nlme.1996.0050.

Restivo, L., Vetere, G., Bontempi, B., & Ammassari-Teule, M. (2009). The formation of recent and remote memory is associated with time-dependent formation of dendritic spines in the hippocampus and anterior cingulate cortex. *Journal of Neuroscience, 29*(25), 8206−8214. http://dx.doi.org/10.1523/29/25/8206, [pii] 10.1523/JNEUROSCI.0966-09.2009.

Robinson, M. J. F., & Franklin, K. B. J. (2010). Reconsolidation of a morphine place preference: impact of the strength and age of memory on disruption by propranolol and midazolam. *Behavioural Brain Research, 213*(2), 201−207. http://dx.doi.org/10.1016/j.bbr.2010.04.056.

Robitsek, R. J., Fortin, N. J., Koh, M. T., Gallagher, M., & Eichenbaum, H. (2008). Cognitive aging: a common decline of episodic recollection and spatial memory in rats. *Journal of Neuroscience, 28*(36), 8945−8954. http://dx.doi.org/10.1523/JNEUROSCI.1893-08.2008.

Rodriguez-Ortiz, C. J., De la Cruz, V., Gutiérrez, R., & Bermudez-Rattoni, F. (2005). Protein synthesis underlies post-retrieval memory consolidation to a restricted degree only when updated information is obtained. *Learning & Memory, 12*(5), 533−537. http://dx.doi.org/10.1101/lm.94505.

Roozendaal, B., Brunson, K. L., Holloway, B. L., McGaugh, J. L., & Baram, T. Z. (2002). Involvement of stress-released corticotropin-releasing hormone in the basolateral amygdala in regulating memory consolidation. *Proceedings of the National Academy of Sciences of the United States of America, 99*(21), 13908−13913. http://dx.doi.org/10.1073/pnas.212504599 212504599.

Ross, R. S., & Eichenbaum, H. (2006). Dynamics of hippocampal and cortical activation during consolidation of a nonspatial memory. *Journal of Neuroscience, 26*(18), 4852−4859, 26/18/4852 10.1523/JNEUROSCI.0659-06.2006.

Rossato, J. I., Bonini, J. S., Coitinho, A. S., Vianna, M. R., Medina, J. H., Cammarota, M., & Izquierdo, I. (2004). Retrograde amnesia induced by drugs acting on different molecular systems. *Behavioural Neuroscience, 118*(3), 563−568. http://dx.doi.org/10.1037/0735-7044.118.3.563.

Rubin, D. C., Boals, A., & Berntsen, D. (2008). Memory in posttraumatic stress disorder: properties of voluntary and involuntary, traumatic and nontraumatic autobiographical memories in people with and without posttraumatic stress disorder symptoms. *Journal of Experimental Psychology. General, 137*(4), 591−614. http://dx.doi.org/10.1037/a0013165.

Sacco, T., & Sacchetti, B. (2010). Role of secondary sensory cortices in emotional memory storage and retrieval in rats. *Science, 329*(5992), 649−656, 329/5992/649 10.1126/science.1183165.

Santini, E., Ge, H., Ren, K., Peña de Ortiz, S., & Quirk, G. J. (2004). Consolidation of fear extinction requires protein synthesis in the medial prefrontal cortex. *Journal of Neuroscience, 24*(25), 5704−5710. http://dx.doi.org/10.1523/JNEUROSCI.0786-04.2004.

Sara, S. J. (2000). Strengthening the shaky trace through retrieval. *Nature Reviews Neuroscience, 1*(3), 212−213. http://dx.doi.org/10.1038/35044575.

Schiller, D., Monfils, M.-H., Raio, C. M., Johnson, D. C., LeDoux, J. E., & Phelps, E. A. (2010). Preventing the return of fear in humans using reconsolidation update mechanisms. *Nature, 463*(7277), 49−53. http://dx.doi.org/10.1038/nature08637.

Sirota, A., Csicsvari, J., Buhl, D., & Buzsaki, G. (2003). Communication between neocortex and hippocampus during sleep in rodents. *Proceedings of the National Academy of Sciences of the United States of America, 100*(4), 2065−2069. http://dx.doi.org/10.1073/pnas.0437938100.

Slipczuk, L., Bekinschtein, P., Katche, C., Cammarota, M., Izquierdo, I., & Medina, J. H. (2009). BDNF activates mTOR to regulate GluR1 expression required for memory formation. *PLoS ONE, 4*(6). http://dx.doi.org/10.1371/journal.pone.0006007. e6007.

Smith, C. N., & Squire, L. R. (2009). Medial temporal lobe activity during retrieval of semantic memory is related to the age of the memory. *Journal of Neuroscience, 29*(4), 930−938, 29/4/930 10.1523/JNEUROSCI.4545-08.2009.

Sorg, B. A. (2012). Reconsolidation of drug memories. *Neuroscience and Biobehavioral Reviews, 36*(5), 1400−1417. http://dx.doi.org/10.1016/j.neubiorev.2012.02.004.

Squire, L. R., & Alvarez, P. (1995). Retrograde amnesia and memory consolidation: a neurobiological perspective. *Current Opinion in Neurobiology, 5*(2), 169−177.

Squire, L. R., Clark, R. E., & Knowlton, B. J. (2001). Retrograde amnesia. *Hippocampus, 11*(1), 50−55. http://dx.doi.org/10.1002/1098-1063(2001)11, 1<50::AID-HIPO1019> 3.0.CO;2-G.

Squire, L. R., Stark, C. E., & Clark, R. E. (2004). The medial temporal lobe. *Annual Review of Neuroscience, 27*, 279−306. http://dx.doi.org/10.1146/annurev.neuro.27.070203.144130.

Staddon, J. E., & Cerutti, D. T. (2003). Operant conditioning. *Annual Review of Psychology, 54*, 115−144. http://dx.doi.org/10.1146/annurev.psych.54.101601.145124 101601. 145124.

Stickgold, R., Hobson, J. A., Fosse, R., & Fosse, M. (2001). Sleep, learning, and dreams: off-line memory reprocessing. *Science, 294*(5544), 1052−1057. http://dx.doi.org/10.1126/science.1063530.

Suárez, L. D., Smal, L., & Delorenzi, A. (2010). Updating contextual information during consolidation as result of a new memory trace. *Neurobiology of Learning and Memory, 93*(4), 561−571. http://dx.doi.org/10.1016/j.nlm.2010.02.004.

Suris, A., Smith, J., Powell, C. M., & North, C. S. (2012). Interfering with the reconsolidation of traumatic memory: sirolimus as a novel agent for treating veterans with posttraumatic stress disorder. *Annals of Clinical Psychiatry.* in press.

Suzuki, A., Josselyn, S. A., Frankland, P. W., Masushige, S., Silva, A. J., & Kida, S. (2004). Memory reconsolidation and extinction have distinct temporal and biochemical signatures. *Journal of Neuroscience, 24*(20), 4787−4795. http://dx.doi.org/10.1523/JNEUROSCI.5491-03.2004.

Takehara-Nishiuchi, K., & McNaughton, B. L. (2008). Spontaneous changes of neocortical code for associative memory during consolidation. *Science, 322*(5903), 960−963. http://dx.doi.org/10.1126/322/5903/960, [pii] 10.1126/science.1161299.

Taubenfeld, S. M., Milekic, M. H., Monti, B., & Alberini, C. M. (2001a). The consolidation of new but not reactivated memory requires hippocampal C/EBPbeta. *Nature Neuroscience, 4*(8), 813−818. http://dx.doi.org/10.1038/90520.

Taubenfeld, S. M., Muravieva, E. V., Garcia-Osta, A., & Alberini, C. M. (2010). Disrupting the memory of places induced by drugs of abuse weakens motivational withdrawal in a context-dependent manner. *Proceedings of the National Academy of Sciences of the United States of America, 107*(27), 12345−12350. http://dx.doi.org/10.1073/pnas.1003152107.

Taubenfeld, S. M., Riceberg, J. S., New, A. S., & Alberini, C. M. (2009). Preclinical assessment for selectively disrupting a traumatic memory via postretrieval inhibition of glucocorticoid receptors. *Biological Psychiatry, 65*(3), 249−257. http://dx.doi.org/10.1016/j.biopsych.2008.07.005.

Taubenfeld, S. M., Wiig, K. A., Monti, B., Dolan, B., Pollonini, G., & Alberini, C. M. (2001b). Fornix-dependent induction of hippocampal CCAAT enhancer-binding protein β and δ co-localizes with phosphorylated cAMP response element-binding protein and accompanies long-term memory consolidation. *Journal of Neuroscience, 21*(1), 84–91, 21/1/84.

Taubenfeld, S. M., Wiig, K. A., Bear, M. F., & Alberini, C. M. (1999). A molecular correlate of memory and amnesia in the hippocampus. *Nature Neuroscience, 2*(4), 309–310. http://dx.doi.org/10.1038/7217.

Teixeira, C. M., Pomedli, S. R., Maei, H. R., Kee, N., & Frankland, P. W. (2006). Involvement of the anterior cingulate cortex in the expression of remote spatial memory. *Journal of Neuroscience, 26*(29), 7555–7564. http://dx.doi.org/10.1523/26/29/7555, [pii] 10.1523/JNEUROSCI.1068-06.2006.

Tollenaar, M. S., Elzinga, B. M., Spinhoven, P., & Everaerd, W. (2009). Immediate and prolonged effects of cortisol, but not propranolol, on memory retrieval in healthy young men. *Neurobiology of Learning and Memory, 91*(1), 23–31. http://dx.doi.org/10.1016/j.nlm.2008.08.002.

Touzani, K., Puthanveettil, S. V., & Kandel, E. R. (2007). Consolidation of learning strategies during spatial working memory task requires protein synthesis in the prefrontal cortex. *Proceedings of the National Academy of Sciences of the United States of America, 104*(13), 5632–5637. http://dx.doi.org/10.1073/pnas.0611554104.

Tronel, S., & Alberini, C. M. (2007). Persistent disruption of a traumatic memory by post-retrieval inactivation of glucocorticoid receptors in the amygdala. *Biological Psychiatry, 62*(1), 33–39. http://dx.doi.org/10.1016/j.biopsych.2006.09.009.

Tronel, S., Milekic, M. H., & Alberini, C. M. (2005). Linking new information to a reactivated memory requires consolidation and not reconsolidation mechanisms. *PLoS Biology, 3*(9). http://dx.doi.org/10.1371/journal.pbio.0030293. e293.

Tronson, N. C., Wiseman, S. L., Olausson, P., & Taylor, J. R. (2006). Bidirectional behavioral plasticity of memory reconsolidation depends on amygdalar protein kinase A. *Nature Neuroscience, 9*(2), 167–169. http://dx.doi.org/10.1038/nn1628.

Valjent, E., Corbillé, A.-G., Bertran-Gonzalez, J., Hervé, D., & Girault, J.-A. (2006). Inhibition of ERK pathway or protein synthesis during reexposure to drugs of abuse erases previously learned place preference. *Proceedings of the National Academy of Sciences of the United States of America, 103*(8), 2932–2937. http://dx.doi.org/10.1073/pnas.0511030103.

Vetere, G., Restivo, L., Cole, C. J., Ross, P. J., Ammassari-Teule, M., Josselyn, S. A., & Frankland, P. W. (2011). Spine growth in the anterior cingulate cortex is necessary for the consolidation of contextual fear memory. *Proceedings of the National Academy of Sciences of the United States of America, 108*(20), 8456–8460, 1016275108 10.1073/pnas.1016275108.

von Hertzen, L. S., & Giese, K. P. (2005). Memory reconsolidation engages only a subset of immediate-early genes induced during consolidation. *Journal of Neuroscience, 25*(8), 1935–1942, 25/8/1935 10.1523/JNEUROSCI.4707-04.2005.

Wiltgen, B. J., Brown, R. A., Talton, L. E., & Silva, A. J. (2004). New circuits for old memories: the role of the neocortex in consolidation. *Neuron, 44*(1), 101–108. http://dx.doi.org/10.1016/j.neuron.2004.09.015 S0896627304005793.

Wiltgen, B. J., & Silva, A. J. (2007). Memory for context becomes less specific with time. *Learning & Memory, 14*(4), 313–317. http://dx.doi.org/10.1101/lm.430907.

Winocur, G., Moscovitch, M., & Bontempi, B. (2010). Memory formation and long-term retention in humans and animals: convergence towards a transformation account of hippocampal-neocortical interactions. *Neuropsychologia, 48*(8), 2339–2356, S0028-3932(10)00162-4 10.1016/j.neuropsychologia.2010.04.016.

Winocur, G., Moscovitch, M., & Sekeres, M. (2007). Memory consolidation or transformation: context manipulation and hippocampal representations of memory. *Nature Neuroscience, 10*(5), 555–557, nn1880 10.1038/nn1880.

Winters, B. D., Tucci, M. C., & DaCosta-Furtado, M. (2009). Older and stronger object memories are selectively destabilized by reactivation in the presence of new information. *Learning & Memory, 16*(9), 545−553. http://dx.doi.org/10.1101/lm. 1509909.

Xue, Y.-X., Luo, Y.-X., Wu, P., Shi, H.-S., Xue, L.-F., Chen, C., & Lu, L. (2012). A memory retrieval-extinction procedure to prevent drug craving and relapse. *Science, 336*(6078), 241−245. http://dx.doi.org/10.1126/science.1215070.

Yehuda, R., Tischler, L., Golier, J. A., Grossman, R., Brand, S. R., Kaufman, S., & Harvey, P. D. (2006). Longitudinal assessment of cognitive performance in Holocaust survivors with and without PTSD. *Biological Psychiatry, 60*(7), 714−721. http://dx. doi.org/10.1016/j.biopsych.2006.03.069.

Zhang, Y., Fukushima, H., & Kida, S. (2011). Induction and requirement of gene expression in the anterior cingulate cortex and medial prefrontal cortex for the consolidation of inhibitory avoidance memory. *Molecular Brain, 4*, 4, 1756-6606-4-4 10.1186/1756-6606-4-4.

Chapter six

Memory Reconsolidation Versus Extinction

Satoshi Kida

Tokyo University of Agriculture, Tokyo, Japan

6.1 MEMORY RECONSOLIDATION VERSUS CONSOLIDATION

Short-term memory (STM) is labile. To generate long-term memory (LTM), STM is stabilized via memory consolidation (Davis & Squire, 1984; Flexner *et al.*, 1965; McGaugh, 1966, 2000). Memory consolidation is thought of as a process of storage; that is, memories become increasingly immune to disruption as they mature (McGaugh, 1966). Importantly, studies show that inhibiting protein synthesis around the time of learning blocks the formation of LTM without affecting STM, indicating that the formation of LTM, but not STM, depends on gene expression (Abel *et al.*, 1997; Kida *et al.*, 2002; Suzuki *et al.*, 2004). Therefore, the critical biochemical feature of memory consolidation is a requirement for gene expression (Abel *et al.*, 1997; Davis & Squire, 1984; Flexner *et al.*, 1965; McGaugh, 2000).

There is increasing evidence that memory retrieval initiates a dynamic process that either reinforces or alters consolidated memories (Anokhin *et al.*, 2002; Judge & Quartermain, 1982; Lewis, 1979; Mactutus *et al.*, 1979; Misanin *et al.*, 1968; Nader *et al.*, 2000a; Pedreira *et al.*, 2002; Przybyslawski *et al.*, 1997, 1999; Sara, 2000; Schneider & Sherman, 1968). Studies show that blocking gene expression with inhibitors of translation or transcription disrupts long-term post-reactivated memory without affecting short-term post-reactivated memories (Debiec *et al.*, 2002; Kida *et al.*, 2002; Nader *et al.*, 2000a; Suzuki *et al.*, 2004; Taubenfeld *et al.*, 2001;). This experimental evidence suggests that following retrieval, the retrieved memory is first destabilized, returning to a labile state similar to STM, and then restabilized through gene-expression-dependent memory reconsolidation for re-storage (Debiec *et al.*, 2002; Kida *et al.*, 2002; Nader *et al.*, 2000a; Taubenfeld *et al.*, 2001). Memory reconsolidation is thought to serve to update or integrate new information into long-term memories (Dudai, 2002; Nader *et al.*, 2000b; Sara, 2000). **119**

Memory Reconsolidation. http://dx.doi.org/10.1016/B978-0-12-386892-3.00006-8

The majority of these studies used conditioned fear to examine reconsolidation (Anokhin *et al.*, 2002; Debiec *et al.*, 2002; Kida *et al.*, 2002; Kraus *et al.*, 2002; Milekic & Alberini, 2002; Nader *et al.*, 2000a; Pedreira *et al.*, 2002; Taubenfeld *et al.*, 2001). Further studies extended these observations and showed that nearly all types of memory, including spatial memory, object recognition memory, cocaine-seeking behavior, incentive memory, and conditioned place preference, undergo reconsolidation following retrieval (Eisenberg *et al.*, 2003; Lee *et al.*, 2005; Miller *et al.*, 2005; Milton *et al.*, 2008; Rossato *et al.*, 2007; Suzuki *et al.*, 2004; Tronel *et al.*, 2005; Wang *et al.*, 2005; but see Blum *et al.*, 2006; Morris *et al.*, 2006). Moreover, the phenomenon of memory reconsolidation has been observed in all levels of animals from nematodes to crab, medaka fish, chicken, and mammals, including rodents and human (Anokin *et al.*, 2002; Eisenberg *et al.*, 2003; Pedreira *et al.*, 2002; Rose *et al.*, 2006; Sangha *et al.*, 2003a, 2003b; Walker *et al.*, 2003).

Additional studies identified some of the molecular mechanisms underlying the restabilization of reactivated memory (Duvarci *et al.*, 2005; Kida *et al.*, 2002; Lee *et al.*, 2004; Miller & Marshall, 2005; Taubenfeld *et al.*, 2001; Tronson *et al.*, 2006; von Hertzen & Giese, 2005). Restabilization engages molecular processes that are similar to, but distinct from, those of the initial consolidation. Activation of cAMP response element binding (CREB)-mediated transcription is required for both consolidation and reconsolidation of fear memory (Kida *et al.*, 2002). On the other hand, brain-derived neurotrophic factor (BDNF) and Zif268 are required in the hippocampus for consolidation and reconsolidation, respectively, of contextual fear memory (Lee *et al.*, 2004). Interestingly, CAAT/enhancer-binding protein β (C/EBPβ)-mediated transcription in hippocampus is required for consolidation, but not for reconsolidation, of inhibitory avoidance memory (Taubenfeld *et al.*, 2001); in contrast, reconsolidation of such memory requires C/EBPβ-mediated transcription in the amygdala, whereas consolidation does not (Tronel *et al.*, 2005). These findings suggest that mechanisms of memory consolidation and reconsolidation are dissociable at the molecular and anatomical levels.

6.2 MEMORY EXTINCTION VERSUS CONSOLIDATION

In Pavlovian fear conditioning, a conditioned stimulus (CS; e.g., a context) is paired with an unconditioned stimulus (US; e.g., footshock). When the animal is placed back in the conditioned context, it displays conditioned fear responses such as freezing, in the absence of the US. Experimentally, cued recall typically involves re-exposing subjects to the CS without the US. This reminder initiates not only reconsolidation but also extinction in which the CS comes to predict no US and loses its ability to evoke a conditioned response (Baum, 1988; Bouton, 1993; Myers & Davis, 2002; Pavlov, 1927). Memory extinction is thought to reflect new learning of a CS—no US association that inhibits the conditioned response (Konorski, 1967; Rescorla & Heth, 1975; Rescorla, 2001; Robbins, 1990). Most important, similar to the molecular signatures of memory consolidation, extinction of fear memory was shown to be consolidated through new gene expression (Mamiya *et al.*, 2009; Quirk *et al.*, 2000; Santini *et al.*, 2004).

Extinction is thought to depend on the medial prefrontal cortex (mPFC; Morgan & LeDoux, 1995, 1999; Morgan *et al.*, 1993; Morrow *et al.*, 1999; Quirk *et al.*, 2000; Teich *et al.*, 1989) and amygdala (Herry *et al.*, 2008; Myers & Davis, 2002; Quirk *et al.*, 2000). The amygdala plays significant roles in the acquisition of tone fear extinction and consolidation of contextual fear extinction, whereas the mPFC, especially the prelimbic cortex, is implicated in its consolidation (Mamiya *et al.*, 2009; Quirk *et al.*, 2000; Santini *et al.*, 2004). Interestingly, a recent study identified a population of "extinction" neurons in the basolateral amygdala, whose activation decreases high fear behavior (Herry *et al.*, 2008).

6.3 MEMORY RECONSOLIDATION VERSUS EXTINCTION: BEHAVIORAL LEVEL

As described previously, memory retrieval initiates two opposite processes: reconsolidation and extinction. Reconsolidation may serve to strengthen or modify the existing memory trace, whereas extinction involves the formation of an inhibitory memory that competes with the original memory. Several studies have examined whether a single retrieval session (re-exposure to the CS without the US) induces memory reconsolidation or extinction using behavioral paradigms in which animals learn a CS–US association. A few examples are described here.

6.3.1 Contextual fear memory in mice

In contextual fear conditioning (Kim & Fanselow, 1992), mice receive electrical footshocks (US) in the conditioned chamber (CS). Upon re-exposure to the conditioned chamber, they retrieve contextual fear memory and display freezing responses. In this paradigm, 24 hr after conditioning with a single electrical footshock (0.4 mA), short re-exposure to the CS (3 min; placed back in the conditioning context) triggers memory reconsolidation (Figure 6.1A). The inhibition of protein synthesis with a systemic injection of protein synthesis inhibitor (anisomycin (ANI)) before or immediately after this re-exposure disrupts the retrieved fear memory (Figure 6.1B). In contrast, longer re-exposure to the CS (30 min) triggers extinction of contextual fear memory (Figure 6.1A). The inhibition of protein synthesis before or immediately after this re-exposure blocks consolidation of extinction memory (long-term extinction) while leaving the contextual fear memory unaffected (Figure 6.1B; Suzuki *et al.*, 2004). Importantly, inducible inhibition of CREB-mediated transcription in forebrain also demonstrated effects similar to those following the inhibition of protein synthesis by ANI; the inhibition of CREB-mediated transcription before and after the re-exposure to the CS for 3 or 30 min blocked reconsolidation and long-term extinction, respectively (Figure 6.1C; Kida *et al.*, 2002; Mamiya *et al.*, 2009). These observations indicated the temporal dynamics determining the fate of retrieved memory at the behavioral level; reconsolidation and extinction are not induced independently following memory retrieval.

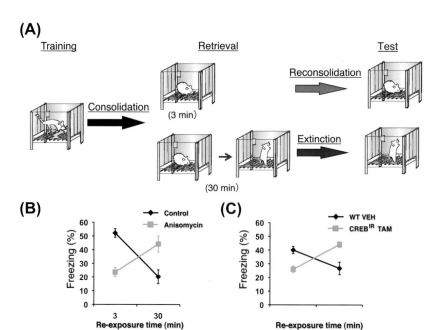

FIGURE 6.1 Reconsolidation and extinction of contextual fear memory after retrieval. (A) Reconsolidation and extinction are initiated by re-exposure to the conditioned context (CS) 24 hr after contextual fear conditioning. Effects of inhibiting protein synthesis (B; Suzuki et al., 2004) and CREB-mediated transcription (C; Mamiya et al., 2009) are summarized. Inhibition of protein synthesis via anisomycin or CREB-mediated transcription (Kida et al., 2002) blocked reconsolidation and long-term extinction induced by short (3 min) and long (30 min) re-exposure, respectively, to the CS. Error bars are SEM (*n* = 9–12).

6.3.2 Context-signal memory in crab

In the *Chasmagnathus* model of context–signal memory (CSM; Pedreira & Maldonado, 2003; see also Chapter 7), the crab learns an association between the training context (CS) and a visual danger stimulus (VDS) (US; the features, such as an opaque rectangle, passing overhead). After the conditioning, consisting of multiple representations of VDS in the context, the crab displays strong freezing responses to the VDS in the training context but not the escape responses that it displayed before the conditioning. Similar to the results of contextual fear memory in mice, short re-exposure to the training context (<1 hr) triggers reconsolidation of the CSM. Inhibiting protein synthesis with cycloheximide (CHX) disrupted CSM; following the re-exposure session with protein synthesis inhibition, the crab that received CHX displays escape, but not freezing, responses to the VDS in the context, as it responded to the VDS before the conditioning. In contrast, longer re-exposure to the CS (>1 hr) results in extinction of the CSM. Inhibiting protein synthesis blocks CSM extinction while leaving CSM unaffected; following re-exposure, the crab that received CHX displayed freezing, but not escape, responses to the VDS in the context, as it responded to the VDS after the conditioning. Importantly, further studies using crab/CMS paradigms showed that CS offset (termination of re-exposure to the CS) is required to induce reconsolidation (destabilization followed by restabilization) and extinction following the re-exposure to the CS for a short or longer time, respectively (Pedreira & Maldonado, 2003; Pedreira *et al.*, 2004; Perez-Cuesta *et al.*, 2007). For example, studies showed that CS offset followed by re-exposure to the training context for 120 min triggered the acquisition of CSM extinction and that, interestingly, this CMS extinction acquisition was completed in less than 45 sec, but not 27 sec, after CS offset (Perez-Cuesta *et al.*, 2007).

6.3.3 Fear conditioning in medaka fish

In the fear conditioning of medaka fish (Eisenberg *et al.*, 2003), the fish is conditioned to learn an association between light (CS) and mild electrical shock (US). After the conditioning, the fish displays a fear response (change in locomotion; conditioned response) when re-exposed to the CS. Similar to observations in mice and crabs, a single retrieval session of re-exposure to the CS without the US triggers reconsolidation of fear memory, whereas repeated re-exposure to the CS ($10 \times$ CS) triggers memory extinction. Treatment of conditioned fish with an anesthetic drug (MS222) after a single or 10 retrieval trials disrupted retrieved fear memory and blocked fear memory extinction, respectively (Eisenberg *et al.*, 2003). Thus, retrieval duration-dependent induction of either reconsolidation or extinction is observed in medaka fish as well as in mice and crabs.

6.3.4 Conditioned taste aversion in rats

In conditioned taste aversion (CTA; Bures *et al.*, 1988), rodents learn an association between taste (CS; e.g., saccharin) and delayed visceral malaise following a single systemic injection of LiCl. In contrast to the previous observations, a study using rats showed that a single retrieval trial of re-exposure to the CS (saccharin) without the US 24 hr after a single training session is enough to trigger extinction of the CTA-memory (Eisenberg *et al.*, 2003). On the other hand, the same single retrieval trial 24 hr after intensive training consisting of two training sessions triggered reconsolidation of CTA-memory. Indeed, 24 hr following one or two (intensive) training sessions, inhibition of protein synthesis in the insular cortex by a microinfusion of ANI immediately after the retrieval trial blocked long-term extinction, while leaving the original CTA memory unaffected, and disrupted retrieved CTA-memory, respectively (Eisenberg *et al.*, 2003). These observations suggest that in this paradigm, whether disruption of protein synthesis at the time of retrieval disrupts the original CTA memory trace or extinction memory trace depends on the dominance of the memory trace.

6.3.5 Spatial memory in rodents

In the Morris water maze task (Morris, 1984), rodents learn the position of a hidden platform in a water pool and form a spatial memory for the platform position during training sessions. In the probe trial, in which the hidden platform is removed, rodents retrieve the spatial memory by searching for the missing platform. A study using mice showed that a single retrieval (probe) trial 24 hr after the last training session triggers reconsolidation of the spatial memory formed by training for 6 trials/day for 2 days, whereas 10 retrieval trials at 1-min intervals 24 hr after the last training trial triggers extinction of this memory (Suzuki *et al.*, 2004). Moreover, inhibiting protein synthesis by a systemic injection of ANI before a single or 10 retrieval sessions disrupted the retrieved spatial memory or blocked extinction consolidation without affecting the original spatial memory, respectively (Suzuki *et al.*, 2004). It is important to note that further study has shown that the reconsolidation of spatial memory under these experimental conditions depends on new gene expression in the hippocampus (Kim *et al.*, 2011). Thus, retrieval duration-dependent induction of either reconsolidation or extinction is observed not only in fear conditioning paradigms but also in nonconditioning paradigms, such as spatial memory.

However, in contrast to the results using mice, a study using rats showed that when spatial memory was retrieved in a single probe test 72 hr after the last training trial, a microinfusion of ANI into the hippocampus failed to disrupt the retrieved spatial memory formed by training trials consisting of 4 trials/day for 6 days (Morris *et al.*, 2006). Furthermore, the same microinfusion of ANI into the hippocampus following 8 probe trials also failed to block extinction consolidation of spatial memory. However, the same infusion of ANI into the hippocampus disrupted the retrieved spatial memory formed by a delayed matching-to-place training, consisting of 4 trials/day for 6 days (the position of the platform was changed every day), when the spatial memory was retrieved 72 hr after the last training trial (Morris *et al.*, 2006). These results suggest that the reconsolidation of spatial memory is induced in the hippocampus only when new information is encoded at the time of memory retrieval. Thus, the retrieval duration-dependent induction of either reconsolidation or extinction observed in mice was not observed in rats. However, it is possible that, as described later (stronger memory is immune to amnesic effects of protein synthesis inhibition), differences in the memory strengths between the two studies (total of 12 training trials in mice vs. a total of 24 training trials in rats) strongly affected the stability of spatial memories after retrieval. In addition, these observations do not exclude the possibility that reconsolidation and extinction of spatial memory require new gene expression in regions other than the hippocampus because another study showed that extinction consolidation of hippocampus-dependent contextual fear memory depends on new gene expression in mPFC but not hippocampus (Mamiya *et al.*, 2009).

6.4 RELATIONSHIP BETWEEN RECONSOLIDATION AND EXTINCTION AT THE BEHAVIORAL LEVEL: INTERACTION OF TWO MEMORY PHASES

As described previously, except for cued fear memory in rats (Duvarci *et al.*, 2006), memory reconsolidation and extinction are not induced simultaneously after retrieval. The initiation of either reconsolidation or extinction depends, in part, on the duration of the retrieval episode; reconsolidation is the dominant process following shorter duration re-exposures, whereas extinction is the dominant process following longer duration re-exposures (Debiec *et al.*, 2002; Eisenberg *et al.*, 2003; Nader, 2003; Pedreira & Maldonado, 2003; Suzuki *et al.*, 2004; but see Duvarci *et al.*, 2006). Moreover, blocking protein synthesis during brief re-exposure disrupts the original memory, whereas blocking protein synthesis during longer re-exposure blocks the formation of a new extinction memory (Eisenberg *et al.*, 2003; Pedreira & Maldonado, 2003; Suzuki *et al.*, 2004). The requirement for protein synthesis in the formation of a new extinction memory is not surprising; however, the fact that inhibiting protein synthesis selectively affects the formation of the extinction memory and leaves the original memory unaffected is surprising because it is expected that both reconsolidation and extinction are initiated under these conditions. As described previously, it is important to note that this relationship between reconsolidation and extinction of contextual fear memory was also observed when CREB-mediated-transcription was inhibited in forebrain. Thus, there might be an interaction between the phases of extinction and reconsolidation at the behavioral level; the acquisition of a new extinction memory may stabilize the original memory, thereby protecting it from being disrupted by protein synthesis inhibition.

In addition, as described previously, studies using crab have shown that the CS offset is critical for the induction of reconsolidation or extinction following re-exposure to the CS for a short or longer time, respectively (Pedreira *et al.*, 2004; Perez-Cuesta *et al.*, 2007). These observations suggest that CS offset as well as the duration of re-exposure to the CS act as switches determining reconsolidation or extinction after retrieval.

6.5 RELATIONSHIP BETWEEN RECONSOLIDATION AND EXTINCTION: ANATOMICAL LEVEL

The extinction consolidation of tone fear memory requires protein synthesis and NMDA receptor-dependent bursting in the mPFC (Burgos-Robles *et al.*, 2007; Santini *et al.*, 2004). On the other hand, reconsolidation of fear memories is mediated by the amygdala (Nader *et al.*, 2000a) and the hippocampus (Debiec *et al.*, 2002). To compare the mechanisms responsible for reconsolidation and extinction of contextual fear memory at the anatomical level, brain regions activated during these two processes were analyzed (Mamiya *et al.*, 2009). Because CREB-mediated transcription is required for reconsolidation and extinction of contextual fear memory (Mamiya *et al.*, 2009), the activity of CREB (i.e., the level of CREB phosphorylation at Serine 133) was measured following brief (3 min) or prolonged (30 min) re-exposure to the conditioning context, which induces reconsolidation or extinction, respectively (Figure 6.2). When mice were briefly re-exposed to the context, CREB activity was increased in the hippocampus and the amygdala but not in the mPFC.

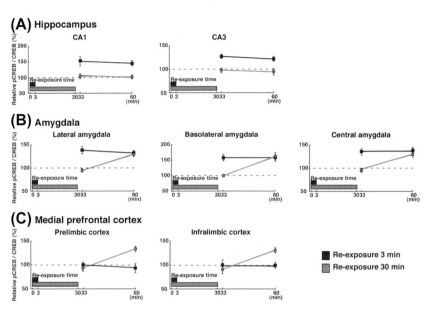

FIGURE 6.2 Regulation of CREB activity in the hippocampus, amygdala, and mPFC during the reconsolidation and extinction phases of contextual fear memory. Time course of CREB activation in the hippocampus (A), amygdala (B), and mPFC (C) from the beginning of the reconsolidation (3 min) and extinction (30 min) re-exposure to the context (using the identical time schedule) 24 hr after the contextual fear conditioning (Mamiya et al., 2009). Error bars are SEM ($n = 9-11$). CREB activation (relative pCREB/CREB levels) was calculated by normalizing the number of phosphorylated CREB (pCREB)-positive cells to the total number of CREB-positive cells. Data for CREB activation for each group were then expressed as percentages of the averaged values in the control group (dashed lines at 100%) that were exposed and re-exposed to the training context without receiving the electrical footshocks (no US).

Consistent with this, pharmacological studies using the microinfusion of ANI into these brain regions indicated that reconsolidation of the contextual fear memory depends on new gene expression in the hippocampus and amygdala but not in the mPFC (Mamiya *et al.*, 2009). In contrast, following prolonged re-exposure to the context (30 min), CREB activity was increased in the amygdala and the mPFC but not in the hippocampus. Likewise, pharmacological studies indicated that extinction consolidation of contextual fear memory depends on new gene expression in the mPFC and amygdala but not the hippocampus (Mamiya *et al.*, 2009). These observations extend behavioral observations showing that re-exposure to the CS triggers two distinct, time-dependent processes—reconsolidation and extinction—and indicate that these processes are dissociable at the anatomical level.

Restabilization of retrieved contextual fear memory requires new gene expression in the hippocampus (Debiec *et al.*, 2002; Mamiya *et al.*, 2009; Suzuku *et al.*, 2008). In contrast, inhibiting protein synthesis in the hippocampus did not affect extinction consolidation (Mamiya *et al.*, 2009), suggesting that new protein synthesis in the hippocampus does not contribute to the extinction consolidation. These contrasting observations suggest that the hippocampus plays distinct roles in reconsolidation and extinction of contextual fear memory. Interestingly, the hippocampus plays critical roles in the extinction of contextual fear. Indeed, cyclin-dependent kinase-5 (cdk5) signaling, activation of proteasome-dependent protein degradation, activation of CB1 receptors, and actin rearrangement in the hippocampus are required for extinction of contextual fear memory (de Oliveira Alvares *et al.*, 2008; Fischer *et al.*, 2004; Lee *et al.*, 2008; Sananbenesi *et al.*, 2007). Therefore, it is possible that the hippocampus regulates contextual fear extinction through activation of these pathways without activating gene expression. Suppression of gene expression in the hippocampus might be a critical step leading to long-term extinction. Further studies are required to investigate the regulatory roles of the hippocampus in memory extinction.

Studies showed that gene expression was activated in the amygdala during both reconsolidation and extinction phases (Herry & Mons, 2004; Herry *et al.*, 2008; Mamiya *et al.*, 2009). However, the observation that the time course of amygdaloid CREB activation differed during the reconsolidation and extinction phases of contextual fear memory (Figure 6.1B; Mamiya *et al.*, 2009) raises the possibility that distinct populations of amygdaloid neurons are activated during these phases. Consistent with this, Reijmers *et al.* (2007) demonstrated that retrieval of a contextual fear memory reactivates basolateral amygdaloid neurons that are activated during contextual fear conditioning, whereas extinction learning prevents their activation. Furthermore, two distinct populations of these neurons (fear and extinction neurons) were identified, whose activities were reversely correlated with low and high fear behavior (Herry *et al.*, 2008). Therefore, it is important to examine whether identical or different populations of neurons are activated in the reconsolidation and extinction phases of contextual fear memory.

6.6 RELATIONSHIPS BETWEEN RECONSOLIDATION AND EXTINCTION AT THE MOLECULAR LEVEL

6.6.1 Molecular signatures shared by reconsolidation and extinction: Do similar molecular mechanisms underlie memory reconsolidation and extinction?

The observation that there is an interaction between the reconsolidation and extinction phases of contextual fear memory at the behavioral level raises the possibility that molecular processes engaged during extinction may also regulate the stability of the original memory trace (reconsolidation) after retrieval. Recent pharmacological and mouse genetics studies indicate that the downstream signaling transduction pathways involving L-type voltage-gated calcium channel (LVGCC), cannabinoid receptor 1 (CB1), cdk5 signaling, NMDA glutamate receptor (NMDAR), activation of the ubiquitin-proteasomal pathway, actin rearrangement, and BDNF are required for extinction of fear memory (de Oliveira Alvares *et al.*, 2008; Fischer *et al.*, 2004; Lee *et al.*, 2008; Marsicano *et al.*, 2002; Peters *et al.*, 2010; Sananbenesi *et al.*, 2007).

Abundant studies have focused on investigating the mechanisms for restabilizing (reconsolidating) retrieved memories (Duvarci *et al.*, 2005; Kida *et al.*, 2002; Lee *et al.*, 2004; Miller & Marshall, 2005; Taubenfeld *et al.*, 2001; Tronson *et al.*, 2006). In contrast, the molecular mechanisms underlying the initial destabilization remain poorly understood. A report demonstrated the importance of activating NMDAR in the destabilization of retrieved cued fear memory (Ben Mamou *et al.*, 2006). Ben Mamou *et al.* showed that blocking the NMDAR but not the AMPA glutamate receptor in the amygdala inhibited the disruption of reactivated cued fear memory induced by protein synthesis inhibitors. This evidence indicates that activating the NMDAR triggers the induction of destabilization of retrieved memory. Interestingly, another study showed that the destabilization of retrieved contextual fear memory requires the activation of protein degradation via the proteasome in the hippocampus (Lee *et al.*, 2008), suggesting that retrieved memory is destabilized via protein degradation, thereby requiring protein synthesis-dependent restabilization (reconsolidation). Studies also indicated that the activation of LVGCC and CB1 is required for destabilizing contextual fear memory following its retrieval (Suzuki *et al.*, 2008). Similar to the blockade of NMDARs or proteasome-dependent protein degradation, Suzuki *et al.* also showed that pharmacological blockade of these molecules protected retrieved memories from the amnestic effects of protein synthesis inhibition. Collectively, these findings suggest the existence of an active process inducing the destabilization of reactivated memory at the molecular level.

Thus, the activation of LVGCCs, CB1s, and proteasome-dependent protein degradation are required for extinction of contextual fear memory (Cain *et al.*, 2002; Lee *et al.*, 2008; Marsicano *et al.*, 2002; Suzuki *et al.*, 2004), whereas these signal transduction pathways are also required in the hippocampus for the destabilization of retrieved contextual fear memory (Lee *et al.*, 2008; Suzuki *et al.*, 2004, 2008). These findings suggest that molecular processes involved in fear extinction in the hippocampus also regulate the stability of the original fear memory after retrieval; the regulations of reconsolidation (destabilization) and extinction of the retrieved fear memory share similar molecular mechanisms—activation of LVGCCs, CB1, NMDAR, and proteasome-dependent protein degradation. Furthermore, these findings suggest that memory retrieval triggers the activation of LVGCCs, CB1 receptors, and proteosome-dependent protein degradation, leading to destabilization and/or extinction of contextual fear memory, and they support the interaction between reconsolidation and extinction at the molecular level. Therefore, it is important to evaluate whether acquisition of contextual fear extinction prevents the destabilization of retrieved memory or whether the original contextual fear memory is destabilized and then restabilized (inactivated) in the extinction phase in a gene expression-independent manner (e.g., the redistribution or relocalization of pre-existing proteins).

Importantly, to further understand the roles of signal molecules regulating memory destabilization and extinction, it is necessary to characterize "destabilized memory" at the molecular, synaptic, and cellular levels. Furthermore, studies are required to investigate at the cellular level whether the destabilization and extinction of contextual fear memory are induced in the same neuronal populations or different ones.

6.6.2 Interaction of reconsolidation and extinction phases at the molecular level

As described previously, differences in CREB activity during the reconsolidation and extinction phases identified the hippocampus and the amygdala as candidate anatomical loci for the interaction between these two processes at the molecular level (Figure 6.2; Mamiya *et al.*, 2009). First, an increase in CREB activity was observed in the hippocampus following short, but not longer, re-exposure to the CS (Figure 6.2A), suggesting that gene expression in the hippocampus undergoes distinct regulation in the reconsolidation and extinction phases. The observation that CREB-mediated gene expression was not induced in the extinction phase, even though contextual fear memory was retrieved, indicates that such induction must be actively suppressed when within-session extinction occurs. Second, differences in the time courses of CREB activation in the amygdala were observed in the reconsolidation and extinction phases (Figure 6.2B), indicating that amygdaloid CREB activation is differentially regulated in these two memory phases and also that the amygdaloid CREB activation observed in the extinction phase is not simply due to fear memory reactivation. Moreover, inhibition of protein synthesis in the amygdala following prolonged re-exposure blocked long-term extinction without affecting the subsequent expression of the original fear memory, whereas such inhibition following brief re-exposure disrupted the fear memory. Collectively, this evidence suggests that the interaction between the reconsolidation and extinction phases occurs in both the hippocampus and the amygdala at the molecular level.

Observations that the phosphorylation of CREB at S133 is increased or actively inhibited in the hippocampus in the reconsolidation and extinction phases, respectively, of contextual fear memory raise the possibility that hippocampal regulation of CREB activity, involving dephosphorylation as well as phosphorylation of CREB S133, functions as a critical molecular switch to determine the fate of memory: reconsolidation or extinction. Interestingly, a recent study investigated molecular cascades regulating the induction of either reconsolidation or extinction phases of contextual fear memory in the hippocampus (de la Fuente *et al.*, 2011). In the reconsolidation phase induced by a short re-exposure (5 min) to the conditioning context, the transcription factor nuclear factor-κB (NF-κB) was activated in the hippocampus. Consistently, hippocampal inhibition of NF-κB activation in the reconsolidation phase disrupted retrieved contextual fear memory. These observations indicated that, consistent with a previous report (Lubin & Sweatt, 2007), activation of NF-κB is required for reconsolidation of contextual fear memory. More important, similar to the regulation of CREB in the hippocampus after retrieval of contextual fear memory, the activation of NF-κB observed in the reconsolidation phase was not observed in the extinction phase induced by prolonged re-exposure (30 min) to the context. Taken together, these findings suggest that within-session extinction actively prevents the hippocampal activation of transcription factors, including CREB and NF-κB, that are required for reconsolidation of contextual fear memory.

Interestingly, the same study suggests that calcineurin, which positively and negatively regulates the transcription factor nuclear factor of activated T cells (NFAT) and NF-κB, respectively, plays a critical role as a molecular switch in the transition from reconsolidation to extinction phases (de la Fuente et al., 2011). In the extinction phases induced by prolonged re-exposure to the conditioning context (30 min), the activity of NF-κB was inhibited and, conversely, translocalization of NFAT into the nucleus was facilitated. Consistent with this, the inhibition of calcineurin or NFAT in the extinction phase blocked extinction consolidation of contextual fear. Interestingly, the inhibition of NF-κB enhanced extinction of contextual fear memory, supporting the role of calcinuerin as an upstream negative regulator of NF-κB in the induction of memory extinction. Further studies are required to investigate whether hippocampal regulations of CREB and calcineurin signal transductions required for the regulation of retrieved fear memory occur in the same neuronal populations or different ones and the possibility of cross talk between CREB and calcineurin signal transductions after retrieval of contextual fear memory.

6.7 PARAMETERS AFFECTING MEMORY RECONSOLIDATION AND EXTINCTION

The phenomenon of reconsolidation raises a fundamental question: Does memory always become labile following retrieval? Several studies have examined this question. Twenty-four hours after contextual fear conditioning, inhibiting protein synthesis along with re-exposure to the context (3 min) disrupted retrieved fear memory, indicating that this duration of fear memory retrieval induces memory reconsolidation (Kida et al., 2002; Suzuki et al., 2004). In contrast, inhibiting protein synthesis along with a shorter contextual re-exposure (1 min) failed to disrupt retrieved fear memory, even though the mice displayed fear memory retrieval (high levels of freezing behavior; Suzuki et al., 2004). These observations indicate that brief retrieval leaves the original memory unaffected and that the important variable that determines the stability of a retrieved memory is the duration of its retrieval.

Whereas the initial encoding and storage of fear memories depend on the hippocampus, permanent storage is thought to depend on the neocortex (Anagnostaras et al., 1999, 2001; Eichenbaum et al., 1994; Frankland et al., 2001; Kim & Fanselow, 1992; LeDoux, 2000; McClelland et al., 1995; McGaugh, 2000; Quevedo et al., 1999; Squire & Alvarez, 1995). Studies demonstrated that retrieved remote memories (~28 days) of inhibitory avoidance and contextual fear in rodents were resistant to the inhibition of protein synthesis (Eisenberg & Dudai, 2004; Milekic & Alberini, 2002; Suzuki *et al.*, 2004; but see Debiec *et al.*, 2002), indicating that another important variable that determines the stability of a retrieved memory is its age.

Similar to the features of remote memory, stronger memories are more resistant to reconsolidation than weaker memories. For example, retrieved contextual fear memory conditioned by three footshocks, but not a single footshock, was immune to the disruptive effects of protein synthesis inhibition (Suzuki *et al.*, 2004). A similar observation was made when strong cued (tone) fear memory formed after 10 pairings of the CS–US was tested (Wang *et al.*, 2009). These findings suggest that an additional important variable that determines the stability of a retrieved memory is its strength.

Thus, boundary conditions affecting the induction of reconsolidation have been identified; re-exposure duration, the age of the memory, and the strength of the memory influence the stability of retrieved memory in tasks that model declarative memory. These observations also indicate that memory does not always become labile when retrieved.

Further investigations of the boundary conditions for inducing reconsolidation demonstrated that even strong or old memories of contextual fear undergo reconsolidation with longer re-exposure (Suzuki *et al.*, 2004). The retrieval of strong or old memories induced memory reconsolidation when mice were re-exposed to the conditioning context (CS) for 10 min but not for 3 min. Re-exposure to the context for 10 min, but not for 3 min, along with the inhibition of protein synthesis disrupted both reactivated strong and remote contextual fear memories, whereas re-exposure to the context for only 3 min in the presence of protein inhibitors, which was sufficient to disrupt reactivated weak and recent memories, did not.

Importantly, these parameters (durations of memory retrieval and the strength and age of memory) also affect the induction of memory extinction. The extinction acquisition of stronger and older contextual fear memory requires more duration of re-exposure to the conditioning context (Suzuki and Kida, unpublished results). Interestingly, a recent study demonstrated that repeated retrieval (three times) of inhibitory avoidance memory by re-exposure to the light compartment (10 sec per day every 2 days) leads to memory strengthening when the memory is recent but leads to memory extinction when it is remote, suggesting that the age of memory has a major impact on the fate of the memory (Inda *et al.*, 2011). Therefore, it is important to investigate whether these parameters affect interaction of reconsolidation and extinction phases at the anatomical, cellular, and molecular levels.

6.8 CLINICAL IMPORTANCE OF UNDERSTANDING THE RELATIONSHIPS BETWEEN RECONSOLIDATION AND EXTINCTION FOR THE TREATMENT OF EMOTIONAL DISORDERS

The finding that LTM may be more dynamic and plastic than previously thought may have important clinical implications for the treatment of emotional disorders (Delgado *et al.*, 2008; Phelps & LeDoux, 2005; Rauch *et al.*, 2006).

Understanding the circumstances in which maladaptive memories become plastic (and modifiable) is of clear clinical relevance. As described previously, studies have shown that LVGCCs, CB1, and protein degradation via proteasome-dependent processes are all important in weakening (destabilizing and extinguishing) fear memories (Lee et al., 2008; Marsicano et al., 2002; Suzuki et al., 2004, 2008). Thus, they might serve as useful therapeutic targets for the treatment of conditions such as post-traumatic stress disorder (PTSD) and phobias. On the other hand, exposure therapy for the treatment of such emotional disorders as PTSD is thought to reflect some aspect of the biological basis of memory extinction (Delgado et al., 2008; Phelps & LeDoux, 2005; Rauch et al., 2006). Thus, blocking the reconsolidation and facilitation of extinction are thought to be candidates for reducing acquired fear that leads to emotional disorders.

Interestingly, a study using rats showed that a systemic injection or intra-amygdala (basolateral amygdala) infusion of a partial NMDAR agonist D-cycloserine before short (1 min) or long re-exposure (1 min $\times$ 10 times at 1-min intervals) to the CS (tone) potentiated retrieved cued fear memory and extinction of this memory, respectively; whether the same drug enhances or weakens cued fear memory depends on the duration of memory retrieval (Lee et al., 2006). These observations emphasize the importance of estimating whether the status of memory is in reconsolidation or extinction phases when clinical treatments, such as exposure therapy combined with drugs such as D-cycloserine, are performed. Therefore, from a clinical perspective, it is also important to understand the mechanisms by which retrieved memory is reconsolidated or extinguished at the molecular level.

6.9 SUMMARY

Memory retrieval initiates two opposite processes: reconsolidation and extinction. Reconsolidation is a process to maintain or enhance retrieved memory, whereas memory extinction tends to weaken the original memory. Memory reconsolidation and extinction are not independent processes; rather, abundant evidence suggests that these phases interact with one another at behavioral as well as anatomical and molecular levels. Importantly, studies using amnesic drugs or transgenic mice suggest that the acquisition of extinction (within-session extinction) seems to leave the original memory unaffected; the original memory is immune to amnesic treatment even though this memory is retrieved. Because memory extinction is thought to be a new learning or updating of a fear episode, understanding the mechanisms by which the original memory is inactivated when memory extinction is acquired may open windows to understanding the fundamental mechanisms for updating memory.

REFERENCES

Abel, T., Nguye, P. V., Barad, M., Deuel, T. A., Kandel, E. R., & Bourtchouladze, R. (1997). Genetic demonstration of a role for PKA in the late phase of LTP and in hippocampus-based long-term memory. *Cell, 88*, 615–626.

Anagnostaras, S. G., Maren, S., & Fanselow, M. S. (1999). Temporally graded retrograde amnesia of contextual fear after hippocampus damage in rat: within-subjects examination. *Journal of Neuroscience, 19*, 1106—1114.

Anagnostaras, S. G., Gale, G. D., & Fanselow, M. S. (2001). Hippocampus and contextual fear conditioning: recent controversies and advances. *Hippocampus, 11*, 8—17.

Anokhin, K. V., Tiunova, A. A., & Rose, S. P. R. (2002). Reminder effects—Reconsolidation or retrieval deficit? Pharmacological dissection with protein synthesis inhibitors following reminder for a passive-avoidance task in young chicks. *European Journal of Neuroscience, 15*, 1759—1765.

Baum, M. (1988). Spontaneous recovery from the effects of flooding (exposure) in animals. *Behaviour Research and Therapy, 26*, 185—186.

Ben Mamou, C., Gamache, K., & Nader, K. (2006). NMDA receptors are critical for unleashing consolidated auditory fear memories. *Nat. Neurosci., 9*, 1237—9.

Blum, S., Runyans, J. D., & Dash, P. K. (2006). Inhibition of prefrontal protein synthesis following recall does not disrupt memory for trace fear conditioning. *BMC Neuroscience, 7*, 67.

Bouton, M. E. (1993). Context, time, and memory retrieval in the interference paradigms of Pavlovian learning. *Psychological Bulletin, 114*, 80—99.

Bures, J., Buresova, O., & Krivanek, J. (1988). *Brain and behavior: Paradigms for research in neural mechanisms.* New York: Wiley.

Burgos-Robles, A., Vidal-Gonzalez, I., Santini, E., & Quirk, G. J. (2007). Consolidation of fear extinction requires NMDA receptor-dependent bursting in the ventromedial prefrontal cortex. *Neuron, 53*, 871—880.

Cain, C., Blouin, A., & Barad, M. G. (2002). L-type voltage-gated calcium channels are required for extinction, but not for acquisition or expression, of conditioned fear in mice. *Journal of Neuroscience, 22*, 9113—9121.

Davis, H. P., & Squire, L. R. (1984). Protein synthesis and memory. *Psychological Bulletin, 96*, 518—559.

Debiec, J., LeDoux, J. E., & Nader, K. (2002). Cellular and systems reconsolidation in the hippocampus. *Neuron, 36*, 527—538.

Delgado, M. R., Nearing, K. I., Ledoux, J. E., & Phelps, E. A. (2008). Neural circuitry underlying the regulation of conditioned fear and its relation to extinction. *Neuron, 59*, 829—838.

de la Fuente, V., Freudenthal, R., & Romano, A. (2011). Reconsolidation or extinction: transcription factor switch in the determination of memory course after retrieval. *Journal of Neuroscience, 31*, 5562—5573.

de Oliveira Alvares, L., Pasqualini Genro, B., Diehl, F., Molina, V. A., & Quillfeldt, J. A. (2008). Opposite action of hippocampal CB1 receptors in memory reconsolidation and extinction. *Neuroscience, 154*, 1648—1655.

Dudai, Y. (2002). Molecular bases of long-term memories: a question of persistence. *Current Opinion in Neurobiology, 12*, 211—216.

Duvarci, S., Mamou, C. B., & Nader, K. (2006). Extinction is not a sufficient condition to prevent fear memories from undergoing reconsolidation in the basolateral amygdala. *European Journal of Neuroscience, 24*, 249—260.

Duvarci, S., Nader, K., & LeDoux, J. E. (2005). Activation of extracellular signal-regulated kinase-/mitogen-activated protein kinase cascade in the amygdala is required for memory reconsolidation of auditory fear conditioning. *Eur. J. Neurosci., 21*, 283—289.

Eichenbaum, H., Otto, T., & Cohen, N. J. (1994). Two functional components of the hippocampal memory system. *Behavioral and Brain Sciences, 17*, 449—518.

Eisenberg, M., Kobilo, T., Berman, D. E., & Dudai, Y. (2003). Stability of retrieved memory: inverse correlation with trace dominance. *Science, 301*, 1102—1104.

Eisenberg, M., & Dudai, Y. (2004). Reconsolidation of fresh, remote, and extinguished fear memory in Medaka: old fears don't die. *European Journal of Neuroscience, 20*, 3397—3403.

Fischer, A., Sananbenesi, F., Schrick, C., Spiess, J., & Rdulovic, J. (2004). Distinct roles of hippocampal *de novo* protein synthesis and actin rearrangement in extinction of contextual fear. *Journal of Neuroscience, 24*, 1962—1966.

Flexner, L. B., Flexner, J. B., & Stellar, E. (1965). Memory and cerebral protein synthesis in mice as affected by graded amounts of puromycin. *Experimental Neurology, 13*, 264−272.

Frankland, P. W., O'Brien, C., Ohno, M., Kirkwood, A., & Silva, A. J. (2001). Alpha-CaMKII-dependent plasticity in the cortex is required for permanent memory. *Nature, 411*, 309−313.

Herry, C., & Mons, N. (2004). Resistance to extinction is associated with impaired immediate early gene induction in medial prefrontal cortex and amygdala. *European Journal of Neuroscience, 20*, 781−790.

Herry, C., Ciocchi, S., Senn, V., Demmou, L., Muller, C., & Luthi, A. (2008). Switching on and off fear by distinct neuronal circuits. *Nature, 454*, 600−606.

Inda, M. C., Muravieva, E. V., & Alberini, C. M. (2011). Memory retrieval and the passage of time; From reconsolidation and strengthening to extinction. *Journal of Neuroscience, 31*, 1635−1643.

Judge, M. E., & Quartermain, D. (1982). Alleviation of anisomycin-induced amnesia by pretest treatment with lysine-vasopressin. *Pharmacology Biochemistry and Behavior, 16*, 463−466.

Kida, S., Josselyn, S. A., deOrtiz, S. P., Kogan, J. H., Chevere, I., Masushige, S., & Silva, A. J. (2002). CREB required for the stability of new and reactivated fear memories. *Nature Neuroscience, 5*, 348−355.

Kim, J. J., & Fanselow, M. S. (1992). Modality-specific retrograde amnesia of fear. *Science, 256*, 675−677.

Kim, R., Moki, R., & Kida, S. (2011). Molecular mechanisms for the destabilization and restabilization of reactivated spatial memory in the Morris water maze. *Molecular Brain, 4*, 9.

Konorski, J. (1967). Some new ideas concerning the physiological mechanisms of perception. *Acta Biologiae Experimentalis. (Warsz), 27*, 147−161.

Kraus, M., Schicknick, H., Wetzel, W., Ohl, F., Staak, S., & Tischmeyer, W. (2002). Memory consolidation for the discrimination of frequency-modulated tones in Mongolian gerbils is sensitive to protein-synthesis inhibitors applied to the auditory cortex. *Learning & Memory, 9*, 293−303.

LeDoux, J. E. (2000). Emotion circuits in the brain. *Annual Review of Neuroscience, 23*, 155−184.

Lee, J. L., Di Ciano, P., Thomas, K. L., & Everitt, B. J. (2005). Disrupting reconsolidation of drug memories reduces cocaine-seeking behavior. *Neuron, 47*, 795−801.

Lee, J. L., Everitt, B. J., & Thomas, K. L. (2004). Independent cellular processes for hippocampal memory consolidation and reconsolidation. *Science, 304*, 839−843.

Lee, J. L., Milton, A. L., & Everitt, B. J. (2006). Reconsolidation and extinction of conditioned fear: inhibition and potentiation. *Journal of Neuroscience, 26*, 10051−10056.

Lee, S. H., Choi, J. H., Lee, N., Lee, H. R., Kim, J. I., Yu, N. K., Choi, S. L., Lee, S. H., Kim, H., & Kaang, B. K. (2008). Synaptic protein degradation underlies destabilization of retrieved fear memory. *Science, 319*, 1253−1256.

Lewis, D. J. (1979). Psychobiology of active and inactive memory. *Psychological Bulletin, 86*, 1054−1083.

Lubin, F. D., & Sweatt, J. D. (2007). The IkappaB kinase regulates chromatin structure during reconsolidation of conditioned fear memories. *Neuron, 55*, 942−957.

Mactutus, C. F., Riccio, D. C., & Ferek, J. M. (1979). Retrograde amnesia for old (reactivated) memory: some anomalous characteristics. *Science, 204*, 1319−1320.

Mamiya, N., Fukushima, H., Suzuki, A., Matsuyama, Z., Homma, S., Frankland, P. W., & Kida, S. (2009). Brain region-specific gene expression activation required for reconsolidation and extinction of contextual fear memory. *Journal of Neuroscience, 29*, 402−413.

Marsicano, G., Wotjak, C. T., Azad, S. C., Bisogno, T., Rammes, G., Cascio, M. G., Hermann, H., Tang, J., Hofmann, C., Zieglgansberger, W., Di Marzo, V., & Lutz, B. (2002). The endogenous cannabinoid system controls extinction of aversive memories. *Nature, 418*, 530−534.

McClelland, J. L., McNaughton, B. L., & O'Reilly, R. C. (1995). Why there are complementary learning systems in the hippocampus and neocortex: insights from the successes and failures of connectionist models of learning and memory. *Psychology Review, 102,* 419−457.

McGaugh, J. L. (1966). Time-dependent processes in memory storage. *Science, 153,* 1351−1358.

McGaugh, J. L. (2000). Memory—a century of consolidation. *Science, 287,* 248−251.

Milekic, M. H., & Alberini, C. M. (2002). Temporally graded requirement for protein synthesis following memory reactivation. *Neuron, 36,* 521−525.

Miller, C. A., & Marshall, J. F. (2005). Molecular substrates for retrieval and reconsolidation of cocaine-associated contextual memory. *Neuron, 47,* 873−884.

Milton, A. L., Lee, J. L., & Everitt, B. J. (2008). Reconsolidation of appetitive memories for both natural and drug reinforcement is dependent on β-adrenergic receptors. *Learning & Memory, 15,* 88−92.

Misanin, J. R., Miller, R. R., & Lewis, D. J. (1968). Retrograde amnesia produced by electroconvulsive shock after reactivation of a consolidated memory trace. *Science, 160,* 554−555.

Morgan, M. A., & LeDoux, J. E. (1995). Differential contribution of dorsal and ventral medial prefrontal cortex to the acquisition and extinction of conditioned fear in rats. *Behavioral Neuroscience, 109,* 681−688.

Morgan, M. A., & LeDoux, J. E. (1999). Contribution of ventrolateral prefrontal cortex to the acquisition and extinction of conditioned fear in rats. *Neurobiology of Learning and Memory, 72,* 244−251.

Morgan, M. A., Romanski, L. M., & LeDoux, J. E. (1993). Extinction of emotional learning: contribution of medial prefrontal cortex. *Neuroscience Letters, 163,* 109−113.

Morris, R. (1984). Developments of a water-maze procedure for studying spatial learning in the rat. *Journal of Neuroscience Methods, 11,* 47−60.

Morris, R. G., Inglis, J., Ainge, J. A., Olverman, H. J., Tulloch, J., Dudai, Y., & Kelly, P. A. (2006). Memory reconsolidation: Sensitivity of spatial memory to inhibition of protein synthesis in dorsal hippocampus during encoding and retrieval. *Neuron, 50,* 479−489.

Morrow, B. A., Elsworth, J. D., Rasmusson, A. M., & Roth, R. H. (1999). The role of mesoprefrontal dopamine neurons in the acquisition and expression of conditioned fear in the rat. *Neuroscience, 92,* 553−564.

Myers, K. M., & Davis, M. (2002). Behavioral and neural analysis of extinction. *Neuron, 36,* 567−584.

Myers, K. M., & Davis, M. (2002). Behavioral and neural analysis of extinction. *Neuron, 36,* 567−584.

Nader, K. (2003). Memory traces unbound. *Trends in Neuroscience, 26,* 65−72.

Nader, K., Schafe, G. E., & Le Doux, J. E. (2000a). Fear memories require protein synthesis in the amygdala for reconsolidation after retrieval. *Nature, 406,* 722−726.

Nader, K., Schafe, G. E., & Le Doux, J. E. (2000b). The labile nature of consolidation theory. *Nature Reviews Neuroscience, 1,* 216−219.

Pavlov, I. P. (1927). *Conditioned reflexes.* London: Oxford University Press.

Pedreira, M. E., Perez-Cuesta, L. M., & Maldonado, H. (2002). Reactivation and reconsolidation of long-term memory in the crab *Chasmagnathus*: protein synthesis requirement and mediation by NMDA-type glutamatergic receptors. *Journal of Neuroscience, 22,* 8305−8311.

Pedreira, M. E., & Maldonado, H. (2003). Protein synthesis subserves reconsolidation or extinction depending on reminder duration. *Neuron, 38,* 863−869.

Pedreira, M. E., Pérez-Cuesta, L. M., & Maldonado, H. (2004). Mismatch between what is expected and what actually occurs triggers memory reconsolidation or extinction. *Learning & Memory, 11,* 579−585.

Pérez-Cuesta, L. M., Hepp, Y., Pedreira, M. E., & Maldonado, H. (2007). Memory is not extinguished along with CS presentation but within a few seconds after CS-offset. *Learning & Memory, 14,* 101−108.

Peters, J., Dieppa-Perea, L. M., Melendez, L. M., & Quirk, G. J. (2010). Induction of fear extinction with hippocampal-infralimbic BDNF. *Science, 328*, 1288—1290.

Phelps, E. A., & LeDoux, J. E. (2005). Contributions of the amygdala to emotion processing: from animal models to human behavior. *Neuron, 48*, 175—817.

Przybyslawski, J., & Sara, S. J. (1997). Reconsolidation of memory after its reactivation. *Behavioural Brain Research, 84*, 241—246.

Przybyslawski, J., Roullet, P., & Sara, S. J. (1999). Attenuation of emotional and nonemotional memories after their reactivation: role of beta adrenergic receptors. *Journal of Neuroscience, 19*, 6623—6628.

Quevedo, J., Vianna, M. R., Roesler, R., de-Paris, F., Izquierdo, I., & Rose, S. P. (1999). Two time windows of anisomycin-induced amnesia for inhibitory avoidance training in rats: protection from amnesia by pretraining but not pre-exposure to the task apparatus. *Learning & Memory, 6*, 600—607.

Quirk, G. J., Russo, G. K., Barron, J. L., & Lebron, K. (2000). The role of ventromedial prefrontal cortex in the recovery of extinguished fear. *Journal of Neuroscience, 20*, 6225—6231.

Rauch, S. L., Shin, L. M., & Phelps, E. A. (2006). Neurocircuitry models of posttraumatic stress disorder and extinction: human neuroimaging research—Past, present, and future. *Biological Psychiatry, 60*, 376—382.

Reijmers, L. G., Perkins, B. L., Matsuo, N., & Mayford, M. (2007). Localization of a stable neuronal correlate of associative memory. *Science, 317*, 1230—1233.

Rescorla, R. A., & Heth, C. D. (1975). Reinstatement of fear to an extinguished conditioned stimulus. *Journal of Experimental Psychology: Animal Behavior Processes, 1*, 88—96.

Rescorla, R. A. (2001). Experimental extinction. In R. R. Mowrer, & S. Klein (Eds.), *Handbook of contemporary learning theories* (pp. 119—154). Mahwah, NJ: Erlbaum.

Robbins, S. J. (1990). Mechanisms underlying spontaneous recovery in autoshaping. *Journal of Experimental Psychology: Animal Behavior Processes, 16*, 235—249.

Rose, J. K., & Rankin, C. H. (2006). Blocking memory reconsolidation reverses memory-associated changes in glutamate receptor expression. *Journal of Neuroscience, 8*, 11582—11587.

Rossato, J. I., Bevilaqua, L. R., Myskiw, J. C., Medina, J. H., Izquierdo, I., & Cammarota, M. (2007). On the role of hippocampal protein synthesis in the consolidation and reconsolidation of object recognition memory. *Learning & Memory, 14*, 36—46.

Sananbenesi, F., Fischer, A., Wang, X., Schrick, C., Neve, R., Radulovic, J., & Tsai, L. H. (2007). A hippocampal Cdk5 pathway regulates extinction of contextual fear. *Nature Neuroscience, 10*, 1012—1019.

Sangha, S., Scheibenstock, A., & Lukowiak, K. (2003a). Reconsolidation of a long-term memory in Lymnaea requires new protein and RNA synthesis and the soma of right pedal dorsal 1. *Journal of Neuroscience, 23*, 8034—8040.

Sangha, S., Scheibenstock, A., Morrow, R., & Lukowiak, K. (2003b). Extinction requires new RNA and protein synthesis and the soma of the cell right pedal dorsal 1 in *Lymnaea stagnalis*. *Journal of Neuroscience, 23*, 9842—9851.

Santini, E., Ge, H., Ren, K., deOrtiz, S. P., & Quirk, G. J. (2004). Consolidation of fear extinction requires protein synthesis in the medial prefrontal cortex. *Journal of Neuroscience, 24*, 5704—5710.

Sara, S. J. (2000). Retrieval and reconsolidation: toward a neurobiology of remembering. *Learning & Memory, 7*, 73—84.

Schneider, A. M., & Sherman, W. (1968). Amnesia: a function of the temporal relation of footshock to electroconvulsive shock. *Science, 159*, 219—221.

Squire, L. R., & Alvarez, P. (1995). Retrograde amnesia and memory consolidation: a neurobiological perspective. *Current Opinion in Neurobiology, 5*, 169—177.

Suzuki, A., Josselyn, S. A., Frankland, P. W., Masushige, S., Silva, A. J., & Kida, S. (2004). Memory reconsolidation and extinction have distinct temporal and biochemical signatures. *Journal of Neuroscience, 24*, 4787—4795.

Suzuki, A., Mukawa, T., Tsukagoshi, A., Frankland, P. W., & Kida, S. (2008). Activation of LVGCCs and CB1 receptors required for destabilization of reactivated contextual fear memories. *Learning & Memory, 15*, 426—433.

Taubenfeld, S. M., Milekic, M. H., Monti, B., & Alberini, C. M. (2001). The consolidation of new but not reactivated memory requires hippocampal C/EBPbeta. *Nature Neuroscience, 4*, 813–818.

Tronel, S., Milekic, M. H., & Alberini, C. M. (2005). Linking new information to a reactivated memory requires consolidation and not reconsolidation mechanisms. *PLoS Biology, 3*, 1630–1638.

Tronson, N. C., Wiseman, S. L., Olausson, P., & Taylor, J. R. (2006). Bidirectional behavioral plasticity of memory reconsolidation depends on amygdalar protein kinase A. *Nature Neuroscience, 9*, 167–169.

Teich, A. H., McCabe, P. M., Gentile, C. C., Schneiderman, L. S., Winters, R. W., Liskowsky, D. R., & Schneiderman, N. (1989). Auditory cortex lesions prevent the extinction of Pavlovian differential heart rate conditioning to tonal stimuli in rabbits. *Brain Research, 480*, 210–218.

von Hertzen, L. S., & Giese, K. P. (2005). Memory reconsolidation engages only a subset of immediate-early genes induced during consolidation. *Journal of Neuroscience, 25*, 1935–1942.

Walker, M. P., Brakefield, T., Hobson, J. A., & Stickgold, R. (2003). Dissociable stages of human memory consolidation and reconsolidation. *Nature, 425*, 616–620.

Wang, S. H., de Oliveira Alvares, L., & Nader, K. (2009). Cellular and systems mechanisms of memory strength as a constraint on auditory fear reconsolidation. *Nature Neuroscience, 12*, 905–912.

Wang, S. H., Ostlund, S. B., Nader, K., & Balleine, B. W. (2005). Consolidation and reconsolidation of incentive learning in the amygdala. *Journal of Neuroscience, 25*, 830–835.

Chapter seven

Memory Reconsolidation and Extinction in Invertebrates: Evolutionarily Conserved Characteristics of Memory Reprocessing and Restabilization

María Eugenia Pedreira, Arturo Romano

*Laboratorio de Neurobiología de la Memoria, FCEN UBA, IFIBYNE-CONICET,
Buenos Aires, Argentina*

*In memoriam to our science mentor Héctor Maldonado—a true
scientist who inspired us with his illimitable creativity.*

7.1 INTRODUCTION

The concept of memory consolidation was established by pioneer studies on human memory by Müller and Pilzecker (1900) and was further formalized after the accumulation of experimental evidence on retrograde amnesia in rodents (McGaugh, 1966). The requirement of both transcription and translation

139

Memory Reconsolidation. http://dx.doi.org/10.1016/B978-0-12-386892-3.00007-X

during a discrete period of time after acquisition has become widely accepted for memory stabilization and persistence (Davis & Squire, 1984; Kandel, 2004). According to the classical version of consolidation theory, once stability is reached, memory becomes resistant to further challenges over time. However, soon after the formalization of the theory, the studies of Lewis and Misanin (Lewis, 1979; Lewis & Maher, 1965; Misanin, Miller, & Lewis, 1968) on cue-dependent amnesia suggested, for the first time, that the process was more complex and pointed to a more dynamic nature of memory processing. The phenomenon of cue-dependent amnesia states that a consolidated memory can undergo retrograde amnesia if a cue or reminder is presented just prior to the disrupting agent. The concept was later extended to the possibility of post-retrieval memory enhancement (Devietti, Conger, & Kirkpatrick, 1977). According to the original formulation of these authors, the modulation of memory occurs only when memory is active—that is, initially, during, and soon after acquisition and later, when memory is reactivated. Reactivation can be spontaneous or can be induced by internal or external events, such as the presence of a reminder. Twenty years later, the idea of memory labilization and reprocessing after retrieval was recovered (Nader, Schafe, & LeDoux, 2000; Przybyslawski & Sara, 1997) and was termed reconsolidation. Such an idea gained interest in the neurobiological community not only because of its theoretical and mechanistic importance but also because of its potential application in therapeutic strategies for memory-related pathologies.

After a decade of intense studies in this field, the concepts of cue-dependent amnesia and reconsolidation have become more complex and have been integrated into a more comprehensive hypothesis, as discussed in other chapters in this book. In addition, the concepts are now integrated with the study of another retrieval-dependent process, memory extinction. The study of memory has also advanced to encompass knowledge of the molecular mechanisms involved in both reconsolidation and extinction.

However, the initial studies mentioned previously, and many subsequent studies, focused mainly on rodent models of memory reconsolidation. Despite the unquestioned value of the rodent studies, a question soon arose regarding the universality of this phenomenon: Was reconsolidation a particular characteristic of rodents or mammals?

In this chapter, we focus on findings obtained using a context–signal memory model in crabs and describe the parametrical conditions for memory labilization and reconsolidation. We also review the studies at the mechanistic level, describing the molecular features involved in memory reconsolidation and extinction. Then, on the basis of the findings in crab studies, we present comparative studies in rodents that are performed using another contextual memory paradigm, fear conditioning.

A wide variety of animal models, ranging from *Caenorhabditis elegans* to humans, are available for the study of memory. Each model system has benefits and drawbacks. Using this broad spectrum of species, learning and memory have been studied at the behavioral, systems, neuronal, and subcellular levels. Invertebrate models have provided central insights into the underlying mechanisms of learning and memory formation (Carew, 2000; Kandel, 2004).

Research using nonhuman animals has produced more than 300 papers on reconsolidation in the past 10 years alone, and invertebrate research accounted for approximately 10% of these. Many invertebrate models can be used to study memory. However, to our knowledge, only seven invertebrate models have been used to study the process of reconsolidation: the terrestrial slug *Limax* (Sekiguchi, Yamad, & Suzuki, 1997), the pond snail *Lymnaea* (Sangha, Scheibenstock, & Lukowiak, 2003), the terrestrial snail *Helix locorum* (Gainutdinova *et al.*, 2005), the mollusk *Hermissenda* (Child, Epstein, Kuzirian & Alkon 2003), the worm *Caenorhabditis elegans* (Rose & Rankin, 2006), the honeybee *Apis melifera* (Stollhoff, Menzel, & Eisenhardt, 2008), and the crab *Chasmagnatus*. Although the results on reconsolidation obtained in the mentioned models are important, due to space limitations, this chapter focuses on the context–signal memory in the crab *Chasmagnatus*.

7.2 CONTEXT-SIGNAL MEMORY IN THE CRAB *CHASMAGNATHUS*

During approximately the past 25 years, a research effort has been focused on the study of learning and memory in the grapsid crab *Chasmagnathus granulatus* (recently reclassified as *Neohelice granulata*). The crab's associative learning paradigm is based on its escape response, which is elicited by the presentation of a visual danger stimulus (VDS), an opaque rectangle passing over the animal. Upon the iterative presentation of the VDS, the crab's escape response declines, and a strong freezing response is developed (Pereyra, Saracco, & Maldonado, 1999). The decline in escape response lasts for at least 5 days (Lozada, Romano, & Maldonado, 1990; Pedreira, Dimant, Tomsic, Quesada-Allue, & Maldonado, 1995). The memory that is formed is based on the association between the environmental features of the training place (the context) and the features of the screen moving over the animal (the signal) (Tomsic, Pedreira, Romano, Hermitte, & Maldonado, 1998). This type of memory was termed context–signal memory (CSM). Indeed, this association was revealed by experiments that evaluated context specificity, in which a training-to-testing context shift abolished CSM retention. Moreover, another relevant aspect of this type of learning is the presence of both latent inhibition and extinction (Hepp, Pérez-Cuesta, Maldonado, & Pedreira, 2010; Tomsic *et al.*, 1998). Thus, these findings strongly support the associative nature of CSM and, specifically, the existence of an associative link between the signal and the context (spatial and temporal) as distinctive features of this memory process.

For more than 15 years, our laboratory has performed studies to determine the mechanisms underlying consolidation of the CSM. In brief, we have shown that CSM consolidation is blocked by protein synthesis inhibitors (Hermitte, Pedreira, Tomsic, & Maldonado, 1999; Pedreira *et al.*, 1995; Pedreira, Dimant, & Maldonado, 1996), is positively modulated by angiotensins (Delorenzi *et al.*,

1996, 2000), is selectively regulated by a muscarinic cholinergic mechanism (Berón de Astrada & Maldonado, 1999), and is mediated by N-methyl-D-aspartic acid (NMDA)-like glutamate receptors (Troncoso & Maldonado, 2002).

At the molecular level, it was demonstrated that the cAMP signal pathway (Locatelli, Maldonado, & Romano, 2002; Romano, Delorenzi, Pedreira, Tomsic, & Maldonado, 1996a; Romano, Locatelli, Delorenzi, Pedreira, & Maldonado, 1996b) and the MAPK kinase pathway (Feld, Dimant, Delorenzi, Coso, & Romano, 2005) are involved in memory formation. Regarding the regulation of gene expression, the nuclear factor kappa B (NF-κB) transcription factor pathway (Freudenthal & Romano, 2000; Freudenthal *et al.*, 1998; Merlo, Freudenthal, & Romano, 2002) and the epigenetic mechanism of histone acetylation (Federman, Fustiñana, & Romano, 2009) are engaged in CMS consolidation (Romano *et al.*, 2006b).

7.3 THE PARAMETRICAL CONDITIONS OF CSM RECONSOLIDATION AND EXTINCTION

7.3.1 CSM reconsolidation

The studies of Lewis and colleagues in the late 1960s (Misanin *et al.*, 1968) defined the criteria that an experimental protocol of reconsolidation should follow. The reactivation of a consolidated memory is obtained as a result of the presentation of a cue reminder. The administration of a disrupting treatment is used to reveal the presence of reconsolidation after reactivation. The testing session must occur after the time window for reconsolidation has closed (long-term testing). By observing these criteria, we adapted the protocol for CSM to study labilization-reconsolidation. Our first study was aimed at determining whether the CSM of the crab could be reactivated by a short re-exposure to the context (reminder) after a period during which the crab was impervious to amnesic agents. This labilization was revealed by impairing the restabilization process using amnesic agents. In addition, the initial research was oriented to characterize retrieval properties and to ascertain whether reconsolidation requires part of the same cellular machinery as consolidation, starting with the protein synthesis requirement. In these experiments, designed to demonstrate that the amnesic effect was a consequence of CSM labilization and blockade of reconsolidation, the experimental series included groups in which the animals were exposed to the training context (standard context) and others in which crabs were confronted with a novel context (different context) during the treatment session.

Previous experiments demonstrated that cycloheximide (CHX), at a dose that inhibits at least 90% of protein synthesis for 2 hr, impairs newly acquired CSM when administered from 1 hr before up to 6 hr after training (Pedreira *et al.*, 1995). Consequently, to test whether the consolidated memory could be reactivated by a reminder and converted into a labile state, a similar dose of CHX was given 1 hr before the crab's exposure to a standard or to a different context. The results revealed that when crabs were exposed to the different

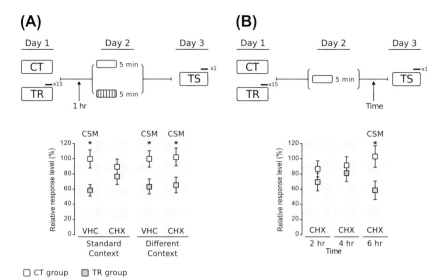

FIGURE 7.1 Context—signal memory (CSM) reconsolidation. (A) (Top) Experimental protocol: A 3-day experiment. CT, control groups; TR, training groups; white box, standard context; hatched box, different context. The black hyphen at the end of each box represents the visual danger stimulus (VDS) trial; ×1 and ×15 are the number of VDSs presented in the session. The arrow indicates the time-point for the injection; ×15, 15 training trials. (Bottom) Testing session. CHX, cicloheximide-injected groups; CSM, CSM retention; VHC, vehicle-injected groups. Mean responses ± SEM during VDS presentation, normalized with respect to the mean response of the CT—VHC group. White squares represent the CT groups and gray squares represent the TR groups' curves; *$P < 0.05$. (B) CSM reconsolidation time window. (Top) Experimental protocol: A 3-day experiment. Symbols as in panel A; time is the interval between the context re-exposure (reminder) and the injection. (Bottom) Testing session: Symbols as in panel A. Times at the bottom are the hours between the reminder presentation and the injection.

context, CHX failed to disrupt memory (Figure 7.1A). Another experiment was performed that aimed to determine whether the amnesic effect of CHX could be observed in short-term testing carried out immediately after 5 min of re-exposure to the standard context. No memory-disrupting effect was found in this case.

The next step aimed to determine the time window of the restabilization process using treatment at diverse time intervals after re-exposure to the standard context on Day 2. CSM was blocked by a CHX injection administered 2 or 4 hr after, but not 6 hr after, reactivation (Figure 7.1B). Finally, the last experiment was performed to explore to what extent CSM reconsolidation could be affected when the time interval between training and contextual re-exposure was doubled (i.e., 48 hr instead of 24 hr). Memory impairment was found in the case of CHX injection. Thus, it was demonstrated that a protein synthesis blocker can impair the restabilization of an older CSM.

These experiments provide clear evidence that the robust CSM acquired by the crab through spaced training (Freudenthal *et al.*, 1998; Locatelli *et al.*, 2002; Locatelli, LaFourcade, Maldonado, & Romano, 2001; Pedreira *et al.*,

1995; Romano *et al.*, 1996a, 1996b) becomes labile again after 5 min of re-exposure to the learning context and is vulnerable to CHX. The results are interpreted according to the view, stemming from findings obtained in vertebrates (Nader *et al.*, 2000), that a memory retrieved by a reminder passes from a dormant and stable state to an active and labile state (destabilization) and then undergoes a time-dependent consolidation process (reconsolidation) (Przybyslawski, Roullet, & Sara, 1999; Przybyslawski & Sara, 1997; Sara, 2000).

It is important to note that in accordance with the interpretive model of CSM retrieval (Hermitte, Pedreira, *et al.*, 1999; Maldonado, 2002; Tomsic *et al.*, 1998), re-exposure of a trained crab to the learning context evoked a CSM representation that induced a freezing response as soon as the animal was faced with the VDS. Until the use of experimental designs that evaluated CSM reconsolidation, no previous evidence had shown that such a memory representation was already present before the VDS was displayed. However, the outcome obtained in reconsolidation experiments supported this proposal. The mere re-exposure to the original learning context, even in the absence of the VDS, is enough to render the memory labile and vulnerable to interruption of reconsolidation by an amnesic agent. Thus, these findings support the associative nature of CSM and, specifically, the existence of an associative link between signal and context as the basis of this memory process.

In summary, these results are in line with two main tenets of the reactivation/reconsolidation hypothesis: (1) Reactivation converts memory from a dormant−stable state to an active−labile state, and (2) the post-acquisition cascade of intracellular events is recapitulated to some extent whenever memory is reactivated. It is worth noting that the present findings in a crustacean model, together with the previously mentioned findings in other invertebrate models, suggest the persistence through evolution of the molecular mechanisms serving both consolidation and reconsolidation phases of memory. The shared mechanisms would be the basic tools used by evolution to promote adaptive changes through phylogenetically disparate animals (Carew, 2000).

7.3.2 The relationship between CSM reconsolidation and CSM extinction

From the beginning of the resurgence of memory reconsolidation, other results cast doubt on the consistency of the reconsolidation theory (Myers & Davis, 2002). The most salient conflicting point is related to the very nature of the reminder—that is, the episode that claims to trigger reconsolidation. The reminder generally consists of presenting an unreinforced conditioned stimulus (CS), which is tantamount to giving an extinction trial and thus contributes to the development of a new second memory (extinction memory) that is stored without destroying the old one but suppresses its expression (Brooks & Bouton, 1994). Therefore, if an agent such as anisomycin is given in relation to the reminder, impairment of the new memory and retention of the old memory should be expected at testing. Such a prediction was confirmed in two studies that appeared in parallel with the reinstatement of the reconsolidation hypothesis (Berman & Dudai, 2001; Vianna, Szapiro, McGaugh, Medina, & Izquierdo, 2001). To reconcile the conflicting data, it was proposed by different authors (Dudai, 2002; Debiec, LeDoux, & Nader, 2002) that extinction and reconsolidation compete on a molecular level. Therefore, if anisomycin is given and retention of the original memory is shown at testing, this means that the dominant protein synthesis process underlies extinction. Conversely, if the original memory is abolished, the dominant process is reconsolidation. In line with this view, Myers and Davis (2002) proposed extinction and reconsolidation as two separate but competing processes that are active following a reactivation/extinction episode, and they envisaged some procedural variables whose manipulation would allow discrimination between impaired extinction and disrupted reconsolidation. Therefore, the next step of our characterization of the reconsolidation process focused on this issue.

Considering the demonstration of memory labilization-reconsolidation in CSM (Pedreira, Perez-Cuesta, & Maldonado, 2002) and other results showing that exposure to the context without VDS presentation produced extinction (Tomsic *et al.*, 1998), we explored the relationship between extinction and reconsolidation in the *Chasmagnathus* memory model. Specifically, our working hypothesis was that re-exposure of the crab to the learning context (reminder) 24 hr after the training session would induce reconsolidation or extinction according to the duration of the re-exposure. If so, the re-exposure duration would be, in the terms of Myers and Davis (2002), the procedural variable that would allow us to dissect two novel processes triggered by the same episode.

We first explored the effect of diverse periods of context re-exposure on CSM retention. Thus, during the treatment session on Day 2, animals were exposed to the standard context or a novel context for a variable time period without VDS presentation (from 5 to 120 min). A test for retention was then administered on Day 3, in which animals were returned to the standard context and a single VDS was presented.

In this way, we determined the point at which the duration of context re-exposure renders CSM vulnerable to extinction. In particular, re-exposure of less than 60 min does not produce an effect on CSM retention. In contrast, re-exposures equal to or longer than 60 min results in extinction of the CSM. Moreover, memory extinction depends on the similarity between the training and reminder contexts, as shown by the fact that exposure to a different context, as opposed to the standard context, did not induce extinction of CSM, regardless of exposure duration (Figure 7.2A).

Thus, we determined a parametrical condition for the reminder. Five minutes of context re-exposure labilized the original memory, and 60 min of exposure induced the formation of the extinction memory. Using this feature of the reminder, we compared the effect of CHX on CSM in relation to variable durations of context re-exposure. Memory impairment was evident when the animals were confronted with the standard context for 5 min. In contrast,

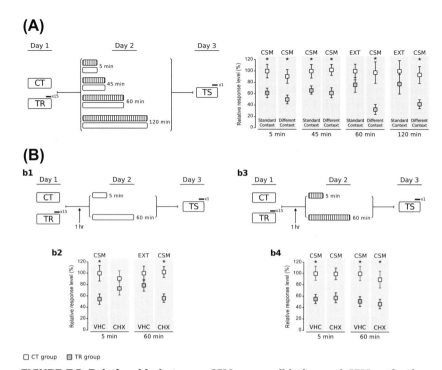

FIGURE 7.2 Relationship between CSM reconsolidation and CSM extinction.
(A) (Left) Experimental protocol: A 3-day experiment. Symbols as in Figure 7.1. (Right)
Testing session: Symbols as in Figure 7.1. EXT, extinction memory retention. (B) Effect
of CHX on CSM reconsolidation and extinction memory. (b1) Experimental protocol:
Symbols as in Figures 7.1 and 7.2A. (b2) Testing session: Symbols as in Figure 7.1.
(b3) Experimental protocol: Symbols as in Figures 7.1 and 7.2A. (b4) Testing session:
Symbols as in Figure 7.1.

when the animals spent 1 hr in the standard context (i.e., extinction training),
the inhibition of protein synthesis prevented the consolidation of extinction
memory. Thus, the CSM was recalled and expressed at testing (Figure 7.2B).

Moreover, we evaluated the time window for the CHX effect on extinction
memory consolidation. Injections of CHX either 1 hr before or 2 hr after context
re-exposure resulted in the impairment of extinction memory consolidation.
However, when the reminder injection interval was extended to 6 hr, the
CHX-injection was unable to impair extinction memory. A central conclusion
stemming from these results is that the consolidation of the crab's CSM extinction is dependent on protein synthesis. Moreover, the results support the idea
that extinction is a form of new learning and that protein synthesis mediates
extinction memory consolidation.

At this junction, we proposed a framework for the interpretation of these
findings: The same intervention (i.e., cycloheximide treatment) can either
abolish or preserve the original memory depending on the duration of context
re-exposure. Thus, when the crab was exposed to the original training

context, the learned context—VDS association was recalled and the animal remained still, expecting the appearance of the danger stimulus (Maldonado, 2002). As a consequence, the mechanisms underlying either extinction or reconsolidation become operative once the non-occurrence of the expected VDS is confirmed. This confirmation occurs when the crab is removed from the training context. Note that the crab's removal is proposed as a switch that leads either to memory retention (reconsolidation) or to memory impairment (extinction); however, this does not necessarily imply that the mechanisms underlying such options are mutually exclusive. Thus, it is unlikely that both processes compete at the molecular level and that the expression of either the old memory or the new memory is dependent on the dominant mechanism (Debiec *et al.*, 2002). We discuss this point later in the chapter.

Returning to the beginning of this section, the conflicting results obtained using other animal models (Berman & Dudai, 2001; Vianna *et al.*, 2001) could reflect differences in terms of the learning tasks employed or the region specificity studied. However, the conflicting results may also be reconciled by the finding that the same reminder triggers two alternative processes depending on the duration of exposure to the reminder. In accordance with other studies (Eisenberg & Dudai, 2004; Suzuki *et al.*, 2004), it was demonstrated that manipulation of a procedural variable would allow us to discriminate impaired extinction from disrupted reconsolidation.

7.3.3 The relevance of the mismatch component on the triggering of memory reconsolidation or extinction

As discussed in the previous section, unreinforced re-exposure to the learning context acts as a switch that guides the memory toward reconsolidation or extinction, depending on reminder duration (Pedreira & Maldonado, 2003). This proposal implies that the system computes the total exposure time to the context and, therefore, that the reminder presentation must be terminated in order for the switching mechanism to become operative. In this section, we investigate to what extent the requirement of re-exposure to the training context without reinforcement is necessary. Previous results support the view that CHX can be used to test the lability state of memory at different time points. Using CHX, which is a protein synthesis blocker, as a tool, we focused our study on the retrieval-labilization-reconsolidation sequence. As we showed previously, CSM was reactivated by re-exposure to the learning context without reinforcement (VDS) for 5 min; CHX injected 2 hr later impaired CSM reconsolidation. In contrast, when the VDS was presented during the last minute of context re-exposure, the CHX injection had no effect, even though the CHX was administered within the appropriate time window, suggesting that no reconsolidation, and thus no labilization, was produced by context re-exposure when it included a VDS trial. Similar results were obtained when the injection was administered immediately after the reminder (Figure 7.3A, right).

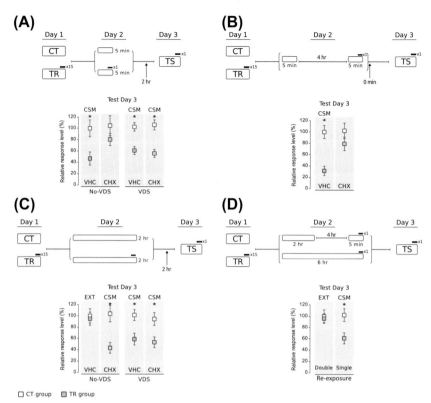

FIGURE 7.3 Relevance of the mismatch component on the triggering of memory reconsolidation or extinction. (A) Effect of VDS inclusion in the reminder presented to trigger the CSM reconsolidation. (Top) Experimental protocol: A 3-day experiment. Symbols as in Figure 7.2. (Bottom) Testing session: Symbols as in Figure 7.2. No VDS, context re-exposure without VDS presentation. (B). Effect of separated presentation of the reminder from the VDS on Day 2. (Top) Experimental protocol: A 3-day experiment. Symbols as in Figures 7.1 and 7.2. O hr, injection given immediately after the context re-exposure with the VDS presentation. (Bottom) Testing session: Symbols as in Figure 7.2. (C) Effect of VDS inclusion in the reminder presented to trigger the CSM extinction. (Top) Experimental protocol: A 3-day experiment. Symbols as in Figure 7.2. (Bottom) Testing session: Symbols as in Figure 7.2. (D) Effect of separated presentation of the reminder from the VDS on Day 2. (Top) Experimental protocol: A 3-day experiment. Symbols as in Figure 7.2. (Bottom) Testing session: Symbols as in Figure 7.2. Double, the two re-exposures to the training context; single, one re-exposure to the training context.

In short, memory labilization appeared to be strictly dependent on the fulfillment of two conditions:(1) the closure of the learning context re-exposure and (2) the absence of the VDS during the entire presentation of the training context. We then predicted that training context re-exposure with the VDS would show intact but labile memory if it was preceded by a genuine reminder without reinforcement—that is, by a previous unreinforced context re-exposure that triggered reconsolidation. This prediction was confirmed experimentally when crabs were exposed to the training context twice for 5 min each time, separated by a 4-hr interval. The first exposure did not include the VDS, but the second exposure included the VDS during the last minute. Vehicle (VHC) or CHX was injected immediately after the second context re-exposure. Memory emerged intact when tested with one VDS presentation on Day 2, and amnesia was revealed only for the CHX groups when they were tested for CSM retention with VDS presentation on Day 3 (Figure 7.3A, left). Therefore, in keeping with the prediction, memory during the last minute of the second re-exposure remained intact but labile as a consequence of the previous unreinforced re-exposure.

To explore the issues under study in connection with extinction, we performed experiments that were similar to those of the first series but had a learning context re-exposure of 2 hr instead of 5 min. As we previously showed, memory was extinguished when context re-exposure lasted 2 hr, but extinction memory was abolished by CHX injected 2 hr after the re-exposure to the training context. In contrast, if a single VDS trial was included during the last minute of context re-exposure, CHX injection had no effect even though the CHX was administered within the time window of vulnerability (Figure 7.3B, right). These results indicate that inclusion of a reinforcement during the reminder presentation left the original memory not only intact but also insensitive to CHX—that is, intact and consolidated. Furthermore, 2 hr of re-exposure with the inclusion of a VDS in the last minute of exposure hindered the possibility of acquiring the extinction memory. However, this lack of extinction could be accounted for in terms of reinstatement of the old memory by the reinforcement—that is, the recovery of behavior when the subject was exposed to the unconditioned stimulus after extinction (Bouton, 2002). To explore this interpretation, a double context re-exposure versus a simple re-exposure to the training context was compared. In the double re-exposure experiment, the animals were placed in the training context for 2 hr without reinforcement, followed 4 hr later by a 5-min re-exposure with a VDS presentation. When we performed the single re-exposure experiment, the crabs were re-exposed to the context for 6 hr and received a VDS trial during the last minute of this period. Extinction was shown when the context presentation was interrupted but not when the context presentation was continuous on both Day 2 and Day 3. Therefore, extinction, similarly to reconsolidation, is a result of the finalization of training context re-exposure without reinforcement. That is, extinction, similarly to reconsolidation, is induced not by the beginning of context presentation (retrieval) but by the end of an unreinforced reminder.

In summary, two new parametrical conditions are revealed for the reconsolidation and extinction processes. No reinforcement during the reminder and no reinforcement during the ending of context re-exposure are the necessary conditions for both processes to occur. Moreover, regardless of the reminder duration, CSM retention appears at testing when the evaluation is performed during the re-exposure. These results strongly suggest that neither reconsolidation nor extinction is concomitant with re-exposure. The main conclusion is that either process can only be triggered once the definitive incongruence between what is expected and what actually occurs (mismatch) is confirmed. Here, the mismatch emerges with the termination of the reminder re-exposure without the expected reinforcement.

7.3.4 CSM reconsolidation and extinction: Can they coexist?

It has been proposed that although mechanistically different, reconsolidation and extinction share an important functional feature; that is, they are both involved in the acquisition of new information related to previous learning (Forcato, Argibay, Pedreira, & Maldonado, 2009; Monfils, Cowansage, Klann, & LeDoux, 2009). Given this functional relationship between memory reconsolidation and extinction, and given that either process can be triggered by exposure to a CS, the study of the mechanistic relationship between these two processes is of particular interest. As previously shown in our model, certain parametric features of the re-exposure, such as duration and the absence of reinforcement, determine the fate of the memory (i.e., reconsolidation or extinction). Mutual exclusion upon a single CS presentation (Pedreira & Maldonado, 2003; Suzuki *et al.*, 2004) could be a consequence of an interaction between these two processes (Mamiya *et al.*, 2009) or could imply the lack of such an interaction (Pedreira, Perez-Cuesta, & Maldonado, 2004). If mutual exclusion does depend on an interaction (e.g., one process inhibits the other), this would assume that both processes must be triggered at some point, and then, upon the putative interaction, one process develops while the other does not. However, if either process is triggered only after the CS offset, a point at which the conditions are irreversibly met for only one process and not for the other, the possibility of an interaction should be ruled out. In this respect, our previous work with crabs shows that memory extinction is not triggered until the CS is terminated and strongly suggests similar dynamics for reconsolidation (Pedreira, Perez-Cuesta, & Maldonado, 2004; Pérez-Cuesta, Hepp, Pedreira, & Maldonado, 2007). Given mutual exclusion, an important issue is whether either process intrinsically constitutes a constraint on the other or whether the processes can, in some circumstances, develop in parallel. To address this issue, Perez-Cuesta and Maldonado (2009) exposed trained crabs to a series of two unreinforced context re-exposures—a reconsolidation-inducing short context re-exposure followed 15 min later by an extinction-inducing prolonged exposure—and they investigated the occurrence of both processes.

When the crabs were tested soon after the end of the long exposure to the context, a short-term extinction memory was disclosed. This memory was impervious to CHX treatment; therefore, it is protein synthesis-independent memory (Pérez-Cuesta *et al.*, 2007). At a 24-hr test, long-term extinction memory was found and was dependent on protein synthesis (Pedreira & Maldonado, 2003; Pedreira *et al.*, 2004; Pérez-Cuesta *et al.*, 2007). Finally, the original memory spontaneously reappeared after extinction at a 48-hr test, or upon reinstatement (Merlo & Romano, 2008). Using these defined characteristics and the combination of a short re-exposure followed by a long re-exposure to the context, the authors evaluated whether a short exposure was capable of inducing memory labilization despite a subsequent extinction process. They used CHX to evaluate labilization and found that the corresponding CHX-injected crabs showed persistent amnesia, revealing impairment in CSM reconsolidation. Thus, a short CS exposure was capable of inducing CSM labilization regardless of subsequent extinction training. Hence, the extinction induced by the prolonged exposure did not prevent, or reverted in some way, the CSM labilization-reconsolidation process triggered by the first short re-exposure. Moreover, in addition to extinction acquisition and ongoing extinction memory consolidation, CSM reconsolidation was effectively taking place at some point after labilization in the case of animals injected with the vehicle. These animals expressed the extinction memory at testing, and after that, the original memory appeared as a consequence of spontaneous recovery. Therefore, the authors concluded that the memory processes, reconsolidation and extinction, were being triggered serially (Pérez-Cuesta & Maldonado, 2009).

Whether memory reconsolidation and memory extinction are mutually exclusive processes or whether they coexist in time depends only on behavioral experience—that is, on whether they are triggered by a single context exposure or by successive context exposures. Thus, when they do exclude each other by single context exposure, a consequence is not that each process places a constraint on the other (as in competition for molecular substrates) but, rather, that an outcome of an amnesic mechanism drives memory to one of them. In the last section of this chapter, we analyze the particular molecular processes that differentially determine the fate of memory after retrieval.

In addition to experiments with the translation inhibitor CHX, the crab *Chasmagnathus* animal model has been used during approximately the past 10 years to characterize the neurotransmitters and modulators that affect memory, in the sense of impairing or improving the reconsolidation process. Due to space limitation, we do not provide an extensive discussion of these studies here. We only mention that the actions of glutamate via the NMDA-type receptors, γ-aminobutyric acid (GABA) as the major inhibitory neurotransmitter, angiotensin II neuropeptide, and real-life episodes that increase the endogenous levels of this peptide and the biogenic amine octopamine were studied. All these mechanisms are involved in reconsolidation (Carbó-Tano, Molina, Maldonado, & Pedreira, 2009; Frenkel, Maldonado, & Delorenzi, 2005; Kaczer & Maldonado, 2009; Pedreira et al., 2002; Perez-Cuesta et al., 2007).

7.4 MOLECULAR MECHANISMS INVOLVED IN RECONSOLIDATION AND EXTINCTION OF CSM

The development of memory models in different species, particularly in invertebrates such as mollusks and insects, has led to considerable progress in understanding the molecular mechanisms underlying memory formation and processing (Crow, 2004; Dubnau *et al.*, 2003; Kandel, 2001; Menzel, 2001; Roberts & Glanzman, 2003). In the search for the molecular mechanisms that are involved in such processes, we have used the CSM model for more than a decade to study the roles of cAMP-dependent protein kinase (PKA), extracellular signal-regulated kinase (ERK), and the NF-κB transcription factor in memory processing. In this section, we describe the molecular processes involved in CSM reconsolidation and extinction and some recent comparative studies on rodents in which the role of the molecular mechanisms described in the crab were evaluated using contextual fear conditioning.

7.4.1 Gene expression in consolidation and reconsolidation

There is a great deal of evidence for the role of transcription in consolidation, beginning with pioneering work on brightness discrimination in rats (Matthies, 1989), on the avoidance task in chickens (Rose, 1991), on long-term facilitation in the mollusk *Aplysia* (Goelet, Castellucci, Schacher, & Kandel, 1986), and in several recent reports. Among the transcription factors (TFs) that have been found to regulate gene expression during memory consolidation (for a revision, see Alberini, 2009), two of them—cAMP response element binding protein (CREB) and NF-κB—show relatively high basal expression. Such a characteristic warrants the presence of the proteins prior to the neuronal activity that occurs during information acquisition. This fact implies that TFs can be promptly activated by synaptic activity and extracellular signals. Such activation takes place via protein–protein interactions or by covalent modifications, usually phosphorylations. In this way, the induction of transcription is rapidly achieved by the presence of TFs in regulatory regions of different genes.

Three additional families of TFs that have been found to play critical roles in memory—C/EBP, ZIF268 (also known as EGR-1), and AP-1—are immediate early genes. The basal expression levels of these genes are very low, and they require induction to reach the protein levels necessary for the action of the TF in the nucleus. There is evidence that C/EBP is regulated, at least in part, by CREB (Alberini, Ghirardi, Metz, & Kandel, 1994), whereas NF-κB is involved in the regulation of Zif268 (Lubin & Sweatt, 2007).

NF-κB participates in the regulation of memory-related genes, including brain-derived neurotrophic factor (BDNF), Zif268, c-Fos, JunB and JunD, angiotensinogen, the proteasome subunit LMP2, inducible NO synthase (iNOS), and neural cell adhesion molecule (N-CAM) (Romano, Freudenthal, Merlo, & Routtenberg, 2006a).

7.4.2 NF-κB transcription factor in memory reconsolidation

The first evidence that links the NF-κB family to memory formation was obtained in CSM of the crab *Chasmagnathus*. CSM formation strongly correlated with NF-κB activation in the nucleus of the crab central brain. The activation showed two phases. The first phase of activation was transient and occurred immediately after training, decaying to basal levels after 3 hr. The second phase peaked at 6 hr and was more persistent. In contrast, NF-κB was not activated after massed training (Freudenthal & Romano, 2000). In subsequent experiments, an NF-κB inhibitor was shown to impair memory consolidation. Sulfasalazine, an inhibitor of the specific protein kinase IκB (IKK), which activates NF-κB, induced amnesia when administered during, but not after, the two periods in which NF-κB was active (Merlo *et al.*, 2002).

In an initial study of the molecular mechanisms involved in crab memory reconsolidation, we evaluated whether NF-κB was required for memory restabilization after a brief 5-min re-exposure to the training context. We found that when animals were re-exposed to the same training context 24 hr after training, NF-κB was reactivated. Furthermore, NF-κB was not activated in animals that were re-exposed to the training context after a weak training protocol that was insufficient to induce long-term memory. NF-κB activation took place very rapidly and was transient. Central brain samples were obtained soon after the 5-min period of re-exposure. At this time point, NF-κB activity was significantly higher than in controls, but it returned to basal levels after 30−45 min. Furthermore, sulfasalazine impaired reconsolidation when administered 20 min before re-exposure to the training context but was not effective when a different context was used (Merlo, Maldonado, & Romano, 2005). These findings revealed, for the first time, that NF-κB is involved in memory reconsolidation. NF-κB was specifically activated by retrieval, and activation of NF-κB was required for memory reconsolidation, supporting the view that this molecular mechanism plays a key role in both consolidation and reconsolidation. Such a conclusion is in line with the view that the basic molecular mechanisms required in consolidation are necessary for restoring the reactivated memory.

7.4.3 NF-κB and memory extinction

As mentioned previously, in consolidated associative memories, retrieval induced by CS presentation without reinforcement may induce two mutually exclusive processes, reconsolidation and extinction. A body of evidence supports the view that the original memory is not disrupted by extinction but that its expression is temporarily inhibited (Rescorla, 2004). The fact that extinction requires protein synthesis during a certain period of time led to the assumption that extinction involves a new memory that must be consolidated, as the original one was previously. However, the temporary nature of extinction, in contrast to the persistent nature of the original memory, points to mechanistic differences between both processes. In fact, studies support distinct molecular requirements, such as the participation of protein phosphatases and endocannabinoids (Mansuy, 2003; Suzuki *et al.*, 2004).

As mentioned previously, NF-κB activation plays a critical role in consolidation and reconsolidation. We therefore investigated the possible participation of NF-κB in memory extinction. Under the hypothesis that extinction is a new memory that has similar characteristics to the original consolidated memory, we expected this TF to be required for the consolidation of extinction. However, we found that administration of the NF-κB inhibitor sulfasalazine prior to the extinction session enhanced extinction. Moreover, reinstatement experiments showed that the original memory was not affected and that NF-κB inhibition by sulfasalazine impaired or delayed spontaneous recovery, thus strengthening the ongoing memory extinction process. Interestingly, in animals with a fully consolidated memory, a brief re-exposure to the training context induced NF-κB activation in the brain, whereas prolonged re-exposure induced NF-κB inhibition in correlation with memory extinction (Merlo & Romano, 2008). Such inhibition was found 45 min after the beginning of re-exposure, and NF-κB activity recovered to basal levels at 2 hr, when a clear extinction level had been acquired. Together, the data on NF-κB dynamics in reconsolidation and extinction indicate that NF-κB is initially activated during re-exposure to the training context. However, after some time, an NF-κB inhibition mechanism becomes active after prolonged re-exposure (Figure 7.4A). Limited data are available in the field of molecular mechanisms for memory reprocessing. The study of NF-κB dynamics in the crab brain provides new information regarding the molecular mechanisms involved in the switch that determines if a memory will be reconsolidated or extinguished.

On the basis of these findings, we propose a working model for the role of NF-κB in memory after retrieval. The initial process of retrieval-induced transcriptional activation would be mediated by protein kinases. In particular, the activation of the IKK and PKA protein kinases induces the activation and translocation of NF-κB to the nucleus. The prolonged presence of the training context would induce the activation of other mediators, such as protein phosphatases, which may increase the levels of the NF-κB inhibitor IκB and thus induce its nuclear exportation (Arenzana-Seisdedos *et al.*, 1997). Under this interpretation, the administration of NF-κB inhibitors during memory reactivation would reinforce the effect of prolonged exposure to the CS, inducing extinction strengthening (Figure 7.5). We return to this point later.

Our interpretation is consistent with the view that extinction formation recruits some mechanisms that are different from the mechanisms of original memory consolidation and that weakening of the original consolidated circuits is a neural correlate of memory extinction. However, we cannot exclude the requirement of reinforcement mechanisms in other circuits, independent of the NF-κB pathway, that mediate the same extinction process. In summary, the evidence reviewed here supports the view that extinction does not require the activity of NF-κB, a key TF involved in consolidation and reconsolidation, but actually requires its inhibition.

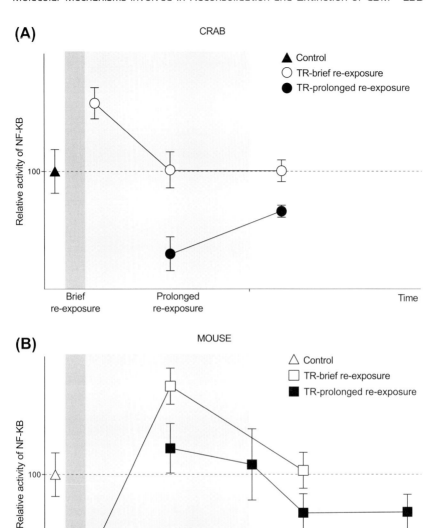

FIGURE 7.4 Time course of NF-κB activity during memory reconsolidation and extinction. The relative activity of NF-κB in reference to an untrained control is represented as a function of the time after brief or prolonged re-exposure to the training context. (A) Data from crab central brain. (B) Data from mouse hippocampus. TR-brief re-exposure, trained groups re-exposed for 5 min to the training context and sacrificed at different time points after re-exposure; TR-prolonged re-exposure, trained group re-exposed for different prolonged time points.

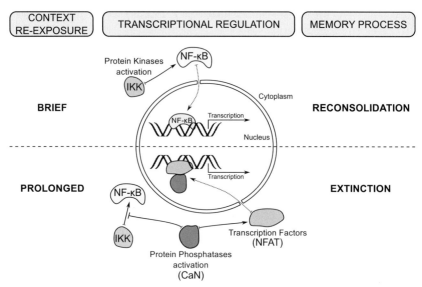

FIGURE 7.5 Transcription factor switching between reconsolidation and extinction. Under a brief re-exposure to the training context, protein kinases are activated and then transcription factor NF-κB is activated and translocates to the nucleus, where it induces the expression of target genes involved in reconsolidation. In contrast, if the stimulus is prolonged, protein phosphatases are activated and block NF-κB activation, allowing other transcription factors (e.g., NFAT in mice) nuclear translocation. Once in the nucleus, these transcription factors are able to regulate gene expression involved in extinction.

7.5 BUT WHAT ABOUT MY MOUSE?

The findings reviewed in the previous section regarding the role of NF-κB and IKK in memory reconsolidation and extinction led us to the following question: Is the role of NF-κB in reconsolidation and extinction, together with the proposed molecular switch for the determination of memory reprocessing after retrieval, a specific characteristic of crab memory or an evolutionarily conserved mechanism? To begin to answer this question, we performed experiments in mice using a different paradigm of contextual associative memory—contextual fear conditioning. In this task, mice associate the contextual characteristics of a training chamber with a mild footshock. During testing, the percentage of freezing response is determined. As in crab CSM, once memory is consolidated, a brief re-exposure to the training context (5 min) induces memory labilization-reconsolidation, whereas a prolonged re-exposure (30 min) induces memory extinction. The hippocampal formation is a key brain structure for the formation of contextual memories because it is involved in the processing and identification of contextual characteristics of different places and in the coding of a US associated with a particular place (Fanselow, 1986). We studied the dynamics of NF-κB activation in the hippocampus in the consolidation, reconsolidation, and extinction of contextual fear memory (de la Fuente, Freudenthal, & Romano, 2011). After three training trials, an initial inhibition of hippocampal

NF-κB was observed, which reverted to an activation that peaked 45 min after training. When animals were re-exposed for 5 min to the training context 1 day after training (once memory consolidation was fully achieved), a labilization-reconsolidation process occurred. After an initial inhibition, NF-κB showed a peak of activation in the hippocampus 15 min after the animal was removed from the context. However, if the mice received a prolonged re-exposure of 30 min (a treatment that induces memory extinction), NF-κB was not activated either during or after the extinction session. Instead, a tendency for a decrease in activity was observed up to 45 min after re-exposure (Figure 7.4B). All of these findings led us to postulate that NF-κB is activated after memory reactivation as part of the molecular mechanisms involved in memory reconsolidation. In contrast, if the re-exposure is prolonged, a mechanism that actively restrains NF-κB activation should be part of the molecular mechanisms of memory extinction formation. As in the case of crab memory, we postulated that NF-κB is necessary for memory reconsolidation and that its inhibition is required for memory extinction. Furthermore, we postulated that the phosphatase calcineurin is involved in the inhibition of NF-κB (Figure 7.5). To test these hypotheses, we performed inventive experiments in which, by means of local administration of NF-κB inhibitors in the hippocampus, we evaluated the requirements of these molecular mechanisms in reconsolidation and extinction. NF-κB was directly inhibited by means of the κB decoy DNA strategy. The DNA decoy consists of a double stranded DNA oligonucleotide containing a TF consensus sequence, which sequesters NF-κB from its normal sites of action. To inhibit NF-κB function, the κB decoy DNA was administered in the dorsal hippocampus to compete with endogenous TF and suppress its function. This oligonucleotide enters the cells and induces NF-κB inhibition 15 min after intrahippocampal injection (Boccia *et al.*, 2007; Freudenthal *et al.*, 2005). A mutated decoy oligonucleotide (mdecoy) was used as a control for the nonspecific actions of DNA administration in the hippocampus. mdecoy is a stringent control; the entire composition of the bases is conserved except for the position of one base in the consensus sequence that is mutated, impeding NF-κB binding (Boccia *et al.*, 2007). The infusion of κB decoy immediately after a brief re-exposure caused memory impairment when animals were tested a day after, but not 4 h after, re-exposure or when the mice were not re-exposed. The memory deficit was present even when the mice were tested 2 weeks later, supporting a permanent impairment in memory. In another experiment, we administered κB decoy into the dorsal hippocampus immediately after a 30-min extinction session. In complete agreement with the previous results in crabs, NF-κB inhibition resulted in extinction enhancement. Such an enhancement is manifested as a delay in spontaneous recovery. Effectively, the extinction session caused a significant reduction in freezing (the conditioned response) that was present 1 day after extinction induction, but freezing recovered 1 week later for the control group. However, decoy-injected animals continued to express low levels of freezing. Two weeks later, the decoy-injected mice completely recovered the freezing response, indicating that the original memory was intact and that spontaneous recovery was delayed. The extinction enhancement is equivalent to that previously found in crabs when another NF-κB inhibitor, sulfasalazine, was administered during prolonged re-exposure to the training context.

As mentioned previously, we postulated that a protein phosphatase is activated during prolonged re-exposure to the training context to block the NF-κB activation that normally occurs when memory is reactivated. The activation of NF-κB requires the phosphorylation of IκB, a protein that inhibits NF-κB in its normal inactive condition, and thus the action of the phosphatase can impede NF-κB activation. Calcineurin (CaN; also called PP2b), a protein phosphatase that is present in synaptic terminals, was found to be involved in neuronal plasticity and memory (Mansuy, 2003). Some experimental data support the idea that CaN can interact with IκB (Pons & Torres-Aleman, 2000). To evaluate the requirement of CaN in contextual fear extinction, we administered the specific CaN inhibitor FK506 into the dorsal hippocampus prior to the extinction session. This drug completely impaired extinction, allowing the injected mice to show normal levels of freezing, similar to those shown by nonextinguished animals. It is important to note that the same FK506 dose administered prior to a 5-min re-exposure reconsolidation session did not induce changes in the original fear memory. The previous findings suggest that CaN does not act during memory reconsolidation but is involved in memory extinction.

We next asked whether CaN is involved in NF-κB blocking during prolonged re-exposure to the learning context. We found that if FK506 is injected into the hippocampus prior to the extinction session, NF-κB is activated 15 min after the session, as it is after a reconsolidation session. This finding suggests that CaN blocks retrieval-dependent NF-κB activation during extinction. As mentioned previously, the behavioral consequence of CaN inhibition during the extinction session is that the original memory is expressed, and the animals show normal levels of freezing. All of this evidence supports the hypothesis that CaN inhibition of NF-κB is a part of the switch mechanism that determines, at least in the hippocampus, the occurrence of memory extinction instead of memory reconsolidation (Figure 7.2).

On the one hand, NF-κB is a TF that promotes synaptogenesis (Boersma et al., 2011; Gutierrez, Hale, Dolcet, & Davies, 2005), and the experimental inhibition of NF-κB blocks activity-dependent synaptic generation. On the other hand, CaN activity has been associated with long-term depression, a plasticity mechanism that reduces synaptic efficacy and induces synaptic elimination (Lisman, 2001). We hypothesized that during extinction, a temporary reduction in synaptic efficacy occurs in the hippocampal representation of the memory trace as part of the mechanism of memory extinction.

Although the inhibition of the original memory that occurs during extinction is transient in nature, it is considered to be a new memory that is present for one or more days. It is widely established that different types of memory require transcriptional regulation to persist. We postulate that during extinction formation, CaN induces transcriptional regulation to ensure the persistence of memory extinction for some days. In other cellular systems, CaN associates with nuclear factor of activated T cells (NFAT), a transcription factor that shares homology with the NF-κB family. CaN is able to produce NFAT dephosphorylation and nuclear translocation (Sugiura, Sio, Shuntoh, & Kuno, 2001). Once in the nucleus, NFAT regulates the expression of different genes. We detected CaN and NFAT nuclear translocation 45 min after the extinction session. Furthermore, a specific NFAT inhibitor that acts by interfering with the binding site of NFAT with CaN impaired extinction when it was administered into the hippocampus after the induction of extinction.

7.6 A CONSERVED MECHANISM

Together, the results obtained in crabs and mice support an evolutionarily conserved molecular mechanism that determines the course of memory after reactivation. Furthermore, the molecular processes described in mice, both for reconsolidation and for extinction, take place after the finalization of context re-exposure. These observations support the hypothesis proposed by the crab model regarding the boundary condition for both the mismatch component and the duration of the reminder. Under such a hypothesis, a decision between reconsolidation and extinction is expected after the reminder presentation. Accordingly, we found that the molecular switch occurred after context termination: NF-κB activation in reconsolidation takes place 15 min after re-exposure, and NF-κB blockade in extinction, together with CaN and NFAT nuclear translocation, occurs 45 min after re-exposure finalization. In the crab model, regarding the parametrical conditions for memory reprocessing after reactivation, time computing is a key component (Pedreira & Maldonado, 2003). Here, it may be represented by CaN activation induced as a function of prolonged CS presentation (Figure 7.2).

In summary, the evidence obtained in crabs and mice reviewed in this chapter supports the proposed model of a point of decision between memory reconsolidation and extinction at the end of the CS presentation. The non-reinforced reminder and the end of the training context re-exposure are the necessary conditions for both processes to occur. The results strongly suggest that neither reconsolidation nor extinction is concomitant with the onset of re-exposure. Either process could only be triggered once the definitive incongruence between what was expected and what actually occurred (mismatch) was confirmed. At the moment of the termination of the reminder, the duration of the reminder can be determined, defining which process will prevail after memory retrieval.

ACKNOWLEDGMENTS

We thank Dr. Liliana Orelli for language correction and Lic. Martín Carbó-Tano for the figure art.

REFERENCES

Alberini, C. M. (2009). Transcription factors in long-term memory and synaptic plasticity. *Physiological Reviews, 89*(1), 121−145.

Alberini, C. M., Ghirardi, M., Metz, R., & Kandel, E. R. (1994). C/EBP is an immediate-early gene required for the consolidation of long-term facilitation in *Aplysia. Cell, 76*(6), 1099−1114.

Arenzana-Seisdedos, F., Turpin, P., Rodriguez, M., Thomas, D., Hay, R. T., Virelizier, J. L., & Dargemont, C. (1997). Nuclear localization of I kappa B alpha promotes active transport of NF-kappa B from the nucleus to the cytoplasm. *Journal of Cell Science, 110*(3), 369−378.

Berman, D. E., & Dudai, Y. (2001). Memory extinction, learning anew, and learning the new: dissociations in the molecular machinery of learning in cortex. *Science, 291*(5512), 2417−2419.

Berón de Astrada, M., & Maldonado, H. (1999). Two related forms of long-term habituation in the crab *Chasmagnathus* are differentially affected by scopolamine. *Pharmacology, Biochemistry, and Behavior, 63*(1), 109−118.

Boccia, M., Freudenthal, R., Blake, M., de la Fuente, V., Acosta, G., Baratti, C., & Romano, A. (2007). Retrieval activation of hippocampal NF-kappaB is required for memory reconsolidation. *Journal of Neuroscience, 27*(49), 13436−13445.

Boersma, M. C., Dresselhaus, E. C., De Biase, L. M., Mihalas, A. B., Bergles, D. E., & Meffert, M. K. (2011). A requirement for nuclear factor-κB in developmental and plasticity-associated synaptogenesis. *Journal of Neuroscience, 31*(14), 5414−5425.

Bouton, M. (2002). Context, ambiguity, and unlearning: source of relapse after behavioural extinction. *Biological Psychiatry, 52*, 976−986.

Brooks, D. C., & Bouton, M. E. (1994). A retrieval cue for extinction attenuates response recovery (renewal) caused by return to the conditioning context. *Journal of Experimental Psychology: Animal Behavior Processes, 20*, 366−379.

Carew, T. J. (2000). *Behavioral Neurobiology: The Cellular Organization of Natural Behaviour.* Sunderland, MA: Sinauer.

Child, F. M., Epstein, H. T., Kuzirian, A. M., & Alkon, D. L. (2003). Memory reconsolidation in *Hermissenda. Biology Bulletin, 205*(2), 218−219.

Crow, T. (2004). Pavlovian conditioning of *Hermissenda*: current cellular, molecular, and circuit perspectives. *Learning & Memory, 11*, 229−238.

Davis, H. P., & Squire, L. R. (1984). Protein synthesis and memory: a review. *Psychological Bulletin, 96*, 518−559.

de la Fuente, V., Freudenthal, R., & Romano, A. (2011). Reconsolidation or extinction: transcription factor switch in the determination of memory course after retrieval. *Journal of Neuroscience, 31*(15), 5562−5573.

Debiec, J., LeDoux, J. E., & Nader, K. (2002). Cellular and systems reconsolidation in the hippocampus. *Neuron, 36*(3), 527−538.

Delorenzi, A., Dimant, B., Frenkel, L., Nahmod, V. E., Nässel, D. R., & Maldonado, H. (2000). High environmental salinity induces memory enhancement and increases levels of brain angiotensin-like peptides in the crab *Chasmagnathus granulatus. Journal of Experimental Biology, 203*(Pt 22), 3369−3379.

Delorenzi, A., Pedreira, M. E., Romano, A., Garcia, S. I., Pirola, C. J., Nahmod, V. E., & Maldonado, H. (1996). Angiotensin II enhances long-term memory in the crab *Chasmagnathus. Brain Research Bulletin, 41*(4), 211−220.

Devietti, T. L., Conger, G. L., & Kirkpatrick, B. R. (1977). Comparison of the enhancement gradients of retention obtained with stimulation of the mesencephalic reticular formation after training or memory reactivation. *Physiology & Behavior, 19*(4), 549−554.

Dubnau, J., Chiang, A. S., & Tully, T. (2003). Neural substrates of memory: from synapse to system. *Journal of Neurobiology, 54*, 238−253.

Dudai, Y. (2002). Molecular bases of long-term memories: a question of persistence. *Current Opinion in Neurobiology, 12*, 211−216.

Eisenberg, M., & Dudai, Y. (2004). Reconsolidation of fresh, remote, and extinguished fear memory in Medaka: old fears don't die. *European Journal of Neuroscience, 20*(12), 3397−3403.

Fanselow, M. S. (1986). Associative vs. topographical accounts of the immediate shock-freezing deficit in rats: implication for the response selection rules governing species-specific defensive reactions. *Learning and Motivation, 17,* 16−39.

Federman, N., Fustiñana, M. S., & Romano, A. (2009). Histone acetylation is recruited in consolidation as a molecular feature of stronger memories. *Learning & Memory, 16*(10), 600−606.

Feld, M., Dimant, B., Delorenzi, A., Coso, O., & Romano, A. (2005). Phosphorylation of extra-nuclear ERK/MAPK is required for long-term memory consolidation in the crab *Chasmagnathus. Behavioural Brain Research, 158*(2), 251−261.

Forcato, C., Argibay, P. F., Pedreira, M. E., & Maldonado, H. (2009). Human reconsolidation does not always occur when a memory is retrieved: the relevance of the reminder structure. *Neurobiology of Learning and Memory, 91*(1), 50−57.

Frenkel, L., Maldonado, H., & Delorenzi, A. (2005). Memory strengthening by a real-life episode during reconsolidation: an outcome of water deprivation via brain angiotensin II. *European Journal of Neuroscience, 22*(7), 1757−1766.

Freudenthal, R., & Romano, A. (2000). Participation of Rel/NF-kappaB transcription factors in long-term memory in the crab *Chasmagnathus. Brain Research, 855*(2), 274−281.

Freudenthal, R., Locatelli, F., Hermitte, G., Maldonado, H., Lafourcade, C., Delorenzi, A., & Romano, A. (1998). Kappa-B like DNA-binding activity is enhanced after spaced training that induces long-term memory in the crab *Chasmagnathus. Neuroscience Letters, 242*(3), 143−146.

Freudenthal, R., Boccia, M. M., Acosta, G. B., Blake, M. G., Merlo, E., Baratti, C. M., & Romano, A. (2005). NF-κB transcription factor is required for inhibitory avoidance long-term memory in mice. *European Journal of Neuroscience, 21,* 2845−2852.

Gainutdinova, T. H., Tagirova, R. R., Ismailova, A. I., Muranova, L. N., Samarova, E. I., Gainutdinov, K. L., & Balaban, P. M. (2005). Reconsolidation of a context long-term memory in the terrestrial snail requires protein synthesis. *Learning & Memory, 12*(6), 620−625.

Goelet, P., Castellucci, V. F., Schacher, S., & Kandel, E. R. (1986). The long and the short of long-term memory—A molecular framework. *Nature, 322*(6078), 419−422.

Gutierrez, H., Hale, V. A., Dolcet, X., & Davies, A. (2005). NF-κB signalling regulates the growth of neural processes in the developing PNS and CNS. *Development, 132,* 1713−1726.

Hepp, Y., Pérez-Cuesta, L. M., Maldonado, H., & Pedreira, M. E. (2010). Extinction memory in the crab *Chasmagnathus*: recovery protocols and effects of multi-trial extinction training. *Animal Cognition, 13*(3), 391−403.

Hermitte, G., Pedreira, M. E., Tomsic, D., & Maldonado, H. (1999). Context shift and protein synthesis inhibition disrupt long-term habituation after spaced, but not massed, training in the crab *Chasmagnathus. Neurobiology of Learning and Memory, 71*(1), 34−49.

Kaczer, L., & Maldonado, H. (2009). Contrasting role of octopamine in appetitive and aversive learning in the crab *Chasmagnathus. PLoS One, 4*(7). http://dx.doi.org/10.1371/journal.pone.0006223. e6223.

Kandel, E. R. (2004). The molecular biology of memory storage: a dialog between genes and synapses. *Bioscience Reports, 24,* 475−522.

Kandel, E. R. (2001). The molecular biology of memory storage: a dialog between genes and synapses. *Bioscience Reports, 21*(5), 565−611.

Lewis, D. J. (1979). Psychobiology of active and inactive memory. *Psychological Bulletin, 86*(5), 1054−1083.

Lewis, D. J., & Maher, B. A. (1965). Neural consolidation and electroconvulsive shock. *Psychological Review, 72,* 225−239.

Lisman, J. E. (2001). Three Ca^{2+} levels affect plasticity differently: the LTP zone, the LTD zone and no man's land. *Journal of Physiology, 532,* 285.

Locatelli, F., LaFourcade, C., Maldonado, H., & Romano, A. (2001). Characterisation of cAMP-dependent protein kinase isoforms in the brain of the crab *Chasmagnathus*. *Journal of Comparative Physiology: B Biochemical, Systemic, and Environmental Physiology, 171*(1), 33–40.

Locatelli, Fernando, Maldonado, H., & Romano, A. (2002). Two critical periods for cAMP-dependent protein kinase activity during long-term memory consolidation in the crab *Chasmagnathus*. *Neurobiology of Learning and Memory, 77*(2), 234–249. http://dx.doi.org/10.1006/nlme.2001.4007.

Lozada, M., Romano, A., & Maldonado, H. (1990). Long-term habituation to a danger stimulus in the crab *Chasmagnathus granulatus*. *Physiology & Behavior, 47*(1), 35–41.

Lubin, F. D., & Sweatt, J. D. (2007). The IkappaB kinase regulates chromatin structure during reconsolidation of conditioned fear memories. *Neuron, 55*(6), 942–957.

Maldonado, H. (2002). Crustaceans as models to investigate memory illustrated by extensive behavioral and physiological studies in *Chasmagnathus*. In K. Wiese (Ed.), *The Crustacean Nervous System* (pp. 314–327). Berlin: Springer.

Mansuy, I. M. (2003). Calcineurin in memory and bidirectional plasticity. *Biochemical and Biophysical Research Communications, 311*, 1195–1208.

Matthies, H. (1989). In search of cellular mechanisms of memory. *Progress in Neurobiology, 32*(4), 277–349.

McGaugh, J. L. (1966). Time-dependent processes in memory storage. *Science, 153*(742), 1351–1358.

Menzel, R. (2001). Searching for the memory trace in a mini-brain, the honeybee. *Learning & Memory, 8*, 53–62.

Merlo, E., Maldonado, H., & Romano, A. (2005). Activation of the transcription factor NF-kappaB by retrieval is required for long-term memory reconsolidation. *Learning & Memory, 12*(1), 23–29.

Merlo, E., Freudenthal, R., & Romano, A. (2002). The IkappaB kinase inhibitor sulfasalazine impairs long-term memory in the crab *Chasmagnathus*. *Neuroscience, 112*(1), 161–172.

Merlo, Emiliano, & Romano, A. (2008). Memory extinction entails the inhibition of the transcription factor NF-kappaB. *PLoS One, 3*(11). http://dx.doi.org/10.1371/journal.pone.0003687. e3687.

Misanin, J. R., Miller, R. R., & Lewis, D. J. (1968). Retrograde amnesia produced by electroconvulsive shock after reactivation of a consolidated memory trace. *Science, 160*(3827), 554–555.

Monfils, M.-H., Cowansage, K. K., Klann, E., & LeDoux, J. E. (2009). Extinction–reconsolidation boundaries: key to persistent attenuation of fear memories. *Science, 324*(5929), 951–955. http://dx.doi.org/10.1126/science.1167975.

Müller, G. E., & Pilzecker, A. (1900). Experimentelle Beitraege zur Lehre vom Gedaechtnis. *Zeitschrift fur Psychologie.* Suppl.1.

Myers, K. M., & Davis, M. (2002). Behavioral and neural analysis of extinction. *Neuron, 36*(4), 567–584.

Nader, K., Schafe, G. E., & LeDoux, J. E. (2000). Fear memories require protein synthesis in the amygdala for reconsolidation after retrieval. *Nature, 406*(6797), 722–726.

Pedreira, M. E., Dimant, B., & Maldonado, H. (1996). Inhibitors of protein and RNA synthesis block context memory and long-term habituation in the crab *Chasmagnathus*. *Pharmacology, Biochemistry, and Behavior, 54*(3), 611–617.

Pedreira, M. E., Dimant, B., Tomsic, D., Quesada-Allue, L. A., & Maldonado, H. (1995). Cycloheximide inhibits context memory and long-term habituation in the crab *Chasmagnathus*. *Pharmacology, Biochemistry, and Behavior, 52*(2), 385–395.

Pedreira, M. E., & Maldonado, H. (2003). Protein synthesis subserves reconsolidation or extinction depending on reminder duration. *Neuron, 38*(6), 863–869.

Pedreira, M. E., Perez-Cuesta, L. M., & Maldonado, H. (2002). Reactivation and reconsolidation of long-term memory in the crab *Chasmagnathus*: protein synthesis requirement and mediation by NMDA-type glutamatergic receptors. *Journal of Neuroscience, 22*(18), 8305–8311.

Pedreira, M. E., Perez-Cuesta, L. M., & Maldonado, H. (2004). Mismatch between what is expected and what actually occurs triggers memory reconsolidation or extinction. *Learning & Memory, 11*(5), 579–585.

Pereyra, P., Saraco, M., & Maldonado, H. (1999). Decreased response or alternative defensive strategy in escape: two novel types of long-term memory in the crab *Chasmagnathus*. *Journal of Physiology, 184*, 301–310.

Pérez-Cuesta, L. M., & Maldonado, H. (2009). Memory reconsolidation and extinction in the crab: mutual exclusion or coexistence? *Learning & Memory, 16*(11), 714–721. http://dx. doi.org/10.1101/lm.1544609.

Pérez-Cuesta, L. M., Hepp, Y., Pedreira, M. E., & Maldonado, H. (2007). Memory is not extinguished along with CS presentation but within a few seconds after CS-offset. *Learning & Memory, 14*(1), 101–108. http://dx.doi.org/10.1101/lm.413507.

Pons, S., & Torres-Aleman, I. (2000). Insulin-like growth factor-I stimulates dephosphorylation of ikappa B through the serine phosphatase calcineurin (protein phosphatase 2B). *Journal of Biological Chemistry, 275*, 38620–38625.

Przybyslawski, J., & Sara, S. J. (1997). Reconsolidation of memory after its reactivation. *Behavioural Brain Research, 84*(1-2), 241–246.

Przybyslawski, J., Roullet, P., & Sara, S. J. (1999). Attenuation of emotional and nonemotional memories after their reactivation: role of beta adrenergic receptors. *Journal of Neuroscience, 19*(15), 6623–6628.

Rescorla, R. A. (2004). Spontaneous recovery. *Learning & Memory, 11*(5), 501–509.

Roberts, A. C., & Glanzman, D. L. (2003). Learning in *Aplysia*: looking at synaptic plasticity from both sides. *Trends in Neuroscience, 26*, 662–670.

Romano, A., Delorenzi, A., Pedreira, M. E., Tomsic, D., & Maldonado, H. (1996a). Acute administration of a permeant analog of cAMP and a phosphodiesterase inhibitor improve long-term habituation in the crab *Chasmagnathus*. *Behavioural Brain Research, 75*(1–2), 119–125.

Romano, A., Freudenthal, R., Merlo, E., & Routtenberg, A. (2006a). Evolutionarily-conserved role of the NF-kappaB transcription factor in neural plasticity and memory. *European Journal of Neuroscience, 24*(6), 1507–1516. http://dx.doi.org/10.1111/j. 1460-9568.2006.05022.x.

Romano, A., Locatelli, F., Delorenzi, A., Pedreira, M. E., & Maldonado, H. (1996b). Effects of activation and inhibition of cAMP-dependent protein kinase on long-term habituation in the crab *Chasmagnathus*. *Brain Research, 735*(1), 131–140.

Romano, A., Locatelli, F., Freudenthal, R., Merlo, E., Feld, M., Ariel, P., Lemos, D., Federman, N., & Fustinana, M. S. (2006b). Lessons from a crab: molecular mechanisms in different memory phases of Chasmagnathus. *Biology Bulletin, 210*, 280–288.

Rose, J. K., & Rankin, C. H. (2006). Blocking memory reconsolidation reverses memory-associated changes in glutamate receptor expression. *Journal of Neuroscience, 26*(45), 11582–11587.

Rose, S. P. (1991). The biochemistry of memory. *Essays in Biochemistry, 26*, 1–12.

Sangha, S., Scheibenstock, A., & Lukowiak, K. (2003). Reconsolidation of a long-term memory in *Lymnaea* requires new protein and RNA synthesis and the soma of right pedal dorsal 1. *Journal of Neuroscience, 23*(22), 8034–8040.

Sara, S. J. (2000). Retrieval and reconsolidation: toward a neurobiology of remembering. *Learning & Memory, 7*(2), 73–84.

Sekiguchi, T., Yamada, A., & Suzuki, H. (1997). Reactivation-dependent changes in memory states in the terrestrial slug *Limax flavus*. *Learning & Memory, 4*(4), 356–364.

Stollhoff, N., Menzel, R., & Eisenhardt, D. (2008). One retrieval trial induces reconsolidation in an appetitive learning paradigm in honeybees (*Apis mellifera*). *Neurobiology of Learning and Memory, 89*(4), 419–425.

Sugiura, R., Sio, S. O., Shuntoh, H., & Kuno, T. (2001). Molecular genetic analysis of the calcineurin signaling pathways. *Cellular and Molecular Life Sciences, 58*, 278–288.

Suzuki, A., Josselyn, S. A., Frankland, P. W., Masushige, S., Silva, A. J., & Kida, S. (2004). Memory reconsolidation and extinction have distinct temporal and biochemical signatures. *Journal of Neuroscience, 24*(20), 4787–4795.

Tomsic, D., Pedreira, M. E., Romano, A., Hermitte, G., & Maldonado, H. (1998). Context—US association as a determinant of long-term habituation in the crab *Chasmagnathus*. *Animal Learning & Behavior, 26,* 196—209.

Troncoso, J., & Maldonado, H. (2002). Two related forms of memory in the crab *Chasmagnathus* are differentially affected by NMDA receptor antagonists. *Pharmacology, Biochemistry, and Behavior, 72*(1-2), 251—265.

Vianna, M. R., Szapiro, G., McGaugh, J. L., Medina, J. H., & Izquierdo, I. (2001). Retrieval of memory for fear-motivated training initiates extinction requiring protein synthesis in the rat hippocampus. *Proceedings of National Academy of Science of the United States of America, 98*(21), 12251—12254.

Chapter | eight

Using Reconsolidation and Extinction to Weaken Fear Memories in Animal Models

Carolyn E. Jones, Marie-H. Monfils

The University of Texas at Austin, Austin, Texas

8.1 INTRODUCTION TO FEAR CONDITIONING

Animal models of fear conditioning provide insight into the neural mechanisms underlying fear acquisition and also ways to reduce the intensity of the fear memory and its associated response. Rodents, such as rats and mice, are popular choices for studying fear in animals because they are relatively easy to house and care for and have stereotyped fear responses that are easily quantified. In Pavlovian fear conditioning, pairing an initially neutral conditioned stimulus (CS) (e.g., tone, light, or context) to an aversive unconditioned stimulus (US) (e.g., a footshock or tailshock) leads to the formation of a fear memory such that later presentation of the CS in the absence of the US elicits a conditioned response (Pavlov, 1927).

Fear conditioning has been performed in a number of different animal species, including humans. Unlike humans, however, most animals cannot provide a declarative account of fear, thus requiring scientists to observe behavioral methods of fear expression. Each species of animal exhibits stereotyped defensive responses to threat (in fear conditioning, that threat is the US) that can manifest as attempts to escape, fighting behavior, immobilization, or vocalizations (Bolles, 1970; Blanchard *et al.*, 1986) depending on the fear conditioning paradigm and species of animal used. In rats, fear is commonly measured as freezing, or the amount of time that the rat ceases any movement (Blanchard & Blanchard, 1969, 1971; Bolles & Collier, 1976). In a number of animals, fear can be measured by activation of the sympathetic nervous system, including increases in heart rate, blood pressure, and pupil dilation (De Toledo & Black, 1966); potentiated startle response to acoustic stimuli (Brown *et al.*, 1951; Davis *et al.*, 1993; Leaton & Borszcz, 1985); vocalizations **165**

Memory Reconsolidation. http://dx.doi.org/10.1016/B978-0-12-386892-3.00008-1

(Blanchard *et al.*, 1991); defecation (Fanselow & Kim, 1992); and hypoalgesia (fear-induced analgesia) (for review, see Fanselow, 1991; Helmstetter & Bellgowan, 1993). Classical fear conditioning is one of the most common methods of studying fear learning in animals. In rats, the conditioned response that is typically measured is either the amount of freezing exhibited during the presentation of a CS or the magnitude of the startle response shown when the CS is presented. When freezing is observed, the rat will stop moving and usually assume a crouching position in response to the CS (Blanchard & Blanchard, 1969). This can then be expressed as a percentage of time that the rat is freezing through the duration of the cue. Potentiated startle can also be used to assess fear. In such a paradigm, the experimenter makes use of a natural acoustic startle reflex of the rat and can measure the increase in this startle response after the pairing of a CS and US, based on the amplitude of movements made by the rat (Brown *et al.*, 1951; Davis & Astrachan, 1978). In both of these paradigms, fear is positively correlated with the measurement used, where greater amounts of freezing or startle response indicate higher levels of fear to the CS.

In addition to classical fear conditioning, in which a CS is simply paired with a US and a conditioned response is measured as an expression of fear, many animal models of fear learning make use of paradigms involving indirect measures of fear, such as either conditioned suppression or avoidance behavior (Table 8.1). Conditioned suppression allows a way to study conditioned fear in which the animal is first trained in an operant paradigm (e.g., pressing a bar for food) or allowed to perform a natural behavior (e.g., licking a drinking spout when the animal has been deprived of water) and subsequently fear conditioned to a CS once a baseline level of the operant behavior is established. Upon later presentation of the now fear-inducing CS, the animal will suppress the operant response in order to express a fear response. Fear can then be quantified as the amount of time it takes the animal to make a specific number of operant responses, the number of operant responses the animal makes while the CS is present, or a suppression ratio that is calculated as the number of responses made during the presentation of the CS divided by the total number of responses made before and during the presentation of the CS. A suppression ratio of 0 represents the highest level of fear, whereas a suppression ratio of 0.5 indicates no change in behavior (Estes & Skinner, 1941; Kamin, 1965; Leaf & Muller, 1965).

TABLE 8.1 Summary of Common Fear Conditioning Paradigms in Rodents

Paradigm	CS	US	Measure of Fear
Cued fear conditioning	Tone or light	Footshock	Freezing; fear potentiated startle
Contextual fear conditioning	Context (chamber or cage)	Footshock	Freezing
Approach avoidance	Tone or light	Footshock	Response latency
Inhibitory avoidance	Chamber or floor	Footshock	Latency to enter chamber

Avoidance procedures are another way to observe fear in nonhuman animals (Brogden *et al.*, 1938). Two common methodologies employed are inhibitory avoidance (Kim & McGaugh, 1992; Liang *et al.*, 1982; Parent *et al.*, 1995) and approach avoidance (Miller & Kraeling, 1952; Montgomery, 1955; Olds & Olds, 1963). In approach avoidance, animals are trained to perform a task (e.g., drink from a water bottle) and then later are punished through the administration of a shock for performing the previously trained task. Fear learning is then measured by the amount of time it takes the animal to complete the task (this is termed *response latency*) on a following day, with a larger response latency indicating greater levels of fear. Inhibitory avoidance also uses latency as a measure of fear but does not require training prior to the fear conditioning session. In a typical inhibitory avoidance paradigm, a rodent is placed in the light portion of a two-compartment chamber; the other compartment is dark. Rodents prefer dark contexts to light ones; thus, when the door separating the two chambers is opened, the rodent will have a natural inclination to enter the dark chamber. However, when the animal does enter the dark chamber, the entryway closes and the rat receives an electrical shock. When the animal is tested later, the latency to enter the dark chamber is used as a measure of fear memory retention because an animal with no recollection of the shock will quickly scurry into the dark chamber. In this situation, the inhibitory response is the animal remaining in the light chamber. Inhibitory avoidance is also sometimes referred to as passive avoidance because in order to avoid the aversive outcome, the animal is not actually required to perform any action or task. Approach avoidance, on the other hand, is considered as active avoidance and requires the animal to complete a trained task in order to avoid or terminate the US; this is not discussed further in this chapter.

Essential to survival in the wild, once learned, fear memories are extremely persistent. Reducing fear responses has thus proven a difficult task both in the laboratory, in animal models of fear conditioning, and in clinical settings (e.g., for anxiety and fear disorders, including post-traumatic stress disorder and specific phobias). Animal models of fear conditioning resemble pathological fear and anxiety conditions seen in humans (Rosen & Schulkin, 1998; Wolpe, 1981; for review, see Delgado *et al.*, 2006), and finding an effective method for reducing fear in these models is critical to our efforts to understand and treat fear conditions in the clinic.

Much recent research has focused on ways to reduce fear in animal models outside of immediately targeting the memory during its acquisition; this ranges from 1 day to several weeks after conditioning. These methods include extinction as well as techniques that target the fear memory during the labile reconsolidation period. In nonhuman animals, these methods can vary from non-imposing behavioral manipulations to potentially toxic drug injections and extremely invasive surgical operations. Consequently, researchers are constantly striving to identify practical ways to effectively reduce fear in animals in a manner that is readily translatable to a human population.

8.2 EXTINCTION

One of the oldest, most established approaches to reduce fear is through extinction or exposure therapy. In extinction, repeated presentation of the CS in the absence of the US leads to a progressive decrease in expression of fear to the stimulus (Bouton & Bolles, 1979; Pavlov, 1927; Rescorla & Heth, 1975). Extinction is effective in immediately reducing fear in a number of fear conditioning paradigms. In classical conditioning, extinction can be induced by repeatedly playing the CS without the accompanying US. For example, a rat that had been previously shocked when a tone was played would be returned to the conditioning chambers and hear repeated presentations of the tone without getting a shock. In avoidance paradigms, extinction is accomplished by allowing the animal to complete the previously punished task (drinking from a water bottle or entering the dark chamber) without getting shocked. After repeated presentation, the animal begins to show less of the conditioned or inhibitory response.

In Pavlov's initial conditioning experiments in dogs, extinction of the conditioned response (salivating) to the conditioned stimulus (a metronome) was seen after just a handful of unreinforced presentations of the metronome. Extinction outcomes have since been replicated extensively in fear-inducing paradigms both in animals and in humans using techniques similar to those used in Pavlov's laboratory. The common theme in any extinction paradigm in an animal model of fear learning is that the animal is always presented the CS in the absence of the aversive reinforcer that it had previously learned to associate together, and this unpairing—whether through explicitly unpairing the two stimuli or repeated presentation of just the CS—leads to a reduction in fear response.

Unfortunately, as initially suggested by Pavlov, it was soon confirmed that extinction procedures, although effective in reducing the fear response in the short term, do not generally modify the original fear memory trace and instead form a new, separate memory that is stored in parallel to the original memory of the fear conditioning (Bouton, 1993; Pavlov, 1927). This is evident at the behavioral level when the fear response reliably returns through the phenomena of spontaneous recovery, reinstatement, and renewal. Research on neural mechanisms underlying extinction also suggests that the extinction memory is processed differently than the original fear memory and serves to inhibit responding to the original memory (Milad & Quirk, 2002; Quirk et al., 2000; for review, see Quirk et al., 2006). Understanding these return-of-fear phenomena is essential for developing a system to permanently attenuate fear responding in any animal model.

In spontaneous recovery, the fear response returns after the passage of time (Burdick & James, 1970; Estes, 1955; Pavlov, 1927; for review, see Rescorla, 2004), and it was observed in the first extinction experiments performed by Pavlov with his dogs (Pavlov, 1927). This is commonly noticed by measuring the level of fear response at the end of extinction and comparing it with the level of fear response after a predetermined amount of time has passed.

Spontaneous recovery can also be measured by performing a fear retention test 24 hr after extinction (long-term memory) or a few hours after extinction (short-term memory) and comparing these levels of fear with the response evoked by the CS after a delay of several days. After this delay, if there is an increase in fear responding compared to the response seen at the end of the extinction session, or a previously measured time point soon after extinction, it is termed spontaneous recovery. It is spontaneous in nature because no other manipulations have been introduced to the animal besides simply the passage of time. This provided the first evidence to researchers that extinction does not target the original memory.

The critical component of spontaneous recovery is the amount of time that is allowed to pass between extinction and retention tests. Experiments in rats have shown that conditioned freezing after classical fear conditioning can return to levels equivalent to that seen prior to the extinction session as early as 10 days after the completion of extinction. However, when re-trained in the same extinction paradigm 14 days after the first extinction, rats show a faster rate of extinction than was seen in the first extinction session, which confirms that the animals do retain what they learned during extinction. The coexistence of complete spontaneous recovery and faster learning rate with further extinction training suggests that both the original fear conditioning memory and the extinction memory remain intact (Quirk, 2002).

Pavlov also observed that exposing the animal to the US could lead to the recovery of previously extinguished behavior. Reinstatement refers to the recovery of fear expression in response to the CS after the animal is subjected to an unsignaled US (footshock) or stressor (Rescorla & Cunningham, 1977, 1978; Rescorla & Heth, 1975). Rescorla and Heth (1975) postulated that the decrease in fear responding observed during extinction could be the result of two possible changes in associations for the animal: (1) It could be that the animal has formed a new memory where it no longer associates the CS with the US or (2) the animal may have formed a new representation of the US where the aversive stimuli used as a US is no longer as aversive as it was during fear conditioning. In a series of conditioned suppression experiments in rats, Rescorla and Heth (1975) provided experimental evidence supporting the first hypothesis. They showed that after extinction, the presentation of an aversive stimulus resulted in recovery of the extinguished fear response. In addition, they found this to be the case with the presentation of a US that was different than the one used in conditioning. In this experiment, an aversively loud noise was able to reinstate the extinguished fear response conditioned to a shock. However, the reinstatement effect is context specific. In conditioning experiments, the term *context* usually refers to the physical apparatus in which the animal is trained; however, it can also refer to emotional state (including drug state if the animal has been injected with any pharmacological agents), time of day, or any additional factors that may be present during learning. If the US is presented in a context different from the one in which the animal is later tested, such as a neutral context that the rat has never seen before, the recovery of fear is not as substantial as when the US is delivered in the same context as the testing session (Bouton, 1984; Bouton & Bolles, 1979b; Bouton & King, 1983; Westbrook *et al.*, 2002).

This context specificity of extinction confirms that the original fear memory is not erased during extinction in a new context and that compared to the conditioning memory, the extinction memory does not generalize as readily to new situations. When learned fear is extinguished in a context different than the one in which fear conditioning originally took place, the animal will show an increase in fear response when it is returned to the original fear conditioning context or to a novel context—a phenomenon referred to as renewal (Bouton & Bolles, 1979a; Bouton & King, 1983). There are several different ways in which renewal can be observed through a variety of different contextual modifications. Three important ways that extinction experiments can lead to the renewal of fear response in animal experiments are commonly referred to as ABA, ABC, and AAB conditioning, and each shows a return of fear. These letters represent the context for each stage of the experiment, in the following order: conditioning, extinction, and retention. Therefore, in an ABA design, the rat is fear conditioned in context A, extinguished in context B, and then returned to context A for fear memory retention tests. When the rat is returned to the conditioning context, it will show a renewal of fear response. In addition, in an ABC design, the rat is again fear conditioned in context A and extinguished in context B; however, it is put in a new context (context C) for retention tests and will again show a renewal of fear. Finally, in AAB conditioning (Bouton & Ricker, 1994), the rat is both fear conditioned and extinguished in context A but is put in a context new to the animal (context B) for retention and again shows a renewal of the fear response. Each of these experiments shows that if the rat is tested in a context different than the one in which it receives extinction, it will show a rebound of the fear response, providing further evidence that extinction is context specific (for review, see Bouton (1993) and Bouton, Westbrook, *et al.* (2006)).

Attempts to reduce this context specificity of extinction and create an extinction memory that more readily generalizes to other contexts have had mixed results. For example, Gunther and colleagues (1998) found that in a conditioned suppression paradigm in which drinking was suppressed during fear expression to a noise, if extinction was performed in three different contexts there was less renewal of fear (less licking while the CS was present) when the rats were tested for fear retention in a neutral context. However, Bouton, Garcia-Gutierrez, and colleagues (2006) failed to reduce renewal when extinguished in three separate contexts either when tested in a neutral context or when returned to the fear conditioning context (Figure 8.1).

Because extinction learning does not generalize to situations outside the extinction session, it is not a good candidate for permanent fear reduction. A recent approach to reducing the intensity of fear memories is through reconsolidation update and blockade paradigms.

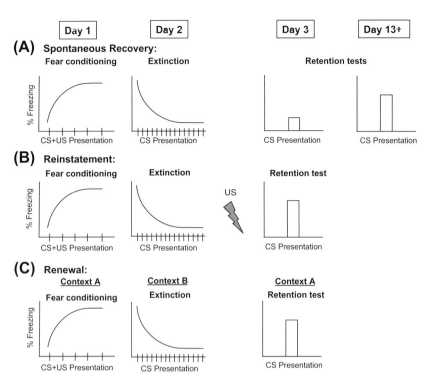

FIGURE 8.1 Graphical representation of freezing behavior of a rat during a traditional extinction experiment following cued Pavlovian fear conditioning and the return of fear seen after spontaneous recovery, reinstatement, and renewal. Percentage freezing, the percentage of time that the rat spends immobilized throughout the duration of the CS presentation, is the measure of fear behavior, where an increase in the percentage freezing represents a greater amount of fear to the CS. Fear conditioning is done 24 hr prior to extinction, and long-term memory tests, or retention tests, are performed 24 hr after the completion of extinction. (A) In spontaneous recovery, the CS is presented 10 days or more after extinction training is complete and an increase in fear response is observed. This increase is generally not present if the CS is presented the day after extinction or immediately after the completion of extinction as it recovers after a delay. (B) Reinstatement of the fear response is seen if the rat receives a footshock during the time between extinction and retention tests. After extinction, the rat is exposed to an unsignaled footshock (US), one that occurs in the absence of the CS, and returned to the same chambers for retention test, where it is exposed to the CS alone. The rat will show an increase in fear response compared to the response seen at the end of extinction; this is evidence that reinstatement of the fear response has occurred. (C) Renewal tests provide evidence of the context specificity of extinction and show that if the rat is fear conditioned in one context (for this example, context A can be a square chamber with a metal grid floor and dark walls and a lemon scent) and receives extinction in a different context (context B, which is a round chamber with plastic flooring, white walls, and peppermint scent), even though the rat will show a decrease of fear responding during extinction (and will maintain this decrease if tested soon after in context B), the rat will show an increase in fear responding if it is returned to the fear conditioning context (context A) at any point after extinction. This is a classic example of ABA fear conditioning. In ABC fear conditioning, the rat would be placed in a third context for the retention test and would demonstrate a similar level of fear response as seen in this ABA example.

8.3 RECONSOLIDATION

Applying reconsolidation update therapies to fear learning paradigms provides a method of inducing amnesia for the fear-inducing event or reducing the fear response by targeting the memory while it is reactivated during this "reconsolidation" period. In fear conditioning studies, these methods can be observed by first creating a fear memory through any of the fear conditioning paradigms described previously. The next day, the memory can be reactivated by presenting the animal with a combination of cues present from the conditioning session, and this is usually followed immediately with one of many techniques shown to interrupt the reconsolidation process. Retention of the fear memory is then quantified the following day by measuring a conditioned response to a CS (e.g., freezing), examining the inhibition of a previously trained task (conditioned suppression), or counting latency to enter into a dark chamber that had previously been the site of a footshock (inhibitory avoidance). The permanent, long-lasting impact of reconsolidation methods is gauged in a manner similar to that of extinction—by examining return of fear through spontaneous recovery, renewal, or reinstatement tests.

When memory reactivation experiments were in their infancy, the most prominent methods of inducing amnesia after a reactivation for previously learned fear events involved administering electroconvulsive shock (ECS) or hypothermia after a reactivation of the memory. These initial studies on reconsolidation-based techniques proved effective in reducing fear to a conditioned stimulus by targeting the original fear memory after a retrieval of the memory. Misanin and colleagues (1968) used a conditioned suppression paradigm in rats trained to drink from a waterspout. Twenty-four hours after Pavlovian fear conditioning, using a white noise CS and a footshock for the US, the fear memory was reactivated by presenting the CS, and the rats immediately received ECS. A second group of rats received ECS but were not exposed to the CS reactivation. In this experiment, fear was measured as the rate at which the rats licked the waterspout while the noise was playing; rats that were afraid of the noise would freeze instead of drink. Misanin *et al.* found that if ECS was administered after a reactivation of the fear conditioning session, rats showed significantly increased lick rate (less fear) than rats that did not have the memory reactivated, and this decrease in fear was equivalent to that seen in rats that received ECS immediately following conditioning. This retrograde amnesia for the fear conditioning memory was duplicated decades later through a number of other animal paradigms, including surgery, hypothermia, and pharmacological methods designed to block reconsolidation or update the memory during the labile reconsolidation period.

Hypothermia, as a technique to induce retrograde amnesia after a reactivation, was used by Mactutus and colleagues (1979) to reduce fear in a passive avoidance task in rats. This task used a two-compartment chamber with one white compartment and one black compartment. If the rat entered the black compartment, it received a footshock. Twenty-four hours after training, some of the rats received a reminder session in which they were exposed to the black compartment where they had previously received a footshock. Following this reactivation, rats were immersed in cold water to induce hypothermia. Twenty-four hours after the hypothermia session, the rats were tested in the same two-compartment chamber for retention of the fear memory. The researchers found that the rats that received the hypothermia treatment after the reactivation of the fear memory showed a drastic reduction in latency to enter the black (feared) compartment, suggesting that they were no longer afraid of the compartment in which they had previously been shocked. Similar results have been obtained using the US and conditioning context as a reactivating stimulus prior to hypothermia (Richardson, 1982).

In addition to electroconvulsive shock therapy and hypothermia, surgical lesions have been found to induce retrograde amnesia in fear settings after a reactivation. Land *et al.* (2000) observed retrograde amnesia to a signaled avoidance task in rats with dorsal hippocampus lesions obtained after a reminder session. Rats were first trained on a three-arm maze to enter the arm with a cue light in order to escape a footshock. Thirty days after training, the rats were returned to the maze and the cue light was turned on and off two times. After this reminder treatment, they received bilateral electrolytic lesions of the dorsal hippocampus. When these rats were tested on the maze, they made significantly more errors in choosing which arm to enter to avoid the shock than rats that were not reminded of the training before lesion and rats that were only reminded of the training but did not undergo surgery.

Pharmacological agents injected after retrieval of the fear memory provided the next major advance in reconsolidation research. These injections, although not without risk, provide a less invasive alternative to the previously mentioned therapies. Of important note is the use of propranolol, a β-adrenergic antagonist frequently used in humans for the treatment of hypertension, to reduce fear responding. When administered systemically to rats after exposure to the conditions in which they were previously shocked, these rats showed poor retention of the fear training previously received in an inhibitory avoidance task when tested for retention 48 hr after the propranolol injection (Przybyslawski *et al.*, 1999). In classical fear conditioning, infusions of propranolol into the lateral and basal nuclei of the amygdala as well as systemic injections of propranolol after a reactivation of the fear memory through the presentation of a single CS resulted in decreased freezing 48 hr after the injections. This decrease in fear response was maintained when the rats were tested again 1 month later (Debiec & LeDoux, 2004). Other pharmacological agents effective at reducing fear during reconsolidation include inhibitors of protein synthesis or kinase activity.

Anisomycin, which inhibits the protein synthesis required for the formation of long-term memories (for review, see Davis & Squire, 1984), can reduce the fear response when infused into the basal lateral nuclei of the amygdala within 4 hr of a reactivation of the original fear memory (Nader *et al.*, 2000). Judge and

Quartermain (1982) were among the first to investigate ways to reduce fear after a reactivation session using pharmacological agents. In a series of experiments in mice, they used subcutaneous injections of anisomycin to reduce fear after reactivation. Using the approach avoidance paradigm described previously, the fear response was measured as the latency for the mice to approach the waterspout and drink for 5 sec after 1 day of water deprivation. Three hours after training, in which the mice received an electrical shock when they approached the water bottle, the mice were exposed to the training context, a context similar to the one used for training, or a context different from the training area and then immediately injected with anisomycin. They observed that in the mice reactivated with the identical or similar context as the one used to train, anisomycin injections resulted in a significant decrease in fear response (latency to approach the water spout) compared to that of animals that received the same reactivation preceding an injection of saline.

Years later, Nader and colleagues (2000) performed an important study in which they showed that in fact when a memory is retrieved, it enters a reconsolidation period during which it requires new protein synthesis before becoming recoded into long-term storage. When that protein synthesis is blocked, as was done through the infusion of anisomycin, freezing (the expression of fear) was drastically reduced to the CS when tested the next day. However, this procedure does not affect fear expression to the CS when tested for short-term retention 4 hr after injections. This was proven to be the case both for newly acquired fear memories (training administered 24 hr before reactivation) and for old fear memories (training administered 14 days before reactivation). In addition, Nader *et al.* showed that the amnesiac effect is sensitive to the time between reactivation and drug injection. When anisomycin was injected immediately after the retrieval, freezing was reduced when tested to the CS 24 hr later. However, when a delay of 6 hr was introduced between the retrieval and injection, there was no significant reduction of freezing during the test session the following day (Figure 8.2).

Reconsolidation blockade as a treatment measure for fear is only advantageous over extinction if the treatment prevents any of the return of fear phenomena seen in extinction. The long-term effectiveness of anisomycin after reactivation was addressed by Duvarci and Nader (2004) by performing spontaneous recovery, renewal, and reinstatement tests in the same manner as frequently performed after extinction studies but instead performed after the injection of anisomycin after a retrieval. Using rats trained to fear a tone when paired with a footshock, they showed that the protein synthesis inhibitor, when administered after retrieval of the CS, prevented the return of fear in spontaneous recovery tests in which the CS was played for the rats 23 days after long-term memory retention tests; renewal tests that placed the rat in a new, neutral context after reactivation (ABC renewal procedure—rats were fear conditioned in context A, the memory was retrieved in context B prior to administration of anisomycin, and then the memory was tested for renewal in context C); or reinstatement after the administration of an unsignaled

Reconsolidation Blockade Protocol:

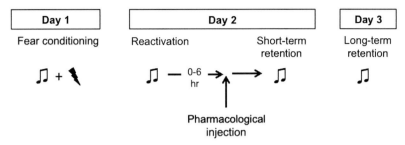

FIGURE 8.2 **Typical reconsolidation blockade protocol for classical tone fear conditioning in a rat using a pharmacological agent.** On Day 1, rats are fear conditioned to a tone paired with a footshock. The following day, rats are returned to the conditioning chambers and exposed to one presentation of the tone; this serves to reactivate the memory trace and initiates the reconsolidation window. After a predetermined amount of time has passed following the completion of the reactivation session (usually ranging from immediate to 1 hr), an injection of the pharmacological agent (e.g., anisomycin) is administered either systemically or into cannulas implanted into the brain. Short-term memory is tested by presenting the tone within a few hours of the injection. Twenty-four hours after the injection, rats are presented with another tone to test for long-term memory retention. If the reconsolidation blockade was successful, rats will show decreased levels of freezing during long-term retention tests compared to rats that were injected with saline and rats that did not receive a reactivation on Day 2. This is a standard protocol for the pharmacological blockade of reconsolidation; however, any of the methods described in this chapter could be administered in place of this injection (e.g., ECS).

footshock. This suggests that reconsolidation blockade with protein synthesis inhibitors such as anisomycin can permanently reduce fear by targeting the original fear memory in classical conditioning paradigms. Alternative protein synthesis inhibitors, such as the drug cycloheximide (Duvarci *et al.*, 2005), have also been used in similar reconsolidation blockade procedures with identical results in reducing fear in rats. However, the protein synthesis required for reconsolidation may have a biochemical signature that differs from that seen after initial learning (Hoeffer *et al.*, 2011), and other learning paradigms have shown that older memories are less receptive to reconsolidation blockade using protein synthesis inhibitors. For example, Milekic and Alberini (2002) showed that in an inhibitory avoidance task, memories showed little disruption if anisomycin was administered after a reactivation if they were older than 14 days. These results suggest that the strength or the age of the fear memory could influence the way in which reconsolidation paradigms are applied to reduce responding (for review, see Alberini, 2005).

Protein kinase A (PKA) activation in the basolateral amygdala has been shown to be required for both the consolidation (Schafe & LeDoux, 2000) and the reconsolidation of fear memories. In addition, inhibiting activation of PKA after the retrieval of the CS results in a reduction of fear (Duvarci *et al.*, 2005; Tronson *et al.*, 2006), whereas enhancing its activation after a retrieval leads to increased reconsolidation (increased freezing) in rats. In an experiment by Tronson and colleagues (2006), rats were fear conditioned to a tone by pairing it with a footshock. The next day, rats underwent a single retrieval of the tone in a new context to initiate the reconsolidation phase and were immediately infused with a PKA inhibitor into cannulas surgically implanted to target the basolateral nuclei of the amygdala. Fear was measured by the amount of freezing observed in the rats during presentation of the tone and was significantly decreased compared to that of rats that received a reactivation followed by an infusion of saline at test both 1 and 7 days after reactivation. In one of many control experiments performed, the authors also confirmed the time-sensitive lability window of reconsolidation-based techniques in which infusion of the PKA inhibitor 6 hr after reactivation of the fear memory did not have an effect on fear expression.

Unfortunately, although these drugs are very effective in rodent studies of fear reduction to a simple CS, anisomycin is toxic in humans and many of these studies require injection of a substance directly into the brain. Therefore, pharmacological reconsolidation blockade provides an excellent avenue to understand the role of protein synthesis in reconsolidation of fear memories and in developing animal models of fear reduction through reconsolidation blockade, but the ability to translate into a clinical setting remains questionable and not without risk.

8.4 BEHAVIORAL RECONSOLIDATION UPDATE

With extinction providing a practical but not permanently effective method to reduce fear responding behaviorally, and reconsolidation blockade providing an effective but impractical method for targeting the original fear memory and reducing fear, a more effective behavioral technique is much desired. Monfils and colleagues (2009) addressed this issue by combining the strengths of both reconsolidation and extinction methods into a behavioral paradigm to permanently reduce fear. In this paradigm, they found that providing a behavioral update using extinction training during the reconsolidation window allows for a persistent updating and prevents the return of fear.

In this experiment, rats were first fear conditioned to a tone paired with a footshock. The following day, rats were returned to the conditioning chambers and exposed to a single presentation of the tone and then immediately returned to their home cages in the animal colony for 1 hr. During this hour, the animals had free access to food and water and were left undisturbed by the experimenter. This retrieval session, of just a single CS, served to initiate the reconsolidation process in the same manner as experimenters have done for decades. However, if the rats were returned to the chambers for an extinction session within the reconsolidation window after the CS retrieval, they showed reduced fear expression after the extinction, which was measured as the percentage of time spent freezing during the duration of the CS; this fear expression did not return when tested in the classic return of fear phenomena: renewal, reinstatement, and spontaneous recovery.

Similar to previous experiments that attempted to reduce fear after a reactivation session, Monfils *et al.* (2009) found that the effectiveness of this paradigm was restricted to a specific temporal range between the retrieval and the extinction session. This retrieval + extinction procedure was equally effective in preventing the spontaneous recovery of freezing if the reactivation and extinction sessions were separated by 10 min or by 1 hr; however, it was not possible to prevent spontaneous recovery if the retrieval and extinction sessions were separated by more than 6 hr (this was tested at an interval of 6 hr and an interval of 24 hr). This window of update is consistent with results from previous experiments on reconsolidation in which the lability window after retrieval was measured. Further investigation of the neural underpinnings of this procedure found that GluR1 glutamate receptors showed reduced phosphorylation, a technique that represents a destabilization of the memory trace, if the interval between CS presentations was 1 hr (representative of the retrieval + extinction paradigm in which the delay is introduced between the first and the second CS presentation) compared to a 3-min interval between the two CSs that would represent a standard extinction session or if the measurement was taken 1 hr or 3 min after just one CS presentation. This further confirms that the time interval between the first and the second CS presentation is the crucial step to targeting the fear memory in this paradigm.

As previously addressed, one method to behaviorally determine which memories are still available to the animal is to subject it to a reconditioning or re-extinction session. Twenty-four hours after retrieval + extinction, rats were exposed to five tone—shock pairings (reconditioning) (Figures 8.3 and 8.4). The rats that had their fear response reduced through the retrieval + extinction paradigm showed significantly reduced rate of reacquiring the fear conditioning response compared to rats that were only exposed to the context during retrieval (in the absence of the CS) and rats that were being fear conditioned for the first time. This provides further evidence that targeting the fear memory during reconsolidation with an extinction session acts to update the original fear memory as less threatening. If the rats were indeed just suppressing the original fear memory with the extinction memory, as has been proven generally happens in traditional extinction paradigms, it would be expected that (a) the fear would return after the passage of time or any of the other return-of-fear phenomena and (2) when exposed to the CS—US pairing after retrieval + extinction, as it was during the reconditioning, the fear would rebound to levels equal to or greater than those seen in the groups receiving fear conditioning for the first time because it would again be reactivating that same fear conditioned memory. In mice, this behavioral manipulation has also been successfully applied to contextual fear conditioning. Mice that received an extinction session 2 hr after reactivation showed a permanent reduction in freezing when tested 17 days later, compared to mice that were not exposed to the reactivation of the context prior to extinction (Rao-Ruiz *et al.*, 2011).

This technique allows for a behavioral paradigm to permanently attenuate fear expression to a conditioned CS in a way that does not involve drugs or

Retrieval+Extinction Protocol:

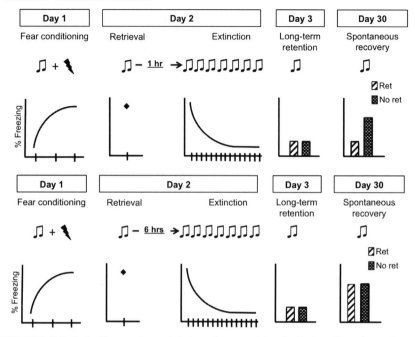

FIGURE 8.3 Extinction performed 1 hr after a retrieval of the CS reduces fear responding and prevents spontaneous recovery after auditory fear conditioning in rats. In this experiment, the fear response is expressed as percentage freezing, where higher percentages equate to increased fear levels. On Day 1, rats are fear conditioned to three pairings of a tone and footshock, and fear is rapidly acquired. The next day, rats receive either a retrieval session, consisting of a single presentation of the tone (ret), or no retrieval, which involves placement in the retrieval context without hearing the tone (no ret). Rats are then returned to their home cages for either 1 hr (top) or 6 hr (bottom), and then both retrieval and no retrieval rats are returned for an extinction session. The extinction session consists of 18 or 19 presentations of the tone in the absence of the footshock. The number of tone presentations (18 or 19) depends on whether the rat heard the tone during the previous retrieval session or not. Rats in the retrieval group receive an extinction session with 18 tones, and the no-retrieval group receives extinction with 19 tones; this ensures that the numbers of presentations of the tone are equal across both groups, with the only difference being the time between the first and second CS presentations. Both groups show reduced freezing during extinction. Long-term retention is tested by playing the tone on Day 3, and both retrieval and no-retrieval groups maintain the reduction in freezing acquired during extinction regardless of whether the time between retrieval and extinction was 1 or 6 hr. When the rats are returned to the chambers 1 month later and tested for spontaneous recovery by playing the same tone, the no-retrieval group shows an increase in fear response and the retrieval group maintains the fear reduction seen during the extinction session if the interval between retrieval and extinction is 1 hr (top), but if the interval is 6 hr, the retrieval rats show the same return of fear as their no-retrieval counterparts (bottom). Intervals of 10 min and 24 hr were also tested, with the 10-min interval group showing lack of spontaneous recovery similar to the 1-hr interval group and the 24-hr interval group showing full spontaneous recovery similar to the 6-hr delay group. These comparisons provide

surgery by slightly modifying the timing between the first and the second presentation of the CS, and it has also been successful in human fear conditioning (Schiller *et al.*, 2010). This retrieval + extinction procedure is not limited to fear memories because similar paradigms (with multiple days of retrieval + extinction training) have been shown to reduce drug cravings in both animal models of drug use and recovering heroin addicts (Xue *et al.*, 2012).

However, recent studies also suggest that there are a number of potential constrictions of behavioral reconsolidation update that should be considered. One critical factor is the age of the original memory. Clem and Huganir (2010) examined this retrieval + extinction procedure in mice in a cued fear conditioning setting and interestingly showed that this behavioral paradigm permanently reduces fear only for newly acquired fear memories. A nearly identical paradigm as that described previously, except with a 30-min interval between the retrieval and extinction sessions, was performed in mice in which the retrieval followed by extinction sessions occurred either 1 or 7 days after conditioning. When a 1 day-old fear conditioning memory was retrieved through a single presentation of the CS and mice were allowed a 30-min delay between retrieval and extinction sessions, they maintained a reduction in freezing when tested for renewal in a context different from the retrieval and extinction context. However, in the 7-day postconditioning group, the same retrieval + extinction paradigm that worked to attenuate the return of fear response in memories that were retrieved 24 hr after conditioning showed a return of fear during spontaneous recovery and renewal tests equal to that of the no retrieval groups that underwent traditional extinction (Clem & Huganir, 2010).

It has been suggested that the reconsolidation period initiates a period of lability in which the original fear memory is open to update (for review, see Tronson & Taylor, 2007). If what happens during this period is indeed updating the memory trace, then all activity that occurs between the retrieval and the extinction period must be closely monitored because the memory trace is now in a highly sensitive state. In fact, some researchers have obtained opposite results in this retrieval + extinction paradigm, with increased return of fear if extinction is administered after a retrieval. Chan *et al.* (2010) performed a similar retrieval + extinction experiment in rats using a 90-min interval between the retrieval and the extinction session and in which both retrieval and extinction were conducted in a context different from the fear conditioning context. However, in this experiment, the researchers found that when rats were returned to the fear conditioning context and exposed to the CS, not only was the

---

a clear depiction of how freezing behavior changes as time passes. When other return-of-fear assays were performed on separate rats with a 1-hr interval between retrieval and extinction, including renewal and reinstatement (data not shown), a similar effect was seen in which the rats preserved the reduced fear response in the retrieval group but not in the no-retrieval group. *Source*: Adapted from Monfils *et al.* (2009).

Reconditioning after Retrieval+Extinction:

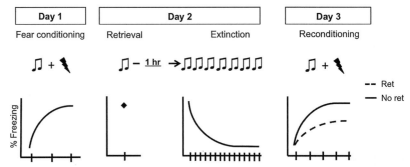

FIGURE 8.4 Twenty-four hours after retrieval + extinction (Day 3), rats showed a significant decrease in the rate of reacquisition when exposed to additional pairings of the tone and shock compared to rats that underwent only extinction and rats that had not been fear conditioned previously. The amount of freezing at each CS presentation was used as a representation of the amount of fear the animal learned. In the reconditioning portion of this experiment, each CS co-terminated with a US, which should cause the animal to freeze to a greater extent with the next presentation of the CS in preparation for an imminent shock if they learned that the CS predicts the US. *Source*: Adapted from Monfils *et al.* (2009).

fear response renewed but also the groups that underwent retrieval 90 min prior to extinction actually showed greater levels of freezing during renewal tests than the rats that did not have a CS retrieval prior to extinction. This suggests that when the memory is labile, it is extremely fragile, and depending on specific circumstances, subtle changes in methodologies may be responsible for updating the memory as benign or re-encoded as more fearful, consistent with experiments on pharmacological reconsolidation update (Tronson *et al.*, 2006).

In addition, it is unclear whether every species of animal undergoes reconsolidation, and there is some disagreement regarding the exact conditions necessary to induce reconsolidation for some learning paradigms (for review, see Nader & Einarsson, 2010). For example, Cammarota and colleagues (2004) found that in a step-down inhibitory avoidance paradigm in which rats were placed on a platform slightly elevated from a metal floor and shocked if they stepped off the platform onto the floor, a reactivation session of up to 40 sec on the platform was not sufficient to reactivate the fear memory and induce reconsolidation. They found that post-retrieval infusions of anisomycin did not reduce the fear response in rats trained in this paradigm. Suzuki and colleagues (2004) further examined the conditions of the reactivation session and found that in mice conditioned to fear a context, re-exposure to the context for 1 min before disruption with anisomycin was not sufficient to reduce fear but re-exposure to the context for 3 min or longer before disruption did result in significant decreases in freezing. In addition, they found that longer context retrieval sessions were necessary to reactivate a stronger memory trace. If the mouse was exposed to three footshocks during conditioning instead of one, a reactivation session of 10 min was required to reduce freezing after anisomycin infusion, whereas no effect was seen with a re-exposure of 3 or 5 min. Whether this means that some fear conditioning paradigms are not capable of undergoing reconsolidation or whether it is simply more difficult to retrieve and generate a window of lability in these paradigms requires additional research because the exact conditions necessary to fully retrieve a fear memory have yet to be completely uncovered. These potential constrictions limit not only pharmacologically induced reconsolidation update but also behavioral paradigms such as extinguishing the conditioned response during the reconsolidation window.

8.5 CONCLUSION

This chapter discussed a number of ways to reduce fear after conditioning in animal models of learning and provided evidence that although basic concepts prevail, slight differences in paradigms or species can yield varied results. Animal models allow us to identify the exact conditions necessary to reduce fear through behavioral means and also provide insight into the neural underpinnings that make this fear reduction possible, which should facilitate therapeutic avenues for fear-related disorders.

REFERENCES

Alberini, C. M. (2005). Mechanisms of memory stabilization: are consolidation and reconsolidation similar or distinct processes? *Trends in Neuroscience, 28*, 51−56.

Blanchard, R. J., & Blanchard, D. C. (1969). Crouching as an index of fear. *Journal of Comparative and Physiological Psychology, 67*, 370−375.

Blanchard, R. J., & Blanchard, D. C. (1971). Defensive reactions in the albino rat. *Learning and Motivation, 2*, 351−362.

Blanchard, R. J., Blanchard, D. C., Agullana, R., & Weiss, S. M. (1991). Twenty-two kHz alarm cries to presentation of a predator, by laboratory rats living in visible burrow systems. *Physiology & Behavior, 50*, 967−972.

Blanchard, R. J., Flannelly, K. J., & Blanchard, D. C. (1986). Defensive behaviors of laboratory and wild *Rattus norvegicus*. *Journal of Comparative Psychology, 100*, 101−107.

Bolles, R. C. (1970). Species-specific defense reactions and avoidance learning. *Psychological Review, 77*, 32−48.

Bolles, R. C., & Collier, A. C. (1976). Effect of predictive cues on freezing in rats. *Animal Learning and Behavior, 4*, 6−8.

Bouton, M. E. (1984). Differential control by context in the inflation and reinstatement paradigms. *Journal of Experimental Psychology: Animal Behavior Processes, 10*, 56−74.

Bouton, M. E. (1993). Context, time, and memory retrieval in the interference paradigms of Pavlovian learning. *Psychological Bulletin, 114*, 80−99.

Bouton, M. E., & Bolles, R. C. (1979a). Contextual control of the extinction of conditioned fear. *Learning and Motivation, 10*, 445−466.

Bouton, M. E., & Bolles, R. C. (1979b). Role of conditioned contextual stimuli in reinstatement of extinguished fear. *Journal of Experimental Psychology: Animal Behavior Processes, 5*, 368−378.

Bouton, M. E., Garcia-Gutierrez, A., Zilski, J., & Moody, E. W. (2006). Extinction in multiple contexts does not necessarily make extinction less vulnerable to relapse. *Behaviour Research and Therapy, 44*, 983−994.

Bouton, M. E., & King, D. A. (1983). Contextual control of the extinction of conditioned fear: tests for the associative value of the context. *Journal of Experimental Psychology: Animal Behavior Processes, 9*, 248−265.

Bouton, M. E., & Ricker, S. T. (1994). Renewal of extinguished responding in a second context. *Animal Learning & Behavior, 22*, 317—324.

Bouton, M. E., Westbrook, F., Corcoran, K. A., & Maren, S. (2006). Contextual and temporal modulation of extinction: behavioral and biological mechanisms. *Biological Psychiatry, 60*, 352—360.

Brogden, W. J., Lipman, E. A., & Culler, E. (1938). The role of incentive in conditioning and extinction. *American Journal of Psychology, 51*, 109—117.

Brown, J. S., Kalish, H. I., & Farber, I. E. (1951). Conditioned fear as revealed by magnitude of startle response to an auditory stimulus. *Journal of Experimental Psychology, 41*, 317—328.

Burdick, C. K., & James, J. P. (1970). Spontaneous recovery of conditioned suppression of licking by rats. *Journal of Comparative and Physiological Psychology, 72*, 467—470.

Cammarota, M., Bevilaqua, L. R. M., Medina, J. H., & Izquierdo, I. (2004). Retrieval does not induce reconsolidation of inhibitory avoidance memory. *Learning & Memory, 11*, 572—578.

Chan, W. Y. M., Leung, H. T., Westbrook, F., & McNally, G. P. (2010). Effects of recent exposure to a conditioned stimulus on extinction of Pavlovian fear conditioning. *Learning & Memory, 17*, 512—521.

Clem, R. L., & Huganir, R. L. (2010). Calcium-permeable AMPA receptor dynamics mediate fear memory erasure. *Science, 330*, 1108—1112.

Davis, H. P., & Squire, L. R. (1984). Protein synthesis and memory: a review. *Psychological Bulletin, 96*, 518—559.

Davis, M., & Astrachan, D. I. (1978). Conditioned fear and startle magnitude: effects of different footshock or backshock intensities used in training. *Journal of Experimental Psychology: Animal Behavior Processes, 4*, 95—103.

Davis, M., Falls, W. A., Campeau, S., & Kim, M. (1993). Fear-potentiated startle: a neural and pharmacological analysis. *Behavioral Brain Research, 58*, 175—198.

De Toledo, L., & Black, A. H. (1966). Heart rate: changes during conditioned suppression in rats. *Science, 152*, 1404—1406.

Debiec, J., & LeDoux, J. E. (2004). Disruption of reconsolidation but not consolidation of auditory fear conditioning by noradrenergic blockade in the amygdala. *Neuroscience, 129*, 267—272.

Delgado, M. R., Olsson, A., & Phelps, E. A. (2006). Extending animal models of fear conditioning to humans. *Biological Psychology, 73*, 39—48.

Duvarci, S., & Nader, K. (2004). Characterization of fear memory reconsolidation. *Journal of Neuroscience, 24*, 9269—9275.

Duvarci, S., Nader, K., & LeDoux, J. E. (2005). Activation of extracellular signal-regulated kinase-mitogen-activated protein kinase cascade in the amygdala is required for memory reconsolidation of auditory fear conditioning. *European Journal of Neuroscience, 21*, 283—289.

Estes, W. K. (1955). Statistical theory of spontaneous recovery and regression. *Psychological Review, 62*, 145—154.

Estes, W. K., & Skinner, B. F. (1941). Some quantitative properties of anxiety. *Journal of Experimental Psychology, 29*, 390—400.

Fanselow, M. S. (1991). Analgesia as a response to aversive Pavlovian conditional stimuli: Cognitive and emotional mediators. In M. R. Denny (Ed.), *Fear, avoidance, and phobias: A fundamental analysis* (pp. 61—86). Hillsdale, NJ: Erlbaum.

Gunther, L. M., Denniston, J. C., & Miller, R. R. (1998). Conducting exposure treatment in multiple contexts can prevent relapse. *Behaviour Research and Therapy, 36*, 75—91.

Helmstetter, F. J., & Bellgowan, P. S. (1993). Lesions of the amygdala block conditional hypoalgesia on the tail flick test. *Brain Research, 612*, 253—257.

Hoeffer, C. A., Cowansage, K. K., Arnold, E. C., Banko, J. L., Moerke, N. J., Rodriguez, R., Schmidt, E. K., Klosi, E., Chorev, M., Lloyd, R. E., Pierre, P., Wagner, G., LeDoux, J. E., & Klann, E. (2011). Inhibition of the interactions between eukaryotic initiation factors 4E and 4G impairs long-term associative memory consolidation but not reconsolidation. *Proceedings of the National Academy of Sciences of the USA, 108*, 3383—3388.

Judge, M. E., & Quartermain, D. (1982). Characteristics of retrograde amnesia following reactivation of memory in mice. *Physiology & Behavior, 28*, 585−590.

Kamin, L. J. (1965). Temporal and intensity characteristics of the conditioned stimulus. In W. F. Prokasy (Ed.), *Classical conditioning*. New York: Appleton-Century-Crofts.

Kim, M., & McGaugh, J. L. (1992). Effects of intra-amygdala injections of NMDA receptor antagonists on acquisition and retention of inhibitory avoidance. *Brain Research, 585*, 35−48.

Land, C., Bunsey, M., & Riccio, D. C. (2000). Anomalous properties of hippocampal lesion-induced retrograde amnesia. *Psychobiology, 28*, 476−485.

Leaf, R. C., & Muller, S. A. (1965). A simple method for CER conditioning and measurement. *Psychological Reports, 17*, 211−215.

Leaton, R. N., & Borszcz, G. S. (1985). Potentiated startle: its relation to freezing and shock intensity in rats. *Journal of Experimental Psychology: Animal Behavior Processes, 11*, 421−428.

Liang, K. C., McGaugh, J. L., Martinez, J. L., Jr., Jensen, R. A., Vasquez, B. J., & Messing, R. B. (1982). Post-training amygdaloid lesions impair retention of an inhibitory avoidance response. *Behavioral Brain Research, 4*, 237−249.

Mactutus, C. F., Riccio, D. C., & Ferek, J. M. (1979). Retrograde amnesia for old (reactivated) memory: some anomalous characteristics. *Science, 204*, 1319−1320.

Misanin, J. R., Miller, R. R., & Lewis, D. J. (1968). Retrograde amnesia produced by electroconvulsive shock after reactivation of a consolidated memory trace. *Science, 160*, 203−204.

Monfils, M. H., Cowansage, K. K., Klann, E., & LeDoux, J. E. (2009). Extinction-reconsolidation boundaries: key to persistent attenuation of fear memories. *Science, 324*, 951−955.

Montgomery, K. C. (1955). The relation between fear induced by novel stimulation and exploratory drive. *Journal of Comparative and Physiological Psychology, 48*, 254−260.

Milad, M. R., & Quirk, G. J. (2002). Neurons in medial prefrontal cortex signal memory for fear extinction. *Nature, 420*, 70−74.

Milekic, M. H., & Alberini, C. M. (2002). Temporally graded requirement for protein synthesis following memory reactivation. *Neuron, 36*, 521−525.

Miller, N. E., & Kraeling, D. (1952). Displacement: greater generalization of approach than avoidance in a generalized approach-avoidance conflict. *Journal of Experimental Psychology, 43*, 217−221.

Nader, K., & Einarsson, E. O. (2010). Memory reconsolidation: an update. *Annals of the New York Academy of Sciences, 1191*, 27−41.

Nader, K., Schafe, G. E., & Le Doux, J. E. (2000). Fear memories require protein synthesis in the amygdala for reconsolidation after retrieval. *Nature, 406*, 722−726.

Olds, M. E., & Olds, J. (1963). Approach-avoidance analysis of rat diencephalon. *Journal of Comparative Neurology, 120*, 259−295.

Parent, M. B., Quirarte, G. L., Cahill, L., & McGaugh, J. L. (1995). Spared retention of inhibitory avoidance learning after posttraining amygdala lesions. *Behavioral Neuroscience, 109*, 803−807.

Pavlov, I. P. (1927). Conditioned reflexes *(G.V. Anrep, Trans.)*. London: Oxford University Press.

Przybyslawski, J., Roullet, P., & Sara, S. J. (1999). Attenuation of emotional and nonemotional memories after their reactivation: role of β adrenergic receptors. *Journal of Neuroscience, 19*, 6623−6628.

Quirk, G. J. (2002). Memory for extinction of conditioned fear is long-lasting and persists following spontaneous recovery. *Learning & Memory, 9*, 402−407.

Quirk, G. J., Garcia, R., & Gonzalez-Lima, F. (2006). Prefrontal mechanisms in extinction of conditioned fear. *Biological Psychiatry, 60*, 337−343.

Quirk, G. J., Russo, G. K., Barron, J. L., & Lebron, K. (2000). The role of ventromedial prefrontal cortex in the recovery of extinguished fear. *Journal of Neuroscience, 20*, 6225−6231.

Rao-Ruiz, P., Rotaru, D. C., van der Loo, R. J., Mansvelder, H. D., Stiedl, O., Smit, A. B., & Spijker, S. (2011). Retrieval-specific endocytosis of GluA2-AMPARs underlies adaptive reconsolidation of contextual fear. *Nature Neuroscience, 14*, 1302–1308.

Rescorla, R. A. (2004). Spontaneous recovery. *Learning & Memory, 11*, 501–509.

Rescorla, R. A., & Cunningham, C. L. (1977). The erasure of reinstated fear. *Animal Learning & Behavior, 5*, 386–394.

Rescorla, R. A., & Cunningham, C. L. (1978). Recovery of the US representation over time during extinction. *Learning and Motivation, 9*, 373–391.

Rescorla, R. A., & Heth, C. D. (1975). Reinstatement of fear to an extinguished conditioned stimulus. *Journal of Experimental Psychology: Animal Behavior Processes, 104*, 88–96.

Richardson, R., Riccio, D. C., & Mowrey, H. (1982). Retrograde amnesia for previously acquired Pavlovian conditioning: UCS exposure as a reactivation treatment. *Physiological Psychology, 10*, 384–390.

Rosen, J. B., & Schulkin, J. (1998). From normal fear to pathological anxiety. *Psychological Review, 105*, 325–350.

Schafe, G. E., & LeDoux, J. E. (2000). Memory consolidation of auditory Pavlovian fear conditioning requires protein synthesis and protein kinase A in the amygdala. *Journal of Neuroscience, 20*, RC96.

Schiller, D., Monfils, M. H., Raio, C. M., Johnson, D. C., LeDoux, J. E., & Phelps, E. A. (2010). Preventing the return of fear in humans using reconsolidation update mechanisms. *Nature, 463*, 49–53.

Suzuki, A., Josselyn, S. A., Frankland, P. W., Masushige, S., Silva, A. J., & Kida, S. (2004). Memory reconsolidation and extinction have distinct temporal and biochemical signatures. *Journal of Neuroscience, 24*, 4787–4795.

Tronson, N. C., & Taylor, J. R. (2007). Molecular memories of memory reconsolidation. *Nature Reviews Neuroscience, 8*, 262–275.

Tronson, N. C., Wiseman, S. L., Olausson, P., & Taylor, J. R. (2006). Bidirectional behavioral plasticity of memory reconsolidation depends on amygdalar protein kinase A. *Nature Neuroscience, 9*, 167–169.

Westbrook, R. F., Iordanova, M., McNally, G., Richardson, R., & Harris, J. A. (2002). Reinstatement of fear to an extinguished conditioned stimulus: two roles for context. *Journal of Experimental Psychology: Animal Behavior Processes, 28*, 97–110.

Wolpe, J. (1981). The dichotomy between classical conditioned and cognitively learned anxiety. *Journal of Behavior Therapy and Experimental Psychiatry, 12*, 35–42.

Xue, Y. X., Luo, Y. X., Wu, P., Shi, H. S., Xue, L. F., Chen, C., & Lu, L. (2012). A memory retrieval-extinction procedure to prevent drug craving and relapse. *Science, 336*, 241–245.

Chapter | nine

Reconsolidation in Humans

Elizabeth A. Phelps[*], **Daniela Schiller**[†]

[*]*New York University, New York, New York; and Nathan Kline Institute, Orangeburg, New York*
[†]*Icahn School of Medicine at Mt. Sinai, New York, New York*

Since the seminal paper by Nader and colleagues (2000) reinvigorated interest in memory reconsolidation, there have been approximately 400 published papers examining the mechanisms, functions, and constraints underlying this important memory phenomenon in nonhuman animals. Interestingly, in this same time period, the number of investigations of reconsolidation in humans is a few dozen. This is somewhat puzzling. Like most neuroscience research in other species, the importance of research on reconsolidation lies not in our greater understanding of the mechanisms of animal behavior but, rather, the possibility that this research will translate to important insights into human memory function and perhaps novel treatments for psychopathology. Given this, one might expect a vigorous effort to investigate these processes in humans.

In this chapter, we provide a comprehensive review of research on reconsolidation in humans to date. We examine the different techniques that have been used to explore memory reconsolidation in humans and highlight some of the unique challenges that arise when investigating reconsolidation in human participants. Through this survey of existing studies, we explore some of the reasons why this science has been slow to emerge, and we suggest some potential avenues for future research.

9.1 HISTORICAL ANTECEDENTS: THE DYNAMIC NATURE OF HUMAN MEMORY

Although most recent investigations of reconsolidation in humans were inspired by the resurgence of research on this topic in nonhuman animals, there is a rich literature in cognitive studies of memory that point to processes with a similar nature. Specifically, this earlier research explored what is proposed to be a primary function of reconsolidation, which is to support the dynamic nature of memory—through either memory strengthening with repeated retrievals

185

Memory Reconsolidation. http://dx.doi.org/10.1016/B978-0-12-386892-3.00009-3

and reconsolidation (Alberini, 2011) or memory modifications through altering or interfering with the reconsolidation process (Dudai, 2012; Monfils *et al.*, 2009). Although these earlier studies did not use the term *reconsolidation*, some of the proposed theoretical explanations suggested mnemonic processes that are reminiscent of what one might call reconsolidation today. Unlike the majority of reconsolidation studies in nonhuman animals, which examine fear memories, these early cognitive studies investigated the dynamic nature of human episodic memory.

The idea that human episodic memory is dynamic was apparent in some of the earliest psychological theories and studies of memory. In his seminal book *Principles of Psychology*, William James (1890) suggested that memory retrieval in different contexts changed the nature of a memory. An early experiment by Bartlett (1932) directly tested the dynamic nature of memory by presenting participants stories from another culture and asking them to recall the stories at a later time. These recollections were not precise but, rather, reflected the participants' interpretations of the stories based on their own cultural and logical expectations. This early research spoke to the reconstructive nature of human memory.

Since this early work, there have been numerous investigations of the dynamic nature of human episodic memory (Tulving & Thompson, 1973), but two lines of research in particular were linked to theoretical models that are conceptually similar to reconsolidation. The first examined the misinformation effect. Introduced by Elizabeth Loftus approximately 30 years ago, studies of this effect explore how introducing new, conflicting information at the time of memory retrieval biased later recollections of the original memory to incorporate this new (mis)information (Loftus, 1979, 1981, 2005a,b; Loftus & Yuille, 1984). In a classic study, Loftus and colleagues (1979) presented participants with slides of an automobile accident that contained either a "stop" sign or a "yield" sign. At a later time, subjects were asked questions that included misinformation about the identity of the sign. For example, if a "yield" sign was presented initially, the questionnaire referred to a "stop" sign. At a subsequent memory test, most of the participants reported the incorrect sign, suggesting this misinformation was incorporated into memory for the accident. These findings and others like it led to debates about the nature of memory that allowed misinformation to be so easily merged into an old memory representation. To explain this effect, Loftus proposed a memory mechanism not so different from reconsolidation. She suggested that new information available at the time of retrieval is integrated into the old memory, essentially rewriting it. In this view, the initial memory no longer exists in its original form but, rather, represents an integration of information available at initial encoding and at the time of retrieval.

The notion that memories can be changed or rewritten with retrieval is suggestive of a process captured by current research on human reconsolidation (Hupbach *et al.*, 2007; Schiller *et al.*, 2010; Walker *et al.*, 2003). At the time, however, this idea was not uniformly embraced by the cognitive science community. Some argued that the misinformation effect occurred not because the original memory trace was altered but, rather, because participants forgot the original event and were lured into responding with the incorrect information (McCloskey & Zaragoza, 1985). Others suggested that the consequences of studies on misinformation could reflect a problem of source memory, in which participants misattributed the context or source of the inconsistent information, with or without an intact original memory trace (Lindsay & Johnson, 1989). The psychological research at the time was not able to resolve these theoretical debates about the mechanistic underpinnings of the misinformation effect.

A second line of research that led to the suggestion of a mnemonic process similar to reconsolidation examined the effects of massed versus distributed practice on memory strength. The massed versus distributed practice effect was first described by the famous memory researcher Ebbinghaus in the late 1800s and has been replicated in hundreds of studies since that time (for a comprehensive review, see Cepeda *et al.*, 2006). The basic premise of this effect is that memory practice that is spaced over time leads to better subsequent memory than similar amounts of practice conducted simultaneously.

There are several theories proposed to account for the benefit of distributed practice on memory strength, but one in particular captures an idea that has been suggested in current models of reconsolidation. Specifically, one view of reconsolidation in the domain of episodic or declarative memory is that a primary function is to enhance lingering memory consolidation and strengthen later memory (Alberini, 2011). This view is similar to the consolidation theory of massed versus distributed practice. This theory suggests that distributed memory practice is superior because it increases the resistance to decay of the memory trace through a process akin to augmenting memory consolidation with repeated presentation (Reed, 1976; Wickelgren, 1972). There are also alternative theoretical accounts to explain the benefits of distributed practice (Cepeda *et al.*, 2006), but much like the misinformation effect described previously, psychological research alone was not sufficient to differentiate the likelihood of these proposed mechanisms.

An important implication of the research on massed versus distributed practice is its potential impact on educational practices. A recent variation of these ideas highlights the benefit of distributed retrieval and testing (as opposed to repeated encoding) on long-term retention (Karpicke & Roediger, 2008). Interestingly, these recent investigations have been linked, theoretically at least, to a reconsolidation mechanism (Lasry *et al.*, 2008).

Finally, unlike nonhuman animal studies of reconsolidation, there are historically very few studies in humans that have explicitly tried to disrupt memories with some type of invasive intervention. One exception is an early literature examining the impact of electroconvulsive therapy (ECT) on memory consolidation (e.g., Squire *et al.*, 1976). This research primarily examined the retention of information learned immediately prior to ECT, which was thought to disrupt memory consolidation. In an extension of this work, there were two attempts in humans to determine if ECT also disrupted older memories if administered immediately following retrieval. The first examined the effect of ECT on symptoms of psychopathology including obsessions and hallucinations. It was found that when patients were prompted to retrieve some of their more disturbing symptoms prior to ECT, the treatment was more effective at diminishing these symptoms (Rubin, 1976). The second was a more direct, experimental investigation of the impact of retrieving remote episodic memories prior to ECT. Consistent with previous studies, Squire and colleagues (1976) found that memories for information learned immediately prior to ECT were impaired following treatment. However, there was no impairment for information learned earlier but retrieved immediately prior to ECT. Based on these results, Squire *et al.* concluded that retrieval did not render older memories labile and that any memory impairment observed with ECT was due to disrupting a time-dependent consolidation process.

The studies on verbal learning in the early days of cognitive science resulted in a wealth of behavioral findings and memory models, many of which have held up over time (for an overview, see Crowder, 1976). However, with rare exceptions, these theoretical accounts of human memory were not informed by neurobiological models derived from research in nonhuman animals. In the past few decades, however, investigations of the neural systems underlying human behavior have become the dominant approach in research on human cognition. One consequence of this cognitive neuroscience approach is the enhanced characterization of multiple types of memory with unique properties that rely on independent but interacting neural systems (Schacter & Tulving, 1994). This shift has also opened the door for animal models of memory mechanisms to inform and inspire our understanding of human memory function. In studies of memory reconsolidation, research with nonhuman animals has suggested two different approaches that could be used to investigate this mnemonic mechanism in humans—pharmacological blockade and behavioral intervention. Next, we describe the emerging research using each approach as it has been applied to different memory systems.

9.2 PHARMACOLOGICAL ALTERATION OF RECONSOLIDATION IN HUMANS

9.2.1 Emotional memory

When using the term *emotional memories*, we are primarily referring to simple associative memories that link neutral stimuli with emotional properties. This type of memory has been most frequently investigated in studies of Pavlovian fear conditioning. Like in other species, fear conditioning studies in humans pair a neutral stimulus, such as a colored square (the conditioned stimulus (CS)), with an aversive outcome, such as a mild shock to the wrist (the unconditioned stimulus (US)). After a few pairings, a fear response is triggered by the CS because of its association with the shock (the conditioned response (CR)). The CR most frequently assessed in human fear conditioning studies is the skin conductance response (SCR), which is an indication of autonomic nervous system arousal (Fredrikson & Ohman, 1979; LaBar *et al.*, 1995). Other measures used have included potentiated eyeblink startle, a reflex response that is enhanced in the presence of negative or aversive stimuli (Grillon *et al.*, 1994), and reaction time, which is thought to be a measure in an emotion-induced interference (Buchel *et al.*, 1998). In addition, some studies examine CS expectancy ratings, which is an online estimation of the likelihood of US delivery, although this explicit measure has been shown to rely on different neural systems than other commonly used measures (Bechara *et al.*, 1995; LaBar *et al.*, 1995).

Importantly, a long line of research in patients with brain lesions and neuro-imaging with healthy participants has shown that Pavlovian fear conditioning in humans relies on the same neural systems as those described in more detailed animal models (for review, see Phelps & LeDoux, 2005). This research in nonhuman animals suggests that the acquisition, storage, and expression of conditioned fear depends on the amygdala. The lateral nucleus of the amygdala is thought to be the site of storage for conditioned fear memories (for review, see LeDoux, 2000). Because of this, animal studies examining fear memory reconsolidation have targeted the amygdala (Duvarci *et al.*, 2005; Jin *et al.*, 2007; Nader *et al.*, 2000).

For example, the study that is generally credited with reinvigorating interest in reconsolidation as an important memory mechanism targeted the amygdala. In this study, Nader and colleagues (2000) trained a rat to fear a tone CS. After waiting a day for this fear memory to consolidate, they presented the tone alone to reactivate the fear memory. This was followed by an injection of a protein synthesis inhibitor into the lateral amygdala. Because protein synthesis is needed for memory storage, this drug was intended to disrupt any re-storage or reconsolidation of the fear memory. Nader and colleagues then tested the rats 1 day later or 2 weeks later, in the absence of the drug. The rats that were exposed to the tone to reactivate the memory prior to the injection no longer showed fear of the tone, compared to rats that received a placebo injection following reactivation or rats that were given the drug without memory reactivation. The protein synthesis inhibitor had no effect when testing the rats 4 hr after reactivation, suggesting that short-term memory was intact, whereas long-term memory was impaired by disrupting reconsolidation.

Due to the potential clinical implications of disrupting fear memories, this study generated a great deal of excitement. At the same time, it highlighted a major obstacle in translating this research to humans. It is not feasible to inject drugs into the lateral amygdala of people, nor is it safe to administer protein synthesis inhibitors to people. This is one of the primary reasons why research on reconsolidation in humans has been so slow to emerge. However, because of the enormous potential clinical applications of altering reconsolidation for the treatment of fear-related disorders, such as post-traumatic stress disorder (PTSD), researchers studying nonhuman animals quickly set out to explore other drugs that might be amenable for use in humans. One such drug is propranolol, a β-adrenergic blocker that has been shown to disrupt the amygdala's modulation of hippocampal-dependent consolidation of episodic memory in both humans and other animals (McGaugh, 2000). It has been suggested that propranolol may impact protein synthesis in the amygdala (Gelinas & Nguyen, 2005) and, as a result, may regulate long-term memory storage of amygdala-dependent memories.

In a series of studies, Debiec and LeDoux (2004) found that, similar to commonly used protein synthesis inhibitors (e.g., anisomycin), propranolol appears to disrupt fear memory reconsolidation in a fear conditioning paradigm mirroring that used by Nader *et al.* (2000). Importantly, they found that propranolol was effective at disrupting later fear expression if it was administered during fear memory reconsolidation either through direct injection into the amygdala or through systemic administration. Although the systematic dose the rats were administered was relatively higher than a dose one might give to humans, this research paved the way for testing whether a systemic dose of propranolol might interfere with fear memory reconsolidation in humans.

We are aware of four studies that have been published or presented at conferences that directly tested whether propranolol administration during reconsolidation impairs the later expression of fear memories in humans, and these have mixed results. The first published study tested the efficacy of propranolol administered after memory retrieval reconsolidation in a clinical population. Brunet and colleagues (2008) examined 19 individuals with PTSD, a chronic syndrome characterized by intrusive and distressing memories of intensely emotional events. The symptoms of PTSD have been linked with amygdala reactivity (Rauch *et al.*, 2006). To reactivate the traumatic memory in this study, the patients were given a script-driven retrieval task. Immediately afterwards, half the patients received propranolol (a short-acting 40-mg pill and a long-acting 60-mg pill 2 hr later) and the other half received placebos. A week later, patients listened to a recording describing their traumatic event to remind them of their memory and were asked to imagine the event at the same time. While listening to this recording, a range of physiological responses were assessed, including measures of autonomic nervous system arousal (heart rate and SCR) and facial expression (electromyogram of the facial frowning muscle). The investigators compared the level of these physiological measures to normative cutoffs for PTSD based on prior research. Heart rate and SCR were above normative PTSD cutoffs in the placebo group but below those in the propranolol group, although not significantly below for SCR. Electromyogram responses were below the normative cutoffs for both groups.

These initial findings were encouraging. They suggested that propranolol given after reactivation of a traumatic memory might be effective in reducing some of the exaggerated physiological responses triggered by the traumatic memory. However, propranolol administration during reconsolidation did not significantly reduce PTSD symptomatology or have a more long-lasting effect on sympathetic arousal (Brunet *et al.*, 2011). Furthermore, attributing the effects of propranolol to the disruption of reconsolidation from these results should be done with caution. There was no control group that received propranolol without memory reactivation, so one cannot rule out the possibility that propranolol had a more general effect on reducing sympathetic arousal that is not related to altered reconsolidation (Nader, 2003).

Despite these concerns, the results of Brunet *et al.* (2008) provided inspiration to further investigate the mechanisms of fear memory reconsolidation in humans using propranolol. To mirror the animal research more closely, other studies have examined Pavlovian fear conditioning in healthy participants. At approximately the same time Brunet and colleagues were exploring the efficacy of propranolol in disrupting reconsolidation in PTSD patients, a study in our laboratory attempted to use propranolol to disrupt conditioned fear memory reconsolidation in humans (for a description, see Schiller & Phelps, 2011). Using a paradigm designed to be similar to those of Nader *et al.* (2000) and LeDoux and Debiec (2004), participants were conditioned to fear a colored square (CS+) by pairing it with a mild shock. Another colored square was never paired with shock and served as a baseline (CS−). After 1 day, the participants returned and two-thirds were shown the CS+ and the CS− to reactivate the memory. Half of the participants were given a 40-mg dose of propranolol immediately after reactivation (drug group), and the other half were given placebo (placebo group). The remaining third of participants were put in a different room and were given propranolol (no reactivation group). On the following day, all participants returned and were given a series of extinction trials in which the CS+ and the CS− were presented repeatedly with no shocks.

The measure of conditioned fear (CR) was the differential SCR to the CS+ minus CS−. The first trial showed evidence of disruption: There was no CR for the drug group, whereas the placebo showed a robust CR. However, there were several caveats to this effect. First, the no reactivation group also failed to a show a CR, suggesting the effect was due to drug administration more broadly. Second, this fear disruption did not last. By the second trial of extinction, there was a robust and significant CR in all three groups. Third, a closer examination of the temporary disruption of the CR revealed it resulted from both a decrease SCR to the CS+ and also an increase SCR to the CS−, suggesting the effect was not specific to the fear memory. Fourth, the temporary disruption effect was only observed in female participants.

Although this initial investigation of the effects of propranolol on reconsolidation was not successful, it suggested avenues for future investigations. The temporary disruption could be due to the fact that explicit knowledge of the CS−US contingency was intact. It has been shown that bilateral human amygdala damage results in impaired expression of conditioned fear as measured with SCR, but explicit knowledge of CS−US contingency is intact unless the hippocampus is damaged as well (Bechara *et al.*, 1995; LaBar & Phelps, 2005; LaBar *et al.*, 1995). It has also been shown that explicit knowledge of the CS−US contingency is sufficient to elicit a fear response to a CS as assessed with either SCR or potentiated startle (Grillon *et al.*, 1994; Phelps *et al.*, 2001). It is possible that this intact, hippocampal-dependent knowledge of the CS−US contingency drove the fear response after the first trial of extinction test. This would suggest future attempts may need to alter explicit expectancies as well.

The temporary CR disruption in the no reactivation group could be due to a nonspecific effect of propranolol, or it may have resulted from the participants mentally reactivating the CSs when placed in the laboratory context, without any explicit reminder from the experimenter. In the latter case, it would point to the obvious difficulty of precisely controlling memory reactivation in human participants.

Altered SCRs to both the CS+ and the CS− could have been due to the fact that both cues were reactivated on Day 2 of this procedure. In the context of fear conditioning, the CS− is not a neutral cue but, rather, a safety cue by virtue of its prediction of no shock (Rogan et al., 2005). In our paradigm, we may have inadvertently disrupted both fear and safety memories. Finally, some studies have indicated that males and females metabolize propranolol differently (Walle et al., 1994a,b), which suggests that it may be necessary to consider the effect of sex in human reconsolidation studies or treatments using propranolol.

In contrast to the findings of Brunet and colleagues (2008), our results were less encouraging. However, they did highlight some unique challenges that may emerge when attempting to alter reconsolidation through drugs or behavioral interventions. Because of the lack of success of our attempt, we ultimately did not publish this finding, but it has been discussed at scientific meetings because it provides insight into some of the challenges one might encounter when attempting to transfer animal research on reconsolidation to humans. In our lab, the study described previously showed a temporary effect of drug administration, but we also conducted additional pilot studies that showed no effect of propranolol administered during reconsolidation on later fear memory. Given the tendency in science not to publish null results, it is possible there are many other labs that have attempted this manipulation.

To date, only one published study using a fear conditioning paradigm in humans has shown some success in consistently diminishing later fear when propranolol was administered during reconsolidation, although this study also had mixed results. A study by Soeter and Kindt (2012a) used a modified version of a fear conditioning paradigm. In this study, two fear-relevant stimuli (spider and gun) were paired with shock during acquisition (CS+), and a third, neutral stimulus (mug) was not (CS−). A day later, one CS+ was presented, reactivating the fear memory. This was followed immediately by a 40-mg dose of propranolol for the drug group. There were also placebo and no reactivation groups. On the third day, participants underwent standard extinction training in which all three CSs were presented without shock. This was followed by a test of fear memory reinstatement. Measures of conditioned fear included potentiated startle and SCR. In addition to passive Pavlovian learning, all participants were asked to explicitly rate the likelihood of shock (shock expectancy) on every trial. On the Day 3 extinction test, participants in the drug group failed to show any evidence of enhanced potentiated startle to the reactivated CS+, in contrast to the nonreactivated CS+, whereas participants in the other groups showed greater potentiated startle to both the reactivated CS+ and the nonreactivated CS+ relative to the CS−. However, participants in the drug group showed evidence of intact conditioned fear to the reactivated CS+ with the autonomic measure of fear (SCR), which did not differ from the nonreactivated CS+ (both of which differed from the CS−).

The dissociation of CR response measures is puzzling because generally autonomic and startle assessments of fear coincide in human fear paradigms (Funayama *et al.*, 2001; Phelps *et al.*, 2001). Soeter and Kindt (2012a) suggest that SCR represents a more explicit measure of fear, perhaps because their CS expectancy ratings, which are known to rely on the hippocampus (Bechara *et al.*, 2005; LaBar & Phelps, 2005), showed a pattern similar to SCR. This argument is difficult to reconcile with the fact that SCR is the only measure of conditioned fear that has been shown to be impaired in humans with discrete bilateral amygdala damage and intact hippocampal function. In these patients, CRs as measured with SCR are dissociable from knowledge of the CS−US contingency (Bechara *et al.*, 1995; Phelps *et al.*, 1998). Furthermore, autonomic measures of fear are a major component of the fear response system, and autonomic CRs are disrupted following amygdala lesions in nonhuman animals (LeDoux, 2000).

The observed dissociation between fear response systems reported by Soeter and Kindt (2012a) suggests that propranolol might have limited effects in disrupting fear reconsolidation in humans. If autonomic fear measures are intact, it would reduce the potential clinical efficacy for this technique. Ironically, the findings of Brunet *et al.* examining the impact of propranolol on fear expression in PTSD patients only showed an effect on reducing autonomic responding, with other measures unaffected (Brunet *et al.*, 2008; 2011b). It is also possible that the pattern observed by Soeter and Kindt could be due to the specific fear conditioning paradigm used. There is evidence that using an online expectancy rating during fear acquisition changes the nature of fear learning and alters its neural representation to make it less amygdala dependent (Coppens *et al.*, 2009). This type of explicit expectancy assessment is obviously a measure that cannot be tested in animals models, so our understanding of the implications of this cognitive manipulation on the neural systems of fear expression is limited.

Interestingly, another study from the same group (Soeter & Kindt, 2012b) examined a similar paradigm but with fears that were learned through verbal instruction (i.e., "When you are presented this CS, you might receive a shock"). In this study, the administration of propranolol after instructed fear reactivation led to a similar disruption of potentiated startle on Day 3 test, with intact SCR and CS expectancy ratings.

So far, the sparse research on the use of propranolol to disrupt fear memory reconsolidation raises more questions than it answers. What is apparent is that this manipulation may be more complicated to translate to humans than the early animal research suggests (Debiec & LeDoux, 2004). This may be due to several factors, including the complex nature of fear representations in humans, the flexibility of the fear learning system (Olsson & Phelps, 2005), and the added difficulty in precisely controlling memory reactivation in human participants. In addition, the relative dose of propranolol systematically given to human participants is less than that used in rats (Debiec & LeDoux, 2004). It is possible that some of the mixed effects observed are the result of inadequate dosage. In order to determine if propranolol can be used successfully to disrupt fear memory reconsolidation in a clinical context, all of these factors will need to be addressed.

A different approach used by some laboratories to examine the efficacy of propranolol on the expression of fear memory is to give the drug prior to memory reactivation. In these studies, propranolol administration is timed so that its peak concentration coincides with fear memory reactivation (Kindt et al., 2009). Research in animal models has shown that propranolol given prior to fear memory reactivation can have different outcomes on later fear expression than propranolol given after reactivation, during reconsolidation (Muravieva & Alberini, 2010). Nevertheless, one cannot rule out the possibility that any observed effect is due, at least in part, to the lingering effects of propranolol during the reconsolidation period.

In a series of studies, Kindt and colleagues examined the effect of administering propranolol prior to memory reactivation on later fear expression using a fear conditioning paradigm (Kindt et al., 2009; Soeter & Kindt, 2010). These studies used a paradigm similar to that described previously examining the impact of propranolol administration during reconsolidation (Soeter & Kindt, 2012a). It was found that propranolol timed to coincide with memory reactivation disrupts later fear expression as assessed with potentiated startle but not SCR or CS expectancy ratings. The similarity between these findings and those of the later study targeting reconsolidation (Soeter & Kindt, 2012a) suggests that reconsolidation may have been effected by the lingering presence of the drug after reactivation. However, like the reconsolidation results, these findings regarding the impact of propranolol on memory reactivation do not extend to autonomic measures of fear, which is a major clinical symptom of fear-related disorders (Rauch et al., 2006).

In a series of studies, Brunet and colleagues (2011b; Poundja et al., 2012) have also examined the efficacy of propranolol administration prior to memory reactivation on later fear expression in patients with PTSD. Unlike their previous study, the primary measure of interest was PTSD symptoms. The Clinician-Administered PTSD Scale (Blake et al., 1995) was used for diagnosis pre- and post-treatment, and interim progress was assessed with the PTSD Checklist (Weathers et al., 1993). For six sessions, propranolol was administered 90 min prior to memory reactivation, with an additional dose given at approximately the time of memory reactivation. The dosage across participants and studies varied, but for most conditions the first was a 40-mg short-acting dose and the second was a 60- or 80-mg long-acting dose. For the first session, participants were asked to provide an account of the event that led to PTSD, and in subsequent sessions they were reminded of this event through a script-driven retrieval task similar to that described previously. The administration of propranolol prior to memory reactivation significantly diminished PTSD symptoms both during treatment and at a 6-month follow-up. A portion of the patients no longer met the diagnostic criteria for PTSD. Interestingly, women improved more than men.

Although these results are exciting because of the clear benefit observed for patients, there are several caveats. The lack of a placebo group or a double-blind design limits any interpretation concerning the drug effect. Although there were control participants who were assessed, these were mostly individuals who chose not to participate in the protocol and did not receive the exposure treatment. In addition, it is possible that any effects observed could be due to the diminished autonomic arousal experienced during retrieval sessions as a result of propranolol administration. In this way, propranolol may have aided extinction (Poundja *et al.*, 2012). Of course, it is also possible that any treatment effect is due to altering fear memory reconsolidation.

It has been argued by Brunet and colleagues (2012), as well as Kindt and colleagues (Kindt *et al.*, 2009; Soeter & Kindt, 2010), that propranolol administration timed so that its peak dose corresponds with reactivation is targeting a reconsolidation mechanism. Furthermore, it has been suggested that it may be necessary to administer propranolol prior to memory reactivation in order to assess its impact on reconsolidation because of the time course of propranolol concentration in the blood following systemic administration. It takes approximately 90 min for propranolol to reach peak plasma concentration in the blood (Gilman & Goodman, 1996). Although the precise timing of the reconsolidation window is not known, manipulations in nonhuman animals administered 1 hr after memory reactivation have been shown to alter reconsolidation (Monfils *et al.*, 2009), and short-term memory of the fear is intact even longer (Nader *et al.*, 2000), suggesting the reconsolidation process is not complete for at least a few hours. This suggests that a post-reactivation administration of propranolol should impact reconsolidation in humans (e.g., consistent with the results of Brunet *et al.* (2008) and Soeter and Kindt (2012a)) and, importantly, would be free from confounds of the effect of the drug on reactivation. From a clinical perspective, we agree with Brunet *et al.* (2011a), who argue that it should not matter if it works. If a treatment is effective, then understanding its underlying mechanism is secondary. However, to understand the process of human memory reconsolidation, it is important that our experimental designs target this mnemomic stage and not others.

9.2.2 Episodic memory

In this chapter, we use the term *episodic memory* to refer to hippocampal-dependent memories that in humans are characterized by explicit or conscious recollection (hence the term "declarative" knowledge). Unlike fear memories that are thought to have a localized representation in the amygdala, episodic representations are thought to be composed of a network of cortical regions whose binding relies on the hippocampus (for reviews, see Davachi (2006) and Dickerson and Eichenbaum (2010)). To our knowledge, there is only one study to date that has examined the influence of a pharmacological agent on reconsolidation of episodic memory in humans. In addition, three studies have examined the impact that pharmacological agents administered prior to memory reactivation have on later memory performance. Like the studies of fear memories mentioned previously, any effects observed in these studies may or may not be linked to altering a reconsolidation process.

For example, a study by Kroes *et al.* (2010) presented participants emotional or neutral nouns. A day later, participants were administered either 40 mg propranolol or placebo 90 min prior to a cued recall retrieval test. Drug administration was timed so the peak concentration coincided with the test. At test, the placebo group showed enhanced memory for the emotional nouns relative to neutral nouns, whereas the propranolol group showed no difference. Importantly, this relative decrement in memory for emotional nouns persisted the following day for the propranolol group when no drug was present. Kroes *et al.* interpret these results as a demonstration of the importance of noradrenaline in emotional memory retrieval, although they suggest there could also be a role for reconsolidation.

A similar paradigm was used in a brain imaging study by Schwabe and colleagues (2012). They examined memory for emotional and neutral scenes. A day after the scenes were encoded, participants were given a 40-mg dose of propranolol or placebo. Seventy minutes later, half of the participants were asked to mentally reactivate memories of the scenes presented the previous day. On the third day, participants were given a forced-choice recognition test in which they were presented new and old scenes. Consistent with the results of Kroes *et al.* (2010), recognition memory for the emotional scenes was diminished for the reactivation drug group. In contrast to the placebo and no reactivation control groups, there was no emotional memory enhancement in the drug group. Interestingly, this group showed enhanced amygdala and hippocampal activation during correct retrieval of emotional scenes. The authors argue that the additional recruitment of these regions may have been necessary given the dampened overall memory due to the drug administration during reactivation.

Whereas both of these studies found evidence that propranolol administration during reactivation impaired later memory for emotional stimuli, a third study failed to find this effect. This study also assessed the impact of another pharmacological manipulation, hydrocortisone, on later memory. On the first day, Tollenaar and colleagues (2009) presented participants with emotional and neutral words and tested their recall. A day later, participants were given propranolol, hydrocortisone, or placebo approximately 80 min prior to test. They were then given a free recall test for the words, followed by a cued recall test. On the third day, participants were again given a free recall test followed by a recognition test. Not surprisingly, there was no difference in memory performance between the groups on the first day recall test, and memory for emotional words was enhanced relative to neutral words overall.

In contrast to the results of Kroes *et al.* (2010), there was no effect of propranolol relative to placebo on memory retrieval on the Day 2 test for emotional or neutral words; however, the group that received hydrocortisone showed reduced memory for both emotional and neutral words (for a similar finding, see de Quervain *et al.*, 2007). On the third day of memory testing, this decrement for the hydrocortisone group persisted. A number of studies have shown that stress hormones and cortisol have decremental effects on the hippocampus and episodic memory in nonhuman animals (McEwen, 2001). These findings are evidence for similar effects in humans, although like the previous studies, we cannot attribute these findings specifically to a disruption of reconsolidation given the pre-reactivation administration of the drug.

The sole study we are aware of that has specifically examined a pharmacological manipulation of episodic memory reconsolidation in humans used clonazepam, a benzodiazepine GABA-A agonist (Rodriguez *et al.*, 2013). In this study, participants were presented five cue syllables and five respective response syllables. A day later, participants were shown the cue syllables to reactivate the memory. This was followed by administering 0.25 or 0.03 mg clonazepam or a placebo. An additional group of participants did not undergo the reactivation procedure but were given the drug. Four hours later, short-term memory for the stimuli was assessed for all groups. The following day, participants were given the cue syllables and asked to generate the response syllables. Memory performance was better in the participants who received the higher drug dose compared to those who received the lower dose or placebo. There was no effect when the drug was administered without retrieval or at the short-term memory testing session. These findings highlight a role for the GABAergic system in the reconsolidation of episodic memory in humans.

9.2.3 Summary and future challenges

As this survey of research on attempts to alter human reconsolidation using a pharmacological agent shows, there is very little consistent evidence for disruption of reconsolidation in humans with this technique. Although neurobiologists did their part by identifying a drug that could be used to disrupt reconsolidations in humans (Debiec & LeDoux, 2004), the few studies that have specifically targeted reconsolidation with this drug have had mixed results, with none showing a lasting fear disruption for autonomic fear responses. Of course, only three studies published to date have targeted reconsolidation (Brunet *et al.*, 2008; Soeter & Kindt, 2012a,b), and one additional unsuccessful attempt has been documented (Schiller & Phelps, 2011). However, there have been additional unsuccessful attempts from our lab, and given the interest in this topic, other labs may also have conducted failed experiments attempting to disrupt reconsolidation with propranolol in humans.

In contrast to the weak evidence for demonstrating an effect for pharmacological disruption of reconsolidation of fear memories in humans, a number of studies have shown some success in disrupting memory reactivation with a drug on later memory expression, although these findings also have their limits.

We have reviewed these papers in this chapter on reconsolidation because some of the authors of these studies claim to be disrupting reconsolidation with this manipulation. Although one cannot rule out a lingering effect of the drug on reconsolidation in these studies, most of them precisely time drug administration so that its peak blood concentration coincides with reactivation, not reconsolidation (e.g., Soeter & Kindt, 2009). Researchers studying nonhumans differentiate pharmacological effects on memory reactivation and memory reconsolidation, and we suggest that researchers studying humans need to be similarly precise if we hope to develop a rigorous science on human reconsolidation. This is not to say that pharmacological effects on memory reactivation are not scientifically interesting or potentially clinically important, but they may very well be different (Muravieva & Alberini, 2010).

This issue raises an important question: How do we effectively administer drugs to humans that could precisely target some stages of memory formation and not others? Studies to date have used oral administration of the drug, but it may be that intravenous administration, which is more precise and faster, is a more effective technique. Of course, the invasive nature of this technique is not ideal for human research, but it is possible. An additional challenge is how to administer a dose to humans that is both safe and effective at targeting reconsolidation. The propranolol dosages used in the studies described previously are mostly based on their demonstrated clinical efficacy in reducing autonomic arousal. Although there are clear limits to the dose that could be safely administered to humans, animal research has not titrated doses to identify the effective range with different means of administration. Animal research on this topic might provide some insight into the limitations of the current studies in humans and also inform future research using this technique.

Finally, with two exceptions, the studies described previously used a single drug, propranolol. Since the important finding of Debiec and LeDoux (2004) showing that this drug might be effective in targeting fear memory reconsolidation, other research has emerged suggesting additional drugs that could be used safely in humans for this purpose (Gamache et al., 2012; Stern et al., 2012). Future studies should expand the range of pharmacological agents used to investigate reconsolidation in humans.

There are many challenges to conducting pharmacological studies in humans, including ethical concerns. Because of these challenges and the limited success of studies examining the pharmacological disruption of reconsolidation in humans to date, researchers have begun to use other techniques to investigate reconsolidation in the laboratory.

9.3 BEHAVIORAL INTERFERENCE OF RECONSOLIDATION

It has been suggested that one primary adaptive function of reconsolidation is to update old memories with new information available at the time of retrieval (Dudai et al., 2012). In this way, memory is dynamic. This could be useful in that information available at the time of retrieval may be relevant to the future use of the memory in prompting adaptive actions. If this is the case, then we should be able to take advantage of this process and modify human memories by precisely timing the introduction of new information to coincide with memory reconsolidation. On the basis of this premise, a few studies have attempted behavioral interventions to modify reconsolidation across different memory systems.

9.3.1 Emotional memory

Studies examining the behavioral interference of emotional memories in humans have explored both conditioned aversive memories and appetitive memories. A common nonpharmacological technique to change conditioned emotional reactions is extinction training. Extinction involves recurrent presentations of the CS without aversive or appetitive outcomes, which leads to a gradual decrease in the CR. Similar to acquisition, extinction is a learning process, but now the CS is associated with no aversive or appetitive outcome. Importantly, there is abundant evidence that standard extinction training results in an additional memory trace representing an alternative value for the CS (e.g., safe). Because the initial aversive or appetitive memory trace still exists, the CR can return after extinction training in a number of circumstances (Bouton, 2002). However, if extinction training occurs during reconsolidation while the memory is still labile, it is possible that this new information will get incorporated into the original memory trace, thus updating the original emotional memory and changing its emotional significance.

Schiller and colleagues (2010) demonstrated this effect using a fear conditioning paradigm. We trained participants to associate a colored square (CS+; e.g., blue) with mild electric shock to the wrist (US) and another square (CS−; e.g., yellow) with no shock. A day later, we reminded two-thirds of the participants of the fear memory using a single presentation of the CS+. Half of these participants then took a 10-min break, and the other half took a 6-hr break. The remaining third of participants (no reactivation group) did not receive the CS+ reminder trial. All the participants then underwent extinction training. In this procedure, the 10-min group received extinction training during reconsolidation, whereas the 6-hr group underwent extinction after reconsolidation (Duvarci & Nader, 2004; Nader et al., 2000; Walker et al., 2003). We tested the memory a day later by presenting the CSs again without shock, constituting another extinction session. The CR was assessed with SCR. As expected, the no reactivation and 6-hr groups showed evidence of fear recovery on the Day 3 test, consistent with previous studies of extinction retention in humans (e.g., Phelps et al., 2004). In contrast, the group that received the CS+ reminder 10 min prior to extinction training showed no evidence of fear recovery. Interestingly, a year later, a subset of participants returned to the laboratory and fear recovery was tested again. Only those participants who received standard extinction training (no reactivation and 6-hr groups) showed a return of fear, suggesting extinction during reconsolidation leads to a persistent fear reduction. In a second study, two colored squares were paired with shock during acquisition (CS+) and another was not (CS−). Ten minutes prior to extinction on the next day, one CS+ was reminded to trigger the reconsolidation process, followed by extinction training for all CSs. A fear recovery test on the third day showed evidence of fear recovery but only for the nonreminded CS+. This suggests that the behavioral interference of fear memory reconsolidation with extinction training is specific to the reactivated fear memory.

Oyarzún and colleagues (2012) replicated this finding using aversive auditory sounds as the US. They trained participants with three conditioned stimuli. Two of them (CS+) were paired with a US, but for each stimulus the US was unique (a girl screaming or a pig squealing); the third stimulus was neutral. A day later, they reminded participants of one CS+ and not the other, followed by extinction training for all CSs 10 min later. They tested reinstatement of conditioned fear a day later (SCR was the index of fear) and found recovery only to the CS+ that was not reminded.

Agren and colleagues (2012a) examined the consequences of such behavioral interference on the neural systems of fear using functional magnetic resonance imaging. In their paradigm, 24 hr after fear conditioning, participants were randomly assigned to two groups. Both groups were reminded of the CS+, but one group underwent extinction training 10 min later and the other 6 hr later (i.e., within and outside the reconsolidation window, respectively). On Day 3, the participants were presented the CSs again for a renewal test, with the shock electrodes attached but no shock delivery. This session was conducted while blood oxygenation level-dependent (BOLD) signal was assessed. On Day 5, subjects were exposed to unsignaled shocks to reinstate the fear memory, followed by CS presentations without the shocks. The index of fear reinstatement was the differential SCR between the first CS trial on Day 5 and the last extinction trial on Day 2. The 6-hr group, but not the 10-min group, showed evidence of fear recovery, consistent with the results of Schiller *et al.* (2010). The 6-hr group also showed amygdala BOLD activity during the renewal session (Day 3), which correlated with the CR on the fear reinstatement (Day 5) and with other brain regions mediating the expression of fear, including the dorsal anterior cingulate cortex and the insula. The authors concluded that the fear memory was "erased" in the amygdala rather than suppressed because they did not observe any negative correlation between amygdala and ventromedial prefrontal cortex that should theoretically exist when extinction memory is retrieved (Milad & Quirk, 2012; Phelps *et al.*, 2004).

The same group (Agren *et al.*, 2012b) also examined how genetic variability might influence reconsolidation of human fear memory. They demonstrated the retrieval−extinction effect on reconsolidation using reacquisition instead of fear recovery tests. Specifically, two groups of participants underwent fear conditioning on Day 1 and then extinction on Day 2 either within (10 min) or outside (6 hr) the reconsolidation window. On Day 3, Agren *et al.* tested how fast the groups would relearn the extinguished association. They found that extinction during reconsolidation retarded reacquisition of the fear association, consistent with similar findings in rats (Monfils et al., 2009). These results suggest that extinction training during reconsolidation incorporates safety information learned during extinction into the original CS representation, thus making it more difficult to reacquire the fear.

Because fear conditioning and extinction are modulated by monoaminergic genetic polymorphisms (Garpenstrand et al., 2001; Hettema et al., 2003; Lonsdorf et al., 2009; Raczka et al., 2011), Agren et al. (2012b) hypothesized that reconsolidation might be affected as well. They found that carriers of the short allele of the serotonin transporter 5-HTTLPR polymorphism (but not long-allele homozygotes) and homozygotes of the val allele (but not met carriers) of the dopamine-related COMT val158met polymorphism showed reconsolidation interference of reacquisition in the 10-min but not the 6-hr group. Long-allele homozygotes of the serotonin transporter length polymorphism and met allele carriers of the dopamine-related COMT val158met polymorphism were indifferent to the reconsolidation manipulation, displaying impaired reacquisition either way. These findings suggest that serotonin- and dopamine-related genes might modulate behavioral interference of reconsolidation.

The previous studies stand in contrast to a failure to replicate these effects of extinction during reconsolidation, reported by Kindt and Soeter (2011). Methodological differences might account for the discrepancy. As mentioned previously, the paradigm commonly used by Kindt and colleagues includes an active, online expectancy rating during the entire conditioning procedure. This subjective, instrumental assessment of learning has been shown to make the task less amygdala-dependent (Coppens et al., 2009), which may explain the conflicting results. In addition, this study used pictures of fear-relevant stimuli as CSs (e.g., pictures of spiders and guns) as well as a higher rate of reinforcement (75% vs. ~37%) than previous studies demonstrating this effect. Finally, Kindt and Soeter included potentiated startle as an additional measure of conditioning. The assessment of the startle reflex requires repeated bursts of loud noise throughout all stages of the conditioning procedures. In many human fear conditioning studies, loud noise is used as a US (LaBar et al.,1995), so it is possible that the repeated loud noise changed the qualitative nature of learning. Although further investigation is needed to determine which, if any, of these factors led to this replication failure, the findings by Kindt and Soeter stand in contrast to a majority of papers showing success with this technique.

The human reconsolidation research on emotional memory has primarily focused on conditioned fear memories in the hope of developing improved treatments for PTSD and other anxiety disorders. However, Pavlovian conditioning also plays a major role in drug addiction and relapse. Conditioned responses to drug-associated cues persist through long periods of drug abstinence and are difficult to extinguish (Stewart et al., 1984). Xue and colleagues (2012) adapted the memory retrieval−extinction procedure for drug addicts (inpatient detoxified heroin addicts) and found long-lasting attenuation in cue-induced drug craving. On Day 1, they took baseline measures of cue-induced heroin craving using the visual analog scale (VAS; as well as heart rate and blood pressure). On Days 2 and 3, similar to the fear paradigm described previously (Schiller *et al.*, 2010), they divided the participants into three groups: One group was reminded of the drug memory (5-min videotapes of heroin cues) and 10 min later had 60-min extinction training (four consecutive sessions of repeated exposures to three different heroin-related cues); the second group had a similar procedure but with a 6-hr break; and the third group had the 60-minute extinction training only. They assessed the change in craving, compared to baseline level, during Day 4, as well as 34 and 184 days later. Only the group that had extinction training 10 min after the drug cue reminder showed significant attenuation in craving that persisted at least 184 days.

Taken together, the previously mentioned studies introduce an aversive and appetitive version of nonpharmacological reconsolidation interference with a retrieval–extinction procedure. The findings with addicts (Xue *et al.*, 2012) are encouraging because they suggest that this technique can be extended to real-life memories, which are naturally older, stronger, and richer in associations. However, it remains to be seen if this technique will be useful in the treatment of fear-related disorders.

9.3.2 Episodic memory

When discussing the historical antecedents of reconsolidation in human memory, the early work on the misinformation effect and massed versus distributed practice highlight effects that may target the adaptive updating or memory-enhancing effects of reconsolidation. Inspired by the renewed interest in the reconsolidation of fear memories, there has also been a growing interest in exploring the reconsolidation of episodic memory in humans. Unlike studies of fear learning, however, which generally show no expression of the original memory following interference, studies of episodic memory show altered, impaired, or enhanced memory, depending on the paradigm.

For example, Hupbach and colleagues (2007, 2009) trained participants to memorize a list of random objects (e.g., tennis ball and envelope), which were pulled from a basket one after the other. A day later, the participants learned a new list of items spread on a table. There were two groups of subjects. One group saw the basket from the previous day, which reminded them of the first list, and then learned the second list. The other group learned the second list in a different context, and with a different experimenter, to avoid any reminder of the list from the first day. A day later, the participants had to recall items from the first list. Hupbach and colleagues found that the group that had learned the second list after being reminded of the first did not show increased forgetting of items from the first list compared to the nonreminded group. Instead, they found items from the second list were more likely to be mistakenly included. This merging of the memories for the two lists was selective, however, in that items from the first list were not more likely to be mistakenly included when recalling the second list.

In another study examining episodic memory updating, Forcato and colleagues (2007) trained participants on a paired associate task, in which they were instructed to associate cue syllables with their respective response syllables (e.g., "ALG" and "MIV"). The next day, they used the cues from this list as a reminder, after which they trained the participants on a second list of paired associates. They found that learning the second list after the reminder cues impaired the memory of the first list. Interestingly, if the Day 2 cue reminder procedure was altered by presenting both cue and response syllables, there was no interference from the second list (Forcato et al., 2010).

These studies exploring the impact of new information presented during reconsolidation on the quality of older episodic memories suggest that interference might modify or update the original memory to include additional information (Forcato et al., 2010; Hubpach et al., 2007, 2009), impair the original memory (Forcato et al., 2007), or have no effect (Forcato et al., 2009), depending on the paradigm. These findings differ from those of studies of repeated, distributed testing, which show an enhancement in later memory strength (Karpicke & Roediger, 2008). In a more explicit test of the memory-strengthening function of reconsolidation, Forcato et al. (2013) conducted a variation of their paradigm in which participants received the cue reminder without the interfering information. It was found that when at least two cue reminders were given, later memory performance was improved. This effect was not observed with a single reminder cue.

In these paradigms, the type of interfering information presented during reconsolidation is not different from that contained in the initial memory (i.e., objects or syllables), which might make the original memories particularly vulnerable to interference. In fact, some have suggested that these effects could be attributed to standard temporal context interference models of episodic memory without invoking a reconsolidation mechanism (Sederberg et al., 2011). However, an additional series of studies demonstrate that qualitatively different emotional cues or triggers can also modify the strength of later episodic memory when presented during reconsolidation.

For example, Strange and colleagues (2010) trained participants to memorize a list of nouns. The next day, they presented the respective word stems from the nous (i.e., the first three letters), and participants had to use these cues to recall the words from Day 1. In this way, Strange and colleagues could monitor which words were retrieved successfully. After cued recall, some nouns were immediately followed by the presentation of a fearful face and some were followed by a neutral face. They found that the presentation of fearful faces impaired memory after 1 day, and this effect persisted when tested 6 days later.

Although the findings by Strange et al. (2010) suggest that emotion may impair episodic memory reconsolidation, many studies have shown that emotion can also enhance episodic memory storage, specifically if the emotion manipulation results in a physiological arousal response (for review, see McGaugh, 2000). To explore whether stress or arousal can also enhance episodic memory reconsolidation, Coccoz and colleagues (2011) trained participants to associate five pairs of cue syllables and their respective response syllables. Six days later, they exposed the participants to a reminder of the paired associate memory. The reminder was one of the cue syllables in the training context, but instead of allowing the participants to respond with the respective paired syllable, they instructed the participants to put their arm inside a container of ice-cold water for approximately 1 min to elicit a mild stress response. When tested the next day (Day 7), all participants in the control conditions showed poor memory retrieval. The participants who were stressed after memory reactivation on Day 6, however, showed enhanced performance. This suggests that mild stress might improve long-term expression of episodic memory via effects on reconsolidation.

In a related study, Finn and colleagues (Finn & Roediger, 2011; Finn *et al.*, 2012) exposed participants to negative emotional pictures after memory reactivation. The participants studied pairs of Swahili–English vocabulary words, which were reminded with a cued recall task. For each pair, cued recall was followed by a blank screen, a neutral scene, or a negative scene. Participants' subsequent memory, assessed by another cued recall test, was best if they saw negative pictures after the cued-recall reminder. Finn and colleagues (2012) verified that this enhancing effect did not occur if the negative pictures were presented before the reminder and it did not extend to positive pictures presented after the reminder. The authors suggest that reconsolidation of episodic memories was thus enhanced, but only when it was concurrent with exposure to negatively arousing stimuli. However, unlike the studies of Strange *et al.* (2010) and Coccoz *et al.* (2011), this study was conducted on a single day, so it is difficult to know if the effects are due to altering reconsolidation or modified initial consolidation.

9.3.3 Motor memory

The first study to provide conclusive evidence for reconsolidation in humans examined motor skill memory (Walker *et al.*, 2003). This is also the only demonstration to date of reconsolidation of a procedural memory in humans. Walker and colleagues trained their participants to perform a five-element sequence composed of four numeric keys (e.g., "3-2-4-1-3") within a 12-trial training session. A day later, they briefly reminded half the participants of the original sequence memory with a 3-trial retention session, after which they trained all the participants on a novel five-element sequence. Immediately after the second sequence, they tested performance (speed and accuracy) on the original sequence to examine short-term memory. Participants' long-term memory for the sequence was assessed on Day 3. The participants who performed the new sequence after the reminder of the original sequence showed worse performance on Day 3 compared to the performance level they achieved on Day 1 (50% reduction in accuracy and nonsignificantly lower speed) and also showed worse performance compared to the no-reminder group. There was no decrease in performance on the short-term memory test, and there was no change in performance of the second sequence. Walker and colleagues concluded that the impaired performance on Day 3 was the result of reminding the first sequence on Day 2, prior to training on the second sequence. This study suggests that behavioral interference during the reconsolidation of motor memories could modify the initial skill memory and impair performance.

9.3.4 Summary and future challenges

Perhaps in part due to the difficulty of pharmacological interventions in humans, there has been relatively more success altering reconsolidation through behavioral interference. However, across different types of memory, the consequence of presenting interfering information during reconsolidation seems to differ. For amygdala-dependent conditioned fear memories, presenting safety information during reconsolidation appears to rewrite the original fear memory, resulting in no evidence for the expression of the original memory as assessed by SCR. For hippocampal-dependent episodic memory, the effect varies. Depending on the type of paradigm, interference during reconsolidation results in impaired, altered, or enhanced episodic memory. For motor skill memory, interference during reconsolidation results in impaired expression of the original memory, but there is evidence that it exists in a degraded form.

Given the extensive literature documenting the differences in the neural systems mediating these different types of memories, diverse effects are not surprising. As outlined previously, fear conditioning results in an association whose neural representation is localized in a relatively discrete manner in the lateral amygdala (LeDoux, 2000), whereas episodic memories rely on the hippocampus, which binds a cortical network of discrete representations that make up the components of the episode or event (Davachi, 2006). Although there are general principles of learning and memory across different memory systems, there are also many unique processes and mechanisms that will tailor the success and qualitative outcome of techniques used to alter reconsolidation.

A primary challenge for the future is to understand the general principles that underlie the success or failure of the different interference techniques used to target reconsolidation in humans. As this review of the literature demonstrates, in addition to the type of memory assessed, many other variables need to be considered, including, but not limited to, the type of interference, the timing of interference, the method of memory reactivation, the method of memory assessment, and the quality of the original memory. Depending on these factors and others, we might expect very different consequences of reconsolidation interference, including enhanced overall memory, impaired overall memory, and qualitatively different memory that is neither better nor worse. Moving forward, a detailed science of human memory reconsolidation will need to specify and characterize these different variables.

One challenge in understanding the mechanisms of reconsolidation interference techniques in humans is that animal models are relatively sparse. In contrast to the abundant research on the pharmacological disruption of reconsolidation, there is very little research on nonhuman animals examining the behavioral interference of reconsolidation (Clem & Huganir, 2010; Monfils *et al.*, 2009; Xue *et al.*, 2012). In addition, in contrast to animal studies of reconsolidation that have focused heavily on fear memories, human memory research has predominantly investigated nonemotional episodic memory. In the absence of good neurobiological models, it may be difficult to verify whether any observed effects are due to reconsolidation mechanisms or other proposed memory mechanisms that might yield similar behavioral results (Sederberg *et al.*, 2011).

9.4 GENERAL CONCLUSIONS

Although research on human reconsolidation was relatively slow to emerge, the pace of research on this topic has accelerated rapidly in the past few years. In this chapter, we tried to provide a comprehensive review of the current literature, highlighting some of the discrepancies and unique challenges that have arisen. This research is clearly in its infancy. Not only are there relatively few studies in comparison to the extensive research with nonhuman animals but also they vary widely in their relative success in altering human memory by targeting reconsolidation.

The importance of this science is clear. The promised potential for novel treatments of psychopathology using these techniques is just beginning to be verified in experimental studies (Xue *et al.*, 2012). For this purpose, understanding the selective disruption of memory reconsolidation through pharmacological manipulations or behavioral interference is critical. However, a secondary goal for research on reconsolidation is enhancing educational practices (Karpicke & Roediger, 2008). If a goal of education is to create lasting knowledge, then understanding how our educational practices might be tailored to fit the constraints and benefits of the neurobiological processes of memory formation is an exciting and alternative way to think about teaching.

One final consequence of a broader understanding of human reconsolidation is an expansion of how we view human memory in everyday life. Despite decades of research demonstrating the dynamic nature of human memory, the layperson account of memory is still akin to a tape recorder laying down a veridical, immutable track of our experiences. This common knowledge assumption has profound consequences not only when choosing to rely on our memories to guide our actions but also in legal contexts, in which the assumed veracity of memory can have important implications. Ideally, human reconsolidation research will result in a more refined understanding of how and when memories are strong and accurate, when they may be misleading, which types of details are likely to be reliable in which circumstances, and when it matters. An adaptive memory is not necessarily an accurate memory of the original experience, but understanding the processes that differentiate the two may be useful in some uniquely human circumstances, such as the courtroom, the classroom, and the clinic.

REFERENCES

Agren, T., Engman, J., Frick, A., Björkstrand, J., Larsson, E. M., Furmark, T., & Fredrikson, M. (2012a). Disruption of reconsolidation erases a fear memory trace in the human amygdala. *Science, 337*, 1550−1552.

Agren, T., Furmark, T., Eriksson, E., & Fredrikson, M. (2012b). Human fear reconsolidation and allelic differences in serotonergic and dopaminergic genes. *Translational Psychiatry, 2*, e76.

Alberini, C. M. (2011). The role of reconsolidation and the dynamic process of long-term memory formation and storage. *Frontiers in Behavioral Neuroscience, 7*, 12.

Bartlett, F. C. (1932). *Remembering: A Study in Experimental and Social Psychology.* Cambridge, UK: Cambridge University Press.

Bechara, A., Tranel, D., Damasio, H., Adolphs, R., Rockland, C., & Damasio, A. R. (1995). Double dissociation of conditioning and declarative knowledge relative to the amygdala and hippocampus in humans. *Science, 269*, 1115−1118.

Blake, D. D., Weathers, F. W., Nagy, L. M., Kaloupek, D. G., Gusman, F. D., Charney, D. S., & Keane, T. M. (1995). The development of a Clinician-Administered PTSD Scale. *Journal of Traumatic Stress, 8*, 75−90.

Bouton, M. E. (2002). Context, ambiguity, and unlearning: sources of relapse after behavioral extinction. *Biological Psychiatry, 52*, 976−986.

Brunet, A., Ashbaugh, A. R., Saumier, D., Nelson, M., Pitman, R. K., Tremblay, J., Roullet, P., & Birmes, P. (2011a). Does reconsolidation occur in humans: a reply. *Frontiers in Behavioral Neuroscience, 5*, 74.

Brunet, A., Orr, S. P., Tremblay, J., Robertson, K., Nader, K., & Pitman, R. K. (2008). Effect of post-retrieval propranolol on psychophysiologic responding during subsequent script-driven traumatic imagery in post-traumatic stress disorder. *Journal of Psychiatric Research, 42*, 503−506.

Brunet, A., Poundja, J., Tremblay, J., Bui, E., Thomas, E., Orr, S., Azzoug, A., Birmes, P., & Pitman, R. (2011b). Trauma reactivation under the influence of propranolol decreases posttraumatic stress symptoms and disorder: 3 open-label trials. *Journal of Clinical Psychopharmacology, 31*, 547−550.

Buchel, C., Morris, J., Dolan, R. J., & Friston, K. J. (1998). Brain systems mediating aversive conditioning: an event-related fMRI study. *Neuron, 20*, 94−957.

Cepeda, N. J., Pashler, H., Vul, E., Wixted, J. T., & Rohrer, D. (2006). Distributed practice in verbal recall tasks: a review and quantitative synthesis. *Psychological Bulletin, 132*, 354−380.

Clem, R. L., & Huganir, R. L. (2010). Calcium-permeable AMPA receptor dynamics mediate fear erasure. *Science, 330*, 1108−1112.

Coccoz, V., Maldonado, H., & Delorenzi, A. (2011). The enhancement of reconsolidation with a naturalistic mild stressor improves the expression of a declarative memory in humans. *Neuroscience, 185*, 61−72.

Coppens, E., Spruyt, A., Vandenbulcke, M., Van Paesschen, W., & Vansteenwegen, D. (2009). Classically conditioned fear responses are presented following unilateral temporal lobectomy in humans when concurrent US-expectancy ratings are used. *Neuropsychologia, 47*, 2496−2503.

Crowder, R. G. (1976). *Principles of Learning and Memory.* Oxford: Erlbaum.

Davachi, L. (2006). Item, context and relational episodic encoding in humans. *Current Opinion in Neurobiology, 16*, 693−700.

Debiec, J., & LeDoux, J. E. (2004). Disruption of reconsolidation but not consolidation of auditory fear conditioning by noradrenergic blockade in the amygdala. *Neuroscience, 129*, 267−272.

Dickerson, B. C., & Eichenbaum, H. (2010). The episodic memory system: neurocircuitry and disorders. *Neuropsychopharmacology, 35*, 86−104.

Dudai, Y. (2012). The restless engram: consolidations never end. *Annual Review of Neuroscience, 35*, 227−247.

Duvarci, S., & Nader, K. (2004). Characterization of fear memory reconsolidation. *Journal of Neuroscience, 24*, 9269−9275.

Duvarci, S., Nader, K., & LeDoux, J. E. (2005). Activation of extracellular signal-regulated kinase-mitogen-activated protein kinase cascade in the amygdala is required for memory reconsolidation of auditory fear conditioning. *European Journal of Neuroscience, 21*, 283−289.

Finn, B., & Roediger, H. L., 3rd. (2011). Enhancing retention through reconsolidation: negative emotional arousal following retrieval enhances later recall. *Psychological Science, 22*, 781−786.

Finn, B., Roediger, H. L., 3rd, & Rosenzweig, E. (2012). Reconsolidation from negative emotional pictures: is successful retrieval required? *Memory & Cognition, 40*, 1031−1045.

Forcato, C., Burgos, V. L., Argibay, P. F., Molina, V. A., Pedreira, M. E., & Maldonado, H. (2007). Reconsolidation of declarative memory in humans. *Learning & Memory, 14*, 295−303.

Forcato, C., Argibay, P. F., Pedreira, M. E., & Maldonado, H. (2009). Human reconsolidation does not always occur when a memory is retrieved: the relevance of the reminder structure. *Neurobiology of Learning & Memory, 91*, 50−57.

Forcato, C., Rodríguez, M. L., Pedreira, M. E., & Maldonado, H. (2010). Reconsolidation in humans opens up declarative memory to the entrance of new information. *Neurobiology of Learning and Memory, 93*, 77−84.

Fredrikson, M., & Ohman, A. (1979). Cardiovascular and electrodermal responses conditioned to fear-relevant stimuli. *Psychophysiology, 16*, 1−7.

Funayama, E. S., Grillon, C., Davis, M., & Phelps, E. A. (2001). A double dissociation in the affective modulation of startle in humans: effects of unilateral temporal lobectomy. *Journal of Cognitive Neuroscience, 13*, 721−729.

Gamache, K., Pitman, R. K., & Nader, K. (2012). Preclinical evaluation of reconsolidation blockade by clonidine as a potential novel treatment for posttraumatic stress disorder. *Neuropsychopharmacology, 37*, 2789−2796.

Garpenstrand, H., Annas, P., Ekblom, J., Oreland, L., & Fredrikson, M. (2001). Human fear conditioning is related to dopaminergic and serotonergic biological markers. *Behavioral Neuroscience, 115*, 358−364.

Gelinas, J. N., & Nguyen, P. V. (2005). Beta-adrenergic receptor activation facilitates induction of a protein synthesis-dependent late phase of long-term potentiation. *Journal of Neuroscience, 25*, 3294−3303.

Gilman, A. G., & Goodman, L. S. (1996). *Goodman and Gilman's the Pharmacological Basis of Therapeutics*. New York: McGraw-Hill.

Grillon, C., Falls, W. A., Ameli, R., & Davis, M. (1994). Safety signals and human anxiety: a fear-potentiated startle study. *Anxiety, 1*, 13−21.

Hettema, J. M., Annas, P., Neale, M. C., Kendler, K. S., & Fredrikson, M. (2003). A twin study of the genetics of fear conditioning. *Archives of General Psychiatry, 60*, 702−708.

Hupbach, A., Gomez, R., Hardt, O., & Nadel, L. (2007). Reconsolidation of episodic memories: a subtle reminder triggers integration of new information. *Learning & Memory, 14*, 47−53.

Hupbach, A., Gomez, R., & Nadel, L. (2009). Episodic memory reconsolidation: updating or source confusion? *Memory, 17*, 502−510.

James, W. (1890). *The Principles of Psychology*. New York: Dover.

Jin, X. C., Lu, Y. F., Yang, X. F., Ma, L., & Li, B. M. (2007). Glucocorticoid receptors in the basolateral nucleus of amygdala are required for postreactivation reconsolidation of auditory fear memory. *European Journal of Neuroscience, 25*, 3702−3712.

Karpicke, J. D., & Roediger, H. L. (2008). The critical importance for retrieval for learning. *Science, 319*, 966−968.

Kindt, M., & Soeter, M. (2011). Reconsolidation in human fear conditioning study: a test of extinction as updating mechanism. *Biological Psychology*. [Epub ahead of print].

Kindt, M., Soeter, M., & Vervliet, B. (2009). Beyond extinction: erasing human fear responses and preventing the return of fear. *Nature Neuroscience, 12*, 256−258.

Kroes, M. C., Strange, B. A., & Dolan, R. J. (2010). Beta-adrenergic blockade during memory retrieval in humans evokes a sustained reduction of declarative emotional memory enhancement. *Journal of Neuroscience, 30*, 3959−3963.

LaBar, K. S., Gatenby, J. C., Gore, J. C., LeDoux, J. E., & Phelps, E. A. (1998). Human amygdala activation during conditioned fear acquisition and extinction: a mixed-trial fMRI study. *Neuron, 20*, 937−945.

LaBar, K. S., LeDoux, J. E., Spencer, D. D., & Phelps, E. A. (1995). Impaired fear conditioning following unilateral temporal lobectomy in humans. *Journal of Neuroscience, 15*, 6846−6855.

Lasry, N., Levy, E., & Tremblay, J. (2008). Making memories, again. *Science, 320*, 1720.

LeDoux, J. E. (2000). Emotion circuits in the brain. *Annual Review of Neuroscience, 23*, 155−184.

Lindsay, D. S., & Johnson, M. K. (1989). The eyewitness suggestibility effect and memory for source. *Memory & Cognition, 17*, 349−358.

Loftus, E. F. (1979). The malleability of human memory. *American Scientist, 67*, 312−320.

Loftus, E. F. (1981). Natural and unnatural cognition. *Cognition, 10*, 193−196.

Loftus, E. F. (2005a). Planting misinformation in the human mind: a 30-year investigation of the malleability of memory. *Learning & Memory, 12*, 361−366.

Loftus, E. F. (2005b). Searching for the neurobiology of the misinformation effect. *Learning & Memory, 12*, 1−2.

Loftus, E. F., & Yuille, J. C. (1984). Departures from reality in human perception and memory. In H. Weingartner, & E. S. Parker (Eds.), *Memory Consolidation: Psychobiology of Cognition* (pp. 163−184). Hillsdale, NJ: Erlbaum.

Lonsdorf, T. B., Weike, A. I., Nikamo, P., Schalling, M., Hamm, A. O., & Ohman, A. (2009). Genetic gating of human fear learning and extinction: possible implications for gene−environment interaction in anxiety disorder. *Psychological Science, 20*, 198−206.

McCloskey, M., & Zaragoza, M. (1985). Misleading postevent information and memory for events: arguments and evidence against memory impairment hypotheses. *Journal of Experimental Psychology: General, 114*, 1−16.

McEwen, B. S. (2001). Plasticity of the hippocampus: adaptation to chronic stress and allostatic load. *Annals of the New York Academy of Sciences, 933*, 265−277.

McGaugh, J. L. (2000). Memory—A century of consolidation. *Science, 287*, 248−251.

Milad, M. R., & Quirk, G. J. (2012). Fear extinction as a model for translational neuroscience: ten years of progress. *Annual Review of Psychology, 63*, 129−151.

Monfils, M. H., Cowansage, K. K., Klann, E., & LeDoux, J. E. (2009). Extinction−reconsolidation boundaries: key to persistent attenuation of fear memories. *Science, 324*, 951−955.

Muravieva, E. V., & Alberini, C. M. (2010). Limited efficacy of propranolol on the reconsolidation of fear memories. *Learning & Memory, 17*, 306−313.

Nader, K. (2003). Memory traces unbound. *Trends in Neurosciences, 26*, 65−72.

Nader, K., Schafe, G. E., & LeDoux, J. E. (2000). Fear memories require protein synthesis in the amygdala for reconsolidation after retrieval. *Nature, 406*, 722−726.

Oyarzún, J. P., Lopez-Barroso, D., Fuentemilla, L., Cucurell, D., Pedraza, C., Rodriguez-Fornells, A., & de Diego-Balaguer, R. (2012). Updating fearful memories with extinction training during reconsolidation: a human study using auditory aversive stimuli. *PLoS ONE, 7*, e38849.

Phelps, E. A., Delgado, M. R., Nearing, K. I., & LeDoux, J. E. (2004). Extinction learning in humans: role of the amygdala and vmPFC. *Neuron, 43*, 897−905.

Phelps, E. A., & LeDoux, J. E. (2005). Contributions of the amygdala to emotion processing: from animal models to human behavior. *Neuron, 48*, 175−187.

Phelps, E. A., O'Connor, K. J., Gatenby, J. C., Grillon, C., Gore, J. C., & Davis, M. (2001). Activation of the left amygdala to a cognitive representation of fear. *Nature Neuroscience, 4*, 437−441.

Poundja, J., Sanche, S., Tremblay, J., & Brunet, A. (2012). Trauma reactivation under influence of propranolol: an examination of clinical predictors. *European Journal of Psychotraumatology, 3*, 15470.

Quervain, D. J., Aerni, A., & Roozendaal, B. (2007). Preventative effect of beta-adrenoceptor blockade on glucocorticoid-induced memory retrieval deficits. *American Journal of Psychiatry, 164*, 967−969.

Raczka, K., Mechias, M. L., Gartmann, N., Reif, A., Deckert, J., Pessiglione, M., et al. (2011). Empirical support for an involvement of the mesostriatal dopamine system in human fear extinction. *Translational Psychiatry, 1*, e12.

Rauch, S. L., Shin, L. M., & Phelps, E. A. (2006). Neurocircuitry models of posttraumatic stress disorder and extinction: human neuroimaging research—Past, present, and future. *Biological Psychiatry, 60*, 376−382.

Reed, A. V. (1976). Recognition memory: one-component strength functions in the "short-term to long-term transition region". *Memory and Cognition, 4*, 453−458.

Rodriguez, M. L., Campos, J., Forcato, C., Leiguarda, R., Maldonado, H., Molina, V. A., & Pedreira, M. E. (2013). Enhancing a declarative memory in humans: the effect of clonazepam on reconsolidation. *Neuropharmacology, 64*, 432−442.

Rubin, R. D. (1976). Clinical use of retrograde amnesia produced by electroconvulsive shock: a conditioning hypothesis. *Canadian Psychiatric Association Journal, 21*, 87−90.

Schacter, D. L., & Tulving, E. (1994). What are the memory systems of 1994? In D. L. Schacter, & E. Tulving (Eds.), *Memory Systems* (pp. 1−38) Cambridge, MA: MIT Press.

Schiller, D., Monfils, M. H., Raio, C. M., Johnson, D. C., LeDoux, J. E., & Phelps, E. A. (2010). Preventing the return of fear in humans using reconsolidation update mechanisms. *Nature, 463*, 49−53.

Schiller, D., & Phelps, E. A. (2011). Does reconsolidation occur in humans? *Frontiers in Behavioral Neuroscience, 5*, 24.

Schwabe, L., Nader, K., Wolf, O. T., Beaudry, T., & Pruessner, J. C. (2012). Neural signature of reconsolidation impairments by propranolol in humans. *Biological Psychiatry, 71*, 380−386.

Sederberg, P. B., Gershman, S. J., Polyn, S. M., & Norman, K. A. (2011). Human memory reconsolidation can be explained using the temporal context model. *Psychonomic Bulletin and Review, 18*, 455−468.

Soeter, M., & Kindt, M. (2010). Dissociating response systems: erasing fear from memory. *Neurobiology of Learning & Memory, 94*, 30−41.

Soeter, M., & Kindt, M. (2012a). Stimulation of the noradrenergic system during memory formation impairs extinction learning but not the disruption of reconsolidation. *Neuropsychopharmcology, 37*, 1204−1215.

Soeter, M., & Kindt, M. (2012b). Erasing fear for an imagined threat event. *Psychoneuroendocrinology, 37*, 1769−1779.

Squire, L. R., Slater, P. C., & Chace, P. M. (1976). Reactivation of recent or remote memory before electroconvulsive therapy does not produce retrograde amnesia. *Behavioral Biology, 18*, 335−343.

Stern, C. A., Gazarini, L., Takahashi, R. N., Guimaraes, F. S., & Bertoglio, L. J. (2012). On disruption of fear memory by reconsolidation blockade: evidence from cannabidiol treatment. *Neuropsychopharmacology, 37*, 2132−2142.

Stewart, J., de Wit, H., & Eikelboom, R. (1984). Role of unconditioned and conditioned drug effects in the self-administration of opiates and stimulants. *Psychological Review, 91*, 251−268.

Strange, B. A., Kroes, M. C., Fan, J. E., & Dolan, R. J. (2010). Emotion causes targeted forgetting of established memories. *Frontiers in Behavioral Neuroscience, 4*, 175.

Tollenaar, M. S., Elzinga, B. M., Spinhoven, P., & Everaerd, W. (2009). Immediate and prolonged effects of cortisol, but not propranolol, on memory retrieval in healthy young men. *Neurobiology of Learning and Memory, 91*, 23–31.

Tulving, E., & Thomson, D. (1973). Encoding specificity and retrieval processes in episodic memory. *Psychological Review, 80*, 352–372.

Walker, M. P., Brakefield, T., Hobson, J. A., & Stickgold, R. (2003). Dissociable stages of human memory consolidation and reconsolidation. *Nature, 425*, 616–620.

Walle, T., Walle, K., Mathur, R. S., Palesch, Y. Y., & Conradi, E. C. (1994a). Propranolol metabolism in normal subjects: association with sex steroid hormones. *Clinical Pharmacology & Therapeutics, 56*, 127–132.

Walle, U. K., Fagan, T. C., Topmiller, M. J., Conradi, E. C., & Walle, T. (1994b). The influence of gender and sex steroid hormones on the plasma binding of propranolol enantiomers. *British Journal of Clinical Pharmacology, 37*, 21–25.

Weathers, F., Litz, B., Herman, D., Huska, J., & Keane, T. (1993). *The PTSD Checklist (PCL): Reliability, Validity, and Diagnostic Utility*. San Antonio, TX: Paper presented at the Annual Convention of the International Society for Traumatic Stress Studies.

Wickelgren, W. A. (1972). Trace resistance and the decay of long-term memory. *Journal of Mathematical Psychology, 9*, 418–455.

Xue, Y. X., Luo, Y. X., Wu, P., Shi, H. S., Xue, L. F., Chen, C., Zhu, W. L., Ding, Z. B., Bao, Y. P., Shi, J., Epstein, D. H., Shaham, Y., & Lu, L. (2012). A memory retrieval–extinction procedure to prevent drug craving and relapse. *Science, 336*, 241–245.

Chapter ten

Reconsolidation of Declarative Memory

María Eugenia Pedreira

*Laboratorio de Neurobiología de la Memoria, FCEN UBA, IFIBYNE-CONICET,
Buenos Aires, Argentina*

*In memoriam of my science mentor, Dr. Hector Maldonado—A true
scientist, with Lorca's "duende."*

10.1 INTRODUCTION

The study of memory is one of the most challenging and exciting areas of basic
and applied neuroscience research. In the past decade, it has been demonstrated
that the storage of information can be updated through the reconsolidation
process (Lee, 2009). The study of declarative memory, which is a hallmark
of humans (Dudai, 2002), not only supports the universality of some mechanisms but also opens avenues to apply this current knowledge in new therapies
for traumatic memories (Kindt, Soeter, & Vervliet, 2009; Schiller & Phelps,
2011). Our research demonstrates the existence of the reconsolidation
process for declarative memory, characterizes its boundary conditions, and
studies its underlying functions.

Animals' brains constantly encode the features of their surrounding environment, which is critical for their everyday survival as well as for the learning
that guides their successful interactions with the external world. In this
context, the process of transforming new information into long-lasting memories has been an object of interest for neurobiology throughout the past
century. The seminal studies of Müller and Pilzecker (1900) used verbal
learning and led to the idea that enduring memories are formed through
a process of consolidation. Their theory assumes that memories are labile
during an initial time window after acquisition but that memories become
stable and resistant to amnesic agents with the passage of time. The consolidation process has been described using behavioral, pharmacological, and
molecular approaches in diverse species, ranging from nematodes to
humans. The traditional paradigm assumes that memory consolidation is

213

Memory Reconsolidation. http://dx.doi.org/10.1016/B978-0-12-386892-3.00010-X

a conserved evolutionary process that requires an initial phase of RNA and protein synthesis (Kandel, 2001; McGaugh, 2000). However, the idea that memories are immutable after consolidation has changed. Since the early study by Misanin, Miller, and Lewis (1968), several reports have shown that the presentation of a specific reminder triggers old memories to pass from a stable state to a reactivated state. This reactivation implies that the memory is labile and that it is once again susceptible to amnesic agents. Such susceptibility decreases over time and leads to a restabilization phase known as reconsolidation. It has been proposed that reconsolidation shares many of the cellular and molecular mechanisms used during consolidation (Nader, Schafe, & LeDoux, 2000a; Suzuki *et al.*, 2004). From the extensive studies that have been conducted during approximately the past decade, a general conclusion has emerged. In fact, the term *reconsolidation* is not used to represent the recapitulation of initial consolidation but, rather, to represent the functional role of the process, which is to restore the stability of memories (Alberini, 2005).

Our laboratory first began studying memory in an invertebrate model more than 25 years ago. Our characterization of the reconsolidation process used the aversive memory paradigm and was first focused on compiling evidence for the evolutionary persistence of molecular mechanisms subserving both consolidation and reconsolidation processes (Pedreira, Perez-Cuesta, & Maldonado, 2002). Shared molecular mechanisms would likely be the basic tools used by evolution to promote adaptive changes among phylogenetically disparate animals (Carew, 2000). At approximately the same time, an unexpected conclusion seemed to emerge from the new research: A memory is reactivated and reconsolidated every time it is recalled (Nader, Schafe, & LeDoux, 2000b; Sara, 2000a). This might initially appear to be counterintuitive, given that the vulnerable reconsolidation stage could potentially jeopardize information that is, in the majority of cases, crucial for animals' survival. Because of this concern, our second research aim was to identify boundary conditions for the reconsolidation process, demonstrating that long exposure to specific reminders triggered the formation of an extinction memory instead of the reconsolidation of the original learning process (Pedreira & Maldonado, 2003). We also demonstrated that a memory passed through the reconsolidation stage only when a mismatch component—that is, a discrepancy between what was learned and what actually occurred—was included in the reminder structure (Pedreira, Perez-Cuesta, & Maldonado, 2004). Thus, a mismatch between what was expected and what actually occurred could result from failed prediction. The labilization-reconsolidation process could play a repair role by enabling the system to integrate new information into the background of past memories. Thus, our research in humans was aimed at demonstrating the existence of a reconsolidation process for a declarative memory, characterizing boundary conditions such as the necessary reminder structure, and studying the possible functions of this process.

10.2 RECONSOLIDATION OF A DECLARATIVE MEMORY IN HUMANS

The studies of Lewis and colleagues in the late 1960s (Lewis, 1969; Misanin *et al.*, 1968) inspired the current criteria with which an experimental protocol of reconsolidation should comply. First, the reactivation of a consolidated memory should be the result of the presentation of a cue reminder. Second, the administration of an experimental treatment should affect reconsolidation after reactivation. Finally, the testing session should occur only after the time window for reconsolidation has closed. Meeting these experimental criteria reveals that the memory is again labile (first criteria) and that treatment impairs memory restabilization (second criteria) while the memory is in the labile state. Consequently, the amnesic effect is long-lasting even after the reconsolidation process is complete. The use of a delayed time window for retesting ensures that restabilization develops over time (third criteria).

Observing these criteria, Walker, Brakefield, Hobson, and Stickgold (2003) published the first study of human reconsolidation memory for a motor skill, using a finger-tapping task. Because this paper was, at the time, the only study of human memory reconsolidation that used the criteria defined by Lewis and followed the principles demonstrated for an invertebrate model, our laboratory advanced the study of the reconsolidation process in humans by using a declarative memory paradigm. The first step in our research was to design a new paradigm to study the reconsolidation of declarative memory. The paradigm (Figure 10.1A) included contextual cues (i.e., context-specific cues such as light, images, and music) and a task, which required memorizing five pairs of nonsense syllables (List 1). The selection of these materials was based on the foundational studies of Müller and Pilzecker (1900).

The experiments were conducted in a dark room with a personal computer. Each participant was provided earphones and was seated facing a monitor placed in front of a large screen on the wall. The task required the participants to learn a list of five pairs of nonsense syllables that were presented on the monitor screen. The list was associated with a specific context. The list was composed of five pairs of nonsense cue response syllables in rioplatense Spanish. In each training trial, the participants were required to write down the corresponding response syllable for each cue syllable presented. Each experiment consisted of a training session in which the list was presented in 10 different trials, a treatment session wherein the reminder and/or the amnesic treatment was administered, and a testing session in which memory retention for the target memory was evaluated.

In most preceding studies, memory reconsolidation was demonstrated through the administration of blockers, which produced amnesic effects (Nader *et al.*, 2000a; Przybyslawski, Roullet, & Sara, 1999), or by behavioral interference (i.e., by learning a new task) (Boccia, Blake, Acosta, & Baratti,

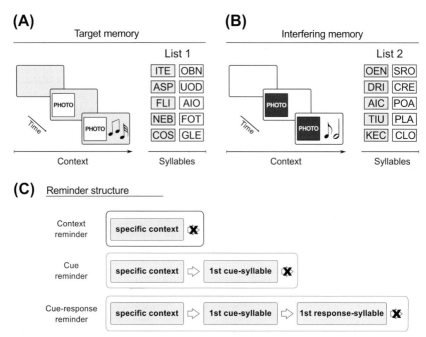

FIGURE 10.1 The paradigm. (A) Each trial was formed by the context—specific sequential combination of a light (color illumination of the room), image (a picture on the monitor), and sound (music melody from earphones)—and by a list of syllables (List 1): Five pairs of cue—response syllables (gray and white boxes, respectively) were presented successively and in random order. (B) Interfering memory: Each trial was formed by the context—different sequential combination of stimuli, light (color illumination of the room), image (a picture on the monitor), and sound (music melody from earphones)—and by a list of syllables (List 2): Five different pairs of cue—response syllables (gray and white boxes, respectively) were presented successively and in random order. (C) Reminder structure. The context reminder consisted of the presentation of specific context and the trial was interrupted before any syllable presentation (top). The cue reminder included the specific context, and then one cue syllable was presented, after which the trial was interrupted, thus not allowing the subject to answer with the respective response syllable (middle). The cue—response reminder included the specific context, and then one cue syllable was presented and subjects were allowed to write down the first response syllable, after which the trial was interrupted (bottom). X's indicate the full stop of each type of reminder.

2005; Walker *et al.*, 2003). Some blockers used in animal models were toxic for humans; therefore, we opted for the use of equivalent learning processes as an interfering agent.

In other studies, the most common method used to induce amnesic effects is to disclose the defective retrieval of the target memory at testing session. Memories are not stored in isolation from other memories; they integrate into complex associative networks (Debiec, Doyère, Nader, & LeDoux, 2006; Levy & Anderson, 2002). The activation of related memory traces may interfere with the desired retrieval trace. Therefore, faulty retrieval at testing may be due to problems in memory encoding, problems in memory storage, or issues related to the simultaneous retrieval of related information (Mayes & Downes, 1997). Consequently, direct retrieval examination becomes less effective in disclosing deficits in memory storage. Thus, we proposed an alternative testing method based on the "forgetting" effect that retrieval of the target memory could have on the recall of other memories that share some features. Such memories are categorically related (Levy & Anderson, 2002). This forgetting of related information, termed retrieval-induced forgetting (RIF) (Anderson, Bjork, & Bjork, 1994; MacLeod & Macrae, 2001), demonstrates that the act of remembering a specific memory can temporarily block the late retrieval of other related memories. To reveal this effect, it is necessary to test the target memory immediately followed by testing the related memory. Recall of the related memory is temporary inhibited, and this effect is expressed as poor performance at testing (Anderson et al., 1994). This effect is possible only when the target memory is intact, and as in the testing condition, its retrieval impairs the posterior retrieval of the other memory. Therefore, the absence of RIF is a good indicator of a defective target memory. In other words, a deficit in the target memory is expressed not only by flaws in its own retrieval but also by the faithful retrieval of a related memory (Forcato et al., 2007). Applying this concept to our experiments, impairments in the target memory are revealed by good retention of the interfering memory when both are evaluated together. On the contrary, the presence of RIF demonstrates that both memories are intact. It is necessary to stress that in our paradigm, the RIF effect was a consequence of the fact that both memories (for List 1 and List 2; Figures 10.1A and 10.1B) shared some items: the experimental room, the experimenter, the trial structure, and the procedural components of the task. These shared components closely link the List 1 and List 2 memories. Consequently, to use the RIF method, the testing session includes the evaluation of List 1 first and then, 5 min later, the evaluation of List 2.

The following experiments were aimed at testing the reconsolidation process (Figure 10.2A). Participants were trained with List 1 on Day 1 and with List 2 on Day 2, 5 min after presentation of the reminder (context cues plus one cue syllable). The results of testing on Day 3 (with List 1 and List 2 evaluated consecutively) showed the absence of RIF for List 1, revealing memory impairment for the list. On the contrary, when the reminder was omitted on Day 2, the presence of the RIF effect (poor List 2 memory with a high number of errors) confirmed that the target memory was intact (Figure 10.2B).

Finally, to determine the time window for memory reconsolidation, the interfering agent was presented either 6 or 10 hr after reactivation by the cue reminder. On Day 3, these experiments showed that the target memory was impaired for the 6-hr time window (i.e., the RIF effect was absent), and the target memory was not affected (the RIF effect was present) when List 2

(A)

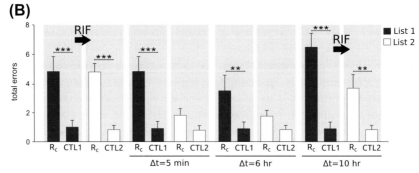

Groups	Day 1	Day 2	Day 3
NR	L1-TR	L2-TR	L1-TS --- L2-TS
$R_c(\Delta t)$	L1-TR	R_Δt_L2-TR	L1-TS --- L2-TS
CTL1	L1-TR	R or no-R	L1-TS
CTL2	--------	L2-TR	L2-TS

(B)

FIGURE 10.2 **Reconsolidation of declarative memory in humans.** (A) Experimental protocol: A 3-day experiment. The table shows the experimental groups. CTL, control groups; L1, List 1; L2, List 2; NR, no reminder; R_C, cue reminder; Δt, the interval between the cue reminder and the L2 presentation; TR, training session; TS, testing session. (B) Mean of total errors $\pm$ SEM on Day 3. Black bars, List 1 performance at testing; white bars, List 2 performance at testing; RIF, retrieval-induced forgetting. **p < 0.01; ***p < 0.001.

training was given 10 hr after target memory reactivation. Thus, behavioral interference affected memory restabilization only when it was administered after memory reactivation in a time window of at least 6 hr.

In summary, our paradigm meets the requirements established by Lewis to study the reconsolidation process. Specifically, our results show reactivation of the consolidated List 1 memory as a result of a cue reminder presentation (List 1 context plus a cue syllable), and this is the only manipulation that induced the memory into a labile state. Second, the administration of an amnesic agent (new interference learning; i.e., List 2) produced an amnesic effect and consequently verified the occurrence of reconsolidation after reactivation. Finally, the testing session occurred 24 hr after the treatment, when the time window for reconsolidation (10 hr for this paradigm) had closed, indicating that the amnesic agent had to be presented when the memory was passing through the reconsolidation phase. This phase was time limited.

Here, it is important to stress a major point. As observed with other models, the effect of memory interference could be reflected in partial amnesia (Debiec et al., 2006; Nader et al., 2000b; Przybyslawski et al., 1999). Because of this possibility and because of the existence of a network of memories that share some components, such as for the elements included in our paradigm, partial amnesia may reflect not only memory interference but also flawed memory retrieval. Based on this alternative interpretation, we considered it essential to evaluate both the target and the interfering memories (Forcato et al.,

2007). The evaluation of only the target memory might yield an incomplete picture of what had actually occurred to this memory.

10.3 SPECIFICITY OF THE REMINDER STRUCTURE

An operational definition of memory reconsolidation generally includes the assertion that the reactivated memory can be disrupted by pharmacological or behavioral agents that hinder the restabilization process (Boccia *et al.*, 2005; Nader *et al.*, 2000b). Taking this statement in its strictest sense could lead us to conclude that whenever a memory is retrieved, it becomes labile and is therefore susceptible to disruption (Nader, 2003). The conclusion that a memory is jeopardized every time it is retrieved initially seems to be counterintuitive. Furthermore, restabilizing a memory that has been previously reactivated, which requires molecular mechanisms with a significant energy cost, seems to be of low adaptive value. However, we have seen in our *Chasmagnathus granulatus* paradigm that changes in some of the reminder parameters could prevent a memory from undergoing reconsolidation (Pedreira *et al.*, 2004). Therefore, we take into account three conditions that define the specific structure of the reminder. First, the duration of the reminder should be limited to induce reconsolidation and not extinction (Eisenberg & Dudai, 2004; Pedreira & Maldonado, 2003). Second, the reminder must be completed to produce the labilization (Pedreira *et al.*, 2004). Third, the reminder must not include reinforcement. Under these conditions, there is an inconsistency (i.e., a mismatch) between what the animal expects and what actually happens. These reminders are referred to as the mismatching component (Morris *et al.*, 2006).

We anticipate that the labilization-reconsolidation process would no longer be observed if these reminder parameters were changed. To identify the reminder structure that best reactivates the memory, we decided to truncate the reminder presentation at different time points. Using this strategy, it is possible to identify the components that are necessary to trigger the reactivation of a declarative target memory.

Using the same paradigm and protocol described previously, we evaluated whether changes in the reminder structure hindered the reactivation of the target memory. We designed three different types of reminders: reminders consisting only of context cues (context reminder; Figure 10.1C, top); reminders consisting of context cues plus one cue syllable, without providing the participants with an opportunity to write down the response one (cue reminder; Figure 10.1C, middle); and reminders consisting of context cues plus one cue syllable, with participants being given an opportunity to write down the response syllable (cue–response reminder; Figure 10.1C, bottom). Only the group that received only the cue reminder prior to learning List 2 showed impairments in the target memory, as indicated by an absence of RIF at testing (i.e., a high number of errors for List 1 and a lower number of errors for List 2). The no-reminder group and the other two reminder groups (the context-reminder and the cue–response-reminder groups, respectively) exhibited an intact List 1 memory, demonstrated by a RIF effect and a poor List 2 memory. The context and cue—response reminders failed to induce memory labilization, leaving the first memory intact. It is important to note that this lack of labilization was due to subtle changes in the reminder structure. Specific context followed by a cue syllable triggers the labilization-reconsolidation process for List 1 memory. However, this phenomenon was not observed if the cue syllable was omitted and only the context was presented, and it was not observed if the participant could answer with the correspondent response syllable. The List 1 memory was not reactivated in the absence of the learned cue (the context-reminder group) or in the absence of the mismatching component of the reminder (the cue—response-reminder group). These findings cast doubt on the idea that every time a memory is recalled, it passes through the labilization-reconsolidation process, and our results define boundary conditions that guide the search for defined roles for this process in determining the fate of a memory.

It is worth emphasizing that in the case of the cue—response-reminder group, the reminder failed to induce memory labilization due to the inclusion of one syllable-response pair in its structure. Such an inclusion represents the beginning of the completion of the learned task and, therefore, the omission of the mismatching component. Results analogous to those from the cue—response-reminder group were obtained with crabs using a model of contextual memory wherein the reinforcement was included during the context re-exposure training (Pedreira *et al.*, 2004). Results with rats in the water maze paradigm (Morris *et al.*, 2006) could be considered to be another example of the opposite effects of a protein synthesis inhibitor (anisomycin), depending on whether the mismatching component was included in the reminder. Given that the platform location changes between trials, there is an inconsistency (i.e., a mismatch) between the expected and the actual position of the platform. It was shown that this irreversible mismatch made the memory susceptible to anisomycin and triggered the updating of the cognitive representation of the new location of the platform. However, in other studies, the reactivation session results seemed identical to the training session. Consequently, the labilization-reconsolidation process seems to be triggered by a breach of the expectations generated based on previous learning experiences. The transgression might be qualitative (the expected reinforcement never comes) or quantitative (the amount of the reinforcement is not fully predicted) (Lee, 2009). In summary, a mismatch between what is expected and what actually occurs could result from failed predictions. Therefore, it seems that labilization-reconsolidation plays a repair role by enabling the system to integrate new information into the background of the past (Pedreira *et al.*, 2004).

10.4 LABILIZATION-RECONSOLIDATION FUNCTIONS: MEMORY UPDATING AND STRENGTHENING VIA THE RECONSOLIDATION PROCESS

It is generally recognized in the field of cognitive psychology that memories can be rebuilt upon their retrieval (Schacter, Norman, & Koutstaal, 1998). Previous studies of human memories clearly suggest that memories are not constant through time. Indeed, they vary not only in content but also in strength (e.g., flashbulb memories (Brown & Kulik, 1977) and misleading post-event information (Loftus, Miller, & Burns, 1978)).

In the field of neurobiology, the reconsolidation process represents a tool that offers a putative mechanism for the modification of acquired information. Two nonexclusive functions have been proposed for this process (Alberini, 2007). Memory updating suggests that destabilization of the original memory after the reminder allows for the integration of new information into the background of the original memory (Dudai, 2004; Lewis, 1979). Another proposal states that the labilization-reconsolidation process strengthens the original memory (Sara, 2000b). Interestingly, memory updating has received experimental support using different paradigms and models. In brief, Morris *et al.* (2006) found that reconsolidation occurs in spatial memory when animals retrieve a memory in circumstances in which new memory encoding is likely to occur. The necessity of updating stored information in these experiments is related to the delayed match-to-place procedure. The critical manipulation in this protocol was that new memory encoding was required each day as the location of the escape platform changed between sessions.

Using a procedure that separates the learning of pure context from footshock-motivated contextual fear learning, Lee (2010) demonstrated that the hippocampal mechanisms of initial context learning and the subsequent updating of the neutral contextual representation (to incorporate the footshock) were doubly dissociable. Contextual memory consolidation was dependent on BDNF expression in the dorsal hippocampus, whereas the footshock-induced modification of the contextual representation required the expression of Zif268.

List-learning procedures have been used to assess reconsolidation in human episodic memory. Hupbach, Gomez, Hardt, and Nadel (2007) instructed participants to memorize a list of objects, and on a subsequent day, the participants were primed to recall the learning episode (reactivation) before memorizing a second list. The authors showed the reconsolidation effect by the expression of a significant number of intrusions from the second list into the target list.

In contrast, only two research papers have investigated the strength of reconsolidation. Lee (2008) found that a second learning trial strengthened a consolidated contextual fear memory, but only following its destabilization. Interestingly, preventing memory destabilization invariably maintains the strength of the original memory. Inda, Muravieva, and Alberini (2011) used rat inhibitory avoidance to test whether reconsolidation mediates memory strength over time. They found that successive reactivations of more recent memories, via re-exposure to the context, resulted in reconsolidation that mediated memory strength, an effect that was temporally limited.

The demonstration of reconsolidation for declarative memories would not only substantially support the universality of this phenomenon but also raise the possibility of discussing the reconsolidation hypothesis in light of a type of memory that is unique to humans (Dudai, 2002). This phenomenon would bring new perspective to the discussion of controversial or conjectural aspects of the reconsolidation hypothesis, such as its function (Debiec *et al.*, 2006; Dudai & Eisenberg, 2004; Sara & Hars, 2006) or the requirements for an appropriate reminder (Pedreira *et al.*, 2004). We first undertook this important study of reconsolidation via the study of its possible biological functions. We studied the incorporation of new information into a previously consolidated memory (Forcato, Rodríguez, Pedreira, & Maldonado, 2010) and the strengthening of previously learned information by successive labilization-reconsolidation processes (Forcato, Rodríguez, & Pedreira, 2011).

10.4.1 Declarative memory updating via the labilization-reconsolidation process

To design a protocol to study the updating of a declarative memory during reconsolidation, we incorporated verbal instruction as a tool in our experiments. Consequently, in this section, we show how proper verbal instruction, which was given consecutively after a memory had just been labilized by a reminder, allowed us to add new information to an existing memory. The target memory was acquired during a training session of 10 trials. In the first trial, the volunteers only read the response syllables, whereas in all other trials they wrote the response syllables down. The new information (INFO) was formed by three pairs of cue—response syllables. In this trial, the participant had only 3 sec to read each cue—response syllables pair. Thus, the participants learned the new syllables by reading them only once. The duration of the training was the main difference between List 1 and INFO. Therefore, the training for each memory condition differed in terms of information volume and in the way participants learned the information. Thus, they received a strong training for the target memory (List 1 memory) and very weak training for the new information (INFO memory). Following a classical experimental protocol for reconsolidation, the experiment lasted 3 days. All the participants received List 1 training on Day 1, INFO training on Day 2, and evaluations of both memories simultaneously on Day 3. Differences between groups emerged from the exhaustive combination of factors presented on Day 2, such as the presence or absence of the reminder and instructions to either incorporate or only read the new information. As a result of the parametric manipulation of these two factors, four unique participant groups were formed. The cue-reminder group was exposed to a cue reminder (the List 1 memory was labilized), given verbal instructions to incorporate the new information, and finally presented with the new information. The no-reminder group was similar to the cue-reminder group in all respects except for the presentation of the reminder. The cue—response-reminder group was similar to the cue-reminder group but was instructed to write down a response syllable; consequently, this group retrieved, but did not reactivate, its List 1 memory. Finally, the no-instruction group differed from the cue-reminder group only in the type of instructions given. In this group, participants were instructed only to read the new information. Despite being tested together (five syllables from

List 1 and three syllables of INFO), we analyzed memory for each list separately (Figure 10.3A).

The performance of each group on Day 3 was estimated by the percentage of errors committed when responding to the cue syllables. For the INFO memory, participants who received the reminder followed by explicit instructions to incorporate it demonstrated better performance than those who were previously given no reminder, those who were only given the cue–response reminder, or those who received instructions that omitted the request to add the INFO to List 1. The cue-reminder group made fewer errors on List 1 than the other groups. These failures in retrieving List 1 pairs as well as the INFO pairs might be explained by the fact that for all groups except the cue-reminder group, the INFO on Day 2 was encoded in a new INFO memory that coexisted with the previous List 1 memory (Figure 10.3A). Consequently, evoking either of the two memories might have recruited items from the other, thus generating retrieval interference (Forcato et al., 2007; McGeoch, 1932; Van Dyke & McElree, 2006). On the contrary, the good performance of the cue-reminder group, demonstrated for both the INFO and List 1 pairs, as well as in the absence of retrieval interference, might indicate that this group actually incorporated the information from both lists into only one memory, namely the early List 1 memory.

Four main conclusions can be drawn from the results discussed in this section. First, when a memory is labilized by the presentation of a reminder, and then verbal instruction and new information are given, the participants can introduce this new information into the recalled memory (memory updating). The labilization of the List 1 memory not only made the incorporation of the new information possible but also made it much faster than in the original acquisition. Second, in the absence of a reminder, new information is not incorporated into the single List 1 memory even if verbal instruction is given. It is instead encoded in a new INFO memory that coexists with the former memory. Third, the use of a reminder that included one syllable-response in its structure hindered the addition of new information into the List 1 memory, confirming that updating only occurs when the parametrical conditions necessary for reconsolidation are fulfilled (Forcato et al., 2009). Fourth, the omission of an explicit order to add INFO in the instruction hindered List 1 memory updating. Hence, in nonexperimental conditions, the relevance of the new information may be the factor that engages the reconsolidation process to update memory information. In this experiment, the relevance of the INFO was engendered by the explicit instruction to incorporate it into the learned list. Consequently, it is possible to identify the parametrical conditions necessary for updating within the reconsolidation framework. Specifically, the reminder needs to be unreinforced and, in this paradigm, explicit verbal instructions must be given to remember the new information while the original memory is labilized to achieve memory modification.

We demonstrated that new information can enter the original memory while it is labilized. Our results contradict the idea that the memory patrimony of an

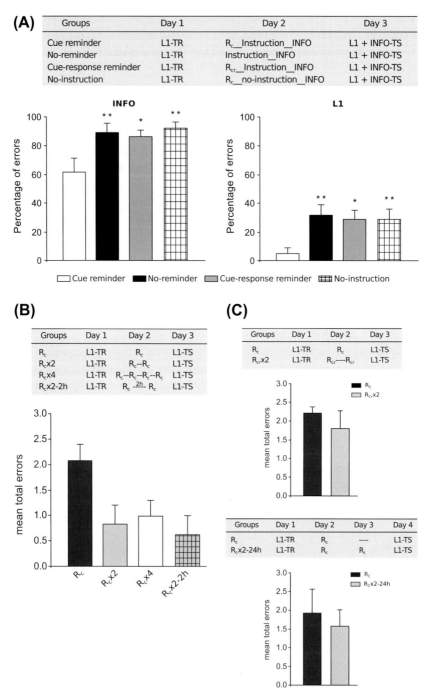

FIGURE 10.3 (A) Declarative memory updating. (Top) Experimental protocol: A 3-day experiment. INFO, new information; L1, List 1; R_c, cue reminder; R_{cr}, cue—response reminder. (Bottom) White bars, the cue-reminder group; black bars, the no-reminder group; gray bars, cue—response-reminder group; cross-hatched bars, no-instruction

animal is confined to memories that are only acquired once and are susceptible only to modification through forgetfulness-induced weakening. This patrimony could instead be conceived as an assembly that is continuously enriched not only by the addition of new memories but also by frequent changes in the content of previous memories. In the case of humans, this scenario is expected to be extremely dynamic because new information can quickly enter the labilized memory via language-related mechanisms.

10.4.2 Declarative memory strengthening via repeated labilization-reconsolidation processes

To study the strengthening of a declarative memory during the reconsolidation process, we repeated our presentation of the reminders. Thus, to evaluate memory strengthening via repeated reactivations, we performed a 3-day experiment with three groups. On Day 1, participants learned a list of five pairs of cue—response syllables (List 1 training session). On Day 2, they received treatment. The cue-reminder group received one cue reminder, the two cue-reminder group received two cue reminders separated by a 5-min interval, and the four cue-reminder group received the cue reminder four times. The cue reminder, which triggered the labilization-reconsolidation process, was formed by the specific context associated with the list plus one cue syllable without providing an opportunity for participants to write down the response syllable. Finally, all participants underwent testing on Day 3 (Figure 10.3B).

The performance of each group on Day 3 was estimated by the mean number of total errors made when responding to the cue syllables of the two testing trials. Participants who received two or four cue reminders successively on Day 2 performed better than those who received only one reminder. Our hypothesis that repeated reactivations would strengthen the memory for List 1 was reflected in a decrease in the number of total errors made at testing (Figure 10.3B). However, we also performed a more detailed analysis by classifying the errors

group. *$p < 0.05$; **$p < 0.01$. All data presented as percentage of errors $\pm$ SEM on Day 3. (B) Declarative memory strengthening. (Top) Experimental protocol: A 3-day experiment. Groups differ in the number of reminders that they received on Day 2. Group R_C received a cue reminder, group R_Cx2 received two cue reminders, and group R_Cx4 received the cue reminder four times. R_Cx2-2h received two cue reminders separated by 2 hr. (Bottom) Mean number of total errors $\pm$ SEM on Day 3. (C) Successive retrievals do not strengthen the declarative memory. (Upper panel, top) Experimental protocol. Group R_C received a cue reminder, and group R_{cr}x2 received the cue—response reminder twice. (Upper panel, bottom) Mean number of total errors $\pm$ SEM on Day 3. (Lower panel, top) Experimental protocol: A 4-day experiment. On Day 1, subjects received the training session (L1-TR), on Day 2 they received the cue reminder (R_c), on Day 3 only one group received the cue reminder, and subjects were tested on Day 4 (L1-TS). Group R_c received a cue reminder on Day 2 but received no treatment on Day 3. Group R_cx2-24h received the cue reminder on Days 2 and 3. (Lower panel, bottom) Mean number of total errors $\pm$ SEM on Day 4.

made at testing into three categories. Void-type errors occurred when no response was written. Intralist-type errors occurred when the response syllable was incorrect but did belong to the list. Finally, confusion-type errors occurred when the response syllable was not included in the list. It is worthwhile to note differences in the types of errors committed by each group. The numbers of void- and intralist-type errors were similar for the three groups. However, when two or four cue reminders were presented on Day 2, participants made fewer confusion-type errors. To discard the alternative hypothesis that this improved performance was a result only of the repeated retrievals (instead of repeated retrievals followed by reactivation–reconsolidation processes), we performed another experiment using two cue–response reminders that were retrieved but did not trigger labilization-reconsolidation of the target memory during the same number of sessions. The cue-reminder group was exposed to one cue reminder. The two cue–response-reminder group received the cue–response reminders twice. The interval between the cue–response reminders was the same as in the previous experiment (i.e., 5 min). The results showed that participants who received either one cue reminder or two cue–response reminders made a similar number of errors on Day 3. Moreover, in this case, the comparison between the error types showed an equivalent number of errors for each type in both groups. Therefore, successive retrievals on Day 2, induced by the cue–response reminders without reactivation (Figure 10.3C), did not improve the retention of the memory, and this effect depended on the repetition of the presentation of reminders (as two cue reminders) that induce the destabilization of the declarative memory.

Up to this point, improvements in memory retention as a consequence of a double reactivation occurred when the cue reminders were given successively in the same treatment session. In real life, outside the laboratory, it should be expected that reactivations occur intermittently and not necessarily immediately after one another. Our next step was to explore the effects of successive reactivations induced by the presentation of cue reminders separated by different time intervals. Considering the time window for reconsolidation previously determined in this paradigm (i.e., a reconsolidation period of at least 6 hr; Forcato, 2007), we designed a participant group with reactivations separated by intervals greater than the effective time to interfere with reconsolidation (24 hr; Figure 10.3C) and another participant group with the second reactivation within the interval of the first triggered labilization-reconsolidation process (2 hr; Figure 10.3B). The presentation of two cue reminders 24 hr apart did not improve the performance of participants compared with that of the group that reactivated the memory only once (Figure 10.3C). However, the participants who reactivated the memory twice within a 2-hr time interval showed a lower number of errors at testing (Figure 10.3B). Specifically, this decrease reflected a lower number of confusion-type errors. Taken together, these results support the view that two labilization-reconsolidation processes strengthen the target memory when the second labilization-reconsolidation occurs within at least 6 hr after the first. On the contrary, when the first reconsolidation finished and a second cue-reminder was presented thereafter, the first memory was not strengthened.

The main conclusion of this section is that when a memory is labilized by the presentation of a genuine reminder and the process is again triggered by the presentation of another cue reminder within the time window of the first, participants can improve their testing performance. This memory strengthening allowed the participants to remember both the three letters and their respective orders, showing an improvement in the precision of the memory.

However, it is necessary to stress that the idea that reactivated memories ensure their long-term storage is not new. According to a widely held conceit, the formation of long-term memories relies on the reactivation and redistribution of newly acquired memory representations from temporal storage to neural networks supporting long-term storage (Rasch & Born, 2007). The standard model of long-term memory consolidation, at least with regard to declarative memory events and facts (Frankland & Bontempi, 2005; Squire & Bayley, 2007), considers that during the offline periods, the newly acquired memory traces are gradually redistributed to neocortical regions via the strengthening of corticocortical connections. Human studies of reactivation patterns during sleep (offline periods) show that the learning of a declarative task is reactivated by the hippocampus during slow-wave sleep (SWS; Peigneux *et al.*, 2004). Using an olfactory stimulus to reactivate declarative memory during sleep, Rasch, Büchel, Gais, and Born (2007) showed that participants who learned a visual–spatial learning task under the presence of an odor and who were subsequently re-exposed to the odor during SWS improved their later retrieval of the task. These results support the hypothesis that once an odor has become associated with the context of learned object locations, re-exposure to the odor during subsequent SWS acts like a context cue, reactivating the new memories and thereby boosting memory consolidation. In other studies, neural signs of memory reactivation have also been revealed during post-learning when the participant was awake (Hoffman & McNaughton, 2002; Kudrimoti, Barnes, & McNaughton, 1999; Peigneux *et al.*, 2006).

Considering that destabilization after memory reactivation during wakefulness could modify the existing memory trace (Dudai, 2006), we decided to apply this logic to the reconsolidation process. Thus, while participants were awake and guided by the cue reminder, repeated reactivations could induce a strengthening of a previously consolidated memory, much like the odor reactivated spatial learning and improved memory consolidation during SWS. This waking reinforcement seems to be impervious to external inputs, which produces a real danger of encountering conflicting information. Surprisingly, in this case, these new data did not interfere with the initiated reconsolidation process.

Finally, speculative analysis of these results suggests the possibility that successive reactivations trigger repetitive labilization processes, which implies successive restabilization processes. Thus, the second restabilization is dependent on the previous restabilization, resulting in repeated activations of the same molecular pathways, which then leads to an increasing number of molecular/macromolecular changes that are necessary or available for the recovery of the stable state. To test this hypothesis, a new paradigm must be developed with an animal model to show a differential effect of repeated labilizations and induce an increase in the number of modifications associated with the plastic state. This increase may be correlated with a specific molecular mechanism that has been improved by repeatedly triggering the process.

To date, we have demonstrated that the presentation of a proper reminder (the cue reminder that triggers the labilization-reconsolidation process) could guide the same memory to be strengthened within the same context or to be updated. The fate of a memory depends on how and where the reactivation takes place. Our general conclusion is that both functions play a crucial role in the reconsolidation process because this phenomenon is not merely an automatic restabilization process that is triggered after retrieval. Instead, it is a truly unique process that represents an opportunity for adaptive modifications of stored information.

10.5 FUTURE INSIGHTS USING THE DECLARATIVE MEMORY PARADIGM

Because our paradigm is well-established, it can be applied to different research questions. It is well-known that memory retention can be enhanced by pharmacological modulation or by real-life events in animal models if the treatment is applied during the labilization-reconsolidation process. By adapting our design and manipulating the properties of the reminder structure, another group in our laboratory investigated whether the same effects occur for human memories. They chose to modulate the acquired memory with a mild stressor, which has had an effect on memory processing in other paradigms (Cahill, Gorski, & Le, 2003; Smeets, Otgaar, Candel, & Wolf, 2008), and to combine this stressor with different reminders. Thus, they presented a cue reminder (which reactivated the target memory) or a cue—response reminder (which only retrieved the original memory), and they applied a mild stressor after the presentation of the reminder (the cold pressor stress). Volunteers learned List 1, and 6 days later, one group reactivated their List 1 memory via exposure to the cue reminder prior to exposure to a mild stressor. Another group received a cue—response reminder before the stress treatment. Poor memory performance was found for the last group at testing on Day 7. Conversely, robust memory retention was shown at testing when the cold pressor stress administration was concurrent with the retrieved labile-memory state. These results revealed that a naturalistic, mild stressor could enhance reconsolidation, thus improving the long-term expression of a declarative memory (Coccoz, Maldonado, & Delorenzi, 2011).

Our paradigm could also be used with pharmacological interventions. Future research may, for instance, study the impact of different drugs administered after reactivation given the relevance of different systems to the reconsolidation process.

Another potential use of our paradigm takes advantage of the fact that we have previously demonstrated the existence of memory strengthening. It would be useful to study the fate of a memory when the strengthening process is triggered and an amnesic agent is administered.

Finally, our promising results obtained from basic research do not answer a central question: Can real traumatic memories be changed? In this chapter, we revisited results indicating ways to demonstrate the reconsolidation process, modify the storage of declarative memories, characterize the boundary conditions of reconsolidation, and determine the function of reconsolidation. Incorporating these results, new treatments may be developed to specifically address traumatic or dysfunctional memories based on the features of memory reconsolidation.

10.6 CONCLUSIONS AND REMARKS

The cognitive tradition considers memory to be a permanent, reconstructive, and dynamic process. Reconsolidation provides a plausible neurobiological mechanism to explain some of the dynamic properties of memory (Nader & Einarsson, 2010). Thus, cognitive psychology research has demonstrated the malleability of human memory (e.g., flashbulb memories (Brown & Kulik, 1977) and misleading post-event information (Loftus *et al.*, 1978)). Both types of memory modification can be explained by postreactivation plasticity and by the subsequent stabilization process (Hardt, Einarsson, & Nader, 2010).

It is important to stress that it is possible to demonstrate the reconsolidation process for a declarative memory and that such memories do not pass through reconsolidation every time they are retrieved. Moreover, the use of different cues presented during training could evoke or even reactivate consolidated memories. These types of reminder manipulations allow us to determine the boundary conditions for the process and guide our studies of the biological significance of this phenomenon. This biological role, which is likely to involve the modification, updating, or strengthening of a consolidated memory, reconciles the cognitive and neurobiological perspectives of memory. Thus, our main conclusion is that reconsolidation is not merely an automatic restabilization triggered after retrieval; it is a unique process that represents an opportunity for the adaptive modification of stored information.

ACKNOWLEDGMENTS

I thank Dr. Forcato C. and Lic. Carbó-Tano for their helpful comments on the manuscript and Lic. Carbó-Tano for figure production.

REFERENCES

Alberini, C. M. (2005). Mechanisms of memory stabilization: are consolidation and recon-solidation similar or distinct processes? *Trends in Neurosciences, 28*(1), 51–56. http://dx.doi.org/10.1016/j.tins.2004.11.001.
Alberini, C. M. (2007). Reconsolidation: the samsara of memory consolidation. *Debates in Neuroscience, 1*(1), 17–24. http://dx.doi.org/10.1007/s11559-007-9000-z.

Anderson, M. C., Bjork, R. A., & Bjork, E. L. (1994). Remembering can cause forgetting: retrieval dynamics in long-term memory. *Journal of Experimental Psychology, 20*(5), 1063−1087.

Boccia, M. M., Blake, M. G., Acosta, G. B., & Baratti, C. M. (2005). Memory consolidation and reconsolidation of an inhibitory avoidance task in mice: effects of a new different learning task. *Neuroscience, 135*(1), 19−29.

Brown, R., & Kulik, J. (1977). Flashbulb memories. *Cognition, 5*, 73−79.

Cahill, L., Gorski, L., & Le, K. (2003). Enhanced human memory consolidation with post-learning stress: interaction with the degree of arousal at encoding. *Learning & Memory, 10*(4), 270−274. http://dx.doi.org/10.1101/lm.62403.

Carew, T. J. (2000). *Behavioral Neurobiology: The Cellular Organization of Natural Behaviour.* Sunderland, MA: Sinauer.

Coccoz, V., Maldonado, H., & Delorenzi, A. (2011). The enhancement of reconsolidation with a naturalistic mild stressor improves the expression of a declarative memory in humans. *Neuroscience, 185*, 61−72. http://dx.doi.org/10.1016/j.neuroscience.2011.04.023.

Debiec, J., Doyère, V., Nader, K., & LeDoux, J. E. (2006). Directly reactivated, but not indirectly reactivated, memories undergo reconsolidation in the amygdala. *Proceedings of the National Academy of Sciences of the USA, 103*(9), 3428−3433. http://dx.doi.org/10.1073/pnas.0507168103.

Dudai, Y. (2002). *Memory from A to Z: Keywords, Concepts and Beyond.* Oxford: Oxford University Press.

Dudai, Y. (2004). The neurobiology of consolidations, or, how stable is the engram? *Annual Review of Psychology, 55*, 51−86. http://dx.doi.org/10.1146/annurev.psych.55.090902.142050.

Dudai, Y. (2006). Reconsolidation: The advantage of being refocused. *Current Opinion in Neurobiology, 16*(2), 174−178. http://dx.doi.org/10.1016/j.conb.2006.03.010.

Dudai, Y., & Eisenberg, M. (2004). Rites of passage of the engram: reconsolidation and the lingering consolidation hypothesis. *Neuron, 44*(1), 93−100.

Eisenberg, M., & Dudai, Y. (2004). Reconsolidation of fresh, remote, and extinguished fear memory in Medaka: old fears don't die. *European Journal of Neuroscience, 20*(12), 3397−3403.

Forcato, C., Argibay, P. F., Pedreira, M. E., & Maldonado, H. (2009). Human reconsolidation does not always occur when a memory is retrieved: the relevance of the reminder structure. *Neurobiology of Learning and Memory, 91*(1), 50−57. http://dx.doi.org/10.1016/j.nlm.2008.09.011.

Forcato, C., Burgos, V. L., Argibay, P. F., Molina, V. A., Pedreira, M. E., & Maldonado, H. (2007). Reconsolidation of declarative memory in humans. *Learning & Memory, 14*(4), 295−303.

Forcato, C., Rodríguez, M. L. C., & Pedreira, M. E. (2011). Repeated labilization-reconsolidation processes strengthen declarative memory in humans. *PLoS ONE, 6*, e23305. http://dx.doi.org/10.1371/journal.pone.0023305.

Forcato, C., Rodríguez, M. L. C., Pedreira, M. E., & Maldonado, H. (2010). Reconsolidation in humans opens up declarative memory to the entrance of new information. *Neurobiology of Learning and Memory, 93*(1), 77−84. http://dx.doi.org/10.1016/j.nlm.2009.08.006.

Frankland, P. W., & Bontempi, B. (2005). The organization of recent and remote memories. *Nature Reviews Neuroscience, 6*(2), 119−130. http://dx.doi.org/10.1038/nrn1607.

Hardt, O., Einarsson, E. O., & Nader, K. (2010). A bridge over troubled water: reconsolidation as a link between cognitive and neuroscientific memory research traditions. *Annual Review of Psychology, 61*, 141−167. http://dx.doi.org/10.1146/annurev.psych.093008.100455.

Hoffman, K. L., & McNaughton, B. L. (2002). Coordinated reactivation of distributed memory traces in primate neocortex. *Science, 297*(5589), 2070−2073. http://dx.doi.org/10.1126/science.1073538.

Hupbach, A., Gomez, R., Hardt, O., & Nadel, L. (2007). Reconsolidation of episodic memories: a subtle reminder triggers integration of new information. *Learning & Memory, 14*(1−2), 47−53.

Inda, M. C., Muravieva, E. V., & Alberini, C. M. (2011). Memory retrieval and the passage of time: from reconsolidation and strengthening to extinction. *Journal of Neuroscience, 31*(5), 1635−1643. http://dx.doi.org/10.1523/JNEUROSCI.4736-10.2011.

Kandel, E. R. (2001). The molecular biology of memory storage: a dialog between genes and synapses. *Bioscience Reports, 21*(5), 565−611.

Kindt, M., Soeter, M., & Vervliet, B. (2009). Beyond extinction: erasing human fear responses and preventing the return of fear. *Nature Neuroscience, 12*(3), 256−258.

Kudrimoti, H. S., Barnes, C. A., & McNaughton, B. L. (1999). Reactivation of hippocampal cell assemblies: effects of behavioral state, experience, and EEG dynamics. *Journal of Neuroscience, 19*(10), 4090−4101.

Lee, J. L. C. (2008). Memory reconsolidation mediates the strengthening of memories by additional learning. *Nature Neuroscience, 11*(11), 1264−1266. http://dx.doi.org/10.1038/nn.2205.

Lee, J. L. C. (2009). Reconsolidation: maintaining memory relevance. *Trends in Neurosciences, 32*(8), 413−420. http://dx.doi.org/10.1016/j.tins.2009.05.002.

Lee, J. L. C. (2010). Memory reconsolidation mediates the updating of hippocampal memory content. *Frontiers in Behavioral Neuroscience, 4*, 168. http://dx.doi.org/10.3389/fnbeh.2010.00168.

Levy, B. J., & Anderson, M. C. (2002). Inhibitory processes and the control of memory retrieval. *Trends in Cognitive Sciences, 6*(7), 299−305.

Lewis, D. J. (1969). Sources of experimental amnesia. *Psychological Review, 76*(5), 461−472.

Lewis, D. J. (1979). Psychobiology of active and inactive memory. *Psychological Bulletin, 86*(5), 1054−1083.

Loftus, E. F., Miller, D. G., & Burns, H. J. (1978). Semantic integration of verbal information into a visual memory. *Journal of Experimental Psychology: Human Learning and Memory, 4*(1), 19−31.

MacLeod, M. D., & Macrae, C. N. (2001). Gone but not forgotten: the transient nature of retrieval-induced forgetting. *Psychological Science, 12*(2), 148−152.

Mayes, A., & Downes, J. (1997). Theories of organic amnesia. *Memory, 5*(1−2), 1−2.

McGaugh, J. L. (2000). Memory—A century of consolidation. *Science, 287*(5451), 248−251.

McGeoch, J. A. (1932). Forgetting and the law of disuse. *Psychological Review, 39*, 352−370.

Misanin, J. R., Miller, R. R., & Lewis, D. J. (1968). Retrograde amnesia produced by electroconvulsive shock after reactivation of a consolidated memory trace. *Science, 160*(3827), 554−555.

Morris, R. G., Inglis, J., Ainge, J. A., Olverman, H. J., Tulloch, J., Dudai, Y., & Kelly, P. A. (2006). Memory reconsolidation: sensitivity of spatial memory to inhibition of protein synthesis in dorsal hippocampus during encoding and retrieval. *Neuron, 50*(3), 479−489.

Müller, G. E., & Pilzecker, A. (1900). Experimentelle Beitraege zur Lehre vom Gedaechtnis. *Zeitschrift fur Psychologie*. Suppl. 1.

Nader, K. (2003). Memory traces unbound. *Trends in Neurosciences, 26*(2), 65−72.

Nader, K., & Einarsson, E. O. (2010). Memory reconsolidation: an update. *Annals of the New York Academy of Sciences, 1191*, 27−41. http://dx.doi.org/10.1111/j.1749-6632.2010.05443.x.

Nader, K., Schafe, G. E., & LeDoux, J. E. (2000a). Fear memories require protein synthesis in the amygdala for reconsolidation after retrieval. *Nature, 406*(6797), 722−726.

Nader, K., Schafe, G. E., & LeDoux, J. E. (2000b). The labile nature of consolidation theory. *Nature Reviews, 1*(3), 216−219.

Pedreira, M. E., & Maldonado, H. (2003). Protein synthesis subserves reconsolidation or extinction depending on reminder duration. *Neuron, 38*(6), 863−869.

Pedreira, M. E., Perez-Cuesta, L. M., & Maldonado, H. (2002). Reactivation and reconsolidation of long-term memory in the crab *Chasmagnathus*: protein synthesis requirement and mediation by NMDA-type glutamatergic receptors. *Journal of Neuroscience, 22*(18), 8305−8311.

Pedreira, M. E., Perez-Cuesta, L. M., & Maldonado, H. (2004). Mismatch between what is expected and what actually occurs triggers memory reconsolidation or extinction. *Learning & Memory, 11*(5), 579–585.

Peigneux, P., Laureys, S., Fuchs, S., Collette, F., Perrin, F., Reggers, J., Phillips, C., et al. (2004). Are spatial memories strengthened in the human hippocampus during slow wave sleep? *Neuron, 44*(3), 535–545. http://dx.doi.org/10.1016/j.neuron.2004.10.007.

Peigneux, P., Orban, P., Balteau, E., Degueldre, C., Luxen, A., Laureys, S., & Maquet, P. (2006). Offline persistence of memory-related cerebral activity during active wakefulness. *PLoS Biology, 4*(4), e100. http://dx.doi.org/10.1371/journal.pbio.0040100.

Przybyslawski, J., Roullet, P., & Sara, S. J. (1999). Attenuation of emotional and nonemotional memories after their reactivation: role of beta adrenergic receptors. *Journal of Neuroscience, 19*(15), 6623–6628.

Rasch, B., & Born, J. (2007). Maintaining memories by reactivation. *Current Opinion in Neurobiology, 17*(6), 698–703. http://dx.doi.org/10.1016/j.conb.2007.11.007.

Rasch, B., Büchel, C., Gais, S., & Born, J. (2007). Odor cues during slow-wave sleep prompt declarative memory consolidation. *Science, 315*(5817), 1426–1429. http://dx.doi.org/10.1126/science.1138581.

Sara, S. J. (2000a). Retrieval and reconsolidation: toward a neurobiology of remembering. *Learning & Memory, 7*(2), 73–84.

Sara, S. J. (2000b). Strengthening the shaky trace through retrieval. *Nature Review in Neuroscience, 1*(3), 212–213.

Sara, S. J., & Hars, B. (2006). In memory of consolidation. *Learning & Memory, 13*(5), 515–521. http://dx.doi.org/10.1101/lm.338406.

Schacter, D. L., Norman, K. A., & Koutstaal, W. (1998). The cognitive neuroscience of constructive memory. *Annual Review of Psychology, 49*, 289–318. http://dx.doi.org/10.1146/annurev.psych.49.1.289.

Schiller, D., & Phelps, E. A. (2011). Does reconsolidation occur in humans? *Frontiers in Behavioral Neuroscience, 5*, 24.

Smeets, T., Otgaar, H., Candel, I., & Wolf, O. T. (2008). True or false? Memory is differentially affected by stress-induced cortisol elevations and sympathetic activity at consolidation and retrieval. *Psychoneuroendocrinology, 33*(10), 1378–1386. http://dx.doi.org/10.1016/j.psyneuen.2008.07.009.

Squire, L. R., & Bayley, P. J. (2007). The neuroscience of remote memory. *Current Opinion in Neurobiology, 17*(2), 185–196. http://dx.doi.org/10.1016/j.conb.2007.02.006.

Suzuki, A., Josselyn, S. A., Frankland, P. W., Masushige, S., Silva, A. J., & Kida, S. (2004). Memory reconsolidation and extinction have distinct temporal and biochemical signatures. *Journal of Neuroscience, 24*(20), 4787–4795.

Van Dyke, J. A., & McElree, B. (2006). Retrieval interference in sentence comprehension. *Journal of Memory and Language, 55*(2), 157–166. http://dx.doi.org/10.1016/j.jml.2006.03.007.

Walker, M. P., Brakefield, T., Hobson, J. A., & Stickgold, R. (2003). Dissociable stages of human memory consolidation and reconsolidation. *Nature, 425*(6958), 616–620.

Chapter | eleven

Episodic Memory Reconsolidation: An Update

Almut Hupbach*, **Rebecca Gomez**[†], **Lynn Nadel**[†]

Lehigh University, Bethlehem, Pennsylvania
[†] *The University of Arizona, Tucson, Arizona*

Research on memory reconsolidation in humans is still in its infancy, in contrast to the extensive research that has been carried out with animals, reflecting the fact that reconsolidation is difficult to study in humans. In particular, the pharmacological agents that have been used to directly interfere with or block (re)consolidation in animals are generally not safe for human use (e.g., protein synthesis inhibitors such as anisomycin). As a consequence, human reconsolidation has been studied mostly using behavioral interference paradigms (for exceptions, see the following: Kindt, Soeter, & Vervliet, 2009; Soeter & Kindt, 2012). Specifically, after reactivating a memory, some new information is presented that is related to or in some cases conflicts with the reactivated memory. After a delay, memory for the original information is tested, and if the new information presented after reactivation modifies the original memory (either by impairing or by updating it), a reconsolidation process is inferred. Importantly, it must also be shown that presentation of the same new information does not affect memory for the original information if this occurs without prior reactivation or outside of the reactivation window.

To date, researchers have successfully demonstrated reactivation-dependent memory modification in humans in fear conditioning (Kindt *et al.*, 2009; Schiller *et al.*, 2010) and procedural memory (Walker, Brakefield, Hobson, & Stickgold, 2003). We and others have asked whether reconsolidation also applies to episodic memories (Forcato, Argibay, Pedreira, & Maldonado, 2009; Forcato, Rodríguez, Pedreira, & Maldonado, 2010; Forcato *et al.*, 2007; Hupbach, Gomez, Hardt, & Nadel, 2007; Hupbach, Gomez, & Nadel, 2009, 2011; Hupbach, Hardt, Gomez, & Nadel, 2008). Episodic memory allows people to re-experience the past by engaging in "mental time travel" (Tulving, 2002). A defining feature of episodic memories is that they not only capture the core content of a previous experience but also can be traced back in time (When **233**

Memory Reconsolidation. http://dx.doi.org/10.1016/B978-0-12-386892-3.00011-1

did it happen?) and space (Where did it happen?). It is widely known that episodic memories are not always accurate (Loftus, 2005). Recently, it has been suggested that some memory distortions might be the result of reconsolidation processes (Hardt, Einarsson, & Nader, 2010). In order to study whether episodic memories undergo a reconsolidation process and, if so, which components of an episodic memory can be changed, we developed an object-learning paradigm that allowed us to create a specific time- and space-stamped memory for a set of objects (Hupbach *et al.*, 2007). In this chapter, we review findings from this paradigm. Note that during the same time period, Forcato and colleagues (2007, 2009, 2010) studied memory reconsolidation in a paired associate learning paradigm that also taps episodic memory, and they showed that reactivation that is followed by new learning can impair memory.

11.1 THE PARADIGM AND BASIC BEHAVIORAL EFFECT

Our object-learning paradigm involves three sessions overall—two encoding sessions and one retrieval session. In Session 1, participants are asked to memorize a set of 20 everyday objects (e.g., a tennis ball, a cup, and a toy car) that are placed one by one into a distinctive basket. The basket is used to create a unique setting for the first encoding session that can be distinguished from the setting involved with the second encoding session, typically administered 24 or 48 hr later. In Session 2, participants memorize a second set of 20 semantically unrelated objects. This time, instead of using a basket, the objects are displayed all at once on a table. Critically, this second session is conducted either under reminder or no-reminder conditions. In the reminder condition, participants are asked to describe in general terms what had happened during the first session (they are given a reminder question). Moreover, in this reminder condition, Session 2 takes place in the same room as Session 1, and the same experimenter administers the procedure. In the no-reminder condition, nothing is mentioned about the previous learning episode, and Session 2 is carried out in a different room and administered by a different experimenter. Twenty-four or 48 hr after Session 2, participants are asked to recall the set of objects they had learned in the first session. This recall session takes place in the same room in which Set 1 was encoded and with the experimenter from Session 1. Although the reminder group and the no-reminder group do not differ in the number of items recalled from Set 1, reminded participants include a significant number of Set 2 items in their Set 1 recall; we refer to these incorrectly-recalled items as "intrusions." In contrast, very few intrusions are observed in the no-reminder group (Figure 11.1). We take this result to demonstrate that reactivated memories become labile and open to the incorporation of new information (Hupbach *et al.*, 2007). Importantly, this reminder effect takes time to evolve. When recall of Set 1 is tested immediately after Set 2 encoding, intrusions from Set 2 into Set 1 recall are not observed. This is in line with the expected time dependency of the reconsolidation process (Nader, Schafe, & LeDoux, 2000).

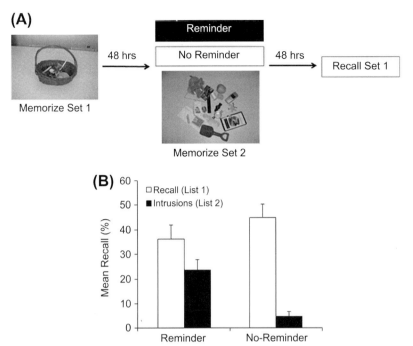

FIGURE 11.1 (A) Experimental design. Participants memorized a set of objects (Set 1) in Session 1. Forty-eight hours later, they were either reminded of Session 1 or not, and then they learned a second set of objects (Set 2). After another 48 hr, recall of Set 1 was tested. (B) Mean percentage of objects correctly and falsely recalled in the reminder and the no-reminder groups. The groups did not differ in the number of items recalled from Set 1, but the reminder group showed significantly more intrusions from Set 2 into Set 1 than the no-reminder group. In all figures, error bars represent standard errors of means. *Note:* Participants were asked to recall objects from Set 1. Objects that were falsely recalled from Set 2 are labeled as "intrusions."

Critically, the reactivation-dependent intrusions from Set 2 into Set 1 recall in the delayed test are not the result of general source confusion (e.g., it is not the case that participants in the reminder group are simply unable to differentiate which objects were presented in which session): When asked to recall Set 2 instead of Set 1 in Session 3, the reminder and no-reminder groups both show very low intrusions of Set 1 items into Set 2. In a follow-up study, we subjected participants to identical learning conditions as described previously, but instead of having participants freely recall Set 1 objects in Session 3, we asked them to recognize Set 1 and Set 2 objects among new fillers and to indicate for each recognized item the session in which they thought it had been presented (Hupbach *et al.*, 2009). As expected, the no-reminder group made few misattributions in either direction. More important, and similar to what we have found in the free recall paradigm, participants in the reminder group misattributed a significant number of Set 2 objects to Session 1 but very few Set 1 objects to Session 2. Interestingly, when asked how confident they were about each source judgment, participants were highly confident about their Set 2 misattributions—as confident as they were about correct source attributions for Set 1 objects. This suggests that the Set 2 items had become integrated into Set 1 memory in the reminder group. However, they were less confident about the few Set 1 items that they misattributed to Session 2.

Taken together, these results show that reactivating memory for a learning episode before presenting new, related information can trigger integration of the new material into the old memory. A similar effect was shown by Forcato *et al.* (2010) in their paired associates learning paradigm. However, in their study, incorporation of List 2 items into List 1 depended on a verbal reminder. These findings illustrate the potential function of memory reconsolidation as a constructive mechanism that allows memories to be updated with new information representing the most current state of knowledge. This function is also explicitly discussed in the animal literature (e.g., Lee, 2009), and several studies have found that reconsolidation only occurs when memory retrieval is coupled with new memory encoding—that is, when there is a mismatch between what is expected based on prior experience and what actually happens in a given situation (Lee, 2010; Morris *et al.*, 2006).

11.2 THE SPECIAL ROLE OF SPATIAL CONTEXT IN REACTIVATING AND UPDATING MEMORIES

In the studies described previously, we reminded participants of the first learning episode by (1) asking them to describe the general procedure of Set 1 learning, (2) using the same room for Set 2 learning, and (3) having the same experimenter administer Session 2. We wondered whether all of these components were necessary to trigger reactivation and subsequent memory updating or if some were more important than others. To address these questions, we created three new conditions, with only one reminder component in each (Hupbach *et al.*, 2008). Neither asking about the general procedure (reminder question) nor encountering the same experimenter during Session 2 caused intrusions from Set 2 into Set 1 in the absence of the other components from the original study (Figure 11.2A). Updating did occur in the spatial context condition, even though the other components were absent (Figure 11.2A). We also wondered whether these various reminders simply differed in strength and whether combining the reminder question and experimenter would induce memory change. To address this, we tested the three possible two-component combinations (reminder question + experimenter, reminder question + spatial context, and experimenter + spatial context). We only observed intrusions in the conditions in which the spatial context was part of the compound (Figure 11.2B), and interestingly, actually being in the context seems essential for the updating effect. Imagining in detail the spatial context in which Set 1 was learned while being in a new context, or briefly revisiting the old context before learning Set 2 in a new context, did not result in later intrusions (Hupbach *et al.*, 2008).

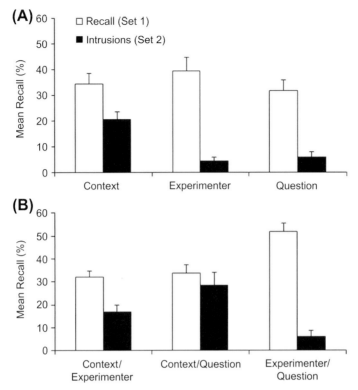

FIGURE 11.2 Mean percentage of objects correctly and falsely recalled in the different reminder groups. (A) In each group, only one reminder component was present—that is, the spatial context, the experimenter, or the reminder question. (B) In each of the three groups, two different reminder components were combined.

What explains this special role of spatial context for memory updating? One of the defining features of episodic memories is that they have a spatial signature, reflecting the fact that it is important for organisms to remember where an event happened. We have argued that the neural representation of spatial context provides a scaffold to which the various elements of an experience can be bound. When an old context is revisited, the relevant scaffold will be reactivated, and new elements, if there are any, can be incorporated. In contrast, when a new context is encountered, an entirely new scaffold is created, reflecting the fact that a new, and distinct, episode is to be remembered. Support for this notion comes from hippocampal place cell recordings in animals. As O'Keefe and Dostrovsky (1971) first showed, principal neurons in the hippocampus of the freely moving rat are activated by the rat occupying a specific place in space. A collection of such place cells in the hippocampus forms the core of a neural system creating "cognitive maps" of the environment (O'Keefe & Nadel, 1978). Place cells retain their specific firing "field" when the animal is returned to the same environment. When an animal encounters moderate changes in a previously visited and mapped environment, the place cells adjust their firing rate while retaining their firing field (rate remapping; Leutgeb *et al.*, 2005). However, when an environment changes more drastically, complete place cell remapping is observed: Specific cells now code for new areas of this novel environment, and any relation between place fields in the original environment is broken in the new environment (Wills, Lever, Cacucci, Burgess, & O'Keefe, 2005). That is, an entirely new map is created—one that appears to be orthogonal to the first map. Our reconsolidation findings resemble these physiological data, leading us to hypothesize that when in the same context, something like rate remapping occurs such that an existing

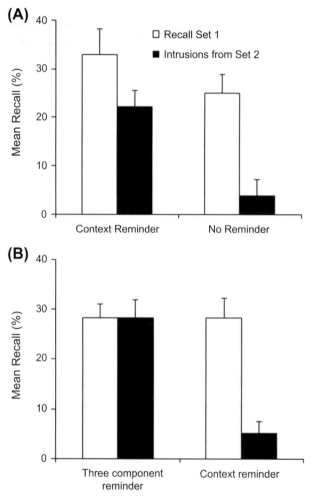

FIGURE 11.3 Mean percentage of objects correctly and falsely recalled by 5-year-olds in the context-reminder and no-reminder groups in an unfamiliar spatial context (A) and in the context-reminder and the three-component-reminder groups in a familiar spatial context (B). Spatial context triggered intrusions from Set 2 into Set 1 only in unfamiliar, but not in familiar, contexts. In familiar contexts, the experimenter and the reminder question caused intrusions.

representation is modified. When in a new spatial context, global remapping occurs instead, creating a new and unrelated memory representation.

The human reconsolidation studies described so far were carried out in a rather unfamiliar spatial environment (an unfamiliar lab space in an otherwise familiar building). We wondered if there might be situations in which spatial context does not trigger memory updating. We reasoned that highly familiar contexts might constitute such a boundary condition. Highly familiar environments (e.g., one's home) are associated with a variety of different episodes (everyday activities but also more unique events such as a birthday party). In familiar environments, the diagnostic value of the spatial context for a specific episode is therefore greatly diminished. Thus, we were interested in whether spatial context would still trigger updating under these conditions (Hupbach *et al.*, 2011). We chose to study 5-year-old children because context familiarity can be easily manipulated in this age group. First, we replicated the adult finding of context-dependent updating in an unfamiliar environment (using rooms in a day care center that were not part of the children's daily routine; Figure 11.3A). Then, we tested children at their homes. All three sessions were carried out in the same place in the children's homes (e.g., the kitchen). Thus, all children received a context reminder in Session 2. In addition, in one condition, the same experimenter was present and he or she asked a reminder question (three-component reminder in Figure 11.3B), whereas in the context-reminder condition, a different experimenter administered Session 2 without a reminder question. If spatial context triggers updating even in a familiar context, we should observe intrusions from Set 2 into Set 1 in both conditions. However, this is not what we found. Children only showed intrusions when the same experimenter and the reminder question were part of Session 2 (Figure 11.3B), but not when the spatial context was the only reminder. Thus, the spatial context appears to be an insufficient reminder in familiar contexts.

11.3 NON-SPATIAL REMINDERS FOR REACTIVATING MEMORY

The study testing children in a familiar spatial context partly answers the question of whether reminders other than the spatial context can also trigger memory updating: In familiar contexts, the experimenter and reminder question can play such a role. In an unpublished set of experiments, we explored other types of reminders and identified the encoding procedure as another way of initiating updating. Specifically, using the basket encoding procedure in Session 1 and in Session 2 results in later intrusions from Set 2 into Set 1, even if the encoding takes place in two different (unfamiliar) locations. At the same time, the updating effect remains unidirectional in that we do not see intrusions from Set 1 into Set 2 recall.

In contrast, and somewhat surprising at first, a variety of other conditions do not seem to trigger updating, although they almost certainly reactivate Set 1 memory prior to Set 2 encoding: (1) explicitly recalling Set 1 once before learning Set 2, (2) briefly viewing Set 1 items again, or (3) having Set 1 items continuously present during Set 2 encoding. Why do these manipulations fail to cause updating even though they seem to go well beyond the subtle reactivation used in our previous studies? They share some common features, which separate them from more subtle reminders in that they might (1) strengthen the memory for Set 1, (2) increase the relative distinctiveness and cohesiveness of the individual sets (for effects of distinctiveness on memory, see, Hunt & Worthen, 2006), and (3) not create a sufficient mismatch between what is expected and what is encountered in the situation (Lee, 2009), thus not triggering reconsolidation. We are currently exploring these possibilities, and we describe our studies manipulating memory strength next. We do not yet have consistent data concerning the distinctiveness and cohesiveness of the object sets.

11.4 MEMORY STRENGTH AND RECONSOLIDATION

How does the strength of a memory affect its potential to be updated or modified? We know from animal studies that strong fear memories, when reactivated, are initially resistant to the reconsolidation process (Bustos, Maldonado, & Molina, 2009; Suzuki et al., 2004; Wang, de Oliveira Alvares, & Nader, 2009). Would we obtain a resistance to updating in our paradigm if we create strong object memories? Similar to what has been done in animals to create strong fear memories, we "overtrained" participants on Set 1. In our previous studies (described previously), we had asked participants to recall the objects after initial encoding. If they recalled fewer than 17 objects, we repeated the encoding procedure. This was continued until participants could recall at least 17 items or for a maximum of four encoding trials. To "overtrain" participants on Set 1, we increased the criterion to a perfect recall of all 20 objects. Moreover, after perfect recall was achieved, we added two additional encoding trials. Set 2 was encoded 48 hr later using our normal encoding procedure (criterion: recall at least 17 items or complete a maximum of four encoding trials). We also manipulated whether participants were reminded of Session 1 before Set 2 encoding or not, utilizing all three components in the reminder condition (experimenter, context, and reminder question). In comparison to our original study (Hupbach et al., 2007), and as expected, overtraining increased recall of Set 1. Most important, overtraining markedly reduced intrusions, although it did not eliminate them; we still found a significant difference in intrusion rates between the overtrained reminder group and the overtrained no-reminder group (Figure 11.4A). Thus, a stronger object memory is somewhat resistant to change but not completely impermeable. It could be the case that stronger memories require different types of reminders or longer reactivation periods in order to return them to a labile state (Bustos et al., 2009; Suzuki et al., 2004).

Some have speculated that the functional role of reconsolidation is to ensure that memories reflect the most current state of knowledge by updating old with new information (e.g., Lee 2009), basing this interpretation on the finding that

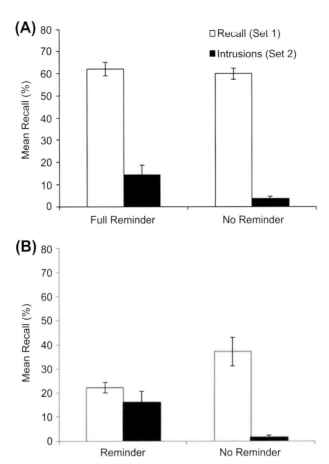

FIGURE 11.4 Mean percentage of objects correctly and falsely recalled in the reminder and the no-reminder groups when participants were overtrained on Set 1 (A) and when participants were overtrained on Set 2 (B). Criterion for overtraining was one perfect recall trial followed by two additional encoding trials. Overtraining on Set 1 reduced intrusions. Overtraining on Set 2 impaired Set 1 recall.

updating only occurs in conjunction with the violation of predictions based on prior experience. For instance, Lee (2010) demonstrated that when animals received a footshock in a previously visited context, a Zif268 expression-dependent reconsolidation process was triggered that updated the context memory by incorporating the footshock (as discussed in Chapter 3). If the context was simply revisited without the administration of footshocks, a knock-down of Zif268 did not impact the reconsolidation of the context memory. Thus, the contextual representation was only updated when the context prediction (neutrality) failed to match what the animal experienced (negative event). One could speculate that we see diminished intrusions from Set 2 into Set 1 in our overtraining study because we increased the relevance of Set 1 in relation to Set 2, and that the new information seems less relevant in comparison. If that is a valid explanation, then we should be able to reverse the effect and increase intrusions by overtraining participants on Set 2. However, data from our lab are not in line with this prediction. When we subjected participants to normal Set 1 training but overtrained them on Set 2, intrusion levels did not increase in comparison to those reported by Hupbach *et al.* (2007). However, we did find evidence for memory impairment: Recall of Set 1 was diminished in the reminder group in comparison to the no-reminder group (Figure 11.4B). This is the first time that we have found significant reactivation-dependent retroactive interference effects (however, for such effects in a different episodic memory task, see Forcato *et al.*, 2007). Thus, it might be the case that "relevance" is reflected less in intrusion levels than in recall of the original memory. Furthermore, it can be speculated that List 2 learning in our previous studies was not strong enough to have caused target memory impairments after reactivation. Further studies are needed to define the exact circumstances leading to changes in memory strength versus memory content.

11.5 AGE OF MEMORY AND STABILITY OF THE UPDATED MEMORY

Related to the previous issue of memory strength is the question of how the age of a memory affects its susceptibility to change. Critics of the reconsolidation account have argued that only rather new memories can be modified (because they are presumably not fully consolidated) but that old and therefore fully consolidated memories cannot be changed through a reconsolidation process (Dudai & Eisenberg, 2004; Milekic & Alberin, 2002). It is difficult to define the exact moment at which a memory can be considered "fully consolidated." Furthermore, if one assumes that strength declines over time because of forgetting, one might actually expect the opposite pattern—that is, that more recent memories are less prone to modification than older ones.

In beginning to explore the relation between memory "age" and reconsolidation, we increased the delays between sessions from 48 hr to 1 week. If Session 1 took place on Monday, Session 2 took place on the Monday of the following week, and final recall (Session 3) was assessed on the Monday 2 weeks after initial encoding. This manipulation tests not only whether 1-week-old memories can be updated but also whether the updating effect remains stable over a 1-week period. In this study, we also manipulated which reminder was given in Session 2. One group received all three components (spatial context, experimenter, and reminder question), whereas two additional groups received only one reminder component—either the spatial context or the encoding procedure. Inserting weeklong time delays between Session 1, 2, and 3 did not change the pattern of the updating effect. Similar to what we have observed with 48-hr delays, we found significant intrusions from Set 2 into Set 1 in all of the reminder conditions but not in the no-reminder group (Figure 11.5).

We also tested the stability of the updated memory by further delaying final recall. Here, Sessions 1 and 2 were scheduled 48 hr apart, but Session 3 was

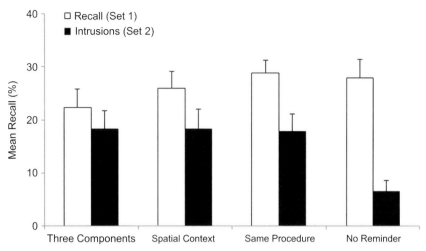

FIGURE 11.5 Mean percentage of objects correctly and falsely recalled in various reminder groups and the no-reminder group when 1-week delays were inserted between Session 1 and Session 2 and between Session 2 and Session 3. *Note:* In all other studies involving adult participants, the delays between sessions were 48 hr.

administered 1 or 2 weeks after Session 2. We found a stable updating effect for both time delays with intrusions from Set 2 into Set 1 but not the other way around.

To date, we have been unsuccessful in implementing time delays that exceed 2 weeks. We suspect that this reflects the limit of our object-learning paradigm rather than a failure to update older memories because recall of both Set 1 and Set 2 is fairly low after 4-week delays. Thus, with time, both the content and the spatiotemporal signature of this relatively neutral memory appear to fade. Creating more memorable episodes might allow us to study whether more remote memories can be modified by reminder and post-reminder treatments.

11.6 THEORETICAL EXPLANATIONS OF THE UPDATING EFFECT

We have interpreted our results of reminder-dependent intrusions from Set 2 into Set 1 within a framework of memory reconsolidation that is largely based on neurobiological findings in animals. The cognitive processes involved in human memory updating remain largely unspecified. Sederberg *et al.* (2011) developed a mechanistic account of our updating finding within the temporal context model (TCM) framework. TCM is a computational model of memory retrieval that can successfully reproduce a variety of episodic retrieval phenomena, such as recency and contiguity effects (Howard & Kahana, 2002; Sederberg, Howard, & Kahana, 2008). The recency effect refers to the phenomenon that recall declines with the passage of time or presentation of additional information. The contiguity effect describes the heightened probability of recalling an item that had been presented in close temporal proximity to a just recalled item. TCM differentiates between an item layer and a mental context layer, which are connected through item—context association matrices. Mental context can be conceptualized as a snapshot of the contextual elements that are present at a given time. As external and internal circumstances change, mental context is assumed to drift slowly over time. The current context contains elements of previous contexts in a gradual recency-weighted manner (more recent contextual elements are represented more strongly). Encoding binds items to the context layer. Retrieval is guided and dependent on the reinstatement of contextual states. A reinstated context activates the items associated with that context, and the items then compete for recall. When an item is recalled, it in turn updates the context layer with a combination of itself and its original encoding context. This new context cues the next recall, and this process continues until the end of the recall period. The recency effect can be explained when one considers that the temporal context that guides initial recall overlaps greatly with the most recent encoding context. It can also be easily understood how this model accounts for the contiguity effect: Items experienced in temporal proximity share contextual features, and the recall of one will trigger the recall of the other through contextual reinstatement.

With regard to our memory-updating effect, Sederberg *et al.* (2011) assume that the reminder in Session 2 triggers reinstatement of Set 1 temporal context. This will cause Set 2 items to be associated with the Set 1 context as well as with their unique Set 2 context. When participants are asked to recall Set 1, the Set 1 temporal context will be reinstated, and because this context is associated not only with Set 1 but also with Set 2, some Set 2 items will be recalled. In the no-reminder condition, the Set 1 context is not associated with Set 2 items, and hence Set 2 items do not intrude into Set 1 recall. In addition, because of the asymmetrical nature of forward cuing in time, the model can also account for the asymmetry of intrusions (Set 1 recall leads to intrusions of Set 2 items and not vice versa): Whereas Set 2 items are associated with a temporal context that contains features of the Set 1 context, the context layer of Set 1 items does not contain contextual features of Set 2 because Set 1 was presented before Set 2.

Although TCM is successful in explaining the basic intrusion effect when spatial context is not a reminder cue, several issues remain unresolved; for example, TCM as currently configured has no way of accounting for the superior role of spatial context in triggering updating (Hupbach *et al.*, 2008). In addition, TCM predicts that during recall in Session 3, Set 1 items should be recalled earlier in the retrieval process than Set 2 intrusions because the cue to recall Set 1 should reinstate the Set 1 encoding context, which is more strongly associated with Set 1 than Set 2 items. We found support for this prediction only in the study in which we tested children in a familiar context (Hupbach *et al.*, 2011). In an unfamiliar context, correctly recalled Set 1 items and Set 2 intrusions do not differ in their relative output positions (i.e.,

Set 1 items are not recalled earlier than Set 2 intrusions). Neither TCM nor we have ready explanations for the differential effects of context familiarity on output position. As described in Sederberg *et al.* (2011), TCM does make a variety of other interesting behavioral predictions for our object-learning paradigm, which we are currently testing.

11.7 WHERE DO WE GO FROM HERE?

In this chapter, we have reported the basic updating findings we observe in our episodic memory reconsolidation paradigm; explored the types of reminders leading to reactivation and the special role of spatial context; manipulated memory strength; and investigated updating effects after longer delays, both between the first two sessions and between updating and final recall. Thus, in our work to date, we have explored many of the boundary conditions on episodic memory reconsolidation. Although we have made substantial progress in the 5 years since our first publication on this topic, a number of questions remain unanswered. In particular, we have recently turned to the neurophysiological mechanisms involved in memory updating and have begun to explore the role played by sleep in the initial formation of "updatable" memories and in subsequent updating. We are also beginning to use imaging techniques to explore differences in the representations of Set 2 items that are eventually incorporated into Set 1 memory versus those that are not, as well as the predictions of alternative models such as TCM. The emphasis in the coming years will be to provide neurophysiological as well as mechanistic accounts of episodic memory updating that will contribute to our growing understanding of memory change.

Hardt *et al.* (2010) expressed the hope that the study of reconsolidation will dissolve the divide between neurobiological and cognitive accounts of memory change. We see real progress in this direction. We developed our paradigm with the goal of replicating animal reconsolidation findings in humans by using noninvasive procedures akin to those used in retroactive interference studies. This much has been accomplished, and the paradigm has taught us a few things about reconsolidation in humans. Building on these behavioral data, computational models might reveal the specific cognitive mechanisms behind our updating effect and ultimately link these to the underlying neurobiology of reconsolidation. A multilevel account of memory reconsolidation would provide a foundation for understanding a number of related phenomena, all of which fall under the rubric of memory malleability. Hindsight bias (Hoffrage, Hertwig, & Gigerenzer, 2000) and the misinformation effect (Loftus, 2005) are two more examples of phenomena defined by changes in memory wrought by subsequent experience. The promise of research on memory reconsolidation is that it addresses the dynamic nature of memory and in so doing helps shift the field of memory research away from the static conceptions of memory it has traditionally favored toward dynamic conceptions of memory that match the way it seems to work in everyday life.

ACKNOWLEDGMENTS

This research was funded by National Science Foundation (NSF) grant BCS-0743988 to L.N., A.H., and R.G.; NSF CAREER Award BCS-0238584 to R.G.; and Arizona Alzheimer's Research Consortium and Arizona Department of Health Services grant HB2354 to L.N.

REFERENCES

Bustos, S. G., Maldonado, H., & Molina, V. A. (2009). Disruptive effect of midazolam on fear memory reconsolidation: decisive influence of reactivation time span and memory age. *Neuropsychopharmacology, 34*, 446–457.

Dudai, Y., & Eisenberg, M. (2004). Rites of passage of the engram: reconsolidation and the lingering consolidation hypothesis. *Neuron, 44*, 93–100.

Forcato, C., Argibay, P. F., Pedreira, M. E., & Maldonado, H. (2009). Human reconsolidation does not always occur when a memory is retrieved: the relevance of the reminder structure. *Neurobiology of Learning and Memory, 91*, 50–57.

Forcato, C., Burgos, V. L., Argibay, P. F., Molina, V. A., Pedreira, M. E., & Maldonado, H. (2007). Reconsolidation of declarative memory in humans. *Learning & Memory, 14*, 295–303.

Forcato, C., Rodrìguez, M. L., Pedreira, M. E., & Maldonado, H. (2010). Reconsolidation in humans opens up declarative memory to the entrance of new information. *Neurobiology of Learning and Memory, 93*, 77–84.

Hardt, O., Einarsson, E., & Nader, K. (2010). A bridge over troubled water: reconsolidation as a link between cognitive and neuroscientific memory research traditions. *Annual Review of Psychology, 61*, 141–167.

Hoffrage, U., Hertwig, R., & Gigerenzer, G. (2000). Hindsight bias: a by-product of knowledge updating? *Journal of Experimental Psychology: Learning, Memory, and Cognition, 26*, 566–581.

Howard, M. W., & Kahana, M. J. (2002). A distributed representation of temporal context. *Journal of Mathematical Psychology, 46*, 269–299.

Hunt, R. R., & Worthen, J. B. (Eds.), (2006). *Distinctiveness and Memory*. New York: Oxford University Press.

Hupbach, A., Gomez, R., Hardt, O., & Nadel, L. (2007). Reconsolidation of episodic memories: a subtle reminder triggers integration of new information. *Learning & Memory, 14*, 47–53.

Hupbach, A., Gomez, R., & Nadel, L. (2009). Episodic memory reconsolidation: updating or source confusion? *Memory, 17*, 502–510.

Hupbach, A., Gomez, R., & Nadel, L. (2011). Episodic memory updating: the role of context familiarity. *Psychonomic Bulletin & Review, 18*, 787–797.

Hupbach, A., Hardt, O., Gomez, R., & Nadel, L. (2008). The dynamics of memory: context-dependent updating. *Learning & Memory, 15*, 574–579.

Lee, J. L. (2009). Reconsolidation: maintaining memory relevance. *Trends Neuroscience, 32*, 413–420.

Lee, J. L. (2010). Memory reconsolidation mediates the updating of hippocampal memory content. *Frontiers in Behavioral Neuroscience, 11*(4), 168.

Leutgeb, S., Leutgeb, J. K., Barnes, C. A., Moser, E. I., McNaughton, B. L., & Moser, M. B. (2005). Independent codes for spatial and episodic memory in hippocampal neuronal ensembles. *Science, 309*, 619–623.

Loftus, E. (2005). Planting misinformation in the human mind: a 30-year investigation of the malleability of memory. *Learning & Memory, 12*, 361–366.

Milekic, M. H., & Alberini, C. M. (2002). Temporally graded requirement for protein synthesis following memory reactivation. *Neuron, 24*, 521–525.

Morris, R. G. M., Inglis, J., Ainge, J. A., Olverman, H. J., Tulloch, J., Dudai, Y., & Kelly, P. A. T. (2006). Reconsolidation of spatial memory: differential sensitivity of distinct spatial memory tasks to local inhibition of protein-synthesis in dorsal hippocampus following memory retrieval. *Neuron, 50*, 479–489.

Nader, K., Schafe, G. E., & LeDoux, J. E. (2000). Fear memories require protein synthesis in the amygdala for reconsolidation after retrieval. *Nature, 406*, 722–726.

O'Keefe, J., & Dostrovsky, J. (1971). The hippocampus as a spatial map: preliminary evidence from unit activity in the freely-moving rat. *Brain Research, 34*, 171–175.

O'Keefe, J., & Nadel, L. (1978). *The Hippocampus as a Cognitive Map*. Oxford: Clarendon.

Schiller, D., Monfils, M. H., Raio, C. M., Johnson, D. C., LeDoux, J. E., & Phelps, E. A. (2010). Preventing the return of fear in humans using reconsolidation update mechanisms. *Nature, 463*, 49–53.

Sederberg, P. B., Gershman, S. J., Polyn, S. M., & Norman, K. A. (2011). Human memory reconsolidation can be explained using the temporal context model. *Psychonomic Bulletin & Review, 18*, 455–468.

Sederberg, P. B., Howard, M. W., & Kahana, M. J. (2008). A context-based theory of recency and contiguity in free recall. *Psychological Review, 115*, 893–912.

Soeter, M., & Kindt, M. (2012). Stimulation of the noradrenergic system during memory formation impairs extinction learning but not the disruption of reconsolidation. *Neuropsychopharmacology, 37*, 1204–1215.

Suzuki, A., Josselyn, S. A., Frankland, P. W., Masushige, S., Silva, A. J., & Kida, S. (2004). Memory reconsolidation and extinction have distinct temporal and biochemical signatures. *Journal of Neuroscience, 24*, 4787–4795.

Tulving, E. (2002). Episodic memory: from mind to brain. *Annual Review of Psychology, 53*, 1–25.

Walker, M. P., Brakefield, T., Hobson, J. A., & Stickgold, R. (2003). Dissociable stages of human memory consolidation and reconsolidation. *Nature, 425*, 616–620.

Wang, S. H., de Oliveira, A. L., & Nader, K. (2009). Cellular and systems mechanisms of memory strength as a constraint on auditory fear reconsolidation. *Nature Neuroscience, 12*, 905–912.

Wills, T. J., Lever, C., Cacucci, F., Burgess, N., & O'Keefe, J. (2005). Attractor dynamics in the hippocampal representation of the local environment. *Science, 308*, 873–876.

Chapter | twelve

Disrupting Consolidation and Reconsolidation of Human Emotional Memory with Propranolol

A Meta-Analysis[1]

**Michelle H. Lonergan[*], Alain Brunet[*],
Lening A. Olivera-Figueroa[†], Roger K. Pitman[‡]**

[*]*McGill University and Douglas Mental Health University Institute, Montreal,
Quebec, Canada*
[†]*Yale University School of Medicine, U.S. Department of Veteran Affairs
Connecticut Healthcare System (VACHS), New Haven, Connecticut*
[‡]*Harvard University, Cambridge, Massachusetts*

Memory consolidation refers to the process of transferring new learning from short- to long-term memory storage, where it is reputed to be permanent (Carlson, 2010). Emotional memories are those that are formed and consolidated during positive or, more often, negative events (Hamann, 2001). It is a well-demonstrated fact that emotion enhances memory encoding and facilitates later recall (Mueller & Cahill, 2010). Such observations have important implications in the realm of psychopathology because many disorders, such as post-traumatic stress disorder (PTSD), have at their core an overly powerful memory, often stemming from a negative life event

---

[1] An earlier version of this work was presented at the 12th European Conference on Traumatic Stress in Vienna, June 2011.

Memory Reconsolidation. http://dx.doi.org/10.1016/B978-0-12-386892-3.00012-3

(Brunet *et al.*, 2001). In order to develop PTSD, one must experience a life threat accompanied by intense negative peritraumatic distress. During trauma exposure, it has been proposed that the release of endogenous stress hormones overconsolidates the traumatic memory (Pitman & Orr, 1990). This memory is subsequently too easily reactivated by contextual cues, thereby eliciting strong conditioned emotional responses in the form of physiological reactivity (Pitman, 1989).

In addition to PTSD, numerous other psychiatric disorders also have at their core an emotional memory. Trauma exposure can increase the risk for other mental disorders, such as specific phobias, social phobias, addiction, depression, panic disorder, and obsessive–compulsive disorder (Gershuny *et al.*, 2008; Heim & Nemeroff, 2001; Spinhoven *et al.*, 2010). Negative life events of lesser magnitude, during development or later, are also believed to increase risk for psychopathology (Dohrenwend, 2000; Labonte *et al.*, 2012). Furthermore, many formerly addicted individuals report having to resist fond memories—manifested in the form of cue-elicited cravings—of their past abuse, which can contribute to relapse (Duka, Crombag, & Stephens, 2010). Thus, decreasing the grip of such memories would seem to have therapeutic value.

One way of decreasing the influence on behavior of an emotional memory would be to interfere with its consolidation, thereby leading to a degraded memory trace. In a landmark study, Cahill and colleagues (1994) found that compared to placebo, propranolol ingested before viewing a set of emotionally disturbing slides prevented the heightened recall of those slides. Since then, many studies have replicated this finding. The robustness of this finding has been explored in a qualitative review paper (Chamberlain, Muller, Blackwell, Robbins, & Sahakian, 2006) but has yet to be investigated by means of meta-analytic review.

In addition to replicating the results of Cahill *et al.* (1994), several researchers have tried to extend them to memory reconsolidation. Reconsolidation theory (Misanin, Miller, & Lewis, 1968) disputes the permanency of consolidated memories. It posits that, in order to persist, a reactivated (i.e., recalled) memory needs to be saved again to long-term memory storage, thereby recapitulating, at least in part, the process of memory consolidation (Nader, Schafe, & Le Doux, 2000; Przybyslawski, Roullet, & Sara, 1999; Przybyslawski & Sara, 1997). Interfering with this process would not necessarily "erase" such memory, but yield a degraded memory trace (Schiller & Phelps, 2011). Although both phenomena are important, from a psychotherapeutic standpoint, the advantages of blocking reconsolidation rather than consolidation are substantial since it could allow reopening the otherwise narrow window of opportunity for blocking unwanted memories.

Although several substances have been used with some success, the substance most frequently used in humans to block memory consolidation and reconsolidation is propranolol. Propranolol is a synthetic β-adrenergic receptor blocker that crosses the blood–brain barrier and exerts peripheral as well as central effects (O'Carroll, Drysdale, Cahill, Shajahan, & Ebmeier,

1999). Propranolol is commonly used to treat migraine (Holroyd, Penzien, & Cordingley, 1991), tachycardia (Raj *et al.*, 2009), and performance anxiety (Brantigan, Brantigan, & Joseph, 1982). It is indicated as a second line of treatment for anxious states.

To help determine whether consolidation and reconsolidation blockade using propranolol has any potential as a psychotherapeutic approach for treating mental disorders that have at their core an emotional memory, we conducted a meta-analytic review on the experimental protocols conducted with healthy and trauma-exposed subjects. Unlike other chapters in this book, this chapter presents like a paper. In conducting the meta-analytic review, we predicted that compared to placebo, propranolol ingested before (or ideally, immediately after) memory consolidation would reduce subsequent recall for negatively valenced material. We made a similar prediction for reconsolidation.

Although the paucity of clinical trials prevented us from conducting separate analyses in clinical populations, several studies examining memory consolidation and reconsolidation blockade in individuals suffering from PTSD were also included. We therefore predicted that propranolol, compared to placebo, would decrease psychophysiological responding to personal trauma scripts when administered either immediately post-trauma exposure (consolidation) or post-memory reactivation (reconsolidation).

12.1 METHODS

12.1.1 Inclusion criteria

Studies involving the recall of negatively valenced material in adults published in any language were included if they randomized subjects to at least one propranolol and one placebo group. We limited our search to articles published after that of Cahill *et al.* (1994)—that is, between January 1995 and December 2012. Unpublished studies were searched for by combing through abstracts from conferences—Society of Biological Psychiatry, International Society for Traumatic Stress Studies, American College of Neuropsychopharmacology, and Society for Neuroscience—and by contacting authors of included studies, other experts in the field, and investigators with studies registered on www.clinicaltrials.gov.

12.1.2 Included experimental paradigms

MEMORY CONSOLIDATION

To assess memory consolidation experimentally in humans, studies have largely replicated the Cahill *et al.* (1994) paradigm. In this protocol, participants watch a series of slides accompanied by either an emotionally upsetting or a neutral verbal narrative for the middle section of the story (slides 5—8). In the emotional section of the story, a young boy is hit by a car and rushed in critical condition to the hospital, where doctors frantically operate to reattach his severed legs. In the neutral version, the young boy witnesses a routine hospital drill performed on a dummy at his father's workplace. Propranolol (or placebo) is administered 60—90 min before viewing the slides so that when memory consolidation begins—that is, immediately after viewing the slides—propranolol is at its peak plasma concentration (Dey *et al.*, 1986). Memory for the viewed material is tested in a surprise forced-choice quiz after a washout period of at least 24 hr (Figure 12.1A).

Other included experimental protocols consisted of fear conditioning paradigms. In the fear conditioning paradigm, a neutral stimulus such as a tone (i.e., conditioned stimulus (CS)) is paired with a feared stimulus (unconditioned stimulus (US)) until presentation of the CS alone elicits the fear response. The experimental protocol in this case consists of administering propranolol or placebo approximately 60 min prior to conditioning, and retention is tested 1 week later. Finally, several clinical trials examined the usefulness of propranolol in blocking trauma memory consolidation by administering

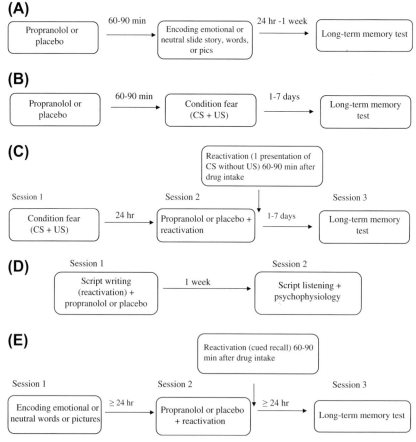

FIGURE 12.1 (A and B) Experimental paradigm for memory consolidation: (A) declarative emotional memory (Cahill et al., 1994) and (B) Pavlovian fear conditioning. (C—E) Experimental paradigm for memory reconsolidation: (C) Pavlovian fear conditioning, (D) script-driven imagery, and (E) declarative emotional memory.

either propranolol or placebo in the days following trauma exposure (Figure 12.1B). Because these studies examined emotional memory consolidation, they were included in the main analysis.

MEMORY RECONSOLIDATION

The experimental protocols used in healthy humans in reconsolidation studies consist of fear conditioning, script-driven imagery, and/or declarative memory tasks. Twenty-four hours after initial learning, propranolol is administered orally 60–90 min before the retrieval of the fear memory. Reactivation of the fear memory is achieved by a single presentation of the CS (i.e., the reactivation cue), and memory is tested after a drug washout period of 1–7 days (Figure 12.1C). One should note that pre-retrieval propranolol (rather than post-retrieval) does represent a departure from the typical reconsolidation protocol (for a discussion of this issue, see Schiller & Phelps, 2011; Brunet *et al.*, 2011). However, in humans this time period is required for pharmacological reconsolidation blockers ingested orally to reach their peak bioavailability (Dey, *et al.*, 1986).

The second method of manipulating memory reconsolidation involves memory reactivation and script-driven imagery tasks (Brunet *et al.*, 2008; Tollenaar, Elzinga, Spinhoven, & Everaerd, 2009b). In this paradigm, subjects are asked to write a script detailing an emotionally negative memory, which serves as the reactivation cue. Propranolol is given during this session. After 1 week, the subjects listen to their script while their physiological responses are recorded (Figure 12.1D). One clinical trial (Brunet *et al.*, 2008) used this protocol in a PTSD population, and the results were included in the initial analysis.

In declarative memory tasks, subjects are instructed to learn a list of emotionally valenced and neutral words. At least 24 hr later, they are given propranolol or placebo 60–90 min before a cued recall task. A second cued-recall task is given after a washout period of at least another 24 hr, which serves as the test for reconsolidation blockade (Figure 12.1E).

Although fear conditioning and declarative memory tasks have different underlying neural mechanisms (Schiller & Phelps, 2011), a literature review suggests that both are referred to as emotional memories and both have been subjected to reconsolidation blockade. This chapter uses the same convention, and the term *emotional memory* is used to refer to both phenomena. However, considering that this has never before been explored formally, on an exploratory basis, we were interested in comparing the magnitude of the effects sizes obtained in studies using episodic retention versus physiological responding as the outcome of interest. No formal hypothesis was made, however.

12.1.3 Outcome measures

In the Cahill *et al.* (1994) paradigm, the outcome of interest was the between-group mean difference in long-term memory performance, as measured by free recall of slides or percentage correct on a recognition task for the emotional (i.e., middle) section of the story. In studies whose methods consisted of fear conditioning and script-driven imagery paradigms, physiological responses (startle, skin conductance, heart rate, and electromyogram responses, respectively) were considered as measures of fear memory.

12.1.4 Search strategy and data extraction

Articles were identified in PsycInfo, PubMed, ISI Web of Science, Cochrane Central, PILOTS, Google Scholar, and at www.clinicaltrials.org using the following as key words: propranolol, emotion, emotional, memory, posttraumatic stress, PTSD, trauma, traumatic stress, consolidation, and reconsolidation. Two investigators independently screened the titles and abstracts to exclude irrelevant articles. Two independent assessments of all potentially relevant full-text articles were made. A third party (A.B.) resolved the disagreement. The reference sections of the included articles were also systematically screened. Data were extracted by two independent reviewers and double-checked by a third party.

Two investigators independently assessed each study with the Quality Assessment tool (Jadad *et al.*, 1996). One point was given respectively for randomization, for double-blind design, and for description of withdrawals/dropouts. A fourth and a fifth point were given if the randomization and blinding methods were considered adequate. Tables 12.1 and 12.2 provide a list of the included studies.

12.1.5 Data analysis

In order to examine the between-group difference on memory performance, we opted for Hedges' g (Borenstein, Hedges, Higgins, & Rothstein, 2009; Higgins & Green, 2009), which produces an adjusted effect size estimate, rather than for Cohen's d (Cohen, 1992) because the latter is upwardly biased with small samples (Lipsey & Wilson, 2001). In behavioral studies, a g-value < 0.2 represents a small, $0.2-0.5$ a moderate, and $0.5-0.8$ a large effect size (Lipsey & Wilson, 2001). For a few reconsolidation studies, g was averaged across outcomes to control for outcome selection bias.

To test our hypotheses, we used a random-effects model, unless there was no observed heterogeneity between studies. When possible, we determined the number of missing negative studies required to nullify our results (Borenstein *et al.*, 2009). Publication bias was not assessed for the reconsolidation analysis due to the smaller number of studies included (Higgins & Green, 2009). All tests were two-sided with an α level < 0.05, unless stated otherwise.

12.2 RESULTS

Figure 12.2 provides a flowchart of the study selection process. Twenty-three experiments across 21 articles were included: 14 pertained to memory consolidation and 9 to reconsolidation. Of the 14 consolidation experiments, 1 was

TABLE 12.1 Characteristics of Included Consolidation Studies

Study	Materials	Subjects (Ppnl/Pl)	Gender (M/F)	Mean Age (Years) (SD)	Study Protocol	Outcome Measures	Jadad Score	Outcome
Cahill et al. (1994)	Emotional slide story	11/8	M: 47% F: 53%	27.4 (27.6)	40 mg 60 min before encoding	% recognition story phase 2	3	Ppnl reduced emotional memory enhancement when tested 1 week later.
van Stegeren et al. (1998)	Emotional slide story	14/13	M: 31% F: 69%	Undergrads	40 mg 60 min before encoding	% recognition story phase 2	3	Ppnl reduced emotional memory enhancement when tested 1 week later.
O'Carroll et al. (1999)	Emotional slide story	12/12	M: 17% F: 83%	21.4 (2.45)	40 mg 60 min before encoding	% recognition story phase 2	3	Ppnl had no effect on emotional memory enhancement when tested 1 week later.
Reist et al. (2001) (a)[a]	Emotional slide story	5/5	M: 100%	44.45 (8.08)	40 mg 60–90 min before encoding	% recognition story phase 2	4	Ppnl reduced emotional memory enhancement when tested 1 week later.
Reist et al. (2001) (b)[a]	Emotional slide story	5/4	M: 100%	50.53 (8.5)	40 mg 60–90 min before encoding	% recognition story phase 2	4	Ppnl reduced emotional memory enhancement 1 week later; no significant difference between clinical and control group.
Pitman et al. (2002)[b]	CAPS; script-driven imagery	18/23	M: 48% F: 52%	34.3 (10)	RCT; 10-day course 40 mg Ppnl vs. Pl 4×/day within 6 hr of trauma; script-driven imagery 3 months later	CAPS score 1 month post-trauma; HR, SC, and EMG from script-driven imagery	3	Ppnl reduced PTSD symptoms 1 month later. Propranolol reduced physiological reactivity to trauma scripts.

(Continued)

TABLE 12.1 Characteristics of Included Consolidation Studies—Continued

Study	Materials	Subjects (Ppnl/Pl)	Gender (M/F)	Mean Age (Years) (SD)	Study Protocol	Outcome Measures	Jadad Score	Outcome
van Stegeren et al. (2002)	Emotional slide story	15/15	M: 23% F: 77%	22.65	40 mg immediately before encoding	% recognition story phase 2	4	Ppnl had no effect on emotional memory enhancement when tested 1 week later.
Maheu et al. (2004), Exp. 1	Emotional slide story	11/13	M: 100%	19–36	40 mg 65 min before encoding	% free recall story phase 2	4	Ppnl had no effect on emotional memory enhancement when tested 1 week later.
Maheu et al. (2004), Exp. 2	Emotional slide story	14/13	M: 100%	20–34	80 mg 90 min before encoding	% free recall story phase 2	4	Ppnl reduced emotional memory enhancement when tested 1 week later.
Strange and Dolan (2004)	Emotionally valenced word list	12/12	M: 50% F: 50%	20–39	40 mg 90 min before encoding	% recognition word list	3	Ppnl had no effect on recognition performance tested 10 hr later.
Grillon et al. (2004)	Fear conditioning	15/15	M: 46% F: 53%	29 (2.8)	40 mg 60 min before conditioning	Retention fear conditioning	4	Ppnl reduced emotional arousal to conditioning context; Ppnl had no effect on acquisition and retention of cued fear conditioning. Memory test 1 week later.

Study	Task	N (a/b)	Sex	Age M (SD)	Intervention	Outcome measure	Quality	Results
van Stegeren et al. (2005)	Emotionally valenced pics; crossover design	28/28	M: 50% F: 50%	20.93 (2.38)	80 mg 90 min before encoding	% recognition pics	3	Ppnl reduced emotional memory enhancement when tested 2 weeks later.
Weymar et al. (2010)	Emotionally valenced pics	23/23	M: 100%	19–31	80 mg 90 min before encoding	% recognition pics	4	Ppnl had no effect on recognition performance when tested 1 week later.
Hoge et al. (2012)[b]	CAPS; script-driven imagery	21/20	M: 44% F: 56%	33 (10)	Preventative RCT; 19-day course of up to 240 mg/day Ppnl vs. Pl	CAPS score 1 month post-trauma; HR, SC, and EMG from script-driven imagery	3	No significant group differences; significant effect for Ppnl on HR and PTSD probability at 5 weeks post-trauma for highly adherent.

CAPS, Clinician Administered PTSD Scale; EMG, electromyogram; F, % female participants; HR, heart rate, M, % male participants; Pl, placebo; Ppnl, propranolol; RCT, randomized controlled trial; SCR, skin conductance response.

[a]The letters "a" and "b" refer to results from two separate populations (healthy and clinical) presented in Reist et al. (2001).
[b]Emotional memory measured by psychophysiological responding.

TABLE 12.2 Characteristics of Included Reconsolidation Studies

Study	Materials	Subjects (Ppnl/Pl)	Gender (M/F)	Mean Age (Years) (SD)	Design	Outcome Measures	Jadad Score	Outcome
Miller et al. (unpublished)[a]	Differential fear conditioning	42/25	M: 50% F: 50%	25 (4.2)	Day 1: Learning Day 2: Ppnl 5 min after reactivation Day 3: LTM test	SCR to CS during extinction Day 3	Could not score	Ppnl had no effect on physiological responses to CS.
de Quervain et al. (2007)	Emotionally valenced word list crossover design	14/14	M: 50% F: 50%	23.9 (2.9)	Day 1: Learning Day 2: 40 mg 60 min before LTM test; 2nd LTM test 2 weeks later	Free recall No. of words	3	Ppnl had no effect on recall of emotional words.
Brunet et al. (2008)	Script driven imagery	9/10	M: 47% F: 53%	35 (10)	RCT. SA 40 mg Ppnl vs. Pl post-trauma memory retrieval; 60 mg LA Ppnl vs. Pl 2 hr later	HR, SCR, EMG from script-driven imagery 1 week after treatment	3	Ppnl reduced HR and SC during script-driven imagery; reduction fell to below normative PTSD cutoff in Ppnl group only.
Kindt et al. (2009)[a]	Differential fear conditioning	40/20	M: 28% F: 72%	20.7 (2.4)	Day 1: Learning Day 2: 40 mg 90 min before reactivation Day 3: LTM test	Fear-potentiated startle to CS during extinction Day 3	4	Ppnl reduced expression of conditioned fear.
Tollenaar et al. (2009a)	Emotionally valenced word list	27/26	M: 100%	20.6 (2.1)	Week 1: Learning Week 2: 80 mg 75 min before memory task Week 3: memory test	% recognition nouns Week 3	3	Ppnl had no effect on recognition performance.

Study	Paradigm	n	Sex	Age	Procedure	Outcome measure		Results
Tollenaar et al. (2009b)	Script-driven imagery	27/26	M: 100%	20.7 (2.2)	Week 1: Script prep Week 2: 80 mg 90 min before script listening Week 3: HR and SCR to emotional script	HR and SCR Week 3	3	Ppnl had no effect on psychophysiological responses.
Soeter and Kindt (2010)[a]	Differential fear conditioning	40/20	M: 25% F: 75%	20.4 (3.8)	Day 1: Learning Day 2: 40 mg 90 min before reactivation Day 3: LTM test	Fear-potentiated startle to CS during extinction Day 3	3	Ppnl reduced expression of conditioned fear.
Kroes et al. (2010)	Emotionally valenced word list	12/12	M: 58% F: 42%	24.4	Day 1: Learning Day 2: 40 mg 90 min before reactivation Day 3: LTM test	% free recall Day 3	4	Ppnl reduced emotional memory enhancement.
Schwabe et al. (2011)	Emotionally valenced pics	13/13	M: 50% F: 50%	18–30	Day 1: Learning Day 2: 40 mg 90 min before reactivation Day 3: LTM test	% recognition pics Day 3	2	Ppnl reduced emotional memory enhancement.

CS, conditioned stimulus; EMG, electromyogram; HR, heart rate; LA, long-acting; LTM, long-term memory; Pl, placebo; Ppnl, propranolol; RCT, randomized controlled trial; SA, short-acting; SCR, skin conductance response.
[a]In Miller et al. (unpublished), Ppnl n = 19, and in Kindt et al. (2009) and Soeter and Kindt (2010), Ppnl n = 20 participants received treatment with no memory reactivation. These data are excluded from statistical analysis.

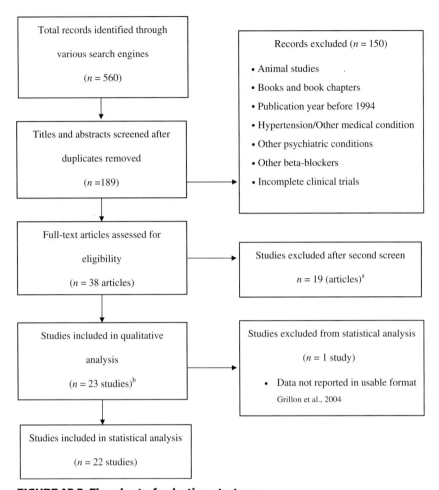

FIGURE 12.2 Flowchart of selection strategy

[a]Reasons for exclusion after full-text screen:

- Outcome measure unrelated to emotional memory, consolidation or reconsolidation, or long-term memory: Harmer, Perrett, Cowen, and Goodwin (2001); Oei, Tollenaar, Elzinga, and Spinhoven (2010); Hurlemann et al. (2005); Maheu, Joober, and Lupien (2005); Schwabe et al. (2009); Strange, Hurlemann, and Dolan (2003); Nielson and Jensen (1994); Stein, Kerridge, Dimsdale, and Hoyt (2007)
- Nonrandomized trials: Brunet et al. (2011), McGhee et al. (2009), Vaiva et al. (2003)
- Insufficient quality assessment: Ioannides et al. (2000)
- Review article or previously reported data: van Stegeren (2008); van Stegeren et al. (2007); Weymar, Low, Melzig, & Hamm (2009); Cahill and van Stegeren (2003); Mueller and Cahill (2010)
- Design does not examine treatment outcome: Orr et al. (2006)
- Treatment outcome in children: Nugent et al. (2010)

[b]Reist et al. (2001) and Maheu et al. (2004) contained two experiments each. Review includes 23 studies across 21 articles.

eventually excluded because it did not report data in a usable format (Grillon, Cordova, Morgan, Charney, & Davis, 2004).

12.2.1 Memory consolidation

QUALITATIVE RESULTS

Table 12.1 provides the characteristics of each memory consolidation study. Overall, 8 of 14 studies closely followed the Cahill *et al.* (1994) study design. Five of those 8 consolidation studies found that propranolol subjects remembered less material than those on placebo (Cahill *et al.*, 1994; Maheu, Joober, Beaulieu, & Lupien, 2004; Reist, Duffy, Fujimoto, & Cahill, 2001; van Stegeren, Everaerd, Cahill, McGaugh, & Gooren, 1998), and 3 studies (Maheu *et al.*, 2004; van Stegeren, Everaerd, & Gooren, 2002) failed to find an effect.

Of the four studies (Grillon *et al.*, 2004; Strange & Dolan, 2004; van Stegeren *et al.*, 2005; Weymar *et al.*, 2010) that used different stimuli (emotionally valenced word lists, pictures, or fear conditioning paradigms), two (Grillon *et al.*, 2004; van Stegeren *et al.*, 2005) found an effect for propranolol.

Two clinical studies (Hoge *et al.*, 2012; Pitman *et al.*, 2002) randomized individuals who had experienced a traumatic event to receive 40 mg of either propranolol or placebo within hours of presenting to the emergency room. Pitman *et al.* instructed patients to continue medication four times a day for 10 days, whereas Hodge *et al.* administered an additional 60 mg propranolol or placebo 1 hr following the original dose. Patients in this trial were instructed to follow a 19-day course of 120 mg, which was tapered down for the last 9 days of treatment. Both studies used script-driven imagery procedures to assess psychophysiological responding to personal traumatic scripts at 5 weeks (Hodge *et al.*, 2012) and 3 months (Pitman *et al.*, 2002) post-trauma. Finally, both these studies found significant effects for propranolol in treatment adherent study participants.

QUANTITATIVE RESULTS

Figure 12.3 presents the pooled results for the memory consolidation analysis. Overall, propranolol-treated subjects ($n = 152$) remembered less aversive material than placebo-treated subjects ($n = 158$) ($g = 0.47$; 95% CI $= 0.22-0.72$). Statistical heterogeneity was not significant ($Q = 14.96$, $P = 0.24$). Between-study variability was considered low ($I^2 = 19.81\%$). Sensitivity analyses revealed no outlier. Effect sizes varied between 0.0 and 1.49. Inspection of Figure 12.4 revealed a slightly asymmetrical funnel plot, with no studies missing in order to completely eliminate the publication bias. The Rosenthal's fail-safe N analysis indicated that 52 studies with null results would be needed in order to bring the combined one-tailed significance to $P > 0.05$.

In order to assess the potential confound of the type of memory tested (i.e., declarative vs. psychophysiological responding), we ran a comparison analysis based on memory type. No significant difference was found between the two groups ($Q = 0.61$, $df = 1$, $P = 0.40$) (Figure 12.3). In addition, the effect

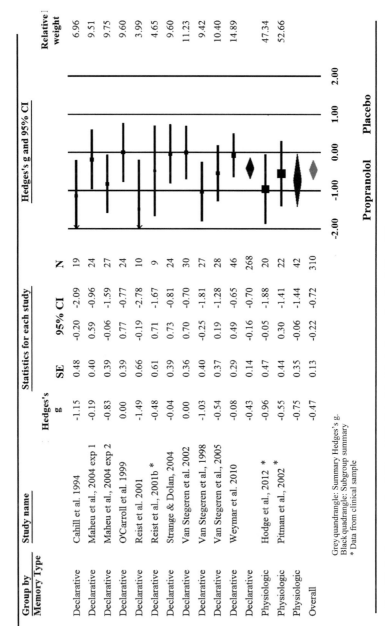

Group by Memory Type	Study name	Statistics for each study					Hedges's g and 95% CI	Relative weight
		Hedges's g	SE	95% CI		N		
Declarative	Cahill et al. 1994	-1.15	0.48	-0.20	-2.09	19		6.96
Declarative	Maheu et al., 2004 exp 1	-0.19	0.40	0.59	-0.96	24		9.51
Declarative	Maheu et al., 2004 exp 2	-0.83	0.39	-0.06	-1.59	27		9.75
Declarative	O'Carroll et al. 1999	0.00	0.39	0.77	-0.77	24		9.60
Declarative	Reist et al. 2001	-1.49	0.66	-0.19	-2.78	10		3.99
Declarative	Reist et al., 2001b *	-0.48	0.61	0.71	-1.67	9		4.65
Declarative	Strange & Dolan, 2004	-0.04	0.39	0.73	-0.81	24		9.60
Declarative	Van Stegeren et al. 2002	0.00	0.36	0.70	-0.70	30		11.23
Declarative	Van Stegeren et al., 1998	-1.03	0.40	-0.25	-1.81	27		9.42
Declarative	Van Stegeren et al., 2005	-0.54	0.37	0.19	-1.28	28		10.40
Declarative	Weymar et al. 2010	-0.08	0.29	0.49	-0.65	46		14.89
Declarative		-0.43	0.14	-0.16	-0.70	268		
Physiologic	Hodge et al., 2012 *	-0.96	0.47	-0.05	-1.88	20		47.34
Physiologic	Pitman et al., 2002 *	-0.55	0.44	0.30	-1.41	22		52.66
Physiologic		-0.75	0.35	-0.06	-1.44	42		
Overall		-0.47	0.13	-0.22	-0.72	310		

Grey quandrangle: Summary Hedges's g.
Black quadrangle: Subgroup summary
* Data from cliniical sample

Propranolol   Placebo

Test of declarative memory: $Z = -3.092$; $p < 0.05$; Test of physiological responding: $Z = -2.10$; $p = 0.03$

Heterogeneity between groups: $Q = 0.61$, $df = 1$, $p = 0.40$, ns

FIGURE 12.3 Propranolol's effects on emotional memory consolidation: Split group by memory mechanism.

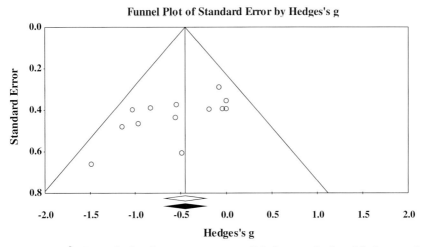

FIGURE 12.4 Funnel plot for memory consolidation analysis with imputed studies.

sizes for studies examining declarative memory ($n = 11$ studies; $g = 0.43$, 95% CI $= 0.16-0.70$) and psychophysiological responding to fear memory ($n = 2$ studies) were significant ($g = 0.75$, 95% CI $= 0.06-1.44$). Because clinical heterogeneity may stem from pooling data from healthy participants with data from the clinical population, we conducted an additional analysis removing the clinical data. Propranolol continued to show an effect on retention of emotional material ($g = 0.44$, 95% CI $= 0.14-0.74$).

12.2.2 Memory reconsolidation

QUALITATIVE RESULTS

As shown in Table 12.2, of the four reconsolidation studies that examined cognitive memory performance similarly to the consolidation studies (de Quervain, Aerni, & Roozendaal, 2007; Kroes, Strange, & Dolan, 2010; Schwabe, Nader, Wolf, Beaudry, & Pruessner, 2011; Tollenaar, Elzinga, Spinhoven, & Everaerd, 2009a), two found a large significant effect (Kroes et al., 2010; Schwabe et al., 2011). Of the remaining five, three aimed at reducing the expression of cue-elicited fear responses and two of those found an effect for propranolol (Kindt, Soeter, & Vervliet, 2009; Soeter & Kindt, 2010). The last two studies (Brunet et al., 2008; Tollenaar et al., 2009b) used a script-driven imagery task—one with healthy participants (Tollenaar et al., 2009b) that failed to find an effect, and one in a PTSD population (Brunet et al., 2008) that found a significant effect for propranolol. In total, 164 participants received propranolol, and 163 received a closely matched placebo. The average Jadad score for the studies included in Tables 12.1 and 12.2 was 3 on a 5-point scale, which is considered good. The most common reason for lost points was failure to report the exact randomization method or failure to report the dropout rate.

QUANTITATIVE RESULTS

Figure 12.5 presents the forest plot results for the memory reconsolidation analysis. Although heterogeneous ($Q = 25.41$, $P < 0.01$, $I^2 = 68.51\%$), results were significant, and the effect size was large ($g = 0.59$, 95% CI $= 0.16-1.01$). Effect sizes ranged between 0.07 and 1.36. A sensitivity analysis revealed that no single study explained the observed heterogeneity. One source of heterogeneity probably stems from the fact that three out of nine studies failed to find a significant effect. Another source of heterogeneity may stem from the differences in study designs and outcome measures. No significant between-group difference was found when episodic memory retention studies ($g = 0.58$) were examined separately from studies measuring physiological responses to fear conditioning ($g = 0.59$). Removing the clinical study of Brunet *et al.* (2008) from the analyses did not change the results: $g = 0.56$, 95% CI $= 0.13-1.00$.

12.3 DISCUSSION

Learning under the influence of propranolol led to subsequent recall deficits congruent with consolidation blockade when the stimuli consisted of negatively valenced slides, pictures, word lists, and fear conditioned stimuli. Recall of previously learned material under the influence of propranolol had a similar effect: It led to subsequent recall deficits congruent with reconsolidation blockade when the material consisted of negatively valenced emotional words, or it reduced the expression of previously learned cue-elicited fear responses. However, in the case of reconsolidation, the evidence is considered less strong, despite the larger effect size, because of the heterogeneity across studies. Caution should be applied in interpreting this result until more studies are published and heterogeneity is reduced. Finally, the observed effects of propranolol on memory apply to moderately emotional material as tested in an experimental design with healthy adults. It remains to be determined if more strongly valenced idiosyncratic memories can also be decreased by propranolol in clinical populations suffering from a mental disorder.

12.3.1 Study limitations

UNDERLYING MECHANISMS

There are a number of issues that this meta-analysis does not address, such as the question of underlying mechanisms of the phenomena observed. Although the results in healthy subjects are congruent with a consolidation and reconsolidation blockade explanation, other explanations remain plausible. Ideally, the propranolol should be given immediately after the memory task (post-retrieval) rather than 60–90 min beforehand to eliminate a possible confounding effect of propranolol on memory encoding (consolidation) or retrieval (reconsolidation). This bias is controlled, in principle, by the fact that in the studies using the protocol from Cahill *et al.* (1994), both propranolol and placebo groups have equal memory performance on the neutral material. Importantly, the only

Group by Memory Mechanism	Study name	Statistics for each study					Hedges's g and 95% CI	Relative weight
		Hedges's g	SE	95% CI		N		
Declarative	de Quervain et al. 2007	-0.46	0.37	-1.19	0.27	28		24.91
Declarative	Kroes et al. 2010	-1.09	0.43	-1.94	-0.24	23		22.43
Declarative	Schwabe et al. 2011	-1.04	0.41	-1.83	-0.24	26		23.51
Declarative	Tollenaar et al. 2009a	0.09	0.27	-0.45	0.62	53		29.15
Declarative		-0.58	0.33	-1.23	0.08	130		
Physiologic	Brunet et al., 2008 *	-0.76	0.46	-1.66	0.14	19		16.30
Physiologic	Kindt et al. 2009	-1.08	0.34	-1.74	-0.42	40		20.15
Physiologic	Miller et al., unpublished	-0.07	0.28	-0.62	0.49	48		21.79
Physiologic	Soeter et al. 2010	-1.36	0.35	-2.03	-0.68	40		19.83
Physiologic	Tollenaar et al. 2009b	0.15	0.28	-0.40	0.70	51		21.94
Physiologic		-0.59	0.29	-1.16	-0.02	197		
Overall		-0.59	0.22	-1.01	-0.16	327		

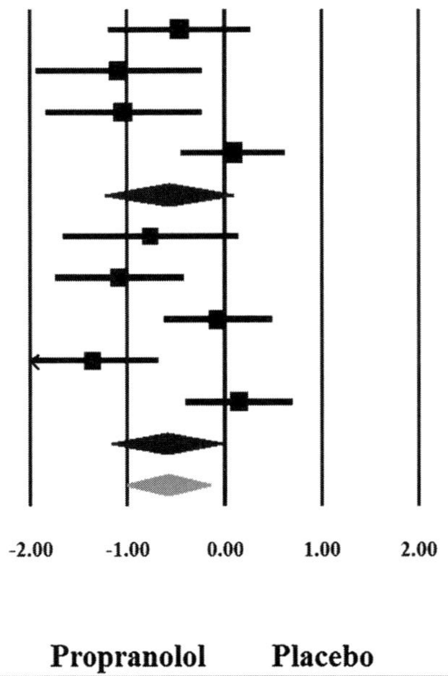

Grey quandrangle: Summary Hedges's g.
Black quadrangle: Subgroup summary
* Data from clinical sample

Propranolol   Placebo

Test of declarative memory: $Z = -1.73$; $p = 0.08$ ns; Test of physiological responding: $Z = -2.04$; $p = 0.04$

Heterogeneity between sub-groups: $Q = 0.001$, df = 1, $p = 0.97$, ns

FIGURE 12.5 Propranolol's effects on emotional memory reconsolidation: Split group by memory mechanism.

study to administer propranolol after reactivating the memory failed to find a sustained effect of propranolol (Miller *et al.*, unpublished results).

SELECTION OF THE EMOTIONAL MATERIAL

Some stimuli may be more susceptible to propranolol-induced forgetting. Because of the limited number of studies currently available for review, a fine-grained analysis taking into consideration the type of stimuli presented could not be performed. However, among the studies reporting negative findings in healthy participants, especially those that did not use the material of Cahill *et al.* (1994), it is possible that the stimuli used were not powerful enough to effectively demonstrate the effect of propranolol in blocking consolidation or reconsolidation of negatively valenced emotional material. In other words, in some cases, the "emotional" material could have ended up being quite neutral, therefore explaining the lack of results in some studies. If some negative findings were explained by the fact that the emotional stimuli are not powerful enough, the effect size reported in this meta-analysis may well be a conservative estimate.

MEASUREMENT OF RECALL

In contrast to Cahill *et al.* (1994), Strange and Dolan (2004) examined propranolol's effects on long-term recognition memory performance for emotionally valenced word lists. Furthermore, Weymar *et al.* (2010) and van Stegeren *et al.* (2005) examined emotional memory performance using a set of unrelated pictures. It is unclear whether the nonsignificant results obtained by Strange and Dolan and by Weymar *et al.* are due in part to the way they measured recall, the fact that they used a different set of stimuli, or both.

The way recall is measured may also have another type of impact on the results. In the consolidation studies, the most reliable finding seems to be that, compared to the placebo group, propranolol subjects failed to recall specific elements of the slides that were accompanied by the emotionally distressing narrative. This is a form of declarative memory. This failure to recall is also found in two of three studies examining reconsolidation (de Quervain *et al.*, 2007; Kroes *et al.*, 2010), although results from de Quervain *et al.*'s study were not significant. However, in two other reconsolidation studies, subjects displayed reduced expression of cue-elicited fear conditioned responses (a form of emotional memory) while declarative memory remained intact (Kindt *et al.*, 2009; Soeter & Kindt, 2010). Future studies will need to explore whether memory reactivation under propranolol decreases the strength of emotional or declarative memory or both and also whether this effect is long-lasting.

DRUG DOSAGE AND GENDER EFFECTS

Contrary to others, Maheu *et al.* (2004) did not find significant results using 40 mg of propranolol. However, 80 mg of propranolol yielded significant results. Using a fixed low dose of propranolol may not work equally well with everybody because of varying body mass or other reasons. A gender difference has also been found (Cahill & van Stegeren, 2003), with women being more affected by propranolol than men. Three studies in this meta-analysis were conducted with samples composed of men only, thereby potentially underestimating the effect size that would be observed in a sample composed of an equal number of men and women. Because most studies did not report gender differences, an analysis by gender was not possible. Dose effects and gender effects will need to be further explored in the future.

12.3.2 Can propranolol effectively block memory consolidation or reconsolidation in memory-related mental disorders?

The effect of propranolol on memory observed in this meta-analysis applies to moderately negative emotional material as tested in an experimental design with healthy adults. Single doses of propranolol have also shown promise in animals in reducing avoidance conditioning (Przybyslawski & Sara, 1997), fear conditioning (Nader *et al.*, 2000), and craving in cocaine and nicotine dependence (Chiamulera, Tedesco, Zangrandi, Giuliano, & Fumagalli, 2010; Kampman *et al.*, 2001). However, recent animal data suggest that the effects of propranolol may not generalize to all types of fear memories (Muravieva & Alberini, 2010).

In humans, Reist *et al.* (2001) replicated the Cahill *et al.* (1994) results in both a healthy population and a clinical (PTSD) sample, finding no between-group difference. However, this study did not involve deeply ingrained traumatic memories. Thus far, one small randomized controlled trial (Brunet *et al.*, 2008) used propranolol in a sample of individuals suffering from unremitting PTSD of more than 10 years' duration on average, in an attempt to decrease the strength of a traumatic memory. In this study, the strength of the trauma memory was lower after a single dose of propranolol compared to placebo, as measured 1 week later by psychophysiologic responses while listening to audiotaped personal trauma narratives. This study is important because psychophysiologic responding to trauma scripts (1) is the most replicated biological finding in PTSD, (2) is less prone to demand characteristics, and (3) directly tackles the issue of the strength of the emotional memory. Anecdotally, all the subjects of that study retained a declarative memory of their traumatic event.

12.4 CONCLUSION

The consideration that motivated this review was that pharmacological reconsolidation blockade might have the potential to become a novel treatment in psychiatry. By summarizing the currently available evidence from placebo-controlled experimental studies involving healthy subjects, this meta-analysis represents a small but important step in this direction. In this review, propranolol was found to be effective in reducing memory for both new and previously learned emotional material in healthy adults. Future studies will have to test whether more powerful idiosyncratic emotional memories can be durably weakened as well, and whether this weakening can bring about lasting symptomatic relief in various clinical populations.

ACKNOWLEDGMENTS

Dr. Brunet holds a salary award from the Fonds de Recherche en Santé du Québec (FRSQ). Michelle H. Lonergan holds a graduate student fellowship from the Canadian Institutes of Health Research (CIHR). Dr. Olivera holds a Postdoctoral Fellowship Merit Award from the Fernand-Seguin Research Center.

REFERENCES

Borenstein, M., Hedges, L. V., Higgins, J. P. T., & Rothstein, H. R. (2009). *Introduction to Meta-Analysis*. Chichester, UK: Wiley.

Brantigan, C. O., Brantigan, T. A., & Joseph, N. (1982). Effect of beta blockade and beta stimulation on stage fright. *American Journal of Medical Genetics, 72*(1), 88–94.

Brunet, A., Ashbaugh, A. R., Saumier, D., Nelson, M., Pitman, R. K., Tremblay, J., & Birmes, P. (2011). Does reconsolidation occur in humans: a reply. *Frontiers in Behavioral Neuroscience, 5*, 74. http://dx.doi.org/10.3389/fnbeh.2011.00074.

Brunet, A., Orr, S. P., Tremblay, J., Robertson, K., Nader, K., & Pitman, R. K. (2008). Effect of post-retrieval propranolol on psychophysiologic responding during subsequent script-driven traumatic imagery in post-traumatic stress disorder. *Journal of Psychiatric Research, 42*(6), 503–506. http://dx.doi.org/10.1016/j.jpsychires.2007.05.006.

Brunet, A., Weiss, D. S., Metzler, T. J., Best, S. R., Neylan, T. C., Rogers, C., & Marmar, C. R. (2001). The Peritraumatic Distress Inventory: A proposed measure of PTSD criterion A2. *American Journal of Psychiatry, 158*(9), 1480–1485.

Cahill, L., Prins, B., Weber, M., & McGaugh, J. L. (1994). Beta-adrenergic activation and memory for emotional events. *Nature, 371*(6499), 702–704. http://dx.doi.org/10.1038/371702a0.

Cahill, L., & van Stegeren, A. (2003). Sex-related impairment of memory for emotional events with beta-adrenergic blockade. *Neurobiology of Learning and Memory, 79*(1), 81–88.

Carlson, N. R. (2010). Learning and memory. In *Physiology of Behavior* (10th ed.). (pp. 440–484). Boston: Allyn & Bacon.

Chamberlain, S. R., Muller, U., Blackwell, A. D., Robbins, T. W., & Sahakian, B. J. (2006). Noradrenergic modulation of working memory and emotional memory in humans. *Psychopharmacology (Berl), 188*(4), 397–407. http://dx.doi.org/10.1007/s00213-006-0391-6.

Chiamulera, C., Tedesco, V., Zangrandi, L., Giuliano, C., & Fumagalli, G. (2010). Propranolol transiently inhibits reinstatement of nicotine-seeking behaviour in rats. *Journal of Psychopharmacology, 24*(3), 389–395. http://dx.doi.org/10.1177/0269881108097718.

Cohen, J. (1992). A power primer. *Psychological Bulletin, 112*(1), 155–159. http://dx.doi.org/10.1037/0033-2909.112.1.155.

de Quervain, D. J., Aerni, A., & Roozendaal, B. (2007). Preventive effect of beta-adrenoceptor blockade on glucocorticoid-induced memory retrieval deficits. *American Journal of Psychiatry, 164*(6), 967–969. http://dx.doi.org/10.1176/appi.ajp.164.6.967.

Dey, M., Brisson, J., Davis, G., Enever, R., Pray, K., Zaim, B., & Dvornik, D. (1986). Relationship between plasma propranolol concentration and dose in young, healthy volunteers. *Biopharmaceutics & Drug Disposition, 7*(2), 103–111.

Dohrenwend, B. P. (2000). The role of adversity and stress in psychopathology: Some evidence and its implications for theory and research. *Journal of Health and Social Behavior, 41*(1), 1–19.

Duka, T., Crombag, H. S., & Stephens, D. N. (2010). Experimental medicine in drug addiction: towards behavioral, cognitive and neurobiological biomarkers. *Journal of Psychopharmacology, 25*, 1235−1255. http://dx.doi.org/10.1177/0269881110388324.

Gershuny, B. S., Baer, L., Parker, H., Gentes, E. L., Infield, A. L., & Jenike, M. A. (2008). Trauma and posttraumatic stress disorder in treatment-resistant obsessive−compulsive disorder. *Depression and Anxiety, 25*(1), 69−71. http://dx.doi.org/10.1002/da.20284.

Grillon, C., Cordova, J., Morgan, C. A., Charney, D. S., & Davis, M. (2004). Effects of the beta-blocker propranolol on cued and contextual fear conditioning in humans. *Psychopharmacology (Berl), 175*(3), 342−352. http://dx.doi.org/10.1007/s00213-004-1819-5.

Hamann, S. (2001). Cognitive and neural mechanisms of emotional memory. *Trends in Cognitive Sciences, 5*(9), 394−400.

Harmer, C. J., Perrett, D. I., Cowen, P. J., & Goodwin, G. M. (2001). Administration of the beta-adrenoceptor blocker propranolol impairs the processing of facial expressions of sadness. *Psychopharmacology (Berl), 154*(4), 383−389. http://dx.doi.org/10.1007/s002130000654.

Heim, C., & Nemeroff, C. B. (2001). The role of childhood trauma in the neurobiology of mood and anxiety disorders: Preclinical and clinical studies. *Biological Psychiatry, 49*(12), 1023−1039.

Higgins, J. P., & Green, S. (Eds.). (2009). *Cochrane Handbook for Systematic Reviews of Interventions, Version 5.0.2 [updated September 2009]. The Cochrane Collaboration.* Available from. www.cochrane-handbook.org.

Hoge, E. A., Worthington, J. J., Nagurney, J. T., Chang, Y., Kay, E. B., Feterowski, C. M., & Pitman, R. K. (2012). Effect of acute posttrauma propranolol on PTSD outcome and physiological responses during script-driven imagery. *CNS Neuroscience & Therapeutics, 18*(1), 21−27. http://dx.doi.org/10.1111/j.1755-5949.2010.00227.x.

Holroyd, K. A., Penzien, D. B., & Cordingley, G. E. (1991). Propranolol in the management of recurrent migraine: A meta-analytic review. *Headache, 31*(5), 333−340.

Hurlemann, R., Hawellek, B., Matusch, A., Kolsch, H., Wollersen, H., Madea, B., & Dolan, R. J. (2005). Noradrenergic modulation of emotion-induced forgetting and remembering. *Journal of Neuroscience, 25*(27), 6343−6349. http://dx.doi.org/10.1523/jneurosci.0228-05.2005.

Ioannides, A., Liu, L., Theofilou, D., Dammers, J. R., Burne, T., Ambler, T., & Rose, S. (2000). Real-time processing of affective and cognitive stimuli in the human brain extracted from MEG signals. *Brain Topography, 13*(1), 11−19. http://dx.doi.org/10.1023/a:1007878001388.

Jadad, A. R., Moore, R. A., Carroll, D., Jenkinson, C., Reynolds, D. J., Gavaghan, D. J., & McQuay, H. J. (1996). Assessing the quality of reports of randomized clinical trials: Is blinding necessary? *Controlled Clinical Trials, 17*(1), 1−12.

Kampman, K. M., Volpicelli, J. R., Mulvaney, F., Alterman, A. I., Cornish, J., Gariti, P., & O'Brien, C. (2001). Effectiveness of propranolol for cocaine dependence treatment may depend on cocaine withdrawal symptom severity. *Drug and Alcohol Dependence, 63*(1), 69−78.

Kindt, M., Soeter, M., & Vervliet, B. (2009). Beyond extinction: Erasing human fear responses and preventing the return of fear. *Nature Neuroscience, 12*(3), 256−258. http://dx.doi.org/10.1038/nn.2271.

Kroes, M. C., Strange, B. A., & Dolan, R. J. (2010). Beta-adrenergic blockade during memory retrieval in humans evokes a sustained reduction of declarative emotional memory enhancement. *Journal of Neuroscience, 30*(11), 3959−3963. http://dx.doi.org/10.1523/JNEUROSCI.5469-09.2010.

Labonte, B., Yerko, V., Gross, J., Mechawar, N., Meaney, M. J., Szyf, M., & Turecki, G. (2012). Differential glucocorticoid receptor exon 1(B), 1(C), and 1(H) expression and methylation in suicide completers with a history of childhood abuse. *Biological Psychiatry, 72*, 41−48. http://dx.doi.org/10.1016/j.biopsych.2012.01.034.

Lipsey, M. W., & Wilson, D. B. (2001). *Practical Meta-Analysis.* Thousand Oaks, CA: Sage.

Maheu, F. S., Joober, R., Beaulieu, S., & Lupien, S. J. (2004). Differential effects of adren-ergic and corticosteroid hormonal systems on human short- and long-term declarative memory for emotionally arousing material. *Behavioral Neuroscience, 118*(2), 420−428. http://dx.doi.org/10.1037/0735-7044.118.2.420.

Maheu, F. S., Joober, R., & Lupien, S. J. (2005). Declarative memory after stress in humans: Differential involvement of the beta-adrenergic and corticosteroid systems. *Journal of Clinical Endocrinology & Metabolism, 90*(3), 1697−1704. http://dx.doi.org/10.1210/jc.2004-0009.

McGhee, L. L., Maani, C. V., Garza, T. H., DeSocio, P. A., Gaylord, K. M., & Black, I. H. (2009). The effect of propranolol on posttraumatic stress disorder in burned service members. *Journal of Burn Care & Research, 30*(1), 92−97. http://dx.doi.org/10.1097/BCR.1090b1013e3181921f3181951.

Mueller, D., & Cahill, S. P. (2010). Noradrenergic modulation of extinction learning and exposure therapy. *Behavioural Brain Research, 208*(1), 1−11. http://dx.doi.org/10.1016/j.bbr.2009.11.025.

Muravieva, E. V., & Alberini, C. M. (2010). Limited efficacy of propranolol on the reconso-lidation of fear memories. *Learning & Memory, 17*(6), 306−313. http://dx.doi.org/10.1101/lm.1794710.

Nader, K., Schafe, G. E., & Le Doux, J. E. (2000). Fear memories require protein synthesis in the amygdala for reconsolidation after retrieval. *Nature, 406*(6797), 722−726. http://dx.doi.org/10.1038/35021052.

Nielson, K. A., & Jensen, R. A. (1994). Beta-adrenergic receptor antagonist antihypertensive medications impair arousal-induced modulation of working memory in elderly humans. *Behavioral and Neural Biology, 62*(3), 190−200. http://dx.doi.org/10.1016/S0163-1047(05)80017-2.

Nugent, N. R., Christopher, N. C., Crow, J. P., Browne, L., Ostrowski, S., & Delahanty, D. L. (2010). The efficacy of early propranolol administration at reducing PTSD symptoms in pediatric injury patients: A pilot study. *Journal of Traumatic Stress, 23*(2), 282−287. http://dx.doi.org/10.1002/jts.20517.

O'Carroll, R. E., Drysdale, E., Cahill, L., Shajahan, P., & Ebmeier, K. P. (1999). Memory for emotional material: A comparison of central versus peripheral beta blockade. *Journal of Psychopharmacology, 13*(1), 32−39.

Oei, N. Y. L., Tollenaar, M. S., Elzinga, B. M., & Spinhoven, P. (2010). Propranolol reduces emotional distraction in working memory: A partial mediating role of propranolol-induced cortisol increases? *Neurobiology of Learning and Memory, 93*(3), 388−395. http://dx.doi.org/10.1016/j.nlm.2009.12.005.

Orr, S. P., Milad, M. R., Metzger, L. J., Lasko, N. B., Gilbertson, M. W., & Pitman, R. K. (2006). Effects of beta blockade, PTSD diagnosis, and explicit threat on the extinction and retention of an aversively conditioned response. *Biological Psychology, 73*(3), 262−271. http://dx.doi.org/10.1016/j.biopsycho.2006.05.001.

Pitman, R. K. (1989). Post-traumatic stress disorder, hormones, and memory. *Biological Psychiatry, 26*(3), 221−223.

Pitman, R. K., & Orr, S. P. (1990). The black hole of trauma. *Biological Psychiatry, 27*(5), 469−471, doi: 0006-3223(90)90437-7 [pii].

Pitman, R. K., Sanders, K. M., Zusman, R. M., Healy, A. R., Cheema, F., Lasko, N. B., & Orr, S. P. (2002). Pilot study of secondary prevention of posttraumatic stress disorder with propranolol. *Biological Psychiatry, 51*(2), 189−192.

Przybyslawski, J., Roullet, P., & Sara, S. J. (1999). Attenuation of emotional and nonemo-tional memories after their reactivation: Role of beta adrenergic receptors. *Journal of Neuroscience, 19*(15), 6623−6628.

Przybyslawski, J., & Sara, S. J. (1997). Reconsolidation of memory after its reactivation. *Behavioural Brain Research, 84*(1-2), 241−246.

Raj, S. R., Black, B. K., Biaggioni, I., Paranjape, S. Y., Ramirez, M., Dupont, W. D., & Robertson, D. (2009). Propranolol decreases tachycardia and improves symptoms in the postural tachycardia syndrome: Less is more. *Circulation, 120*(9), 725−734. http://dx.doi.org/10.1161/CIRCULATIONAHA.108.846501.

Reist, C., Duffy, J. G., Fujimoto, K., & Cahill, L. (2001). Beta-adrenergic blockade and emotional memory in PTSD. *International Journal of Neuropsychopharmacology, 4*(4), 377–383. http://dx.doi.org/10.1017/S1461145701002607.

Schiller, D., & Phelps, E. A. (2011). Does reconsolidation occur in humans? *Frontiers in Behavioral Neuroscience, 5*(24), 1–12. http://dx.doi.org/10.3389/fnbeh.2011.00024.

Schwabe, L., Nader, K., Wolf, O. T., Beaudry, T., & Pruessner, J. C. (2011). Neural signature of reconsolidation impairments by propranolol in humans. *Biological psychiatry, 71*, 380–386. http://dx.doi.org/10.1016/j.biopsych.2011.10.028.

Schwabe, L., Romer, S., Richter, S., Dockendorf, S., Bilak, B., & Schächinger, H. (2009). Stress effects on declarative memory retrieval are blocked by a β-adrenoceptor antagonist in humans. *Psychoneuroendocrinology, 34*(3), 446–454. http://dx.doi.org/10.1016/j. psyneuen.2008.10.009.

Soeter, M., & Kindt, M. (2010). Dissociating response systems: Erasing fear from memory. *Neurobiology of Learning and Memory, 94*(1), 30–41. http://dx.doi.org/10.1016/j.nlm. 2010.03.004.

Spinhoven, P., Elzinga, B. M., Hovens, J. G., Roelofs, K., Zitman, F. G., van Oppen, P., & Penninx, B. W. (2010). The specificity of childhood adversities and negative life events across the life span to anxiety and depressive disorders. *Journal of Affective Disorders, 126*(1-2), 103–112. http://dx.doi.org/10.1016/j.jad.2010. 02.132.

Stein, M. B., Kerridge, C., Dimsdale, J. E., & Hoyt, D. B. (2007). Pharmacotherapy to prevent PTSD: Results from a randomized controlled proof-of-concept trial in physically injured patients. *Journal of Traumatic Stress, 20*(6), 923–932. http://dx.doi.org/10.1002/ jts.20270.

Strange, B. A., & Dolan, R. J. (2004). Beta-adrenergic modulation of emotional memory-evoked human amygdala and hippocampal responses. *Proceedings of the National Academy of Sciences USA, 101*(31), 11454–11458. http://dx.doi.org/10.1073/pnas. 0404282101.

Strange, B. A., Hurlemann, R., & Dolan, R. J. (2003). An emotion-induced retrograde amnesia in humans is amygdala- and β-adrenergic-dependent. *Proceedings of the National Academy of Sciences USA, 100*(23), 13626–13631. http://dx.doi.org/10. 1073/pnas.1635116100.

Tollenaar, M. S., Elzinga, B. M., Spinhoven, P., & Everaerd, W. (2009a). Immediate and prolonged effects of cortisol, but not propranolol, on memory retrieval in healthy young men. *Neurobiology of Learning and Memory, 91*(1), 23–31. http://dx.doi.org/ 10.1016/j.nlm.2008.08.002.

Tollenaar, M. S., Elzinga, B. M., Spinhoven, P., & Everaerd, W. (2009b). Psychophysiological responding to emotional memories in healthy young men after cortisol and propranolol administration. *Psychopharmacology (Berl), 203*(4), 793–803. http://dx.doi.org/10. 1007/s00213-008-1427-x.

Vaiva, G., Ducrocq, F., Jezequel, K., Averland, B., Lestavel, P., Brunet, A., & Marmar, C. R. (2003). Immediate treatment with propranolol decreases posttraumatic stress disorder two months after trauma. *Biological Psychiatry, 54*(9), 947–949, doi: S0006322303004128 [pii].

van Stegeren, A. H. (2008). The role of the noradrenergic system in emotional memory. *Acta Psychologica, 127*(3), 532–541. http://dx.doi.org/10.1016/j.actpsy.2007.10.004.

van Stegeren, A. H., Everaerd, W., Cahill, L., McGaugh, J. L., & Gooren, L. J. (1998). Memory for emotional events: Differential effects of centrally versus peripherally acting beta-blocking agents. *Psychopharmacology (Berl), 138*(3-4), 305–310.

van Stegeren, A. H., Everaerd, W., & Gooren, L. J. (2002). The effect of beta-adrenergic blockade after encoding on memory of an emotional event. *Psychopharmacology (Berl), 163*(2), 202–212. http://dx.doi.org/10.1007/s00213-002-1163-6.

van Stegeren, A. H., Goekoop, R., Everaerd, W., Scheltens, P., Barkhof, F., Kuijer, J. P., & Rombouts, S. A. (2005). Noradrenaline mediates amygdala activation in men and women during encoding of emotional material. *Neuroimage, 24*(3), 898–909. http:// dx.doi.org/10.1016/j.neuroimage.2004.09.011.

van Stegeren, A. H., Wolf, O. T., Everaerd, W., Scheltens, P., Barkhof, F., & Rombouts, S. A. R. B. (2007). Endogenous cortisol level interacts with noradrenergic activation in the human amygdala. *Neurobiology of Learning and Memory, 87*(1), 57—66. http://dx.doi.org/10.1016/j.nlm.2006.05.008.

Weymar, M., Löw, A., Melzig, C. A., & Hamm, A. O. (2009). Enhanced long-term recollection for emotional pictures: Evidence from high-density ERPs. *Psychophysiology, 46*(6), 1200—1207. http://dx.doi.org/10.1111/j.1469-8986.2009.00869.x.

Weymar, M., Low, A., Modess, C., Engel, G., Grundling, M., Petersmann, A., & Hamm, A. O. (2010). Propranolol selectively blocks the enhanced parietal old/new effect during long-term recollection of unpleasant pictures: A high density ERP study. *Neuroimage, 49*(3), 2800—2806. http://dx.doi.org/10.1016/j.neuroimage.2009.10.025.

Chapter thirteen

The Translational Potential of Memory Reconsolidation

Philip R. Corlett, Jane R. Taylor

Yale University School of Medicine, Connecticut Mental Health Center,
New Haven, Connecticut

13.1 INTRODUCTION

Memories allow us to draw upon our past experience in order to respond adaptively in the present and plan for our future (Dudai & Eisenberg, 2004). However, they are not simply a recording of the past that can be replayed as necessary, and they are not always veridical or adaptive (Estes, 1997). The advent of cognitive neuroscience and its application to problems in psychiatry—cognitive neuropsychiatry—has led clinician scientists to characterize many of the symptoms of mental illness as pathologies of memory formation, maintenance, and utilization (Halligan & David, 2001). In this chapter, we review some of those assertions with regard to memory reconsolidation, either as a pathophysiological mechanism (Corlett *et al.*, 2009) or a potential therapeutic window (Debiec, 2012; Taylor *et al.*, 2009), assessing their veracity against the available clinical data. We discuss the ethical implications of memory modification therapies. We also outline some of what we believe will be practical hurdles and complexities associated with attempting to modify aberrant memories in human patients, highlighted by preclinical work exploring the boundary conditions and idiosyncrasies of memory reconsolidation (Inda *et al.*, 2011).

The phenomenon of memory reconsolidation is observed when, after memory encoding and consolidation, a reminder procedure reactivates the initial memory into a labile state in which it becomes susceptible to interventions that prevent its subsequent consolidation (Misanin *et al.*, 1968; Nader *et al.*, 2000; Przybyslawski & Sara, 1997). These destabilizing interventions can degrade subsequent retrieval of the initial memory, perhaps even erasing it entirely (Kindt *et al.*, 2009). It is of course uncertain whether the memory is truly erased or, rather, overridden and inhibited by novel extinction learning (Osan *et al.*, 2011). The balance between extinction and reconsolidation is another key aspect of the potential

Memory Reconsolidation. http://dx.doi.org/10.1016/B978-0-12-386892-3.00013-5

pathophysiological contribution and therapeutic potential of aberrant memory processes (Corlett *et al.*, 2009; Eisenhardt & Menzel, 2007; Pedreira *et al.*, 2004). The clinical appeal of having the capability to remove or inhibit unwanted memories has long been appreciated; here, Shakespeare's Macbeth implores the Doctor to treat his wife:

> *Canst thou not minister to a mind diseased,*
> *Pluck from the memory a rooted sorrow,*
> *Raze out the written troubles of the brain,*
> *And with some sweet oblivious antidote*
> *Cleanse the stuff'd bosom of that perilous stuff*
> *Which weighs upon the heart?*

That potential has yet to be realized, but there are some intriguing initial findings in treating human patients with post-traumatic stress disorder (PTSD), anxiety, and addiction. Furthermore, considering what function memory reconsolidation might serve (Alberini, 2011; Stickgold & Walker, 2007), theoretical models of some symptoms have implicated excessive memory reconsolidation as a pathophysiological process. For example, the delusions that attend serious mental illnesses such as schizophrenia might be maintained in the face of contradictory evidence because of inappropriate memory reconsolidation (Corlett *et al.*, 2009); that is, if the function of memory reconsolidation is to update and streamline memories in light of new information (Alberini, 2011; Stickgold & Walker, 2007), then excessive reconsolidation might explain the puzzling elasticity of delusional beliefs (Simpson & Done, 2002) whereby, when faced with incontrovertible proof that their delusions do not pertain, patients will deftly incorporate that information into their delusion, rendering the information explicable and strengthening the belief (Milton *et al.*, 1978). Before expanding upon the potential theoretical extensions of reconsolidation, we outline some of the preclinical findings with translational potential in psychiatry.

13.2 PRECLINICAL FINDINGS

Early clinical observations of closed-head injury or other traumatic brain insults described retrograde amnesia for memories more proximal to the insult (Ribot, 1882; Russell & Nathan, 1946). These paved the way for consolidation theory (McGaugh, 1966) with the notion that, once encountered, information went through a period of storage during which time it was susceptible to disruption but after which its retention was locked in. Challenging this theory, however, American football players describe a state of being "dinged" (Yarnell and Lynch, 1973):

> *Getting hit in the head so hard that your memory is affected, although you*
> *can still walk around and sometimes even continue playing. You don't*
> *feel pain, and the only way other players or the coaches know you've*
> *been dinged is when they realize you can't remember the plays. (p. 196)*

They do not forget all plays—just the play that was being currently executed. Preclinical studies of the temporal gradient of consolidation after initial encoding yielded findings consistent with "dinging." The first empirical study to demonstrate the fragility of reactivated memories was published in *Science* in 1968. Misanin *et al.* (1968) characterized the boundaries of retrograde amnesia induced by electroconvulsive shock (ECS). They exposed rats to a contingent relationship between white noise auditory conditioned stimulus (CS+) and an electric shock unconditioned stimulus (US). The animals learned a CS−US association, manifest as lick suppression. That is, the animals were thirsty and when given the opportunity to drink they readily licked at a waterspout. However, in the presence of a cue that predicted electric shock, their licking was dramatically suppressed. Lick suppression was reduced in animals that had been conditioned, were reminded of the conditioning situation, and then received ECS, suggesting that the memory for CS−US association had been weakened by the combination of reactivation and subsequent ECS. This initial demonstration generated debate, controversy, and subsequent studies because the time-dependent gradient of retrograde amnesia confounded both the variables manipulated in the Misanin *et al.* study: time since engaging with the memory and the activity level of the memory. Introducing the reminder treatment made the old inactive memory active once more. The eliciting conditions and myriad other procedural modulations were investigated, including hypothermia post-reactivation as well as pre-reminder (Riccio *et al.*, 2006). The phenomenon descended into relative obscurity. However, since its rediscovery in 2000 (Nader *et al.*, 2000), the techniques of modern neuroscience have been brought to bear on reconsolidation (Tronson & Taylor, 2007); for example, molecular dissociations between extinction and reconsolidation argue in favor of reconsolidation failure being a separable form of learning from extinction (Lee *et al.*, 2004). However, because these techniques have not, for the most part, been applied to human subjects and the data are reviewed elsewhere in this book, we do not focus on them here.

13.3 HUMAN MEMORY RECONSOLIDATION

The resurgence in preclinical investigations of reconsolidation naturally led to studies in humans. Episodic memory reconsolidation has been demonstrated with intervening distracting information (Forcato *et al.*, 2007), and fear memory erasure has been demonstrated with propranolol, a β-adrenergic receptor antagonist (Kindt *et al.*, 2009). In a procedure inspired by preclinical work (Monfils *et al.*, 2009; Quirk *et al.*, 2010), Schiller *et al.* (2010) reactivated a fear memory, and during the reactivation period they extinguished the fear memory, reporting erasure of the memory that lasted for 1 year. Taken together, these data indicate that in some circumstances, human memories undergo reconsolidation. Such observations encouraged recent attempts to treat various mental illnesses by reactivating pathogenic memories.

13.3.1 Targeting mental illnesses by disrupting reconsolidation

Although definitive studies of the clinical efficacy of perturbing the reconsolidation of pathological memories have yet to be done, we discuss initial findings from pilot studies. Just as reconsolidation was discovered, so was its clinical application. Inspired by the Misanin *et al.* data in rodents, the Canadian psychiatrist Richard Rubin tried to reactivate various persistent psychiatric symptoms and then engender retrograde amnesia for them using electroconvulsive therapy (Rubin, 1976). He identified a group of 28 patients with persistent intrusive cognitions ranging from delusions to hallucinations, obsessions, and compulsions. He reasoned that

> *if the patient's attention is strongly directed, by hypnosis if necessary, to his most disturbing feelings and imagery, and if he is instantly given ECT (awake) there should result a significantly greater amelioration and reduction of symptoms than is obtained when ECT is given in the usual way. (p. 88)*

Of course, giving ECT "awake," without anesthesia, is likely to have been very unpleasant for the patient (even though the muscle relaxant succinylcholine was given to reduce fracture risk from involuntary and violent muscle contractions), and as such, there should have been a comparison group in whom the ECT procedure was given without the re-engagement of the symptom. The possibility remains that any symptom improvement is due to an association formed between the symptom and the unpleasant experience of ECT without anesthesia. We know from early work on verbal conditioning with aversive stimuli as well as token economies that patients can learn to suppress their verbal endorsement of beliefs, but this does not necessarily mean that their symptoms are "cured" or "erased" (Chadwick & Lowe, 1990, 1994).

Nevertheless, Rubin (1976) reported that all 28 patients, following a single session as described previously, improved dramatically for periods varying between 3 months and 10 years (at the time of publication). However, the symptoms were not erased per se; patients from each clinical category relapsed. Rudin reported that these relapses were theoretically consistent:

> *Relapse was total and sudden and contingent on an event occurring that served to remind the patient of his forgotten psychopathology.... Thus we cannot expect all symptoms can be permanently cured by single ECT ... but by tracing the associations of the undesirable behavior and administering ECT ... it should be possible to treat more effectively patients whose behavior had been refractory to previous therapy. (p. 89)*

Rubin's (1976) work represents an isolated report, which appears to have had little impact on therapeutic approaches, perhaps due to the unpleasant and invasive nature of the treatment. With the advent of more tolerable approaches to modifying brain function, such as transcranial magnetic stimulation (TMS), it may be possible to re-create the intervention—an approach that has been piloted with some success in treating PTSD.

13.3.2 Post-traumatic stress disorder

PTSD has become a part of the public awareness since its introduction in 1980 in the third edition of the *Diagnostic and Statistical Manual of Mental Disorders* (*DSM*). Earlier conflicts were associated with other terms such as "soldier's heart," "shell shock," and "war neurosis" (Donovan, 2010).

Regarding PTSD, the *DSM-IV-TR* (American Psychiatric Association, 2000) states,

> *The essential features of post-traumatic stress disorder is the development of characteristic symptoms following exposure to an extreme traumatic stressor involving direct personal experience of an event that involves actual or threatened death or serious injury or other threat to one's personal integrity … or witnessing an event that involves death, injury, or a threat of physical integrity to another person.… The person's response to the event must involve intense fear, helplessness, or horror. The full symptom picture must be present for more than 1 month.* (p. 463)

PTSD symptoms can include disturbing dreams and flashbacks, whereby sufferers act or feel like the stressful experience is happening again; physical and emotional experiences occur to events that remind the patient of the stressful event. Neuroendocrine responses at the time of a stressful event and subsequent recall may mediate PTSD symptoms that are conceptualized as an excessive emotional response around retrieval of a memory for a traumatic event. Hence, pharmacological treatments for PTSD aim to curtail stress responses (by targeting the glucocorticoid-mediated stress response system) or emotional memory processing (by targeting noradrenergic function) (Donovan, 2010).

Not all memories respond to noradrenergic interventions, but those with emotional content do (Cahill *et al.*, 1994). Emotional memories are often more strongly consolidated, an effect that can be attenuated by the blockade of β-adrenergic receptors. Adrenal glucocorticoids also interact with memory consolidation and retrieval. However, the primary pharmacological agent that has been examined recently for PTSD treatment is propranolol, a β-adrenergic receptor blocker that has been used to treat hypertension. One of the stated side effects is memory loss; however, James McGaugh stated to the President's Council on Bioethics, "20 milligrams is not going to induce retrograde amnesia" (President's Council on Bioethics, 2003). Indeed, propranolol is routinely used at this dose to help performance anxiety in concert pianists. Those performers do not subsequently forget their performance or the piece that they performed.

In an attempt to dampen the consolidation of memories for stressful events, propanolol has been administered in the emergency room following traumatic experiences. Individuals randomized to propranolol treatment 6 hr or less after a traumatic event were less likely to develop PTSD symptoms than those randomized to placebo treatment. When exposed to reminders of the traumatic event 3 months later, propranolol-treated subjects showed less physiological responsivity than placebo-treated individuals (Pitman *et al.*, 2002; Vaiva *et al.*, 2003).

With regard to reconsolidation-based treatment for PTSD, an early treatment using abreaction, narcoanalysis, or narcosynthesis is currently not very popular and considered by some to be obsolete, but it may be based on the blockade of reconsolidation. Abreaction is a psychoanalytic term for an emotional breakdown engendered in the therapeutic setting in order to assist coping. It involves the exploration of "repressed" traumatic experiences or dissociative episodes triggered by traumatic stimuli. Narcoanalysis and narcosynthesis involve the same uncovering of traumatic experience in the context of drug administration. Sodium amytal, a barbiturate that impacts upon GABAergic function and hence may engender amnesia, is commonly used in this setting (Kolb, 1993). According to some theories, through this procedure the difficult traumatic material becomes available for later integration and synthesis. Some authors have suggested videotaping the entire session and that, after full recovery of consciousness, the patient and therapist should review the tape so that the reactivated information can be incorporated into ongoing psychotherapy. The abreactive interview might allow the traumatic interview to be reactivated in a sedative state in which the information can be reappraised and reconsolidated without re-experiencing, which could of course contribute to the maintenance of PTSD symptoms. Furthermore, if the review of the tape occurred during the reconsolidation window, further erasure of the maladaptive aspects of the memory might take place.

More recently and more clearly directed at memory reconsolidation, reactivated traumatic memories have been targeted using propranolol. Individuals with PTSD have had their traumatic memories reactivated by providing a verbal account of the events (which was recorded). They were then dosed with either propranolol or placebo. When re-exposed to the recording 1 week later, the subjects treated with propranolol showed attenuated physiological responding during the replay relative to those who received placebo (Brunet *et al.*, 2008).

Taking a similar, but much less intrusive, approach to Rudin (1976), Osuch and colleagues (2009) induced reactivation of PTSD symptoms by having patients engage in imagined re-exposure, generating lists of memories associated with their trauma. They then administered low-frequency or slow transcranial magnetic stimulation (≤ 1 Hz, TMS), which passed short-duration magnetic fields undistorted through the skull, engendering electrical fields in small (2 or 3 cm) target regions of the brain (Hoffman, 2007). Slow TMS can curtail synaptic activity and engender long-term depression within a brain region because dorsolateral prefrontal cortex is implicated in memory retrieval (Fletcher & Henson, 2001) and trauma reactivation in PTSD specifically (Rossi *et al.*, 2006). After 20 active treatments, this TMS approach decreased hyperarousal compared to sham-treated controls. Hence, there is preliminary evidence that the excessive emotional responding to traumatic events characteristic of PTSD can be curtailed with pharmacological and physical interventions. Importantly, Kindt and colleagues (2009) dissociated physiological responses (diminished by propranolol) from cognitive declarative memory (unimpaired by propranolol during fear conditioning in healthy subjects). In brief, Kindt and colleagues trained subjects that some pictures of spiders predicted the delivery of an unpleasant unconditioned stimulus, whereas others did not. The following day, they re-presented one of the pictures that predicted the unpleasant stimulus and administered propranolol or placebo. Twenty-four hours later, they tested subjects' implicit memory (physiological startle response) and explicit expectations of unpleasant experiences. Propanolol attenuated the implicit startle response but left the explicit conscious expectation intact (Kindt *et al.*, 2009). This has implications when we address the ethics of memory modification later but also when we consider other illnesses that may be amenable to treatment using memory modification. We turn now to one such illness—drug addiction.

13.3.3 Addiction

Preclinical models of drug self-administration provide perhaps the most valid translation, certainly of the behavioral characteristics, of a human mental illness (Hyman *et al.*, 2006). That translational approach has repeatedly highlighted the effects of drugs of abuse on learning and memory processes (Taylor *et al.*, 2009); specifically, they usurp the brain's dopamine-based learning system, encouraging the attribution of incentive salience to cues associated with access to drugs and actions that lead to drug access (Hyman *et al.*, 2006). Much like trauma memories are associated with an excessively strong emotional response, drug-associated stimuli and actions are ascribed too much importance such that they grab attention and drive action (Robinson & Berridge, 2001). The importance of these cue responses, however, can be exploited to therapeutic ends. Psychotherapies based on cue reactivity involve repeatedly exposing a patient to the sights, smells, and/or paraphernalia associated with a substance in the absence of actual consumption, thus attenuating the power of those cues to elicit an expectation of drug effects over time. Through training, individuals gradually learn that previously learned drug cues no longer readily predict an impending "high" (i.e., the cue—drug associations are extinguished) (Otto *et al.*, 2007). Although "extinction-based" approaches are often effective in the therapeutic setting, they can fail to generalize to the real world outside of the clinic (Otto *et al.*, 2007) — that is, extinction is context dependent (Bouton, 2002; Otto *et al.*, 2007; Taylor *et al.*, 2009). In fact, this context dependency constitutes primary experimental evidence of a central limitation of extinction-based (and even non-extinction-based) therapies. Namely, rather than facilitating the "unlearning" or "erasure" of conditioned responses, such forms of therapy constitute new learning of alternative responses or coping strategies (Havermans & Jansen, 2003) that suppress and/or inhibit entrenched learned drug responses. A key issue in the psychotherapy of cocaine addiction is the transfer of motivation and learned strategies from the clinic into daily life: A weekly 50-min therapy session accounts for less than 1% of a patient's waking life (Otto & Otto, 2000). With the goal of having the 1% of time in the clinic influence the other 99% of time away from the clinic, special attention has to be placed on helping the patient extend the motivations and behaviors evident in the clinic beyond the clinic walls.

By targeting reconsolidation, which is less context bound, it may be possible to enhance the efficacy of cue reactivity-based therapies. Furthermore, a combined cognitive and pharmacological approach is often more efficacious therapeutically (Carroll, 1997). Preclinical data demonstrate the effectiveness of propranolol against reactivated cocaine memories (Lee *et al.*, 2006b; Milton *et al.*, 2008): Reactivating a cocaine memory and administering propranolol attenuates the conditioned reinforcing properties of the cocaine-associated stimulus and decreases its ability to drive action and garner new instrumental learning. In human addicts, less data are available. One transcranial magnetic stimulation study in smokers employed a reactivation treatment, exposing subjects to smoking cues and then administering repetitive TMS over left dorsolateral prefrontal cortex daily for 10 days. Cigarette consumption and cue-induced craving were reduced, but the effects dissipated over time (Amiaz *et al.*, 2009). This study highlights a number of the challenges to the clinical application of memory reconsolidation and perturbation to which we will return later in the chapter. First, there are marked individual differences in cue exposure responses: In some subjects, cue exposure therapy actually elicits craving and may facilitate addictive behaviors (Erblich & Montgomery, 2012), just as challenging a patient with delusions about his or her beliefs may augment the delusions (Erblich & Montgomery, 2012). Thus, cue exposure may prime drug seeking rather than extinction. Furthermore, the issue of asymptotes and habits is pertinent to addiction. If drug seeking has been learned to asymptote, it is possible that drug reminders and cue reactivation will not even return drug representations into a labile state. Indeed, heavy smokers fail to acquire new stimuli as smoking-related discriminative stimuli—that is, salient cues to the association between button pushes and nicotine (Hogarth *et al.*, 2003)—suggesting that the plasticity required for reconsolidation-based erasure might decline with extended exposure and abuse (Moussawi *et al.*, 2009). Clearly, the boundaries of memory strength and choice of reactivation procedure will be crucially important if memory reactivation is to become a beneficial therapeutic approach.

13.3.4 Delusions and reconsolidation

Delusions—the fixed, false beliefs that attend serious mental illness—have long been considered intractable to scientific inquiry (Jaspers, 1963). In recent years, cognitive neuroscience has begun to erode this notion (Coltheart, 2010; Coltheart *et al.*, 2011; Corlett *et al.*, 2010; Fletcher & Frith, 2009; McKay *et al.*, 2007). Theoretical models grounded in translational neuroscience suggest that delusions usurp the brain mechanisms of predictive learning (Corlett *et al.*, 2007a, 2010, 2011; Fletcher & Frith, 2009). These models posit a flexible goal-directed controller that is sensitive to the actual contingencies between actions and their consequences and a cached-value habitual controller that is relatively inflexible to changes to the actual consequences of actions (Daw *et al.*, 2005). Prediction error signals, the mismatches between controller predictions and outcomes, can bias which system controls behavior, with the system that is least uncertain mediating the final choice (Daw *et al.*, 2005). With excessive ruminative self-reinforcement and reconsolidation, the inflexible, self-deceptive system gains control despite corrective feedback (Corlett *et al.*, 2009).

We believe that delusions form due to aberrations of the brain systems that underpin successful anticipation of and adaptation to external and internal events (Corlett *et al.*, 2007a, 2007b, 2009, 2011). Prediction error, the mismatch between our expectancy in a given situation and what we experience, is central to our account (Rescorla, 1972). Prediction errors signal that our current understanding is inadequate and that new learning is required. This learning can be achieved directly (prediction errors drive changes in synaptic plasticity that update future expectancies (Schultz, 1998)) or indirectly through the allocation of attention (unpredictable events are allocated more attention (Schultz & Dickinson, 2000)).

Prediction error theories of delusion formation (Corlett *et al.*, 2007a; Gray *et al.*, 1991; Hemsley, 1994) suggest that under the influence of inappropriate prediction error signals, psychotic individuals attend to, learn about, and associate insignificant and merely coincident events, forming delusions as explanations for their odd experiences (Kapur, 2003; Maher, 1974).

Furthermore, delusions can become so strong as to override current sensation; they are tenacious in the face of contradictory evidence (Crick & Mitchison, 1983; Fletcher & Frith, 2009). The transition between belief formation, embellishment, and maintenance occurs when aberrant prediction errors repeatedly reactivate and reconsolidate delusion-related material, resulting in a transfer from a flexible episodic representation of events to an inflexible belief habit (Corlett *et al.*, 2009).

This theory posits that different memory representations govern the endorsement of a belief and its rejection (Stanton, 2000); these representations compete to control behavior, and prediction error contributes to that competition (Eisenhardt & Menzel, 2007; Pedreira *et al.*, 2004). If an organism is reminded of the link between some stimulus and a reward—for example, by re-exposing the stimulus—the organism is reminded of the predictive relationship, returning the representation of that information into a labile state, and if the reward is not presented and extinction takes place, the organism learns that sometimes the stimulus does not predict reward. Prediction error drives the reminder process and, hence, random prediction errors encourage the reconsolidation and strengthening of delusions. The mere repetition of a statement can lead to increases in the strength of one's belief that the statement is true (Begg et al., 1992). Indeed, even recall of some information can increase an individual's endorsement of its truth (Ozubko & Fugelsang, 2011). Thus, delusions are maintained despite contradictory evidence because the process of engaging with that contrary information is surprising to the patient, engages prediction error, and reminds the patient of his or her delusion, strengthening it (Corlett et al, 2009); this has been observed clinically (Milton et al., 1978; Simpson & Done, 2002).

It is adaptive for an organism to be able to remember salient events for extended periods without the necessity for repeat experiences (Dickinson, 2001). Reactivation of a memory trace for a salient event may increase the stabilization of that trace (as discussed in Chapters 3 and 5). The most salient memories would be reactivated most frequently and would therefore undergo the most reconsolidation-based stabilization (Rasch & Born, 2007), increasing their fixity. This may also be the case in emotional disorders such as anxiety, depression, and PTSD (Alberini, 2007). Reconsolidation may facilitate the automation of behavior—the transition from knowledge to belief (Eichenbaum, 2000)—shifting the representation that mediates behavior from declarative to procedural and thus reducing the demand for executive control. Furthermore, reconsolidation is held to aid the extraction of important details from complex episodic memories and to permit the integration of those details in support of adaptive and efficient behaviors (Stickgold & Walker, 2007), possibly through the construction of a habit or schema (Bartlett, 1932).

In rodents, both dopamine and glutamate function are critical to the formation of stimulus response habits from initially goal-directed behaviors (Bespalov et al., 2007; Hitchcott et al., 2007). At the beginning of learning, behavior is governed by flexible, goal-directed representations that, with overtraining, cede control of behavior to more inflexible habitual behaviors (Adams, 1981), which have been aligned with delusion beliefs because of their tenacity and dopaminergic basis (Corlett et al., 2004; Eichenbaum, 2000). Like reconsolidation and extinction, these representations do not overwrite or erase one another, as demonstrated by Hitchcott and colleagues (2007), who, by infusing dopamine into the prefrontal cortex of overtrained rats, were able to rescue goal-directed behavior. Likewise, the habitual effects of overtraining can be reversed using an AMPA receptor antagonist (Bespalov et al., 2007). This switch from goal-directed to habitual control also occurs in states of stress, often associated with intense emotions, and is influenced by noradrenergic as well as glucocorticoid signaling (Schwabe & Wolf, 2009; Schwabe et al., 2011).

Dopaminergic and glutamatergic prediction error signals may, via their effects on retrieval and reconsolidation, enhance habit formation, speeding the transfer of control of behavior from flexible prefrontal and ventral striatal regions toward the dorsal striatum (Wickens et al., 2007). This transfer is speeded further by excessive subcortical dopamine signaling (Nelson & Killcross, 2006). In schizophrenia, striatal dopamine is elevated (Howes *et al.*, 2009; Kegeles *et al.*, 2000; Laruelle *et al.*, 1999) and prefrontal dopamine signaling is decreased (Abi-Dargham *et al.*, 2002), exactly the conditions in which habits dominate (Hitchcott *et al.*, 2007; Nelson & Killcross, 2006). However, novel dopamine partial agonist drugs such as aripiprazole may provide targeted relief because they may simultaneously enhance prefrontal dopamine signaling (Li *et al.*, 2004) and reduce striatal dopamine levels (Mamo *et al.*, 2007), thus weakening habitual behavior and boosting goal-directedness. Of particular interest in the present framework, aripiprazole has been suggested to specifically target phasic dopamine signaling (Hamamura & Harada, 2007), the signaling mode most closely associated with prediction error registration (Grace, 1991; Schultz & Dickinson, 2000; Schultz *et al.*, 1997).

The reconsolidation hypothesis of delusion fixity remains to be tested empirically, but it does provide an attractive answer to the cognitive mechanisms of belief fixity. It also raises the intriguing possibility of taking a reconsolidation blockade approach to treating delusions.

13.3.5 The ethics of memory modification

The plotlines of science fiction novels and movies often explore the potentially disastrous consequences of memory modification. For example, in the movie *The Eternal Sunshine of the Spotless Mind*, a couple agree to have one another erased from their respective memories to aid their coping with the breakup of their relationship, and in the movie *Total Recall*, the implantation of false memories of a vacation causes the protagonist to have problems distinguishing fantasy from reality, engendering paranoia with violent consequences. Much has been written on the ethics of applying memory modification technologies. The President's Council on Bioethics (2003) advised extreme caution with regard to the modification of memories in pursuit of happiness, citing the Lotus Eaters from Homer's *Odyssey* who consumed blossoms that erased memory entirely and hence destroyed all sense of self.

Of course, there are reasons to be cautious in modifying memories; authenticity as an agent must be retained and meeting obligations to remember, such as witness testimony, must be ensured. Some argue that this caution is premature, based on their skepticism that we will ever be able to achieve memory modification. However, as we have seen, fear memories can be modified in the laboratory and the clinic. Furthermore, anecdotal reports of retrograde amnesia induced without complete consent raise serious ethical concerns.

One prominent theorist, Adam Kolber, recounts an incident described by Dr. Scott Haig, an orthopedic surgeon, in which a young mother was undergoing a biopsy procedure under local, not general, anesthesia. The patient agreed for an anesthetist to be present "just in case." The sample was removed and sent to a pathologist in the hospital, who reported the grave outcomes of his investigation to Haig via the one-way intercom system in the operating theater, unaware that the patient could hear. The woman exclaimed "Oh no, my kids," at which point the anesthetist, aware of the amnestic properties of propofol ("the milk of amnesia") administered an infusion to destabilize the information most proximal to the infusion. The woman awoke from the anesthesia with no recollection of the incident (Kolber, 2008). Although an argument can be made that this was done for the patient's safety—she may have thrashed around and endangered herself during the later stages of the surgical procedure—the infusion was conducted without consent and it also decreased the patient's ability to recall information that may have been used punitively against the medical team. The issue of consent is pertinent here and especially relevant to the application of memory modification technology in psychiatry; patients' symptoms are often ego-syntonic, particularly delusional beliefs. That is, many patients do not believe there is anything wrong with them and their delusions contribute to their sense of self and self-esteem (Hagen, 2008; McKay *et al.*, 2007). The protective or defensive function of delusions seems at odds with their intrusive nature and the often-saddening consequences when delusions drive behavior, including homicide and suicide. We treat delusions with antipsychotic medications to avoid such situations, but should we be doing so? It is likely that no one would argue against treatment of veterans suffering from PTSD by erasing the memories to which they are pathologically and excessively responding (Liao & Sandberg, 2008). However, if delusions do indeed provide some benefit to social functioning, is it right to erase them? What about the case of artists and writers who used their drug addiction as subject matter that both informed and entertained throughout the 20th century (e.g., William Burroughs, Philip K. Dick, and Hunter S. Thompson). Would we have their work if we had an effective means with which we could erase their memories for experiences with drugs? Clearly, some people grow from their aberrant memories (Donovan, 2010), but for those who do not, it seems inappropriate to withhold a viable treatment mechanism. That said, based on the available data, clinical and preclinical, we are not yet in a position to erase problematic memories. In the next section, we discuss some of the theoretical and practical impediments to an effective therapeutic approach based on reconsolidation.

13.4 PRACTICAL ISSUES

There are a number of theoretical conundrums regarding the reconsolidation phenomenon. Is it neurobiologically and cognitively unique? What are its temporal and informational boundaries? These critical details will color our ability to exploit the phenomenon therapeutically (Alberini, 2011). More deeply, we need to consider the purpose of memory reconsolidation. That is, given that memory is so important to our adaptation to the environment, why would it make sense to return memory into labile state following recollection and risk its disruption?

There are a number of possibilities that, again, have implications for our use of the reconsolidation window therapeutically. First, memory may become labile to allow the integration of new information and updating. On the other hand, memories may go through reconsolidation to increase strength and longevity (Alberini, 2011). Of course, these are not mutually exclusive ideas. Updating implies that a memory is first reactivated in light of a distinct experience, and memory for that experience is linked to the first memory. However, a second identical learning experience can be defined as memory updating and is indeed sensitive to some of the same interventions as memory reconsolidation (Lee, 2008). Clearly, these involve different types of updating.

To emphasize the point further, the phenomenon of retrospective revaluation incorporates both the repeated conditioning aspect and the updating of retrieved memories in light of new information. Retrospective revaluation has been demonstrated in rodents and humans; it has been demonstrated for fear conditioning in the galvanic skin response but also in causal judgments. Suppose that you learn that a meal consisting of chicken and fish causes an allergic response in a fictitious patient and then you make some causal inference about the allergenic potential of both foods. If, in a subsequent meal, you eat chicken alone and do not experience the reaction, then you may adjust upwards your rating of the allergenic potential of the absent food (fish) to reflect the fact that this food must have caused the allergy following the meal of both chicken and fish. Such an increment in the response to the absent cue is an example of un-overshadowing because it is assumed to reflect a release from the overshadowing that occurred between the foods during the initial compound meal. Conversely, if you find that eating the chicken alone causes the allergic reaction, there would be grounds for decreasing your belief in the allergenic potential of the absent fish on the assumption that the presence of the chicken in the initial compound meal was sufficient to cause the reaction. This form of causal inference is called backward blocking because the causal attribution to the chicken alone retrospectively blocks the attribution to the fish. There is good evidence for the occurrence of both of these forms of retrospective revaluation in human causal learning (Van Hamme & Wasserman, 1994). The psychological processes mediating these phenomena are the subject of intense debate.

Retrospective revaluation of causal judgments (Dickinson, 1996; Shanks, 1985; Wasserman, 1996; Williams, 1994) is problematic for standard error correcting associative learning rules because they can only modify the associative strengths of cues that were present on a particular episode. Retrospective revaluation changes causal judgments about cues in light of episodes when those cues were not presented. However, modifications to the standard associative account have been made (Dickinson, 1996; Van Hamme & Wasserman, 1994). These modifications involve three assumptions. First, presentation of one cue alone (e.g., chicken) retrieves a representation of the absent cue with which it was previously paired (e.g., fish) through a within-compound association established during initial compound training (chicken–fish meal associated with an allergic reaction) in order to support learning about the absent cue. Second, the presentation or omission of the allergic reaction following the presented cue (chicken) generates a prediction error. Finally, pairing a retrieved representation of an absent cue with a prediction error engenders the opposite change in associative strength to that produced by pairing the same prediction error with a presented cue. Therefore, any prediction error that reduces the associative strength of the chicken should, by contrast, enhance the strength and hence the causal status of the absent cue (fish). Prior work has shown that prediction error signaling is engaged during retrospective revaluation and that it relates to the degree of memory updating (Corlett *et al.*, 2004). We mention retrospective revaluation here not simply because it encapsulates some of the hypothesized processes implicated in memory reconsolidation (prediction error, updating, and new learning) but also because it has been proposed as a metaphor for the therapeutic process in psychiatric illness (Lovibond, 2004). That is, although exposure therapy has been equated with Pavlovian extinction learning, the therapeutic process involves establishing new belief systems rather than the destruction of prior problematic schemas (Pally, 2005), hence the relapsing course of therapy. However, clinicians also encourage patients to generate alternative explanations for the events that provide the problematic kernel for their symptoms. By establishing a partner explanation as a reliable predictor of the salient outcome, patients retrospectively revalue the initial causal explanation (Lovibond, 2004). It remains to be determined whether the therapeutic process engages the neural circuitry of retrospective revaluation. Furthermore, preclinical studies of reconsolidation of second-order conditioning have implications for our understanding of retrospective revaluation. In second-order conditioning, an association is formed between a new cue, stimulus, or event (CS2) and a conditioned response elicited by another cue (CS1) that was previously associated with a salient outcome (US) by pairing the new cue (CS2) with the first cue (CS1)—that is, the formation of CS2−CS1−US association. If CS1 is reactivated and the animal is treated with the protein synthesis inhibitor anisomycin, which blocks reconsolidation, responding to CS1 and CS2 is subsequently attenuated. However, reactivation of CS2 followed by anisomycin only attenuates responding to CS2; CS1 remains unaffected (Debiec *et al.*, 2006). Thus, in order to be clinically effective, the exact memory that is engendering pathophysiological responses must be targeted, not simply one of its associates (although for a contradictory finding, see Tzeng *et al.*, 2012).

13.5 TIME

The time between the original memory event and the attempt to block its reconsolidation (Suzuki *et al.*, 2004) as well as the amount of time and number of times the memory is engaged (Lee *et al.*, 2006a) will also be crucial to the success of any therapeutic application. Across species, older memories are less susceptible to disruption by reconsolidation blockade. Memory strength and intensity also influence whether memories enter a labile state.

Care must be taken when engaging memories because long-lasting reactivation interventions preferentially evoke extinction learning and, hence, combining such manipulations with amnestic drugs might block the consolidation of that extinction learning and thus circumvent any clinical benefit (Lee *et al.*, 2006a). Furthermore, pathological memories might strengthen more rapidly over time because they undergo reactivations during rumination (Rubin *et al.*, 2008a, 2008b). Hence, any therapeutic intervention might need to occur nearer to the formation of a pathophysiological memory before rumination-based strengthening has occurred.

13.6 CONCLUSION

The rediscovery of memory reconsolidation and its popularity as a research concern has renewed interest in its therapeutic potential. We are optimistic about this potential, but we advise careful attention to the nuances and boundaries to the reconsolidation phenomenon during this translation process. In particular, the identification of memories to target and the method with which they are targeted will require a great deal of careful discerning and will likely vary across individuals and illnesses. As the Hippocratic oath states, "First, do no harm." The potential for memory strengthening and hence symptom worsening should be taken seriously. Nevertheless, preliminary human data are encouraging, and we await the continued translation of this curious memory effect into viable treatments.

REFERENCES

Abi-Dargham, A., Mawlawi, O., Lombardo, I., Gil, R., Martinez, D., Huang, Y., Hwang, D. R., & Laruelle, M. (2002). Prefrontal dopamine D1 receptors and working memory in schizophrenia. *Journal of Neuroscience, 22*, 3708−3719.

Adams, C. D., & Dickinson, A. (1981). Actions and habits: variations in associative representations during instrumental learning. In N. E. Spear, & R. R. Miller (Eds.), *Information Processing in Animals: Memory Mechanisms*. Hillsdale, NJ: Erlbaum.

Alberini, C. M. (2007). Reconsolidation: the samsara of memory consolidation. *Debates in Neuroscience, 1*, 17−24.

Alberini, C. M. (2011). The role of reconsolidation and the dynamic process of long-term memory formation and storage. *Frontiers in Behavioral Neuroscience, 5*, 12.

American Psychiatric Association. (2000). *Diagnostic and Statistical Manual of Mental Disorders—Text Revision*. Washington, DC: Author.

Amiaz, R., Levy, D., Vainiger, D., Grunhaus, L., & Zangen, A. (2009). Repeated high-frequency transcranial magnetic stimulation over the dorsolateral prefrontal cortex reduces cigarette craving and consumption. *Addiction, 104*, 653−660.

Bartlett, F. C. (1932). *Remembering*. Cambridge, UK: Cambridge University Press.

Bespalov, A. Y., Harich, S., Jongen-Relo, A. L., van Gaalen, M. M., & Gross, G. (2007). AMPA receptor antagonists reverse effects of extended habit training on signaled food approach responding in rats. *Psychopharmacology (Berl), 195*, 11−18.

Bouton, M. E. (2002). Context, ambiguity, and unlearning: sources of relapse after behavioral extinction. *Biological Psychiatry, 52*, 976−986.

Brunet, A., Orr, S. P., Tremblay, J., Robertson, K., Nader, K., & Pitman, R. K. (2008). Effect of post-retrieval propranolol on psychophysiologic responding during subsequent script-driven traumatic imagery in post-traumatic stress disorder. *Journal of Psychiatric Research, 42*, 503−506.

Cahill, L., Prins, B., Weber, M., & McGaugh, J. L. (1994). Beta-adrenergic activation and memory for emotional events. *Nature, 371*, 702—704.

Carroll, K. M. (1997). Integrating psychotherapy and pharmacotherapy to improve drug abuse outcomes. *Addictive Behaviors, 22*, 233—245.

Chadwick, P. D., & Lowe, C. F. (1990). Measurement and modification of delusional beliefs. *Journal of Consulting and Clinical Psychology, 58*, 225—232.

Chadwick, P. D., & Lowe, C. F. (1994). A cognitive approach to measuring and modifying delusions. *Behaviour Research and Therapy, 32*, 355—367.

Coltheart, M. (2010). The neuropsychology of delusions. *Annals of the New York Academy of Sciences, 1191*, 16—26.

Coltheart, M., Langdon, R., & McKay, R. (2011). Delusional belief. *Annual Review of Psychology, 62*, 271—279.

Corlett, P. R., Aitken, M. R., Dickinson, A., Shanks, D. R., Honey, G. D., Honey, R. A., Robbins, T. W., & Fletcher, P. C. (2004). Prediction error during retrospective revaluation of causal associations in humans: fMRI evidence in favor of an associative model of learning. *Neuron, 44*, 877—888.

Corlett, P. R., Honey, G. D., & Fletcher, P. C. (2007a). From prediction error to psychosis: ketamine as a pharmacological model of delusions. *Journal of Psychopharmacology, 21*, 238—252.

Corlett, P. R., Honey, G. D., Krystal, J. H., & Fletcher, P. C. (2011). Glutamatergic model psychoses: prediction error, learning, and inference. *Neuropsychopharmacology, 36*, 294—315.

Corlett, P. R., Krystal, J. H., Taylor, J. R., & Fletcher, P. C. (2009). Why do delusions persist? *Frontiers in Human Neuroscience, 3*, 12.

Corlett, P. R., Murray, G. K., Honey, G. D., Aitken, M. R., Shanks, D. R., Robbins, T. W., Bullmore, E. T., & Fletcher, P. C. (2007b). Disrupted prediction-error signal in psychosis: evidence for an associative account of delusions. *Brain, 130*, 2387—2400.

Corlett, P. R., Taylor, J. R., Wang, X. J., Fletcher, P. C., & Krystal, J. H. (2010). Toward a neurobiology of delusions. *Progress in Neurobiology, 92*, 345—369.

Crick, F., & Mitchison, G. (1983). The function of dream sleep. *Nature, 304*, 111—114.

Daw, N. D., Niv, Y., & Dayan, P. (2005). Uncertainty-based competition between prefrontal and dorsolateral striatal systems for behavioral control. *Nature Neuroscience, 8*, 1704—1711.

Debiec, J. (2012). Memory reconsolidation processes and posttraumatic stress disorder: promises and challenges of translational research. *Biological Psychiatry, 71*, 284—285.

Debiec, J., Doyere, V., Nader, K., & LeDoux, J. E. (2006). Directly reactivated, but not indirectly reactivated, memories undergo reconsolidation in the amygdala. *Proceedings of the National Academy of Sciences of the United States of America, 103*, 3428—3433.

Dickinson, A. (2001). The 28th Bartlett Memorial Lecture. Causal learning: an associative analysis. *Quarterly Journal of Experimental Psychology, 54*, 3—25.

Dickinson, A., & Burke, J. (1996). Within-compound associations mediate the retrospective revaluation of causality judgements. *Quarterly Journal of Experimental Psychology B, 51*, 397—416.

Donovan, E. (2010). Propranolol use in the prevention and treatment of posttraumatic stress disorder in military veterans: forgetting therapy revisited. *Perspectives in Biology and Medicine, 53*, 61—74.

Dudai, Y., & Eisenberg, M. (2004). Rites of passage of the engram: reconsolidation and the lingering consolidation hypothesis. *Neuron, 44*, 93—100.

Eichenbaum, H., & Bodkin, J. A. (2000). Belief and knowledge as distinct forms of memory. In D. L. Schacter, & E. Scarry (Eds.), *Memory, Brain and Belief*. Cambridge, MA: Harvard University Press.

Eisenhardt, D., & Menzel, R. (2007). Extinction learning, reconsolidation and the internal reinforcement hypothesis. *Neurobiology of Learning and Memory, 87*, 167—173.

Erblich, J., & Montgomery, G. H. (2012). Cue-induced cigarette cravings and smoking cessation: the role of expectancies. *Nicotine & Tobacco Research, 14*, 809—815.

Estes, W. K. (1997). Processes of memory loss, recovery, and distortion. *Psychology Review, 104*, 148–169.

Fletcher, P. C., & Frith, C. D. (2009). Perceiving is believing: a Bayesian approach to explaining the positive symptoms of schizophrenia. *Nature Reviews Neuroscience, 10*, 48–58.

Fletcher, P. C., & Henson, R. N. (2001). Frontal lobes and human memory: insights from functional neuroimaging. *Brain, 124*, 849–881.

Forcato, C., Burgos, V. L., Argibay, P. F., Molina, V. A., Pedreira, M. E., & Maldonado, H. (2007). Reconsolidation of declarative memory in humans. *Learning & Memory, 14*, 295–303.

Grace, A. A. (1991). Phasic versus tonic dopamine release and the modulation of dopamine system responsivity: a hypothesis for the etiology of schizophrenia. *Neuroscience, 41*, 1–24.

Gray, J. A., Feldon, J., Rawlins, J. N. P., Hemsley, D., & Smith, A. D. (1991). The neuropsychology of schizophrenia. *Behavioral and Brain Sciences, 14*, 1–84.

Hagen, E. (2008). Non-bizarre delusions as strategic deception. In S. Elton, & P. O'Higgins (Eds.), *Medicine and Evolution: Current Applications, Future Prospect*. Boca Raton, FL: CRC Press.

Halligan, P. W., & David, A. S. (2001). Cognitive neuropsychiatry: towards a scientific psychopathology. *Nature Reviews Neuroscience, 2*, 209–215.

Hamamura, T., & Harada, T. (2007). Unique pharmacological profile of aripiprazole as the phasic component buster. *Psychopharmacology (Berl), 191*, 741–743.

Havermans, R. C., & Jansen, A. T. (2003). Increasing the efficacy of cue exposure treatment in preventing relapse of addictive behavior. *Addictive Behaviors, 28*, 989–994.

Hemsley, D. R. (1994). Perceptual and cognitive abnormalities as the bases for schizophrenic symptoms. In A. S. David, & J. C. Cutting (Eds.), *The Neuropsychology of Schizophrenia* (pp. 97–118). Hillsdale, NJ: Erlbaum.

Hitchcott, P. K., Quinn, J. J., & Taylor, J. R. (2007). Bidirectional modulation of goal-directed actions by prefrontal cortical dopamine. *Cerebral Cortex, 17*, 2820–2827.

Hoffman, R. E. (2007). A social deafferentation hypothesis for induction of active schizophrenia. *Schizophrenia Bulletin, 33*, 1066–1070.

Hogarth, L., Dickinson, A., & Duka, T. (2003). Discriminative stimuli that control instrumental tobacco-seeking by human smokers also command selective attention. *Psychopharmacology (Berl), 168*, 435–445.

Howes, O. D., Montgomery, A. J., Asselin, M. C., Murray, R. M., Valli, I., Tabraham, P., Bramon-Bosch, E., & Grasby, P. M. (2009). Elevated striatal dopamine function linked to prodromal signs of schizophrenia. *Archives of General Psychiatry, 66*, 13–20.

Hyman, S. E., Malenka, R. C., & Nestler, E. J. (2006). Neural mechanisms of addiction: the role of reward-related learning and memory. *Annual Review of Neuroscience, 29*, 565–598.

Inda, M. C., Muravieva, E. V., & Alberini, C. M. (2011). Memory retrieval and the passage of time: from reconsolidation and strengthening to extinction. *Journal of Neuroscience, 31*, 1635–1643.

Jaspers, K. (1963). *General Psychopathology*. Manchester, UK: Manchester University Press.

Kapur, S. (2003). Psychosis as a state of aberrant salience: a framework linking biology, phenomenology, and pharmacology in schizophrenia. *American Journal of Psychiatry, 160*, 13–23.

Kegeles, L. S., Abi-Dargham, A., Zea-Ponce, Y., Rodenhiser-Hill, J., Mann, J. J., Van Heertum, R. L., & Laruelle, M. (2000). Modulation of amphetamine-induced striatal dopamine release by ketamine in humans: implications for schizophrenia. *Biological Psychiatry, 48*, 627–640.

Kindt, M., Soeter, M., & Vervliet, B. (2009). Beyond extinction: erasing human fear responses and preventing the return of fear. *Nature Neuroscience, 12*, 256–258.

Kolb, L. C. (1993). A perspective and future dreams of PTSD as a psychosomatic disorder. *Psychosomatic Medicine, 55*, 424–425.

Kolber, A. (2008). Freedom of memory today. *Neuroethics, 1,* 145–148.

Laruelle, M., Abi-Dargham, A., Gil, R., Kegeles, L., & Innis, R. (1999). Increased dopamine transmission in schizophrenia: relationship to illness phases. *Biological Psychiatry, 46,* 56–72.

Lee, J. L. (2008). Memory reconsolidation mediates the strengthening of memories by additional learning. *Nature Neuroscience, 11,* 1264–1266.

Lee, J. L., Everitt, B. J., & Thomas, K. L. (2004). Independent cellular processes for hippocampal memory consolidation and reconsolidation. *Science, 304,* 839–843.

Lee, J. L., Milton, A. L., & Everitt, B. J. (2006a). Reconsolidation and extinction of conditioned fear: inhibition and potentiation. *Journal of Neuroscience, 26,* 10051–10056.

Lee, J. L., Milton, A. L., & Everitt, B. J. (2006b). Cue-induced cocaine seeking and relapse are reduced by disruption of drug memory reconsolidation. *Journal of Neuroscience, 26,* 5881–5887.

Li, Z., Ichikawa, J., Dai, J., & Meltzer, H. Y. (2004). Aripiprazole, a novel antipsychotic drug, preferentially increases dopamine release in the prefrontal cortex and hippocampus in rat brain. *European Journal of Pharmacology, 493,* 75–83.

Liao, S. M., & Sandberg, A. (2008). The normativity of memory modification. *Neuroethics, 1,* 85–99.

Lovibond, P. F. (2004). Cognitive processes in extinction. *Learning & Memory, 11,* 495–500.

Maher, B. A. (1974). Delusional thinking and perceptual disorder. *Journal of Individual Psychology, 30,* 98–113.

Mamo, D., Graff, A., Mizrahi, R., Shammi, C. M., Romeyer, F., & Kapur, S. (2007). Differential effects of aripiprazole on D(2), 5-HT(2), and 5-HT(1A) receptor occupancy in patients with schizophrenia: a triple tracer PET study. *American Journal of Psychiatry, 164,* 1411–1417.

McGaugh, J. L. (1966). Time-dependent processes in memory storage. *Science, 153,* 1351–1358.

McKay, R., Langdon, R., & Coltheart, M. (2007). Models of misbelief: integrating motivational and deficit theories of delusions. *Consciousness & Cognition, 16,* 932–941.

Milton, A. L., Lee, J. L., & Everitt, B. J. (2008). Reconsolidation of appetitive memories for both natural and drug reinforcement is dependent on β-adrenergic receptors. *Learning & Memory, 15,* 88–92.

Milton, F., Patwa, V. K., & Hafner, R. J. (1978). Confrontation vs. belief modification in persistently deluded patients. *British Journal of Medical Psychology, 51,* 127–130.

Misanin, J. R., Miller, R. R., & Lewis, D. J. (1968). Retrograde amnesia produced by electroconvulsive shock after reactivation of a consolidated memory trace. *Science, 160,* 554–555.

Monfils, M. H., Cowansage, K. K., Klann, E., & LeDoux, J. E. (2009). Extinction–reconsolidation boundaries: key to persistent attenuation of fear memories. *Science, 324,* 951–955.

Moussawi, K., Pacchioni, A., Moran, M., Olive, M. F., Gass, J. T., Lavin, A., & Kalivas, P. W. (2009). *N*-acetylcysteine reverses cocaine-induced metaplasticity. *Nature Neuroscience, 12,* 182–189.

Nader, K., Schafe, G. E., & LeDoux, J. E. (2000). Fear memories require protein synthesis in the amygdala for reconsolidation after retrieval. *Nature, 406,* 722–726.

Nelson, A., & Killcross, S. (2006). Amphetamine exposure enhances habit formation. *Journal of Neuroscience, 26,* 3805–3812.

Osan, R., Tort, A. B., & Amaral, O. B. (2011). A mismatch-based model for memory reconsolidation and extinction in attractor networks. *PLoS ONE, 6,* e23113.

Osuch, E. A., Benson, B. E., Luckenbaugh, D. A., Geraci, M., Post, R. M., & McCann, U. (2009). Repetitive TMS combined with exposure therapy for PTSD: a preliminary study. *Journal of Anxiety Disorders, 23,* 54–59.

Otto, M. W. (2000). Stories and metaphors in cognitive-behavior therapy. *Cognitive and Behavioral Practice, 7,* 166–172.

Otto, M. W., O'Cleirigh, C. M., & Pollack, M. H. (2007). Attending to emotional cues for drug abuse: bridging the gap between clinic and home behaviors. *Science & Practice Perspectives, 3*, 48–56.

Ozubko, J. D., & Fugelsang, J. (2011). Remembering makes evidence compelling: retrieval from memory can give rise to the illusion of truth. *Journal of Experimental Psychology: Learning, Memory, and Cognition, 37*, 270–276.

Pally, R. (2005). Non-conscious prediction and a role for consciousness in correcting prediction errors. *Cortex, 41*, 643–662, discussion 731–734.

Pedreira, M. E., Perez-Cuesta, L. M., & Maldonado, H. (2004). Mismatch between what is expected and what actually occurs triggers memory reconsolidation or extinction. *Learning & Memory, 11*, 579–585.

Pitman, R. K., Sanders, K. M., Zusman, R. M., Healy, A. R., Cheema, F., Lasko, N. B., Cahill, L., & Orr, S. P. (2002). Pilot study of secondary prevention of posttraumatic stress disorder with propranolol. *Biological Psychiatry, 51*, 189–192.

President's Council on Bioethics. (2003). *Beyond Therapy: Biotechnology and the Pursuit of Happiness*. New York: HarperCollins.

Przybyslawski, J., & Sara, S. J. (1997). Reconsolidation of memory after its reactivation. *Behavioural Brain Research, 84*, 241–246.

Quirk, G. J., Pare, D., Richardson, R., Herry, C., Monfils, M. H., Schiller, D., & Vicentic, A. (2010). Erasing fear memories with extinction training. *Journal of Neuroscience, 30*, 14993–14997.

Rasch, B., & Born, J. (2007). Maintaining memories by reactivation. *Current Opinion in Neurobiology, 17*, 698–703.

Rescorla, R. A., & Wagner, A. R. (1972). A theory of Pavlovian conditioning: variations in the effectiveness of reinforcement and non-reinforcement. In A. H. Black, & W. F. Prokasy (Eds.), *Classical Conditioning II: Current Research and Theory*. New York: Appleton-Century-Crofts.

Ribot, T. (1882). *Diseases of Memory: An Essay in the Positive Psychology*. New York: Appleton.

Riccio, D. C., Millin, P. M., & Bogart, A. R. (2006). Reconsolidation: a brief history, a retrieval view, and some recent issues. *Learning & Memory, 13*, 536–544.

Robinson, T. E., & Berridge, K. C. (2001). Incentive-sensitization and addiction. *Addiction, 96*, 103–114.

Rossi, S., Cappa, S. F., Ulivelli, M., De Capua, A., Bartalini, S., & Rossini, P. M. (2006). rTMS for PTSD: induced merciful oblivion or elimination of abnormal hypermnesia? *Behavioural Neurology, 17*, 195–199.

Rubin, D. C., Berntsen, D., & Bohni, M. K. (2008a). A memory-based model of posttraumatic stress disorder: evaluating basic assumptions underlying the PTSD diagnosis. *Psychological Review, 115*, 985–1011.

Rubin, D. C., Boals, A., & Berntsen, D. (2008b). Memory in posttraumatic stress disorder: properties of voluntary and involuntary, traumatic and nontraumatic autobiographical memories in people with and without posttraumatic stress disorder symptoms. *Journal of Experimental Psychology: General, 137*, 591–614.

Rubin, R. D. (1976). Clinical use of retrograde amnesia produced by electroconvulsive shock: a conditioning hypothesis. *Canadian Psychiatric Association Journal, 21*, 87–90.

Russell, W. R., & Nathan, P. W. (1946). Traumatic amnesia. *Brain, 69*, 280–300.

Schiller, D., Monfils, M. H., Raio, C. M., Johnson, D. C., LeDoux, J. E., & Phelps, E. A. (2010). Preventing the return of fear in humans using reconsolidation update mechanisms. *Nature, 463*, 49–53.

Schultz, W. (1998). Predictive reward signal of dopamine neurons. *Journal of Neurophysiology, 80*, 1–27.

Schultz, W., Dayan, P., & Montague, P. R. (1997). A neural substrate of prediction and reward. *Science, 275*, 1593–1599.

Schultz, W., & Dickinson, A. (2000). Neuronal coding of prediction errors. *Annual Review of Neuroscience, 23*, 473–500.

Schwabe, L., Hoffken, O., Tegenthoff, M., & Wolf, O. T. (2011). Preventing the stress-induced shift from goal-directed to habit action with a beta-adrenergic antagonist. *Journal of Neuroscience, 31*, 17317–17325.

Schwabe, L., & Wolf, O. T. (2009). Stress prompts habit behavior in humans. *Journal of Neuroscience, 29*, 7191–7198.

Shanks, D. R. (1985). Forward and backward blocking of causality judgments. *Quarterly Journal of Experimental Psychology B, 37*, 1–21.

Simpson, J., & Done, D. J. (2002). Elasticity and confabulation in schizophrenic delusions. *Psychological Medicine, 32*, 451–458.

Stanton, B., & David, A. (2000). First-person accounts of delusions. *Psychiatric Bulletin, 24*, 333–336.

Stickgold, R., & Walker, M. P. (2007). Sleep-dependent memory consolidation and reconsolidation. *Sleep Medicine, 8*, 331–343.

Suzuki, A., Josselyn, S. A., Frankland, P. W., Masushige, S., Silva, A. J., & Kida, S. (2004). Memory reconsolidation and extinction have distinct temporal and biochemical signatures. *Journal of Neuroscience, 24*, 4787–4795.

Taylor, J. R., Olausson, P., Quinn, J. J., & Torregrossa, M. M. (2009). Targeting extinction and reconsolidation mechanisms to combat the impact of drug cues on addiction. *Neuropharmacology, 56*(Suppl. 1), 186–195.

Tronson, N. C., & Taylor, J. R. (2007). Molecular mechanisms of memory reconsolidation. *Nature Reviews Neuroscience, 8*, 262–275.

Tzeng, W. Y., Chang, W. T., Chuang, J. Y., Lin, K. Y., Cherng, C. G., & Yu, L. (2012). Disruption of memory reconsolidation impairs storage of other, non-reactivated memory. *Neurobiology of Learning and Memory, 97*, 241–249.

Vaiva, G., Ducrocq, F., Jezequel, K., Averland, B., Lestavel, P., Brunet, A., & Marmar, C. R. (2003). Immediate treatment with propranolol decreases posttraumatic stress disorder two months after trauma. *Biological Psychiatry, 54*, 947–949.

Van Hamme, L. J., & Wasserman, E. A. (1994). Cue competition in causality judgments: the role of nonpresentation of compound stimulus elements. *Learning and Motivation, 25*, 127–151.

Wasserman, E. A., Kao, S. F., Van Hamme, L. J., Katagiri, M., & Young, M. E. (1996). *Causation and Association*. London: Academic Press.

Wickens, J. R., Horvitz, J. C., Costa, R. M., & Killcross, S. (2007). Dopaminergic mechanisms in actions and habits. *Journal of Neuroscience, 27*, 8181–8183.

Williams, D. A., Sagness, K. E., & McPhee, J. E. (1994). Configural and elemental strategies in predictive learning. *Journal of Experimental Psychology: Learning, Memory and Cognition, 20*, 694–709.

Yarnell, P. R., & Lynch, S. (1973). The "ding": amnestic states in football trauma. *Neurology, 23*, 196–197.

Chapter | fourteen

Memory Reconsolidation, Trace Reassociation and the Freudian Unconscious

Cristina M. Alberini[*], Francois Ansermet[†],
Pierre Magistretti[‡,1]

[*] *New York University, New York, New York*
[†] *University of Geneva, Geneva, Switzerland*
[‡] *University of Lausanne, Lausanne, Switzerland; EPFL, Lausanne, Switzerland;*
and KAUST, Thuwal, Kingdom of Saudi Arabia

Memory is a fundamental biological function; we need to have long-term memories to find the best food and sex and to be safe from danger. Memories also shape our identity. We could say that we are who we are because of the conscious experience of thinking, the present physical and psychical state and our memories of the past. As Augustine (Confessions, Book 11, Chapter 20) said,

> *There is nothing like future and past…. There is only the presence of the past, the presence of the presence, and the presence of the future. These three I see in the soul, but I cannot see them independent of it: Present is the memory of the past, present is the perception of the presence, and present is the expectation of the future.*

Why do we have memories? To retain and progressively modify our behavior under the impact of experience. Memory is indispensable in all behavior, making it at once consistent and modifiable. Thus, memory seems the critical function designed to replay the past so that it can integrate selected aspects of it into present behavior. Often, however, our behavior does not act in the best or healthiest mode. In certain cases, it may become mildly or even severely pathological, as in the case of mental malfunctioning and disorders such as anxiety, depression,

---

[1] The authors contributed equally to this chapter and are listed in alphabetical order.

293

Memory Reconsolidation. http://dx.doi.org/10.1016/B978-0-12-386892-3.00014-7

obsession, and compulsion. The mechanisms underlying these psychopathologies are still in large part elusive to our scientific understanding. The impact that mental health disorders have on our society in the United States and throughout the world has long been underestimated. Data collected by the massive Global Burden of Diseases Study (2009) conducted by the World Health Organization, the World Bank, and Harvard University reveal that mental illness, including suicide, accounts for more than 20% of the burden of disease in established market economies, such as the United States. This is more than the disease burden caused by all types of cancers.

For many mental health pathologies, "talking" therapies, in which the patient re-evokes memories and experiences and is guided toward new perceptions and reprocessing of the past, are recommended, especially for the treatment of stress, mood, and anxiety disorders. These types of therapies have their roots in psychoanalysis.

Psychoanalysis has undoubtedly had a profound influence on many aspects of 21st-century culture. As a general theory of individual human behavior, psychoanalytic hypotheses enrich and are enriched by the study of the biological and social sciences, behavior, history, philosophy, art, and literature. As a developmental theory, psychoanalysis contributes to child psychology, education, and family studies. In mental health, it is the basis of all other dynamic approaches to therapy. Although during the past century psychoanalysis has undergone numerous theoretical modifications, there has been, unfortunately, very little rigorous validating research to prove the basic assumptions of psychoanalytic theories. Nevertheless, the insights or theories of psychoanalysis constitute the foundation of most psychotherapeutic approaches employed in general psychiatric practice, in child psychiatry, and in individual, family, and group therapies.

The main goal of psychoanalysis is the examination of the complex relationship between body, brain, and mind and the comprehensive understanding of the role of emotions in health as well as in medical illness. It is centered on the observation that individuals are often unaware or "unconscious" of many of the factors that determine their emotions and behavior. Freud was the preeminent pioneer in understanding the importance of the unconscious. Through his extensive work with patients and his theoretic elaboration, he provided evidence that factors which influence thought and action exist outside of awareness, that unconscious conflicts play a part in determining both normal and abnormal behavior, and that the unconscious past shapes the present.

What is the unconscious process that according to Freud controls the individual behaviors and being? How is it formed, and how is it that through recollection, memory reactivation, and memory updating psychopathologies can be alleviated?

14.1 DIFFERENT TYPES OF UNCONSCIOUS PROCESSES

To begin to address the previous questions, it is important that we first clarify that the unconscious according to Freud (Freudian unconscious) is distinct from other nonconscious processes of the brain and mind, such as the cognitive unconscious.

The cognitive and the Freudian unconscious (FU) refer to distinct processes and are connected merely by the use of the word "unconscious." Indeed, the notion of mental processes that do not reach consciousness has been entertained by a variety of psychological theories (Gazzaniga, Ivry, & Mangun, 2008). Recent neurobiological studies, particularly with neuroimaging approaches, have provided evidence for the existence of unconscious neural processing (Hassin, Uleman, & Bargh, 2005). The type of unconscious processes that were tested in these studies, and that have been dubbed the "cognitive unconscious" (CU) (Kihlstrom, 1987), comprised phenomena such as subliminal perception (Kouider & Dehaene, 2007) and other mechanisms of perception and information processing (Driver & Vuilleumier, 2001; Vuilleumier & Pourtois, 2007) including blindsight (Cowey & Stoerig, 1991; Weiskrantz, 1996), which do not lead to a conscious experience (Dehaene, Changeux, Naccache, Sackur, & Sergent, 2006). These phenomena are operated by input—output mechanisms that are common with those that underlie conscious phenomena (Lau & Passingham, 2007; Rees, 2007; Snodgrass & Shevrin, 2006). However, this type of unconscious does not correspond to what the psychoanalytical theory has postulated on the basis of its clinical practice and theoretical elaborations.

The FU refers to the ensemble of feelings, thoughts, urges, and memories that, outside of consciousness, influence our behavior and experiences. The Freudian hypothesis of the existence of unconscious processes has emerged from the clinical perspective provided by the analysis of dreams (Freud, 1900/1953), parapraxis, slip of the tongue/pen, and neurotic symptoms (Freud, 1915b/1957, pp. 186—189), and the FU operates according to principles that are distinct from those that characterize conscious processes or the CU. A first approach to define the principles of FU functions was based on the analysis of the mental operations of dreaming (Freud, 1915b/1957), during paradoxical sleep (Hobson & Pace-Schott, 2002; Mancia, 2004; Nielsen, 2000; Takeuchi, Miyasita, Inugami, & Yamamoto, 2001). The mental events that emerge in this state are devoid of temporal and spatial dimensions; for example, events can occur simultaneously in different locations and times without any apparent contradiction (Freud, 1901/1960). In the FU, like in dreams, emotional contents can be associated with one another without any logical connection; furthermore, contents can be substituted and displaced (Freud, 1900/1953, pp. 277—508). Although the existence of the FU has nourished an extensive theoretical and clinical psychoanalytical literature, and provided heuristically valid elaborations concerning the determinants of mental life such as drives and repression mechanisms, to date there is no neurobiological explanation for its existence. Some insightful reflections have been proposed (Kandel, 1998, 1999; Shulman & Reiser, 2004), as illustrated by the emergence of the new discipline of neuropsychoanalysis (Solms, 2004). To quote Freud (1920/1955),

The deficiencies in our description would probably vanish if we were already in a position to replace the psychological terms by physiological or chemical ones.... Biology is truly a land of unlimited possibilities. We may expect it to give us the most surprising information and we cannot guess what answers it will return to the questions we have put to it. (p. 60)

Contemporary neuroscience appears to be ready to begin addressing the biological bases of the FU.

Freud distinguished two types of nonconscious mental processes: the primary process, which corresponds to what we defined as FU, and the secondary process, which operates according to logical processes that are common to conscious processes.

Furthermore, according to Freud, at least three mechanisms can be responsible for the production of unconscious processes. The first one can be related to the direct unconscious inscription of traces following a given experience. This type of unconscious can, for example, be produced by subliminal perceptual processing leading to the establishment of traces that do not reach consciousness (Del Cul, Baillet, & Dehaene, 2007). This type of unconscious may be akin to the CU and could be considered as being part of what Freud defined as the latent unconscious or preconscious (Freud, 1923/1961, p. 15). He also called it "*unbemerkt*," meaning "not noticed" (i.e., by consciousness), hence not reaching consciousness (Freud, 1923/1961, p. 16) (Figure 14.1). This allowed him to distinguish this latent unconscious/preconscious (*unbemerkt*, Figure 14.1) from what he called "*unbewusst*," which we now refer to as FU (Figure 14.1).

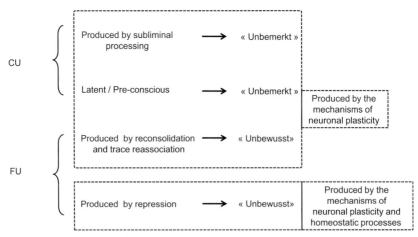

FIGURE 14.1 Summary of the key concepts differentiating the cognitive unconscious (CU) from the Freudian unconscious (FU). *Unbemerkt*, not noticed; *Unbewusst*, not known.

Freud's theory proposed two mechanisms to explain the *unbewusst* (Figure 14.1): one formed by the mechanism of repression and another one for which he had no explanation. Although the former mechanism still represents the historical definition of the unconscious for psychoanalytical theory, Freud hinted that not all unconscious processes could be accounted for by the mechanism of repression (Freud, 1915b/1957, p. 166); he discussed other mechanisms in particular in *Ego and Id* (Freud, 1923/1961, p. 18). Specifically, he proposed the possible existence of "the third unconscious," considering that it would be an addition to the "preconscious" (*unbemerkt*) and to the one formed by repression (*unbewusst*), for which he could not suggest a mechanism nor could he assess its importance in the overall economy of the unconscious (Freud, 1923/1961, pp. 13—18).

In this chapter, we propose a model that may explain the FU, particularly the "third unconscious," based on three fundamental principles of neuroscience and physiology: synaptic plasticity, trace reassociation, and homeostatic processes. On the basis of this model, we speculate that the dynamic processes of memory formation, retrieval, and updating critically contribute to the formation of FU, which includes its psychopathologies as well as their psychoanalytic treatment.

14.2 MEMORY TRACES ACCORDING TO FREUD

At the end of the 1800s and beginning of the 1900s, Freud elaborated on the process of memory and memory traces in numerous writings. Starting with his early *Studies on Hysteria* (Breuer & Freud, 1895/1955), in which he described and discussed the processes of memory and trauma, Freud recognized the existence of a complex network of associations that creates our memories and therefore our identity, which obviously includes our pathologies. Freud was inspired by his early work *On Aphasia* (Freud, 1891/1953), in which he emphasized that the periphery of the body is represented topographically in the brain, and then extended this idea to a complex picture of the formation of words, objects, and their associations. He therefore created a model derived from the spatial and topographical arrangement of the nervous system, which he used as one of the organizing frameworks of psychoanalytic theory. This schematic, spatial arrangement of the mental apparatus was seen as a hierarchical structure of agencies, functions, and organizations that all derived from the combination of simple connections and processes of transference, translation, and transformation.

Freud believed that mnemic traces (*Erinnerungsspur*) are unconscious, whereas the memories of these traces (*Erinnerungen*) are conscious and, based on a hierarchical organization, proposed that the psychical material of hysteric cases is organized by collections of memories or "themes." Each theme is organized in three strata. First, it is arranged linearly as a bundle of documents. Second, it is stratified concentrically around a pathogenic nucleus, which, as Freud writes, "consists of those recollections (of experiences or trains of thoughts) in which the traumatic moment peaked or the pathogenic idea found his purest form." On a third order, according to thought content, there is a nonlinear organization that "contains nodal points at which two or more treads meet, then continue as a single group … several treads either running independently or in places connected by side-paths—flow into the nucleus. In other words often … a symptom … is multiply determined or over-determined" (Breuer & Freud, 1895/1955, pp. 288—290). Based on such concentrically organized, stratified themes or memories, Freud's topographical and spatial models of mental organization emerged.

Hence, Freud's hypothesis of memory includes the idea of networks of associations and representations, part of which become at times active (perhaps the equivalent of conscious) and part that remain inactive (or unconscious). According to Freud, an important aspect of memory is the passage of time because he hypothesized that a sequence of associations that are nonlinearly connected is formed over time and that memories are contained in multiple representations.

Similarly, in *The Aetiology of Hysteria*, Freud (1896/1962) described memories as chains of associations with convergences and divergences through nodal points like a complex network. In addition, in a letter to Fliess, Freud (1950/1985) described memory as a process of continuous elaboration:

> *Our psychic mechanism has come into being by a process of stratification: the material present in the form of memory traces being subjected from time to time to a rearrangement in accordance to fresh circumstances—to a retranscription.… Memory is present not once but several times over.… Successive registrations represents the psychic achievements of successive epochs of life…. At the boundary between two such epochs a translation of the psychic material must take place. (In psychoneuroses such translation does not take place in case of some material.)*

Interestingly, he then added, "A failure of translation—this is what is known clinically as 'repression.' The motive for it is always a release of the unpleasure that would be generated by the translation."

Here, Freud introduced the idea that memories are permanent modifications of the central nervous system but remain in a dynamic state and are continuously updated, unless they are pathogenic. According to his view, pathogenic memories that remain in the unconscious—as might be the case for highly traumatic memories, which lead to mental disorders such as post-traumatic stress disorder (PTSD) and conversion or dissociative disorders (hysteria)—do not change over time (no transcription or retranscription), most likely because of repression. This may perhaps be translated into neuroscientific terms as follows: These memories are not retrieved and therefore not reactivated, perhaps because of a blockade due to repression exerted on the retrieval process per se. Hence, they cannot undergo either reconsolidation or updating.

In the *Project for a Scientific Psychology*, Freud (1950/1966) also elaborated on the cellular mechanisms of memories and proposes that the mnemic trace, a metapsychological construct, results from the facilitation of neurons and the involvement of a differential system of inscription of perceptions so that consciousness and perception are physically distinct from the unconscious and the lasting quality of mnemic traces. He gave a detailed description of what he hypothesized to be the cellular substrates of memory. In Chapter 3 of the *Project*, Freud wrote,

> *We assume that these neurons (the ψ neurons) are permanently altered by the flux of excitation; or rather, if we introduce the contact barrier theory, that their contact barriers are in a state of permanent alteration…. This alteration must depend on the fact that the contact barriers become more capable of conduction and less impermeable, that is, more similar to those of the φ system. We shall describe this situation of the contact barriers as their degree of facilitation. We may therefore state that memory is represented by facilitations that exist between the ψ neurons. (p. 299)*

This is a surprisingly accurate definition of what was discovered in the 1970s and called long-term potentiation, which is now believed to represent the cellular mechanisms underlying memory formation (Bliss & Collingridge, 1993).

From the many letters to Wilhelm Fliess, we know that Freud was interested in understanding the neurobiological bases of psychological functions. However, his enthusiasm turned into frustration because the neuroscience of the late 19th century and early 20th century was too rudimentary to allow for a test of his hypotheses. He decided not to finish the book and even wanted the manuscript to be destroyed. The work remained unpublished until 1950, when it was translated into English with the title *Project for a Scientific Psychology* (Freud, 1950/1966). These hypotheses were not abandoned but instead reformulated in *Interpretation of Dreams* (Freud, 1900/1953), in which he wrote,

> *We may describe as a memory trace and to the function relating to it we give the name of memory…. Memory traces can only consist in permanent modifications of the elements of the system. But, as already pointed out elsewhere, there are obvious difficulties involved in supposing that one and the same system can accurately retain modifications of its elements and yet remain perpetually open to the reception of fresh occasions for modifications…. We must therefore assume that the basis of association lies in the mnemonic systems…. Our memories—not excepting those which are mostly deeply stamped in our minds—are in themselves unconscious. They can be made conscious; but there can be no doubt that they can produce all their effects while in an unconscious condition. (pp. 538–539)*

These conclusions provide important concepts concerning the definition and functioning of memories; that is, memories are built on permanent modification. However, they become active only partially at one time, and only the active parts are open to receiving and making new associations.

It is also important to remember that, as mentioned previously, in addition to the formulation of the theoretical framework of how memories exist in the psychic apparatus and how they can be supported by cellular substrates, Freud elaborated the definition and concepts of memories embedded in a context of trauma. He therefore provided a theoretical view of memories created, stored, and living in traumatic experiences. Freud elaborated on traumatic memories in *Studies on Hysteria* (Breuer & Freud, 1895/1955), in which he wrote,

> *A memory of a psychical trauma enters the great complex of associations, it comes alongside other experiences, which may contradict it, and it is subjected to rectification by other ideas.... In this way a normal person is able to bring about the disappearance of the accompanying affect through the process of association. To this we must add the general effacement of impressions, the ... forgetting.*

> *On the other hand, the memories of ... hysterical phenomena persist for a long time with astonishing freshness and ..., unlike other memories of their past lives, are not at the patient's disposal.... These memories constitute an exception in their relation to all the wearing-away processes.... These memories correspond to traumas that have not been sufficiently abreacted; ... and we find at least 2 sets of conditions under which the reaction to the trauma fails to occur: ... In the first group, ... the nature of the trauma excluded a reaction (loss of a loved person or social circumstances). The second group of conditions are determined by the psychical state in which the patient received the experiences (severely paralyzing fright, semi-hypnotic twilight state of day-dreaming, auto-hypnosis).... Both these conditions that the psychical trauma cannot be disposed. In the first group the patient is determined to forget the experience and exclude them from association; in the second group, the associative working-over fails to occur because there is no associative connection between the normal state of consciousness and the pathological ones in which the ideas made their appearance. (pp. 9–11)*

Therefore, here, in agreement with his writings to Fliess, Freud stresses that traumatic memories are incredibly strong, less flexible than other normal memories, less susceptible to forgetting, and excluded from the activation by retrieval.

14.3 MEMORY TRACES, CONSOLIDATION, AND RECONSOLIDATION ACCORDING TO NEUROSCIENCE AND POTENTIAL LINKS TO PSYCHOANALYSIS

In neuropsychological terms, a memory trace is an *engram*, a hypothetical means by which information is stored as biophysical or biochemical change in the brain (and other neural tissue) in response to external stimuli. It remains unclear which biophysical or biochemical mechanisms underlie or represent an engram. However, a great deal of experimental evidence from both humans and experimental animals throughout the past century has demonstrated that biological changes do indeed occur in the brain following new learning; these changes are required for maintaining information over time or, in other words, to store memories.

Electrophysiological studies show that newly learned information is encoded in the brain as patterns of neuronal activity (Eichenbaum, 2004). With time, this information is transformed into more persistent modifications, which seem to be engrained in molecular or structural forms such as structural modifications of existing synapses or formation of new ones (synaptic plasticity). This process of transforming the activity induced by new learning into stable, long-lasting modifications has been termed *memory consolidation* (McGaugh, 2000). An important feature of the memory consolidation process is that for a limited time after learning, the new trace is labile because it can easily be disrupted by several types of interfering events. In fact, experiments that began at approximately the end of the 1800s and beginning of the 1900s, but then increased significantly in the past 50 years, have shown that if a new memory is exposed to challenges such as brain trauma, seizure, a second learning event, or pharmacological treatments of many sorts, it fades away, and recall tests at later times show amnesia. This has been found in a multitude of types of memories and animal species including humans (Squire, Stark, & Clark, 2004). With time, however, the memory becomes increasingly stable until it is fully insensitive to disruption or consolidated. Indeed, if the interfering challenge is presented sometime after the memory is formed, no effect is seen, and the memory survives perfectly. Hence, there is an opportunity for disrupting newly formed memories immediately after they are formed and for a limited time. How long does this time window of opportunity last? The answer to this is still debated. General interfering events, such as traumas or brain lesions, suggest that memory consolidation takes a relatively long time, which although variable in different memories, can take several years in humans. On the other hand, pharmacological and molecular interferences, such as an acute blockade of *de novo* protein synthesis, disrupt memories only if applied soon after training, but they are ineffective a few hours or days later. This temporal dichotomy seems to be due to different phases of the overall consolidation process (Alberini, 2011; see also Chapter 5).

However, a number of relatively recent studies, extending previous observations first published in the 1960s, showed that memory consolidation is not based on a unique, single process of molecular consolidation, and that once stabilized against these interferences, memories can again revert to a labile state for a limited period of time if retrieved or reactivated. These reactivated memories over time once again become stable and insensitive to disruption—a process that is detailed later and that has been termed *reconsolidation* (Alberini, 2005; Alberini, Milekic, & Tronel, 2006; Dudai, 2004; Nader, 2003; Sara, 2000). The chapters of this book summarize the studies and debated questions that remain to be addressed in this fascinating field.

These findings on memory reconsolidation revolutionized the way we think about long-term memory formation, storage, recall, and stability, or actually the unstable, dynamic nature of memory traces. Knowing that memories after retrieval are fragile, changeable, and disruptable is important for many reasons. For example, in addition to gaining a better understanding of mental processes, this knowledge provides an opportunity to develop more accurate therapeutic protocols in mental health, including psychoanalysis and psychotherapy, that specifically target the intrinsic features and mechanisms of mnemonic processes.

Following the rediscovery of memory reconsolidation, a few studies went on to examine the effect of employing behavioral or the combination of behavioral and pharmacological methods for treating psychopathologies such as PTSD and addiction (Suris, Smith, Powell, & North, 2012; see Chapters 5, 10, 12, and 13).

Our intent here is to discuss the role of trace reactivation in psychoanalysis. Specifically, we elaborate on how trace reactivation is important in psychoanalytic treatment and how it may represent a model for explaining the formation and expression of unconscious processes such as those that characterize the FU.

In 1914, Freud published *Remembering, Repeating and Working-Through*, which clearly established his position on analytic technique, namely that the cathartic method had yielded to the associative method. Freud emphasized that treatment needs to involve real psychic work for the patient for whom passive hypnosis is no longer clinically effective. The goal is to remember and "to fill in gaps in memory," as Freud states, and to "overcome resistances due to repression" (Freud, 1914/1958, p. 148).

What mechanisms are targeted when the patient, in the psychoanalytic setting, goes through the process of remembering and working-through? Obviously, the work of the analyst is to facilitate the re-evoking or reactivation of memories and promote the elaboration and the filling of the gaps. However, remembering, as Freud said and as we can see now in neuroscientific terms, is not a straightforward process.

During psychoanalysis, the subject undertakes the process of becoming aware (or conscious) of the underlying sources of his or her unconscious behavior, both intellectually and emotionally, by re-experiencing them and by redirecting the emotions toward the analyst and then reprocessing them in a new mode. Thus, remembering and elaborating past memories in the new analytic setting is a key component of the psychoanalytic process, whether used to learn about the mind and its functioning or to alleviate disturbances in therapeutic processes. But how does this happen? Why is it that re-experiencing emotions and recalling the past in the new, present setting guided by the analyst allows the subject to recognize his or her unconscious patterns of behavior and ultimately change them to better deal with the realities of adult life? The answer to this question is both important and complex because it is multifaceted.

According to neuroscientific knowledge, and particularly to the emerging view that normal memories exist in a very dynamic state, we can suggest that psychoanalytic therapy and working-through critically implicate new encoding, consolidation of new traces, and reconsolidation of retrieved memories, all of which would provide the tools to fill the gaps and emotionally re-tune and redirect the personal experience. Specifically, with the rediscovery of memory reconsolidation, a great deal of enthusiasm has been directed to this memory process, and major roles for reconsolidation have been hypothesized in psychoanalysis (Bleichmar, 2010; Gorman & Roose, 2011). We note here, for the purpose of discussion, that it is debatable whether or not reconsolidation is a mechanism for memory updating outside of adding onto the same experience (see Tronel *et al.* (2005) and Chapter 5). Hence, although the discovery of reconsolidation critically shifted the way we think about the dynamic nature of long-term memory formation and storage, it is still unclear whether it is reconsolidation that plays a major role in the dynamic rewriting of memory traces or whether instead it is the formation of new memories, which therefore undergo new consolidation processes and, hence, exist in parallel to the old memories. Furthermore, as suggested by reconsolidation studies in animals and humans (see Chapters 5 and 10), the reconsolidation of declarative memories may be limited by time, thus only affecting recent and not yet consolidated memories. As such, it might not be the reconsolidation process that in the psychoanalytic process has the main role of updating memories in changing the representation of experiences. Furthermore, retrieval per se does not weaken or disrupt memories but, rather, can strengthen the memory via reconsolidation. Indeed, if no interference occurs within the time window of fragility, the memory reconsolidates and likely becomes stronger and more long-lasting (see Chapters 3, 5, and 10). On the other hand, we suggest that the new perceptions present in the psychoanalytic treatment, and importantly, the new affect and emotional state of the present while recalling the past, do indeed provide an opportunity for changing consolidated memories via new memory traces (updating) or even, in certain conditions, weakening recent memory traces by interfering with their reconsolidation (extinction or new learning during reconsolidation; see Chapters 8 and 9).

It is also possible, as discussed in Chapter 5, that the reconsolidation of emotional memories that have a more implicit rather than declarative nature may not be (or may be less) restricted by the age of the memory. If this is the case (which still needs to be proven), then reconsolidation, together with the consolidation of new traces, may play a more important role in psychoanalytic settings. This understanding will be important because we do not yet know whether unconscious memory traces are more mechanistically similar to implicit or explicit memories or whether they follow different rules. Along the same lines, another very important question that needs to be addressed, and that is relevant for discussing the role of memory stages and processes in psychoanalysis, is whether or not the memories formed during development follow similar or different rules as those formed in adulthood. Because most studies on the mechanisms of memory consolidation and reconsolidation have been carried out in adults, it is important to question whether the same knowledge applies during development. Studies on consolidation and reconsolidation during developmental stages are greatly needed.

Despite all these questions that remain to be addressed, we believe that, as mentioned previously, consolidation of new traces together with updating of old memories via consolidation, as well as reconsolidation of recent traces, may all contribute to the complex process that occurs in psychoanalytic settings. Next, we propose a mechanistic hypothesis that may explain such a process.

14.4 SYNAPTIC PLASTICITY AND TRACE REASSOCIATION: A WORKING MODEL FOR THE FREUDIAN UNCONSCIOUS

As mentioned previously, experience activates specific synaptic connections and therefore leaves a trace, or engram, in the neuronal networks through the mechanisms of synaptic plasticity (Morris *et al.*, 2003; Neves, Cooke, & Bliss, 2008). The concept of "traces" as the neural counterparts of an encoded experience is represented in Figure 14.2A. Thus, an initial experience will provide an initial pattern of activated synapses; this pattern can be reactivated during recall, upon which the trace becomes prone to modifications (Figure 14.2A) (Braitenberg & Schüz, 1998; Buzsaki & Draguhn, 2004; Fuster, 2006; Gelbard-Sagiv, Mukamel, Harel, Malach, & Fried, 2008; Sakurai, 1999; Sutherland & McNaughton, 2000). In other words, real experiences as well as imaginary events will lead to the production of a trace and therefore of a mental reality through the mechanisms of synaptic plasticity. These mechanisms are common to both CU and FU. In the following section, we propose that trace reassociation is a key mechanism that distinguishes the FU from the CU. Memory traces may only partially maintain direct relationships between experience and representations because memory is dynamic and adaptive and builds on constructions based on selective attention, selective encoding, consolidation, and editing. However, such disconnections between experiences and traces would still contribute to conscious mental processes and, if nonconscious, would occur according to the logic of the secondary process.

Let's consider the possibility that parts of the neuronal assemblies that map for a given perceptual experience (Experience 1 in Figure 14.2B) can reassociate with elements of neuronal assemblies of a different experience (Experience 2, Figure 14.2B). The mechanisms that may drive this reassociation of traces are discussed later. This reassociation of traces will lead to the establishment of a new trace, built from elements of the traces left by the original experiences, producing a novel neuronal assembly and hence a novel representation (Figure 14.2B).

The mechanism of trace reassociation will introduce a discontinuity with the original experiences. Indeed, although primary traces are in a direct relationship with the original experience, the mechanism of trace reassociation produces a new set of traces, which is no longer in a direct relationship with

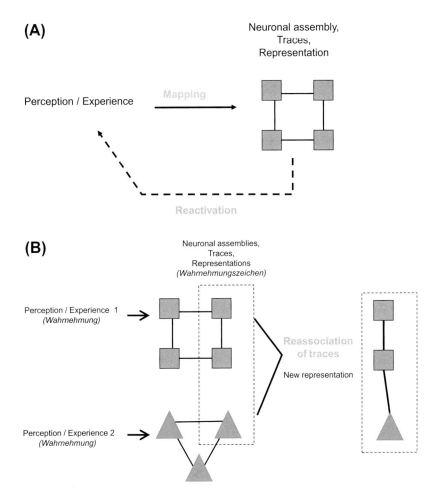

FIGURE 14.2 (A) Perceptual experiences are mapped by the mechanisms of neuronal plasticity onto neuronal assemblies (traces). Reactivation of a given pattern of neuronal assemblies will provide a representation of the initial experience. (B) Neuronal assemblies, or parts thereof, encoding different perceptual experiences (perception/experience 1 and 2) can reassociate, leading to the establishment of a new neuronal assembly and hence a new representation. The geometrical forms represent cells and the connecting lines synaptic connections that would therefore constitute the neuronal assemblies.

the original experience, although it engages parts of the original traces. We hypothesize that the mental reality is constituted of original and reassociated traces, the latter possibly contributing at least in part to the unconscious as defined by Freud. Indeed, the idea that traces (which Freud called *Wahrrneh-mungszeichen*) left by perception (*Wahrnehmung*; Figure 14.2B) can reasso-ciate to establish new traces is a notion initially proposed by Freud in 1895 in the *Project* (1950/1966) and in 1896 in a letter to Fliess (1950/1985).

This notion of trace reassociation can be revisited in light of the recent experimental evidence concerning activation and reactivation of traces during memory formation and recall that we reviewed previously. To summarize this concept briefly, newly learned information becomes a stable memory through memory consolidation. However, stabilized memories, in some circumstances, can become labile if their trace is reactivated. Retrieval results in the reactivation of the memory trace and, importantly, also mediates the formation of new associations. Hence, new as well as reactivated traces can in principle also reassociate with other reactivated traces. We speculate that this integration of traces within other reactivated and temporally dissociated or partial neuronal traces may lead to a condition in which a discontinuity in content and time may exist between the original trace and the new reassociated traces (Figure 14.2B).

From this point of view, these types of reassociated traces do not constitute a factual memory representation, even though they were initially generated by an experience. One can view these new representations constituted from the reassociation of traces as a mechanism that produces unconscious mental representations that may contribute to the establishment of the FU. However, if representations produced by trace reassociation reach consciousness, they might result in what has been defined as "memory distortions," which include false memories, intrusions, and confabulations. For example, inadequate binding of representations of a learned or reactivated event can result in memory failure, in which fragments of an episode are retrieved but there is no recollection of how or when the fragments were acquired.

To recapitulate, one can posit that an internal reality is created by the mechanisms of synaptic plasticity underlying trace inscription, reactivation, and elaboration through reassociations. A discontinuity between experience and traces may emerge through the mechanism of trace reassociation and provides a potential mechanism for the establishment of the FU. In other words, we posit that the discontinuity and synchronic reassociation of traces represent the basic mechanisms of what Freud defined as the primary process. We further conclude that the FU, although being constituted by reassociated traces, is not a factual memory but, rather, an elaboration of an internal reality that is created and maintained by long-term brain plasticity mechanisms.

14.5 HOMEOSTATIC PROCESSES AND SOMATIC STATES

We thus propose that one of the mechanisms through which a component of the FU is established is trace reassociation. As a next step, the nature of the principle(s) that determines the reassociation of traces has to be established. We posit here that the pleasure principle, which is central to Freudian theory, could be one such principle (Freud, 1920/1955, pp. 7–11). With the pleasure principle, Freud postulated that certain aspects of mental life are guided by pleasure-seeking behaviors originating from the unconscious. The principle of pleasure, which supposedly governs mental functions, was also viewed by Freud as a principle of non-displeasure. In addition, in the face of clinical phenomena that indicate a compulsive tendency to repeat unpleasant experiences, Freud recognized the "beyond the pleasure principle." Pleasure and displeasure appeared to be linked, a system of displeasure being triggered and existing in parallel with that of pleasure. Thus, the Freudian pleasure principle is essentially a non-displeasure principle, encompassing those physiological processes that maintain bodily homeostasis.

To address the physiological processes at the basis of the pleasure principle, we consider the theory of emotions as proposed by William James (1890/1950) and its renaissance in the light of contemporary neuroscientific evidence by Antonio Damasio (1994) leading to the somatic markers theory. The fundamental idea is that perceptions, particularly those charged with emotional tones, are associated with a particular somatic state (Figure 14.3). Thus, whereas a perception is emotionally neutral, its somatic state, such as increased heart rate and respiration, will determine its emotional tone, such as fear, rage, or pleasure. For example, on the basis of clinical observations, it has been suggested that the anticipation of a given somatic state is a critical determinant of decision making (Bechara, Damasio, Tranel, & Damasio, 1997). Indeed, the determining factor will be the anticipation of the least unpleasant somatic state that will result from enacting the decision process (Damasio, 1996). This process implies that mental representations are associated with representations of somatic states (Figure 14.4). Interestingly, the Freudian concept of "drive" (Freud, 1915a/1957, p. 122), which is taken as a concept at the interface between the mental and the somatic, resonates with this notion (Figure 14.4). Indeed, a given somatic state S in Figure 14.4 will be perceived through the interoceptive nervous system (Craig, 2003) and will trigger physiological regulatory mechanisms aimed at maintaining homeostasis. Similar regulatory mechanisms will also be triggered by the reactivation of its mapping (S_R in Figure 14.4). Because the somatic state S, or its mapping as S_R, is associated

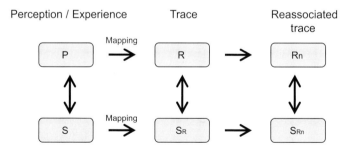

P : perception/experience
R : representation of P (neuronal assembly)
S : somatic state
S_R : representation of S (neuronal assembly)

FIGURE 14.3 Perceptual experiences (P) and their associated somatic state (S) are mapped as traces (R and S_R, respectively) by the mechanisms of synaptic plasticity. These traces can undergo the process of reassociation and yield new sets of traces (R_n and S_{rn}).

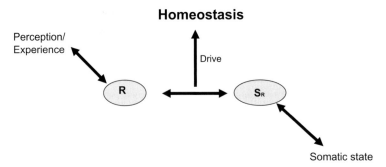

FIGURE 14.4 Representations of perceptual experiences (R) are associated with representations of somatic states (S_R). A given somatic state or the reactivation of its mapping (S and S_R, respectively) is likely to correspond to a departure from the physiological state of homeostasis. A breach in somatic homeostasis will be perceived as unpleasant because it may signal a threat to the organism's integrity. Because the somatic state, or its mapping as S_R, is associated with a representation R of a given experience, the return to a homeostatic state of the body can be operated only through the enactment of an action related to the content of the representation R. The association of R with S_R defines the notion of "drive" and results in an action whose aim is to re-establish homeostasis.

with a representation R of a given experience (Figure 14.4), the return to a homeostatic state of the body can be operated only through the enactment of an action related to the content of the representation R. The association of R with S_R defines the notion of "drive" and results in an action whose aim is to re-establish homeostasis (Figure 14.4). In Freudian theory, the aim of the "drive" is to discharge the internal excitation and to return to a previous state (Freud, 1920/1955, pp. 34–43). Thus, in our view, the Freudian notion of "drive" represents at the level of the FU a parallel with the notion of "decision" taken from a cognitive perspective. Indeed, the anticipation of pleasure and unpleasure as defined in the somatic markers theory (Damasio, 1996) provides a basis to appraise the pleasure principle of Freudian theory (Freud, 1920/1955).

The question of the pleasure principle is intimately related to the psychoanalytic concept of repression. In the Freudian theory, the aim of repression is to prevent unpleasure by removing unwanted, unpleasant representations from consciousness. According to Freud, repression provides one of the mechanisms for the generation of the unconscious (Freud, 1915b/1957; Freud, 1915c/1957, pp. 146–158; Freud, 1923/1961, pp. 13–18). A role of the dorsolateral prefrontal cortex in voluntary suppression of unwanted memories has been proposed (Anderson et al., 2004). Whether this suggestion is relevant to unconscious repression as postulated by Freud remains to be demonstrated.

14.6 THREE DISTINCT MECHANISMS OF THE FU

Based on our previous discussion, we propose that the unconscious (*unbewusst*) that could not be explained by mechanisms of repression in Freudian terms (third unconscious; Figure 14.4) could be produced by the reassociation of traces. As we have seen, representations of experiences are associated with representations of particular somatic states. Through the process of trace re-arrangement, traces encoding both the experience and the associated somatic state become changeable, creating a potential for reassociation. Anticipation of the least unpleasant somatic state will be a key determinant of the nature of the reassociation. Thus, the pleasure principle and its homeostatic function may play a major role in the process of trace reassociation and may contribute to one of the mechanisms for the establishment of the FU.

Through the mechanism of trace reassociation, new representations are created that, although integrating elements of the original experience, are distinct from the original representation. As previously discussed, through this process, a discontinuity between experience and its inscription within a trace network is created that might form one of the basic mechanisms for the FU. This implies that the FU, or at least the component generated by trace reassociation, is not a pure memory trace. Furthermore, the possibility to associate parts of traces left by distinct experiences and to integrate them into a new and unique one (Figure 14.1B) could be viewed as a mechanism to create what Freud described as the process of condensation. According to the Freudian theory, condensation is a process through which a unique representation embeds several associative chains (Freud, 1923/1961, p. 18). Freud viewed this process as the basis of the mental activity operating during dreaming (dream-work) and other manifestations of the unconscious. Typically, in condensation, multiple dream-thoughts are combined into a single element of the manifest dream; this would explain how people and places tend to meld into composite figures in our dreams (Freud, 1900/1953, pp. 279−304). Another mechanism discussed by Freud is displacement; in psychoanalytical terms, the "intensity" associated with a representation is displaced onto another (Freud, 1900/1953, pp. 305−309). A typical example is provided by an unjustified fear (phobia) of neutral objects or situations, such as phobias of harmless animals or of confined spaces. In our model, we propose that a somatic state associated with a given representation can be displaced and associated with another representation through the mechanisms of trace reassociation. This could thus lead to associations that have not been experienced and therefore are part of the FU.

A combined analysis of the Freudian theory and contemporary neuroscience, focused on two cardinal physiological mechanisms—namely synaptic plasticity underlying trace reassociation and homeostatic processes related to somatic states—provides a heuristic within which to identify different kinds of unconscious processes (Ansermet & Magistretti, 2007): (1) the CU, (2) the unconscious produced by repression, and (3) the unconscious resulting from trace reassociation and discontinuity. The proposed classification may provide a framework to orient clinical work. Indeed, clinical interventions should aim at bringing to consciousness the latent form of unconscious, promote the interpretation of the unconscious produced by repression, and use the potential for change offered by the unconscious resulting from trace reassociation.

ACKNOWLEDGMENTS

This work was supported by grants from the National Institute of Mental Health (R01 MH074736, R01 MH065635), National Institute of Drugs of Abuse (R21 CEBRA DA017672), and the Hirschl, NARSAD, and Philoctetes Foundations to Cristina M. Alberini. The authors are grateful to the Agalma Foundation in Geneva for providing support for studies on the relationship between neuroscience and psychoanalysis. We also thank all the members of the Alberini laboratory for their invaluable contributions to the work discussed in this chapter and for their helpful feedback on the manuscript.

REFERENCES

Alberini, C. M. (2005). Mechanisms of memory stabilization: are consolidation and reconsolidation similar or distinct processes? *Trends in Neurosciences, 28*(1), 51–56.

Alberini, C. M. (2011). The role of reconsolidation and the dynamic process of long-term memory formation and storage. *Frontiers in Behavioral Neuroscience, 5*(12). http://dx.doi.org/10.3389/fnbeh.2011.00012.

Alberini, C. M., Milekic, M. H., & Tronel, S. (2006). Mechanisms of memory stabilization and de-stabilization. *Cellular and Molecular Life Sciences, 63*(9), 999–1008.

Anderson, M. C., Ochsner, K. N., Kuhl, B., Cooper, J., Robertson, E., Gabrieli, S. W., et al. (2004). Neural systems underlying the suppression of unwanted memories. *Science, 303*(5655), 232–235.

Ansermet, F., & Magistretti, P. (2007). *Biology of Freedom: Neural Plasticity, Experience and the Unconscious*. New York: Other Press.

Bechara, A., Damasio, H., Tranel, D., & Damasio, A. R. (1997). Deciding advantageously before knowing the advantageous strategy. *Science, 275*(5304), 1293–1295.

Bleichmar, H. (2010). On: memory in a labile state: therapeutic application. *International Journal of Psychoanalysis, 91*(6), 1524–1526.

Bliss, T. V., & Collingridge, G. L. (1993). A synaptic model of memory: long-term potentiation in the hippocampus. *Nature, 361*(6407), 31–39.

Braitenberg, V., & Schüz, A. (1998). *Cortex: Statistics and Geometry of Neural Connectivity*. Berlin: Springer.

Breuer, J., & Freud, S. (1955). Studies on hysteria. In J. Strachey (Ed.), *The Standard Edition of the Complete Psychological Works of Sigmund Freud*, Vol. II. London: Hogarth Press. (Original work published 1895).

Buzsaki, G., & Draguhn, A. (2004). Neuronal oscillations in cortical networks. *Science, 304*(5679), 1926–1929.

Cowey, A., & Stoerig, P. (1991). The neurobiology of blindsight. *Trends in Neurosciences, 14*(4), 140–145.

Craig, A. D. (2003). Interoception: the sense of the physiological condition of the body. *Current Opinion in Neurobiology, 13*(4), 500–505.

Damasio, A. (1994). *Descartes' Error: Emotion, Reason and the Human Brain*. New York: Putnam.

Damasio, A. R. (1996). The somatic marker hypothesis and the possible functions of the prefrontal cortex. Philosophical Transactions of the Royal Society of London - Series. *B: Biological Sciences, 351*(1346), 1413–1420.

Dehaene, S., Changeux, J. P., Naccache, L., Sackur, J., & Sergent, C. (2006). Conscious, preconscious, and subliminal processing: a testable taxonomy. *Trends in Cognitive Sciences, 10*(5), 204–211.

Del Cul, A., Baillet, S., & Dehaene, S. (2007). Brain dynamics underlying the nonlinear threshold for access to consciousness. *PLoS Biol, 5*(10), e260.

Driver, J., & Vuilleumier, P. (2001). Perceptual awareness and its loss in unilateral neglect and extinction. *Cognition, 79*(1–2), 39–88.

Dudai, Y. (2004). The neurobiology of consolidations, or, how stable is the engram? *Annual Review of Psychology, 55*, 51–86.

Eichenbaum, H. (2004). Hippocampus: cognitive processes and neural representations that underlie declarative memory. *Neuron, 44*(1), 109−120.

Freud, S. (1953). *On Aphasia, a Critical Study.* London: Imago. (Original work published 1891).

Freud, S. (1953). The interpretation of dreams. In J. Strachey (Ed.), *The Standard Edition of the Complete Psychological Works of Sigmund Freud*, Vols. IV−V. London: Hogarth Press. (Original work published 1900).

Freud, S. (1955). Beyond the pleasure principle. In J. Strachey (Ed.), *The Standard Edition of the Complete Psychological Works of Sigmund Freud*, Vol. XVIII (pp. 1−64). London: Hogarth Press, (Original work published 1920).

Freud, S. (1957a). Instincts and their vicissitudes. In J. Strachey (Ed.), *The Standard Edition of the Complete Psychological Works of Sigmund Freud*, Vol. XIV (pp. 109−140). London: Hogarth Press, (Original work published 1915).

Freud, S. (1957b). The unconscious. In J. Strachey (Ed.), *The Standard Edition of the Complete Psychological Works of Sigmund Freud*, Vol. XIV (pp. 166−215). London: Hogarth Press, (Original work published 1915).

Freud, S. (1957c). Repression. In J. Strachey (Ed.), *The Standard Edition of the Complete Psychological Works of Sigmund Freud*, Vol. XIV (pp. 1141−1158). London: Hogarth Press, (Original work published 1915).

Freud, S. (1958). Remembering, repeating and working-through. In J. Strachey (Ed.), *The Standard Edition of the Complete Psychological Works of Sigmund Freud*, Vol. XII (pp. 145−156). London: Hogarth Press, (Original work published 1914).

Freud, S. (1960). The psychopathology of everyday life. In J. Strachey (Ed.), *The Standard Edition of the Complete Psychological Works of Sigmund Freud*, Vol. VI (pp. 1−279). London: Hogarth Press, (Original work published 1901).

Freud, S. (1961). The Ego and the Id. In J. Strachey (Ed.), *The Standard Edition of the Complete Psychological Works of Sigmund Freud*, Vol. XIX (pp. 1−59). London: Hogarth Press, (Original work published 1923).

Freud, S. (1962). The aetiology of hysteria. In J. Strachey (Ed.), *The Standard Edition of the Complete Psychological Works of Sigmund Freud*, Vol. III (pp. 187−221). London: Hogarth Press, (Original work published 1896).

Freud, S. (1966). Project for a scientific psychology. In J. Strachey (Ed.), *The Standard Edition of the Complete Psychological Works of Sigmund Freud*, Vol. I (pp. 281−397). London: Hogarth Press, (Original work published 1950).

Freud, S. (1985). Letter to Wilhelm Fliess, December 6, 1896. In J. M. Masson (Ed.), *The Complete Letters of Sigmund Freud to Wilhelm Fliess: 1887−1904* (pp. 207−215). Cambridge, MA: Harvard University Press, (Original work published 1950).

Fuster, J. M. (2006). The cognit: a network model of cortical representation. *International Journal of Psychophysiology, 60*(2), 125−132.

Gazzaniga, M. S., Ivry, R. B., & Mangun, G. R. (2008). *Cognitive Neuroscience: The Biology of the Mind* (3rd ed.). New York: Norton.

Gelbard-Sagiv, H., Mukamel, R., Harel, M., Malach, R., & Fried, I. (2008). Internally generated reactivation of single neurons in human hippocampus during free recall. *Science, 322*(5898), 96−101.

Global Burden of Diseases Study. (2009). *Operations Manual: Final Draft.* Retrieved from http://www.globalburden.org/GBD_Study_Operations_Manual_Jan_20_2009.pdf.

Gorman, J. M., & Roose, S. P. (2011). The neurobiology of fear memory reconsolidation and psychoanalytic theory. *Journal of the American Academy of Psychoanalysis, 59*(6), 1201−1220.

Hassin, R. R., Uleman, J. S., & Bargh, J. A. (Eds.). (2005). *The New Unconscious.* Oxford: Oxford University Press.

Hobson, J. A., & Pace-Schott, E. F. (2002). The cognitive neuroscience of sleep: neuronal systems, consciousness and learning. *Nature Reviews Neuroscience, 3*(9), 679−693.

James, W. (1950). *The Principles of Psychology.* New York: Dover, (Original work published 1890).

Kandel, E. R. (1998). A new intellectual framework for psychiatry. *American Journal of Psychiatry, 155*(4), 457–469.

Kandel, E. R. (1999). Biology and the future of psychoanalysis: a new intellectual framework for psychiatry revisited. *American Journal of Psychiatry, 156*(4), 505–524.

Kihlstrom, J. F. (1987). The cognitive unconscious. *Science, 237*(4821), 1445–1452.

Kouider, S., & Dehaene, S. (2007). Levels of processing during non-conscious perception: a critical review of visual masking. *Philosophical Transactions of the Royal Society of London - Series B: Biological Sciences, 362*(1481), 857–875.

Lau, H. C., & Passingham, R. E. (2007). Unconscious activation of the cognitive control system in the human prefrontal cortex. *Journal of Neuroscience, 27*(21), 5805–5811.

Mancia, M. (2004). The dream between neuroscience and psychoanalysis. *Archives italiennes de biologie, 142*(4), 525–531.

McGaugh, J. L. (2000). Memory—A century of consolidation. *Science, 287*(5451), 248–251.

Morris, R. G., Moser, E. I., Riedel, G., Martin, S. J., Sandin, J., Day, M., et al. (2003). Elements of a neurobiological theory of the hippocampus: the role of activity-dependent synaptic plasticity in memory. *Philosophical Transactions of the Royal Society of London - Series B: Biological Sciences, 358*(1432), 773–786.

Nader, K. (2003). Memory traces unbound. *Trends Neuroscience, 26*(2), 65–72.

Neves, G., Cooke, S. F., & Bliss, T. V. (2008). Synaptic plasticity, memory and the hippocampus: a neural network approach to causality. *Nature Reviews Neuroscience, 9*(1), 65–75.

Nielsen, T. A. (2000). A review of mentation in REM and NREM sleep: « Covert » REM sleep as a possible reconciliation of two opposing models. *Behavioral and Brain Sciences, 23*(6), 851–866, discussion 904–1121.

Rees, G. (2007). Neural correlates of the contents of visual awareness in humans. *Philosophical Transactions of the Royal Society of London - Series B: Biological Sciences, 362*(1481), 877–886.

Sakurai, Y. (1999). How do cell assemblies encode information in the brain? *Neuroscience & Biobehavioral Reviews, 23*(6), 785–796.

Sara, S. J. (2000). Retrieval and reconsolidation: toward a neurobiology of remembering. *Learning & Memory, 7*(2), 73–84.

Shulman, R. G., & Reiser, M. F. (2004). Freud's theory of mind and functional imaging experiments. *Neuro-Psychoanalysis, 6*(2), 133–164.

Snodgrass, M., & Shevrin, H. (2006). Unconscious inhibition and facilitation at the objective detection threshold: replicable and qualitatively different unconscious perceptual effects. *Cognition, 101*(1), 43–79.

Solms, M. (2004). Freud returns. *Scientific American., 290*(5), 82–88.

Squire, L. R., Stark, C. E., & Clark, R. E. (2004). The medial temporal lobe. *Annual Review of Neuroscience, 27*, 279–306.

Suris, A., Smith, J., Powell, C. M., & North, C. S. (2012). Interfering with the reconsolidation of traumatic memory: sirolimus as a novel agent for treating veterans with posttraumatic stress disorder. *Annals of Clinical Psychiatry*. In press.

Sutherland, G. R., & McNaughton, B. (2000). Memory trace reactivation in hippocampal and neocortical neuronal ensembles. *Current Opinion in Neurobiology, 10*(2), 180–186.

Takeuchi, T., Miyasita, A., Inugami, M., & Yamamoto, Y. (2001). Intrinsic dreams are not produced without REM sleep mechanisms: evidence through elicitation of sleep onset REM periods. *Journal of Sleep Research, 10*(1), 43–52.

Tronel, S., Milekic, M. H., & Alberini, C. M. (2005). Linking new information to a reactivated memory requires consolidation and not reconsolidation mechanisms. *PLoS Biol, 3*(9), e293.

Vuilleumier, P., & Pourtois, G. (2007). Distributed and interactive brain mechanisms during emotion face perception: evidence from functional neuroimaging. *Neuropsychologia, 45*(1), 174–194.

Weiskrantz, L. (1996). Blindsight revisited. *Current Opinion in Neurobiology, 6*(2), 215–220.

Index

Page numbers with "f" denote figures; "t" table.